Yemen

the Bradt Travel Guide

Daniel McLaughlin

edition
I

www.bradtguides.com

Bradt Travel Guides Ltd, UK
The Globe Pequot Press Inc, USA

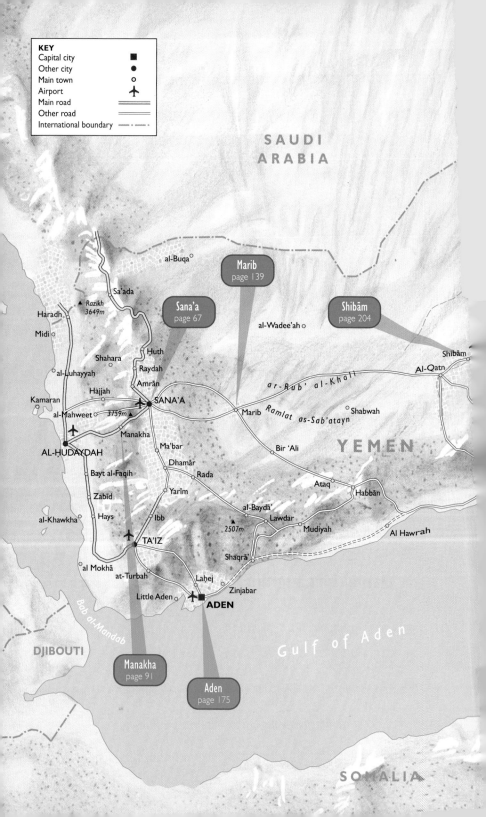

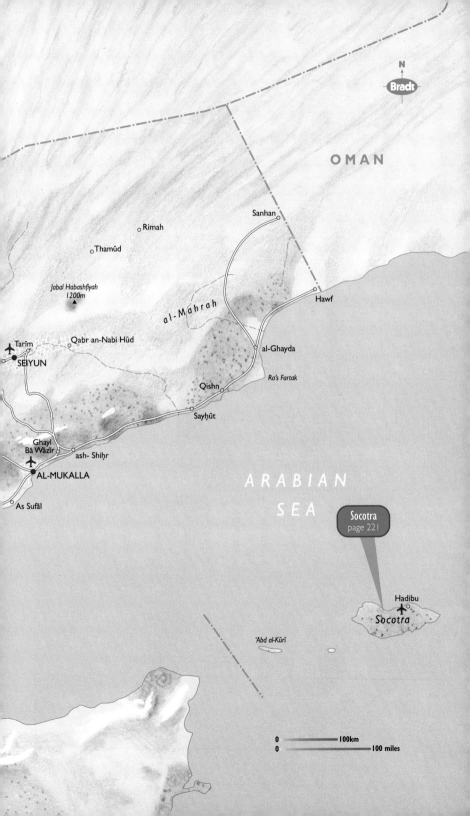

Yemen
Don't
miss...

Old city of Sana'a
(JT) page 82

Qat-chewing sessions
(HR) page 31

Hiking in the Haraz Mountains
(EL) page 91

Sunsets over the desert
The Ramlat as-Sabatayn outside of Marib
(WF/Alamy) page 139

Markets and Souks
Lively fresh fish market at al-Hudaydah
(MF/Alamy) page 166

Old man sits in the souk (EL) page 83

AUTHOR

Daniel McLaughlin first went to Yemen to study Arabic, teach English, and explore the country. He returned for an extensive six months of travel as part of the research for this guide, and he had the time of his life. Having studied music, philosophy, and law, he now works as an international trade attorney in Washington, DC. Somehow he has managed to get paid to travel to Yemen on occasion.

CONTRIBUTORS

I am grateful to the following for their invaluable assistance: Dominic Ashby, Kate Reimer, and David Scoville (natural history and conservation), Sean and Ruth Carroll (Ras Sharma), Alan George (various), Anisa George (weddings), Melanie H P Miller (Arthur Rimbaud), and Allison Otto (Freya Stark)

AUTHOR STORY

Like so many life changing events, my decision to go to Yemen was initially rather random. Scrapping my long-held plans to earn a PhD, I decided to go and study Arabic. I didn't know much about Yemen at the time, but casting a large net out over multiple institutes across the Middle East, I somehow ended up in Sana'a a couple of months later. A year after my return, an article about Bradt Travel Guides in *The Washington Post* sparked my interest in the possibility of writing a new guide on the country (and at the same time, offering a much needed break from law school). Years later, with a great deal of help and flexibility from the Bradt crew, the book is finally being printed.

My time in Yemen was largely dominated by excitement and hospitality. I didn't always appreciate the exhilaration of the moment until afterwards – I was held at gunpoint by an angry guard, suspected of espionage, and nearly thrown from a rickety dhow crossing the Red Sea during 'the time of the big winds'. In retrospect, though, these events are recalled with nothing but fond memories – the soul of satisfaction.

Of course, I'd be lying to say that my daily life in Yemen was so tumultuous. These brief interludes were but the exception to an underlying norm of friendship and hospitality that lasted throughout. I have often told my friends back home that I have been treated better nowhere in the world than in Yemen. It's a contagious sort of hospitality – even among my Western friends in the country we often find ourselves falling in to courtesies and niceties that would not generally be used back home.

The people of Yemen are the country's greatest asset, and it was mainly for their sake that I first decided to write this guide. Though careering through the desert and wandering the streets of the souk definitely have their appeal, there is a simple beauty to a long qat chew filled with interesting conversation among Yemenis that cannot be matched. For the most part, the discussions were excellent, whether they concerned newly heard jokes, politics, or my paltry attempts to write inferior Arabic poetry. I will declare now though, on the public record, that I never again need to hear tales of Cat Stevens converting to Islam or the Hadith of the barrier between the two seas. Conversion talk was always done with the best of intentions though – and I wouldn't give up for a second the memory of the two boys in Mukalla who bubbled with joy when they found out that I was not a Muslim because it meant they had finally met a heathen. Though not for the same reason, I bubble with the same excitement every time I walk through the Old City of Sana'a.

PUBLISHER'S FOREWORD

The first Bradt travel guide was written in 1974 by George and Hilary Bradt on a river barge floating down a tributary of the Amazon. In the 1980s and '90s the focus shifted away from hiking to broader-based guides covering new destinations – usually the first to be published about these places. In the 21st century Bradt continues to publish such ground-breaking guides, as well as others to established holiday destinations, incorporating in-depth information on culture and natural history with the nuts and bolts of where to stay and what to see.

Bradt authors support responsible travel, and provide advice not only on minimum impact but also on how to give something back through local charities. In this way a true synergy is achieved between the traveller and local communities.

* * *

It's rare for a traveller to be truly jolted by a photo; the world is so well documented that there are few surprises left. Yet when I first saw a photograph of the old town of Sana'a I did a double take. I'd never imagined that a capital city so exotically different existed in our uniform world. So I had a bias towards Yemen before I started reading this book – it's always been the Middle Eastern country that I most wanted to visit. And what a good job Daniel McLaughlin has done! This is clearly an insider's account of a much-loved country, rich in personal detail and anecdotes, yet comfortably reassuring on the practicalities of travel.

First published November 2007

Bradt Travel Guides Ltd, 23 High Street, Chalfont St Peter, Bucks SL9 9QE, England.
www.bradtguides.com
Published in the USA by The Globe Pequot Press Inc, 246 Goose Lane,
PO Box 480, Guilford, Connecticut 06475-0480

Text copyright © 2007 Daniel McLaughlin
Maps copyright © 2007 Bradt Travel Guides Ltd
Illustrations copyright © 2007 Individual photographers and artists
Editorial Project Manager: Emma Thomson

ISBN-10: 1 84162 212 5   ISBN-13: 978 1 84162 212 5
British Library Cataloguing in Publication Data
A catalogue record for this book is available from the British Library

Photographs Antonello Lanzellotto/TIPS (Al/TIPS), Daniel McLaughlin (DM), Eric Lafforgue (EL), Hans Rossel (HR), Jorge Tutor (JT), Michelle Falzone/Alamy (MF/Alamy), Wolfgang Kaehler/Alamy (WF/Alamy)
Front cover Men drinking tea (EL)
Back cover Woman's hands decorated with henna tattoos (AL/TIPS)
Title page Yemeni girl in Haraz Mountains (DM), Sana'a Old City (EL), Man wearing the traditional Jambiya dagger (EL)
Illustrations Carole Vincer   **Maps** Dave Priestley, Steve Munns (colour map)
Typeset from the author's disc by Wakewing
Printed and bound in Malta by Gutenberg Press Ltd

Acknowledgements

First and foremost, thank you to my close friend Kamal Frass, who provided invaluable assistance along with tuna, cheese and Nutella sandwiches. (Thanks are given more for the former than the latter.) My deepest gratitude is also given: to Radhwan Frass, for his unending energy, kindness, and thoughtful parting gift; to Fahd Frass, for always assisting with any issue that needed to be resolved; to my good friends David and Aimee Georgetti, Rob and Jenny Cacchioni, Joseph Uccello, Michael Horton, and Jon Oakes for rooftop and courtyard conversations; to Matt Berman, Allison Otto, and Angela Smith, for giving their constant encouragement; to Alan George, Elke Bedehesing, Tim Holmes, Ahmed al-Biel, Mazan Luqman, Borut Zajc, and Anisa George for their friendship in Yemen; to Ambassador Thomas C Krajeski, Hon Frances Fragos Townsend, and H E Abdulwahab A Al-Hajjri for their support; to Hughes Hubbard & Reed for their flexibility while I flirted with all things Yemeni; to Helen Anjomshoaa, Adrian Phillips, Emma Thomson and the folks at Bradt for everything; and lastly to all my friends and family for patiently listening to more Yemen stories than they ever wanted to hear.

FEEDBACK REQUEST

Every effort has been made to ensure that the details contained within this book are as accurate and up to date as possible. Inevitably, however, things move on. Any information regarding such changes, or relating to your experiences in Yemen – good or bad – would be gratefully received. Such feedback is invaluable when compiling further editions. Send your comments to Bradt Travel Guides Ltd, 23 High Street, Chalfont St Peter, Bucks SL9 9QE, England; e info@bradtguides.com.

Contents

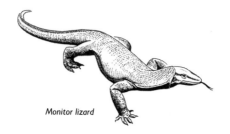

Monitor lizard

Introduction

There is a Yemeni joke that finds Adam and the Archangel Gabriel returning to the earth for a visit. As the pair flies over the various nations of world, Gabriel acts as tour guide. 'That is France, and that Italy,' the angel states. 'There is Greece, and there Jordan.' The whole time, however, Adam looks terribly confused, and finally he confesses: 'Gabriel, I don't recognise anything.' At last, as the two soar over southern Arabia, Adam's face lights up with recognition. 'Ah, there is Yemen,' he exclaims, and in response to Gabriel's quizzical looks, he responds, 'Nothing has changed there!'

Yemen definitely has the feeling of Olde Arabia, especially in comparison to its more oil-rich neighbours. The fact that it's the only country on the Arabian Peninsula without a McDonalds helps with the image, but more than anything it's the culture, traditions, and hospitality of the Yemeni people (be it the desert Bedouin, the mountain tribesmen, the coastal workers in the Tihama, the Sayyids in Hadramawt, and even the average Yemeni in Sana'a) that give you the impression that the very best of old times continues to thrive in the country. As Yemen continues on the path toward development – a course we hope continues – we can only hope its rich culture does not get left behind.

The Yemeni people are the country's gem, but its long history and varied sights and activities hold their own. Perhaps Adam would recognise the country from his heavenly discussions with other religious figures. Apart from clearly being instrumental in the rise of Islam, various claims note that the country holds the site of the Garden of Eden, the resting place of Noah's Ark, and the departing points for the Queen of Sheba and one of the Christ-visiting magi. The latter likely would have brought with him some of the incense in which the ancient Yemeni kingdoms traded to make their vast fortunes. When you are not visiting the ruins of the temples and palaces that these kingdoms left behind, you will have no problem filling your day walking through the souks, admiring the unique architecture, careening through the desert, or simply sitting back with a cheek full of qat and listening to other chewers tell jokes like the one above.

Another Yemeni joke that stands out to me concerns the times before the revolution, when the Imams ruled with iron fists. Supposedly, one particular imam never laughed, despite the attempts of the best jesters throughout the country. Finally, one day a villager from far out in the countryside heard of the ruler's impenetrable sternness, and he made the long trek to the capital. Standing at the gate of the palace, he guaranteed the guards that he could make the imam laugh. As soon as he was brought into the main chamber, he charged the imam and began poking him in the side while yelling, 'Tickle, tickle, tickle!' The imam, who did not even show the faintest hint of a smile, roared with anger, 'Get this man out of here!'

That was the end of the joke. When I first heard it, I was so amused by the joke teller's uproarious laughter that I had to chuckle along with him. To this day, however, I'm not really quite sure what the punch line is supposed to be. I told the joke teller that I didn't understand, he shrugged, and we talked about other things. But whether it's a cultural difference, a bad joke, or just my inability to appreciate fine humour, my lack of understanding here has come to signify for me Yemen's richness. You will never reach the point where you have nothing left to learn about the country. I, for one, can't wait to go back and learn some more.

Bradt Travel Guides is a partner to the 'know before you go' campaign, masterminded by the UK Foreign and Commonwealth Office to promote the importance of finding out about a destination before you travel. By combining the up-to-date advice of the FCO with the in-depth knowledge of Bradt authors, you'll ensure that your trip will be as trouble-free as possible.

www.fco.gov.uk/travel

Part One

GENERAL INFORMATION

Location Southwest corner of the Arabian Peninsula at 15°N, 48°E

Neighbouring countries Saudi Arabia, Oman

Size 527,970km² (*World Factbook*)

Status Republic

President Ali Abdullah Saleh

Prime Minister Abd al-Qadir ba Jamal

Population 21,456,188 (*World Factbook*)

Life expectancy 62.13 years (women 64.11 years; men 60.23 years) (*World Factbook*)

Capital Sana'a; population: 1,747,627 (2004 census)

Other main towns Aden, Mukalla, Hudaydah, Ta'iz

GDP US$19.3 billion (*World Factbook*)

Languages Arabic (official), English, Mahri, Socotri and Bathari

Religion Islam (major sects: Shafi'i, Zaydi, Isma'ili); Christian and Jewish minorities

Currency Yemeni rial (YR)

Exchange rate £1 = 406.44YR; US$1 = 199.14YR; € 1 = 281.32YR (Oct 2007)

National airline Yemenia Airways

International telephone code +967

Regional telephone codes Sana'a and Raimah – 01; Aden, Lahej, adh-Dhali' and Abyan – 02; Hudaydah – 03; Ta'iz and Ibb – 04; Shabwa, Hadhramawt, al-Mahra and Socotra – 05; Dhamar, al-Bayda, Marib and al-Jawf – 06; Hajjah, al-Mahweet and Sa'ada – 07

Time GMT +3

Electric voltage 220V

Flag Three equal horizontal stripes of red, white, and black

National anthem *Oh World, Repeat My Song*

National bird Hoopoe

National flower Arabian Coffee

National sport Football (soccer)

Public holidays Secular: Labour Day (1 May), National Unity Day (22 May), Revolution Day (26 September), National Day (14 October) and Independence Day (30 November). Islamic: Islamic New Year (1 Muharram), Birth of the Prophet (12 Rabi' al-Awwal), Ramadan (month of Ramadan), Eid al-Fitr (1 Shawwal), Eid al-Adha (10–13 Dhu al-Hijja).

I

Background Information

GEOGRAPHY AND CLIMATE

Yemen is located on the southwest corner of the Arabian Peninsula. Although it is dwarfed by its northern neighbour Saudi Arabia, Yemen is the second-largest country on the peninsula, occupying 527,970km². It is bordered to the north by Saudi Arabia and to the east by Oman. As every Yemeni schoolchild knows, the coastline stretches for about 2,000km from Midi in the northwest to Hof in the southeast. The western coastline faces the Red Sea, and the southern coast sits on the Gulf of Aden and the Arabian Sea. The two coasts meet in the southwest corner at Bab al-Mandab, and from there it is only a short 25km sail across the Mandab Straits to the African coast of Djibouti. This narrow channel, shorter than the distance between England and France across the Strait of Dover, is the sole entry point from the Indian Ocean to the Red Sea and the Suez Canal.

Yemen can be divided into four geographical regions: the mountain highlands, the coastal plains, the desert regions, and the eastern plateau. The mountain highlands include the southern end of the 'Asir mountain range from Saudi Arabia and the Sarat Mountains of Yemen. The Sarat Mountains continue from the northern end of the Hajjah and 'Amran governorates through Sana'a, Yarim, and Ta'iz toward the southwest corner of the country, where the range turns eastward, gradually tapering off as it runs along the southern coast. The Sarat Mountains rise gradually from the eastern desert, reaching its highest peak of 3,760m (12,336ft) at Jabal an-Nabi Shu'ayb. Farther to the west, the elevation then falls dramatically in little over 25km between the mountains and the coastal plains of the Tihama. In the easternmost portion of the country, the landscape is dominated by the inhospitable limestone plateau of the Jol, through which the important wadis of Hadhramawt and Do'an traverse. In the centre of Yemen lie the deserts of Ramlat as-Sabatayn and portions of the Empty Quarter, the largest sand desert in the world.

The climate of the country varies according to these geographical regions. The mountain regions are temperate year round. Tihama and the desert, however, are hot and dry during the winter and hotter in the summer, with temperatures rising to 50°C.

The region was nicknamed 'Arabia Felix' due to abundance of rain in the area, especially in comparison with other parts of the Arabian Peninsula. There are two rainy seasons that mostly affect the central and southern mountains. During April–May and August–September these regions are subject to rainfall daily. Sometimes the downpour can be quite torrential – the streets of Sana'a often fill with over a foot of water, bringing all traffic to a virtual standstill. In the easternmost region of the country, parts of al-Mahra experience the monsoon season.

BIBLICAL BEGINNINGS The early history of Yemen is steeped in Old Testament and Koranic lore. According to local tradition, the city of Aden, if not the original earthly paradise of a similar name, is at least the burial site of both Cain and Abel. The same city is claimed to have been the departure point for Noah's Ark during the great deluge. As those floodwaters receded, Noah's son Shem set out and founded the city of Sana'a at the base of Jabal Nuqum.

Shem's great-grandson Eber is equated by some scholars with the Hud, a prophetic giant in the Koran who preached to a nation of giants in Hadhramawt before God wrought their destruction with heavy winds. Eber's son Joktan – identified with Qahtan – is believed to be the ancestor of all Yemenis and the fount of all 'true Arabs'. The Book of Genesis lists his offspring as including Hazarmaveth (the Hebrew version of Hadhramawt), Uzal (an ancient name of the city of Sana'a), and Sheba (a likely reference to the ancient incense kingdom of Saba). From the descendants of Sheba rose the great Sabaean Kingdom, rich in incense and gold, from which the famous biblical queen is said to have visited Solomon.

As always, of course, historical stories drawn from religious sources should be taken with a pillar of salt. Nevertheless, the figures of Shem, Hud, Qahtan, and the Queen of Sheba figure predominantly in the Yemenis' descriptions of their ancient histories.

PREHISTORIC YEMEN Recent excavations in the mountainous regions of Khawlan, the valleys of Wadi Hadhramawt and parts of Tihama, as well as the discovery of early rock drawings near the desert of Ramlat as-Sabatayn, have begun to paint a picture of Yemen in the Palaeolithic, Neolithic and Bronze ages.

As early as 5000BC large settlements existed in the mountains of northern Yemen. Little is known still about these prehistoric Yemenis, and how exactly the transition was made from the Bronze-Age civilizations to the ancient caravan kingdoms. Carbon dating has dated artefacts to roughly near the time the Sabaean and Hadhramawt kingdoms were beginning their rise to power, so it is possible that there was a fluid transition from these early hunters and gatherers to the powerful nations that controlled the incense trade.

THE CARAVAN KINGDOMS
The rise of the caravan kingdoms
For roughly 1,000 years several ancient kingdoms ruled over Yemen and profited greatly from the incense trade that brought frankincense and myrrh across the mainland of the country and onward to the Western world. Of these ancient Yemeni kingdoms, the most well known today by the average layman is that of the **Sabaeans**. Much of this fame draws on the legends of the Queen of Sheba, whose tales have fuelled the imagination of Judeo-Christian-Islamic storytellers for centuries. Even without the popular queen, the considerable achievements and wealth of the Sabaean Kingdom have ensured its proper place in history.

The Sabaean Kingdom rose to power sometime around 1000BC – around the time the Queen of Sheba is believed to have made her trip to visit Solomon. The emergence of the Sabaeans as a strong political force owed much to the domestication of the camel during the tail end of the 2nd millennium BC. With this sturdy beast of burden tamed, the Arabian caravan could be born. Assyrian texts from the 8th century BC document the existence of the camel caravan and the incense trade. The ancient scroll relates how an Assyrian governor had seized myrrh and other goods from a Sabaean caravan some 200 camels strong.

The Sabaean Kingdom lasted for nearly 1,300 years, but its height of power was in the 7th century BC, around the time when construction on the great Marib Dam began. Even as late as the 2nd century BC, the Greek geographer Agatharchides wrote:

> The Sabaeans are the most important people of Arabia and possess all possible opulence. Their land is every bit as productive as our own, and the people exhibit the most remarkable characteristics. They have livestock in abundance. Visitors arriving at their ports are greeted with a divinely pleasurable fragrance from the many balsam and cassia trees that grow near the seashore and which are unspeakably lovely to behold.

As the incense trade grew over the 1st millennium BC, two major routes developed to transport the frankincense and myrrh across Yemen. The first and more important of these routes skirted the edge of the desert, while the second went through the mountain highlands. To protect and profit from the first route, the Sabaeans built their capital at Marib. To oversee the second, they fortified the settlement of Sana'a.

The rulers of the Sabaean Kingdom during its early period assumed the title *mukarrib*, which translates roughly to 'federator', or perhaps more colloquially 'the rally man'. The role of the mukarribs was to bring together the various tribes under the kingdom and preside over them all. In this way, they are somewhat similar to the ruling sheikhs of Yemen's major tribal federations today. In addition to defending the kingdom or leading warriors into battle, the mukarribs presided over large construction projects and officiated at religious ceremonies.

As the Sabaean Kingdom was rising to power in Marib and to the west, the **Kingdom of Hadhramawt** (1000BC–AD320) was establishing itself at its capital of Shabwa and to the east. Far less is known about this kingdom than its Sabaean counterpart, but as both are mentioned in the genealogies of Genesis, it is likely that Hadhramawt is equally as old.

The Kingdom of Hadhramawt began as a vassal of the Sabaean Kingdom. The trees of frankincense and myrrh were all located in the Dhofar region of south Arabia – Hadhramawt's sphere of influence – and so the Sabaeans would need to rein in the Hadhramis if they wished to maximise their profits from the caravan trade.

At the beginning of the 8th century BC the **Awsan Kingdom** (800–685BC) was the only political rival to the Sabaeans. The kingdom was centred in the area of Wadi Markhah, and it held a certain amount of influence in the region for a brief period of time. In the 7th century BC, the Awsan capital was dealt a swift blow by the Sabaean army. In an attack led by the great **Karib'il Watar**, 16,000 soldiers of the Awsan Kingdom were killed and two-and-a-half times as many were taken as prisoners. The damage was crippling, and the tribal confederation crumbled soon thereafter, only to be brought back together by the **Qataban** (800BC–AD190), a tribe that had existed on the fringes during the reign of the Awsan Kingdom but that quickly rose to prominence once that reign ended.

Like the Kingdom of Hadhramawt, the **Ma'in Kingdom** (625BC–AD25) first arose as a vassal of the Sabaeans. Unlike both the Hadhramawt and Sabaean kingdoms, the rulers of the Ma'in Kingdom were more concerned with commercial trade than military conquests. As a result the kingdom, whose people were known as the Minaeans, became much more connected with the world outside Yemen than any of the other ancient kingdoms. The Minaeans were mentioned in ancient Egyptian texts and also traded with the Syrians, Assyrians, and Babylonians. There was even a temple dedicated to the local Minaean god on the Greek island of Delos.

The wars of supremacy In the early centuries of the 1st millennium BC, the Sabaean Kingdom dominated south Arabia. The kingdoms of Hadhramawt and Ma'in were both vassals of the Sabaean Kingdom, and the Sabaean forces were able to exact heavy losses against the Awsan Kingdom under the reign of Karib'il Watar in the 7th century BC. With the help of Hadhramawt and Qataban, the Sabaeans were able to completely annihilate the Awsan Kingdom in subsequent attacks.

By the 5th century BC, the Sabaean vassals were beginning to tire of the kingdom's rule, and the Sabaean ruler Yatha'amar Bayyin found it necessary to quell several rebellions. By the following century both the Minaeans and the Qatabanis broke away and asserted their independence. The Sabaeans' firm hold on power began to collapse – the Qatabanis led several attacks against Marib that severely handicapped the kingdom, the Hadhramawt Kingdom established its independence, and the Minaeans temporarily seized control of most of the caravan routes.

The Sabaean lull in power lasted for over a century, but the old kingdom eventually regained much of its strength. In the 2nd century BC the Sabaeans conquered the Minaeans and put an end to their kingdom. The Sabaean Kingdom reasserted its control over the incense routes, but the lucrative trade would not last for much longer.

THE END OF THE INCENSE TRADE

The Romans in and around Arabia Felix The great wealth that was associated with the trade of incense had piqued Roman curiosity about the possibility of a south Arabian campaign. After all, why pay for the milk when you can crush the cow into submission? With a touch of bitterness, Pliny explained that the tribes of south Arabia were 'the richest races in the world, because vast wealth from Rome and Parthia accumulates in their hands, as they sell the produce they obtain from the sea or their forests and buy nothing in return'.

Alexander the Great was the first to develop schemes of conquering Arabia. On the advice of Aristotle he sent a colony of Greeks to settle on the island of Socotra, but his early death scuttled any plans to secure the mainland. Centuries later, when Roman incense-burning was near its peak, Augustus Caesar carried out the first major attempt to conquer the area. The emperor sent an expedition in 25BC under the command of General Aelius Gallus. Accompanied by a swathe of Roman soldiers numbering in the thousands, Nabataean camel riders and Jewish archers, Gallus marched southward, but the campaign was riddled with illness and disease from the start. Regardless, the army managed to conquer Najran and the old Minaean fortification at Baraqish. The expedition made it as far south as Marib and besieged the city for six days. Before the end of a week, however, disease was rampant and the Roman army was forced to retreat.

Where military strength could not succeed, science prevailed. In the 1st century BC, the Greeks and Romans discovered the secret of the trade winds. As ships began to use the route between the Red Sea and India with greater frequency, the overland caravan route quickly declined in importance, and the prowess of the caravan kingdoms began to fade.

The Himyarite Kingdom Sometime around the early 1st century BC, the Kingdom of Himyar (110BC–AD525) emerged as the new player in the field. Although the new kingdom created a calendar that began in the year 110BC, the first mention of the Himyarites does not occur until about 125 years later, when a Hadhramite inscription detailed the need of building a new fortified wall at a settlement north of modern-day Bir 'Ali to fend off the attacks of the Himyarites.

Before this time, the Himyarites likely existed as a federation of tribes under the Qataban Kingdom. After breaking away in the 2nd century BC, they soon became a powerful political force, conquering parts of Sabaean territory by the beginning of the 1st century AD. The capital of the kingdom was founded at the city of Dhafar, with the seat of power in the palace of Raydan. Pliny recognised the city as the residence of the King of southern Arabia in his *Natural History*. The early Himyarite kings attempted to exert their domination of the Sabaean kingdom nominally by claiming the title of (what would be the first in a series of expanding epithets) 'Kings of Saba' and dhu-Raydan'. As a testament to the initial force the Himyarites had on the scene, the Sabaean rulers soon began to take the same title.

The use of the similar title by two separate kingdoms over several centuries has proven to be quite a mess for historians to sort out. Even the ancient authors got confused. The *Periplus of the Erythraean Sea* noted that Dhafar was 'the metropolis, in which lives Charibael, lawful king of [the] two tribes of Himyar and Saba''. The text places the ruler in Dhafar, capital of the Himyarite Kingdom, but names the king as 'Charibael' – most likely referring to King Karib'il Bayyin, who was the ruler of the Saba' Kingdom when the first version of the *Periplus* likely was published.

Sabaean and Himyarite rivalry The Himyarites and Sabaeans did more than practise linguistic warfare. The two sides often fought against each other bitterly, each having moments of gaining the upper hand. The Kingdom of Saba', however, was in its decline, and the battle would ultimately be won by the Himyarites. The discovery of the trade winds hit the Sabaean economy hard – the money flow from the overland incense trade that had proved nearly inexhaustible in the past had dried up. The Romans now easily loaded their ships at the port of Qana (near modern Bir 'Ali). The Sabaeans were facing more and more internal divisions, as well as threats from the Bedouin tribes.

Conflicts with the other ancient kingdoms continued as well. In the 2nd century AD the Sabaeans and the Hadhramis launched a major attack against the Kingdom of Qataban. The latter force annexed the Qatabani capital of Timna' and agreed to split the defeated kingdom with the Sabaeans.

Over the course of the 3rd century AD, the Sabaean Kingdom continued to have successes. Inscriptions of the period confirm that Sha'irum Awtar was successful in his campaigns against the Ethiopian Abyssinians, with whom his father actually had allied. More importantly for the Sabaeans, Sha'irum was able to deliver a devastating defeat against the Hadhramite army at the Battle of Shuwar'an. The Hadhramite King Il'az Yalit was taken as a prisoner, the capital of Shabwa was heavily damaged, and the wealth of the defeated city was taken back to Marib.

After Abrahah had taken over as ruler of Yemen, he adopted a code of laws that had been promulgated by St Gregentius, the Bishop of Dhafar who had been brought to Yemen from Alexandria by the King of Ethiopia to help spread Christianity. These laws were no doubt heavily influenced by and enacted as a result of the code of Roman law put together by Emperor Justinian several years earlier. Like the Justinian code, the laws were a bit harsh in their efforts to stamp out artistry and sexual promiscuity. Anyone caught performing music, dancing or acting was sent to do a year of hard labour after receiving a fierce whipping. Sex outside of marriage was severely punished: 100 lashes from a whip, the loss of the left ear, and the taking of all property. If the woman involved was married to another at the time of the offence, her left breast was removed and the man was castrated. Pimps had their tongues cut out. If the punishments were properly carried out, a single night of romance could end up with the removal of four separate body parts among three different people!

The Sabaean Kingdom then set out to burn one more blaze of glory before puffing out of existence – the Sabaean brothers and coregents of Ilsharah Yahdub and Ya'zil Bayyin managed to expel the Abyssinians and even to defeat the Himyarites on the field of battle, enabling them once again to rule over large parts of the country. In their last glorious inscription, the two brothers stated that they had vanquished 'all the armies and tribes that rose in battle against them, tribes from the north and south, from sea and land'. Within 30 years of the two rulers' expansive successes, the Sabaean Kingdom finally collapsed under the weight of Himyarite attacks.

With the expulsion of the Abyssinians, the only remaining rival to Himyarite dominance in Yemen was the Kingdom of Hadhramawt, which had been in existence for over 1,300 years. Although the Hadhrami rulers had strengthened their rule with the defeat of the Kingdom of Qataban toward the end of the 2nd century AD, the defeat at the hands of the Sabaean brothers proved to be the beginning of the end. The famous Himyarite King Shamar Yuhar'esh, who had been successful in putting an end to the Sabaean Kingdom, also wrote the final chapter to the Hadhramite story by delivering a stunning defeat in Shabwa. Although there would be smaller rebellions against Himyarite dominance in the decades to come, the end of the Kingdom of Hadhramawt can be pinned to this battle.

With all of the domestic enemies vanquished, and the Abyssinians contained in the Tihama coast, Shamar Yuhar'esh expanded his title to 'King of Saba', Dhu-Raydan, Hadhramawt, and Yamanat'. What exactly 'Yamanat' refers to is anyone's guess. Scholars have postulated that the term could refer to the areas of kingdoms of Qataban and Awsan, but it could also refer to a larger geographical area. In any event, Shamar Yuhar'esh was just trying to tell everyone that he controlled a lot of land. The king even managed to send emissaries abroad – his governor of Saba' was sent as an ambassador to the Persian rulers of the Sasanid Empire in Ctesiphon.

After the rule of Shamar Yuhar'esh, monotheism began to sink roots in Yemen, despite the oft-spoke Muslim claim that the entire Arabian Peninsula was awash in pagan polytheism during the 'age of ignorance' years that led up to the beginning of Islam. An inscription at the dam in Marib makes reference to ar-Rahman, the Lord of the Universe. Christianity and Judaism both appeared in the country around this time. Emperor Constantine II sent a bishop from the island of Socotra who built churches in Dhafar and Aden, and an inscription from a house-builder converted to Judaism contains small sections of Hebrew.

The end of the Himyarite Kingdom In the 6th century AD the Himyarite King Ma'adikarib adopted Christianity as the state religion, and shortly after him Dhu Nuwas, the last of the Himyarite kings, changed the official religion to Judaism. Not remembered as an ecumenical leader, Dhu Nuwas quickly launched campaigns against the Aksumite strongholds, burning the church at Dhafar and slaughtering thousands of Christians in Najran.

The treatment of Christians under Dhu Nuwas prompted an international outcry. With the help of Justinian I, Aksumite forces led by Abrahah returned to south Arabia and defeated Dhu Nuwas. According to local legend, the defeated leader was last seen riding his horse into the sea.

With the assistance of Emperor Justinian in Rome and King Elesbaan in Ethiopia, Abrahah constructed the Qalis – a cathedral of such grandeur and magnificence that it could have been one of the marvels of the world. The Qalis was built with a mind to divert the pilgrims from their annual trip to the Kaaba in Mecca. The fact that the pilgrimage was accompanied by a huge seasonal market didn't hurt either.

Abrahah's scheme did not succeed. Outraged at the construction of a new site to rival the Kaaba, and probably partly worried that the plan would work, tribesmen from the ruling Meccan family of Quraysh arranged to have a man enter the Qalis and defecate within its walls.

For Abrahah, who had always disliked the power the Quraysh wielded, this was the provocation he needed to attack Mecca. The account of Abrahah's march on Mecca is well known by every Muslim and is mentioned in the 105th chapter of the Koran. Claimed to have an army 60,000 strong and accompanied by 13 elephants, Abrahah marched northward toward Mecca, enjoying initial successes along the way. Accordingly, the attack is said to have taken place in 'the Year of the Elephant', cited by Muslims as the year both of the birth of the Prophet Muhammad and the final collapse of the Marib Dam.

As Abrahah and his forces neared Mecca, the Koran states that large flocks of birds flew by, dropping stones and pebbles on the large army and killing most of the soldiers as they fled the onslaught. Islamic tradition adds that whoever was struck by the pebbles started to disintegrate or would fall into fits of scratching until tearing his flesh apart. Another tradition, drawing on less miraculous intervention, holds that an outbreak of smallpox ravaged Abrahah and his army. In any event, the attack on Mecca failed, and Abrahah died before returning to Sana'a.

Sensing an opportunity to rid themselves again of the Aksumite rulers, the Yemenis enlisted the help of the Sassanid Emperor Khosrau I. Persian forces arrived in Yemen and, with the assistance of local tribal forces, the Ethiopian power was driven out of the country for good. The Persians, however, had their own motives in helping the Yemenis drive out the Aksumites. With the former power gone, the Persians settled in for their own occupation.

THE AGE OF ISLAM
Islam makes initial headway in Yemen In AD628, Badhan, the Persian Governor of Sana'a, converted to Islam. Under his rule, the region became a nominally Islamic territory, although it took some while for the new religion to take a firm hold in the area of Yemen. On the one hand, news travelled slowly, and it would take time for the message of Islam to reach the many remote regions of the area. On the other hand, even when news of Islam was available, the local Yemenis were often opposed to the message.

After the conquest of Mecca in AD630, Muhammad was able to devote more attention toward his neighbours to the south. To facilitate Islamic expansion in Yemen, Muhammad sent a number of his close companions to the country, including Mu'adh bin Jabal, who built the first mosque in Yemen in the town of al-Janad, and 'Ali Ibn Abi Talib, Muhammad's cousin and son-in-law and the man who would later become the fourth Rightly Guided Caliph and on whom the Shi'ite sect of Islam, in particular, would place great importance.

To some extent, the missionary messages were successful. 'Ali, for instance, is said to have converted the entire tribe of Hamdan within a single evening. Within the next year, many delegations from Yemen (along with elsewhere from the Arabian Peninsula) went to Mecca to pay their homage to Muhammad and profess their loyalty to Islam.

Early revolts hindered the spread of Islam even during Muhammad's lifetime. A large part of the problem was that the new religion was first accepted by and came to be associated with the Persian occupying forces. Before Islam could take a firm root, nationalism weighed more on the hearts of Yemenis than religious fealty. The highly charismatic speaker and juggler 'Abhalah bin Ka'b al-'Ansi claimed that he also was a prophet in his bid to drive out the Persians. His movement gained ground quickly, and he was able to banish many of Muhammad's emissaries once he captured Sana'a.

'Abhalah's movement was eventually suppressed by northern Muslim forces, but new rebellions continued to spring up and required constant intervention from the authority in Mecca. At the same time, however, Islam was making significant headway in many parts of the country. Tribal delegations from all over Yemen made their way to Mecca to profess their adoption of Islam.

The Four Rightly Guided Caliphs

The Sunni–Shi'a division Muhammad's death sent the Arab world into a short period of chaos. Muhammad had left no instructions as to how his successor should be chosen. This ambiguity led to a division in the Muslim world between Sunni and Shi'a that has persisted and has often played itself out violently up to the present day.

Many Muslims believed that the Imam (or Caliph) – the ruler of Muslim faith – must be a member of Muhammad's family. In particular, these Muslims claimed that the imamate should pass to 'Ali, Muhammad's son-in-law, and afterwards to the descendants of 'Ali and Muhammad's daughter Fatima. Thus, this branch of thought became known as Shi'a, which is short for *Shi'at 'Ali* ('the Party of 'Ali').

The Shi'a Muslims stand in opposition to the Sunni Muslims, who hold that an Imam need not be a member of Muhammad's family, but that he need only be a member of Muhammad's tribe, the Quraish.

The majority of Muslims are Sunni, and they believe that the first four Imams – the Four Rightly Guided Caliphs: Abu Bakr, 'Omar, 'Uthman, and 'Ali – were each elected rightfully. The minority Shi'a Muslims, on the other hand, hold that 'Ali was the first rightfully elected caliph and that the first three, in essence, were usurpers. While there are dogmatic differences between the two sects as well, the origin of the division stems from the passing over of 'Ali as the first caliph.

The Wars of Apostasy Following Muhammad's death there were additional problems within the Muslim community besides those regarding the question of succession. Many of the Bedouin and mountain tribes that had travelled previously to Mecca to profess their adherence to Islam revolted. Believing that the governing forces of Medina would not be as strong after Muhammad's death, many of the tribes revoked their allegiance to Islam, mostly in an effort to avoid paying the alms tax that Muhammad had required of them.

The task fell to Abu Bakr, the first Rightly Guided Caliph, to restore the Arabian Peninsula to Islamic order. Throughout most of his two-year reign as caliph, Abu

Bakr and his forces from Medina were occupied with the Ridda Wars, or the Wars of Apostasy, in an attempt to bring back the wayward tribes to the Islamic fold. Major insurrections arose and were put down in Sana'a, Hadhramawt, and Tihama.

The expansion of the Muslim world Abu Bakr's reign lasted a short two years, and 'Omar succeeded him as the second caliph. Whereas Abu Bakr's main concern fell within quelling the rebellions of the Arabian Peninsula, 'Omar was able to look to Islamic expansion. Outside the Arabian Peninsula, the Byzantine and Persian empires were vying for power. The struggle between the two great powers and also their early dismissal of the Muslim forces allowed for great victories on the Muslim side. The Islamic world grew rapidly.

From the very beginning, Yemenis played a large role in the battles that took place outside the Arabian Peninsula. Even before the end of Abu Bakr's reign, Yemeni tribal forces were arriving in Medina to prepare to leave for Syria. During 'Omar's reign, many more Yemeni forces were sent to the fronts of battles against the Persians in Iraq. Many of the brightest and best of the Yemenis went off on these expeditions, and many of them settled in either Syria or Iraq after the fighting ended.

After 12 years of rule 'Omar was assassinated, and 'Uthman was elected to the caliphate. Like his predecessor, 'Uthman also met his end by an enemy's blade. Hostility against the third caliph began to brew in the newly occupied areas outside the Arabian Peninsula. The Yemenis who had settled in these regions played a large part in the uprising, and when latent hostility turned to active belligerency, Yemenis played a strong role in the numbers and leadership of the rebel party that travelled to Medina from Iraq and Egypt to confront 'Uthman. The rebels surrounded the caliph's house and broke in. Several expatriate Yemenis dealt the final blow.

Civil war in the Islamic world 'Ali was elected as caliph following the assassination of 'Uthman. The move did not heal the varying Islamic factions but resulted in the first Islamic civil war. In particular several groups outside the Arabian Peninsula did not accept 'Ali as the new caliph, putting up their own man in a bid for power. In Iraq, two of Muhammad's companions revolted against 'Ali with the backing of Muhammad's wife 'Aisha, while Mu'awiyah bin Abi Sufyan attempted to seize the caliphate from his power base in Syria.

With the help of large Yemeni numbers in his army, 'Ali was able to quell the 'rebellion of 'Aisha' at the Battle of Camel. 'Ali pardoned 'Aisha for her involvement in the uprising and brought her back to Medina to live.

Mu'awiyah's revolt, however, proved to be 'Ali's greatest threat. In order to cement the loyalty of his Syrian forces, or because he was intent on fulfilling his duty of avenging his fallen relative 'Uthman, Mu'awiyah challenged 'Ali to produce the late caliph's assassins or to admit accomplice liability for 'Uthman's death.

The battle and arbitration at Siffin When Mu'awiyah proclaimed himself the caliph of the western regions, 'Ali was forced to act. The bickering eventually led to the famous Battle of Siffin on the banks of the Euphrates River. Both armies were heavily represented by Yemeni forces, and one of the commanders of 'Ali's army was the previously apostate general al-Ash'ath, who was known for his unkempt hairstyles. Al-Ash'ath headed a group of Yemeni tribesmen that became known as the Sword of 'Ali.

Several months into the fighting, the two sides met on the field of battle for the final encounter. 'Ali's forces acquired the upper hand and had nearly defeated the

Syrian army, when Mu'awiyah and his soldiers held their Korans up on their spears, saying that fighting was silly and that the warring factions should submit to arbitration based on Islamic law.

Pressured by the Yemeni tribes in his forces, 'Ali submitted to the arbitration and sent a Yemeni representative to placate his forces. 'Ali was denied his first choice of a non-Yemeni representative by the Yemeni tribes when it was clear that Mu'awiyah was sending a non-Yemeni as well. Even though the Yemeni representative was not as savvy as 'Ali's first choice or Mu'awiyah's seasoned arbitrator, the Yemeni chiefs are said to have reasoned that a bad decision agreed upon by a Yemeni was better than a good decision in which a Yemeni had no part. Questionable logic carried the day; 'Ali sent the tribes' choice. In the end, the arbitration ended with the recognition of 'Ali as the caliph of much of the Muslim world, but Mu'awiyah returned to Syria and ruled as caliph there.

Perhaps more importantly, the arbitration at Siffin gave rise to a third Muslim sect known as the Kharajites. Although they initially supported the caliphate of 'Ali, they bannered behind the idea that the Siffin arbitration was a violation of divine will – they claimed it was not for mankind to bargain over the divine position of the imamate. 'Ali would later be assassinated by a Kharajite. Further down the road, a more moderate branch of the Kharajite faith, the Ibadhis, would rule over Hadhramawt and Sana'a and continues to this day to constitute the majority in neighbouring Oman.

'Ali and Mu'awiyah continue to vie for power in Yemen In Yemen, the population was divided between supporters for 'Ali and Mu'awiyah even after the arbitration at Siffin. As is often the case, disagreements between the two sides flared into armed conflicts. Both sides sent back messages to their patrons for support. In Iraq, 'Ali was busy fighting the zealous Kharajites and was unable to send reinforcements immediately to Yemen.

Mu'awiyah on the other hand used the opening to send propagandist emissaries and armed forces to help secure a foothold. His plan worked. Under the command of Busr bin Abi Artah al-'Amiri, Mu'awiyah's army marched through Sana'a to the coast and turned east to march toward Hadhramawt. He succeeded in conquering large parts of Yemen. 'Ali, however, eventually sent a large force to counter the growing threat of Mu'awiyah supporters in Yemen.

Neither side was able to enjoy complete success. When 'Ali was killed in AD661, Yemen was a political vacuum. The imamate was passed to 'Ali's son, Hassan, who quickly renounced the position to Mu'awiyah in an attempt to rejoin the factional Islamic world.

The rise of the Umayyad dynasty
With Hassan's abdication of the imamate, rule of the Islamic world was dominated by the Umayyad dynasty – Mu'awiyah and his kin – for the next 90 years. The rulers from Syria appointed governors across the Middle East, including the three Islamic centres of Yemen (Sana'a, al-Janad, and Hadhramawt).

Early rebellions The Umayyad dynasty had a reputation for being particularly cruel and harsh; in Yemen, the governors ruled in the same brutal style. Accordingly, during their tenure, various factions in Yemen launched a series of small revolts against the Umayyad dynasty, but local rulers typically were able to quell the insurrections without much trouble.

Angry with the appointment of caliphs solely from the Umayyad line of the Quraysh tribe, 'Abdullah ibn az-Zubayr followed the lead of his father (who had revolted during the rebellion of Aisha) and proclaimed himself caliph in AD682. He ruled from Medina and controlled much of the Arabian Peninsula, including Yemen. For the next ten years, he appointed the governors to Sana'a. His tenure as self-proclaimed caliph eventually was ended when the fifth Umayyad Caliph Abd al-Malik sent a large Syrian army and defeated him in Mecca.

With the defeat of az-Zubayr the Umayyad Caliphate launched a series of expansive campaigns, enlarging the Islamic world to encompass the land from Spain to India. Although Yemenis had formed the backbone of the Islamic army during the foreign campaigns of the first three caliphs, they took almost no part of the Umayyad battles. The caliphs made no requests to the Yemeni tribal leaders to turn out in droves once more, and the tribes did not feel the need to volunteer their manpower. On the contrary, the Umayyad caliphs largely ignored Yemen, and the country became politically isolated from the rest of the Islamic world.

The Ibadhi revolution In AD746, two men from the Ibadhi sect, a moderate division of the Kharajite branch that formed after the arbitration at Siffin, led another rebellion in Hadhramawt. Talib al-Haqq ('Abdullah ibn Yahya) and Abu Hamza (al-Mukhtar bin 'Awf al-Azdi) are said to have met in Mecca and agreed to spread the Ibadhi faith and overthrow Umayyad rule in Hadhramawt. The two quickly went to work and were very successful initially. Talib al-Haqq and Abu Hamza easily took over Hadhramawt, deposed the Umayyad governor there, and marched out to Sana'a.

The Sana'ani population was growing tired of Umayyad rule. The Ibadhis were able to defeat the governor there without much effort. With Sana'a under his control Talib al-Haqq managed to raise a large army, and he sent Abu Hamza north, occupying Mecca and Medina and challenging the Umayyad control there.

Marwan bin Muhammad, the last caliph of the Umayyad dynasty acted decisively once the Ibadhi rebellion broke into the Hijaz region and threatened his rule in Syria. He despatched an army that quelled the rebellion in Hijaz and Sana'a. The caliph's army marched onward to Hadhramawt and disposed of the remaining Ibadhi soldiers that had fled there. The Ibadhi faith persisted in Hadhramawt for several more centuries, and continues to exist to the east in Oman.

The Abbasid dynasty takes over From AD750 the Abbasid dynasty in Baghdad replaced the Umayyads as rulers of the Islamic world. For the next 100 years, the Abbasid rulers would appoint governors in Yemen as their predecessors had done. With rebellions on the increase, the Abbasid rulers paid more attention to keeping the area of Yemen in line.

The task was not easy – Yemeni tribes were revolting against Abbasid rule and the Abbasid governors themselves were often declaring their own independence from Baghdad. Retribution was often harsh – massacres were perpetrated in Sana'a, al-Janad and Hadhramawt in order to quell the rebellions.

The harsh retribution temporarily calmed the rebellious countryside (especially in Hadhramawt), but uprisings were occurring again in the highlands within two decades. In the areas of Mahweet and Tihama, the Abbasid rulers could not secure a lasting victory. While the Abbasids had considerable control over Sana'a and the areas to the north, they had less of a grasp on the lowlands and coastal area.

The reigns of Harun ar-Rashid and Abu Jafar al-Ma'mun This political situation lasted through the reign of the famous Abbasid caliph, Harun ar-Rashid (who may have been the factual inspiration for the king in the *1001 Arabian Nights* stories). Ar-Rashid continued to appoint governors to Yemen in a series of unsuccessful attempts to bring the area firmly under the Abbasid wing. When Harun ar-Rashid died in AD809, the feuding between his two sons took the Islamic world to another civil war (AD809–14), but Yemen played virtually no role in the conflict.

When the war ended, the victorious Abbasid Caliph Abu Jafar al-Ma'mun was able to focus on a Shi'ite rebellion, led by ibn Tabataba al-Hassani, which was breaking out on the Arabian Peninsula. Under ibn Tabataba's command, a general by the name of Ibrahim bin Musa al-Sadiq had marched toward Sana'a and took the city with relative ease.

Ibrahim bin Musa ruled Sana'a for about a year until al-Ma'mun sent a large army headed by Hamdawayh bin Mahan that defeated the Shi'ite ruler. Al-Ma'mun then appointed Hamdawayh Governor of Sana'a.

In a change of events worthy of a Gilbert and Sullivan operetta, al-Ma'mun appointed Ibrahim bin Musa's brother as heir to the caliphate. While there was no revelation that the two were switched at birth, Ibrahim bin Musa was vindicated and appointed as Governor of Yemen while Hamdawayh became the new enemy. The two continued to fight for several years, but it was bin Musa's successor to the governorship that eventually ousted Hamdawayh from power.

The Yemeni dynasties

The Ziyadids in Zabid Yet another wing of the Shi'ite rebellion rose in the Tihama region. The Abbasids had not been able to secure the region fully in their 70 years of rule, and al-Ma'mun was persuaded to adopt a different strategy. Under the advice of his Persian vizier, Fadl bin Sahl, al-Ma'mun planned to set up a new capital within the unruly coastal area where an additional governor could sit and rule the Tihama tribes directly.

Al-Ma'mun sent Muhammad bin Ziyad to quell the rebellion and set up the new capital. After arriving in Yemen in AD819, bin Ziyad set to the task of pacification by force. The following year he founded the city of Zabid as his seat of power. Over the next 40 years bin Ziyad expanded his domain to include Aden, Hadhramawt and ash-Shihr, solidifying the power base through which his sons, the Ziyadid dynasty would rule.

While the Ziyadid dynasty continued to claim nominal relations with the Abbasid rulers, the Ziyadids eventually established de facto independence. By AD866, Abbasid power had weakened significantly. The last great ruler of that dynasty, al-Mutawakkil, had been assassinated, the capital had been moved from Baghdad to Samarra and internal divisions were creating problems. The Ziyadids were able to effectively sever links with the Abbasids and helped in bringing rule of Yemen back to Yemenis.

The Yu'firid dynasty in Sana'a and al-Janad The power of the Abbasid dynasty was dwindling in Sana'a as well. In AD847, Yu'fir bin Abd al-Rahman al-Hiwali emerged from his home in Shibam Kawkaban to challenge the rule of the increasingly impotent Abbasid-appointed Governor of Sana'a. Yu'fir and his forces eventually prevailed, and the Abbasid governor was forced to hand over control of the city. Once he had seized Sana'a, Yu'fir was able to expand his control southward to al-Janad and Bayhan, the border of the area controlled by the Ziyadids. Historical sources state that the Yu'firids paid tribute to the Ziyadids. Eventually the area of the dynastic rule extended as far north as Sa'ada and Najran.

The Yu'firids claimed to be descended from the Tubba kings of the Himyarite Kingdom, perhaps as a way of legitimising their power. Additionally, like the Ziyadids, the Yu'firids retained nominal allegiance to the waning Abbasid Caliphate.

After 30 years of rule, old age prompted Yu'fir to retire from his position, and he gave control to his son, Muhammad bin Yu'fir. Muhammad continued the dynasty's ostensible recognition of Abbasid authority, and the Abbasid Caliph al-Mu'tamid bestowed *de jure* rule of Sana'a unto the young Yu'firid.

The story of the Yu'firid dynasty heads off in an odd direction. Muhammad appointed his son Ibrahim bin Muhammad to rule Yu'firid territory while the former embarked upon the pilgrimage to Mecca. Muhammad was apparently very moved by the religious trip. When he returned to Yemen he left Ibrahim in power, deciding to abdicate power in favour of a lifetime of devotion to Islam.

For reasons that are not entirely clear, the old, retired Yu'fir plotted with the young, ruling Ibrahim to kill the middle (also retired) Ibrahim. Ibrahim's execution of the plan was literally overkill. In addition to assassinating his father, the young ruler also killed his uncle, his cousin, and even his grandmother.

The tribes of the region revolted; nobody likes a grandma killer. By AD886 Ibrahim retreated to the sanctuary of Shibam and waited six years for the promised reinforcements from the Abbasid Empire. Eventually the Abbasid governor pacified the region. Asa'ad bin Ibrahim (named after the great Himyarite ruler Asa'ad al-Kamil), Ibrahim's son, returned to Sana'a to face the threats that were popping up from all sides.

A complicated struggle for power

So began a battle that none had expected; and it was called the Battle of Five Armies, and it was very terrible.

J R R Tolkien, *The Hobbit*

As the Yu'firids and Ziyadids were settling in, two new important powers appeared that would leave a political and religious impression upon Yemen that would last to the present day. Arriving in the Tihama from Egypt, the first of these powers were the Fatimid missionaries, precursors to Yemen's modern Isma'ilis. The second was the foundation of the Zaydi Imamate, heralded by the arrival of al-Hadi ila al-Haqq.

In the late 9th century the two Fatimid missionaries, Mansur al-Yemen ibn Hawshab and 'Ali bin Fadl, arrived on the coast of the Tihama at Ghulayfigha. They went their separate ways and began to attract followers and conquer land as part of their plan to bring Yemen under the control of the north African Imam Ubayd Allah al-Mahdi. Mansur al-Yemen settled on Jabal Masar in the central mountains, and 'Ali bin Fadl chose the region of Mudhaykhirah as his base of operations.

At the dawn of the 10th century al-Hadi ila al-Haqq, a respected religious scholar, was requested to come to Sa'ada from Medina and mediate between the warring tribes there. Through successful mediation and a large retinue of faithful followers, al-Hadi was able to establish the Zaydi Imamate in Yemen, a political and religious force that would rule in some capacity until the revolution in 1962.

The struggle between these powers usually manifested themselves in Sana'a, and in a period of a decade the city changed hands 20 times. 'Ali bin Fadl was eventually killed when the Yu'firid leader Asa'ad bin Ibrahim (who was serving as bin Fadl's deputy at the time) secretly arranged for a doctor to poison him. Mansur al-Yemen established a brief dynasty, but rivalries within his family quickly ended its hold on power after his death.

The Sulayhids, Najahids and Hamdanids Just as the ornate power struggle of the early 10th century dashed all hopes for lasting peace and tranquillity, the tribal rivalries of the early 11th century turned the country into a jumbled mess. It is described by the local historians as a period of darkness and desolation. From that period rose the Sulayhid dynasty – the second incarnation of the Isma'ili Fatimid cause. The period is remembered fondly by Yemenis today as a time of peace and prosperity, a time when great leaders such as 'Ali al-Sulayhi, Queen Asma and Queen Arwa ruled the land with respect and fairness.

'Ali al-Sulayhi, the founder of the dynasty, was influenced at an early age by an Isma'ili di'a who claimed to have a prized book of the occult that foretold al-Sulayhi's greatness. Al-Sulayhi established himself at Jabal Masar in the Haraz Mountains with the help of 60 loyal tribesmen. His numbers soon grew quickly, enabling him to capture Sana'a. With his popularly loved wife Asma at his side, he transferred the seat of governance to Sana'a, from where he ruled much of the country for nearly 20 years.

The Sulayhids' main rival was the Najahids, a dynasty formed by two former slaves after the fall of the Ziyadid dynasty in Zabid. The two dynasties vied for control over Zabid, and assassinations were common. Ultimately, the Sulayhids dominated the political scene, with minor interruptions from the Najahids in the Tihama.

After 'Ali al-Sulayhi was killed by one of the Najahids, his daughter-in-law Queen Arwa al-Sulayhi eventually took over the dynasty, moving her capital to Jiblah and leaving Sana'a to be taken by the Hamdanid sultans. Queen Arwa ruled from her palace in Jiblah for over 50 years and is remembered as one of the country's greatest rulers.

The Ayyubids, Rasulids and Tahirids The Sulayhid dynasty and the Fatimid missionaries before it had been loyal to the Fatimid Caliphate in Egypt. Within 35 years of Queen Arwa's death, the Fatimid Caliphate was overthrown by Saladin and the Ayyubids. Within several years of their rise to power in Egypt, Saladin sent his brother Turanshah to Yemen to bring the country under Ayyubid control. Following Turanshah's capture of most of the country (except for the Zaydi strongholds of the north), the Ayyubids stayed as the ruling power for about 55 years, unifying much of the country and setting the stage for the glory years of the Rasulids.

When the Rasulids established their capital in Ta'iz in 1229, they heralded in one of the most prosperous periods of Yemeni history. New construction flourished, as did the study of the sciences. Early in their reign, the Rasulids had signed a treaty with the Zaydis, giving the former control of Sana'a. The agreement was honoured for about 50 years before altercations between the two powers erupted in the city. To the north, the Zaydis had clear control of the mountains, and the Rasulids continued to maintain a firm hold on the southern mountains and the Tihama – a political situation that remained throughout much of the 200 years of Rasulid rule.

When the Rasulid dynasty came to an end in 1454, the Tahirids took control of southern Yemen and maintained tenuous relationships with the Zaydis in the north. Unlike the Rasulids, the Tahirids had little desire to continually fight the northern imams for control of Sana'a. While attempts were made to capture the city at various points over the next 75 years, the Tahirids for the most part were content to rule their stretch of land in the south of Yemen.

The age of colonialism
The first Ottoman occupation and afterwards The 16th century was awash with activity in Yemen. The Kathiri Sultanate had recently risen to power in Hadhramawt and was establishing its new capital in Tarim. The Portuguese had been seen off the western Tihama coast and had briefly established a colony on Socotra. Egyptian Mamluk forces arrived and quickly spread across the country, only to withdraw shortly thereafter when their home country was conquered by the Ottomans. The Zaydis were able to capitalise on the vacuum created by the Mamluks' withdrawal and spread their dominion far farther south than had been previously possible.

Eager to prevent Portuguese incursion into the area, the Ottomans soon launched a massive campaign to take control of Yemen. With the exception of the Zaydi stronghold in Shahara, the Ottoman forces dominated much of western Yemen for the next century.

In addition to these political developments, the 16th century also witnessed the rebirth of Yemen as a major exporter on the world market. As the coffee trade began to flourish, parts of the country enjoyed an economic boom that, while not nearly as lucrative, hearkened back to the days when the country shipped frankincense and myrrh to the rest of the world. Yemen maintained its monopoly on the coffee trade until the late 17th century, and continued lucrative trading up until the mid 18th century, exporting the beans from the western port of al-Mokha, which gave rise to the term *mocha* coffee.

The first Ottoman occupation ended as the 17th-century Zaydi Imam Qasim the Great gathered support and launched a concerted effort to expel the Turks from the country. Following his death in 1620, Imam Qasim's son continued the task, and by 1636 the Ottoman forces had completely left the country. The withdrawal of the Ottomans initiated another period of Zaydi control in much of northern Yemen. In the south, the Sultanate of Lahej took control of Aden, and the sultanates of the Kathiris, Qu'aitis and Mahris fought in Hadhramawt. The picture that took shape in Yemen – of the self-isolated Zaydi imams in the north, governing the Shafi'i population in the Tihama, and control of the south in the hands of various sultanates – would remain even through the next occupations and up unto the modern era.

British and Ottoman interests British interest in south Arabia materialised in the beginning of the 19th century. Initial settlements on the islands of Perim and Socotra were abandoned as the British finally occupied the city of Aden in 1839. At this time the sultanates of Hadhramawt were entrenched in a bitter war that lasted for several decades. The fighting between the sultanates mostly came to an end when the British imposed peace on the area. In 1882, the Qu'aitis signed a treaty of friendship with the British. Treaties of friendship with other sultanates soon followed, leading to the establishment of the Aden Protectorates.

The second Ottoman occupation began in 1849, when the Turks returned and conquered much of the north. Battles between the forces of the Ottomans and the Zaydis were nearly continuous until Imam Yahya and the Turkish Pasha signed the Treaty of Da'in in 1911, giving the Tihama to the Ottomans and reserving the highlands for the imamate. Up until the end of World War I, the Ottomans and the Imam Yahya each maintained their hold on their respective areas, with the British in Aden exerting control over the southern and eastern protectorates.

After the war the Ottoman Empire collapsed, and the British gave control of the Tihama to Muhammad al-Idrisi, who had fought against the Ottomans with British support during the previous decade. Following his death, squabbling between his descendants prompted the downfall of Idrisid control of the area, and

Beginning in 1949, two years after the founding of the state of Israel, the majority of Jews in Yemen were airlifted to the new formed state from Aden in a mission known as Operation Magic Carpet. The mass exodus posed a serious problem for the Yemeni economy – the Jews were the only artisans in the country. After all, less than 200 years ago the Imam of Sana'a had banned all of the country's Jewish population to the Red Sea coast, only to plead for their return when he realised the city was in desperate need of their skills. Imam Ahmed, however, agreed to let many of the Jews emigrate after a crash-course apprenticeship was held with local Muslims. In the course of a year, some 45,000 Jews were transported to Israel. The Yemeni art of silver crafting has never recovered.

Imam Yahya and the rulers of Saudi Arabia quickly competed to grab up the land. As tensions mounted, the two countries went to war, and Imam Yahya lost much of Yemen's northern and coastal land. The Saudis eventually withdrew from the Tihama cities of Hudaydah and al-Luhayyah, but in return Imam Yahya agreed not to challenge Saudi control of Asir, Jizan, and Najran – the northern areas lost in the war. The border between Yemen and Saudi Arabia remained largely undemarcated until the recent border agreement was finalised in 2004.

For the next 40 years the imams controlled the highlands and the west, adopting an extreme isolationist policy, while the British controlled Aden and the protectorates in the east. Seeds of revolution were forming in both halves of the country though. In 1948, the Free Yemeni Movement attempted a coup in the north, assassinating Imam Yahya and declaring 'Abdullah al-Wazir the new imam. The movement had failed to kill Yahya's son Ahmed, who gathered tribal forces in Hajjah and decisively ended the coup attempt with massive executions.

Although Imam Ahmed had been able to dodge the attempt on his life in 1948 and a further one in 1955, he finally fell to the assassins' bullet in 1961. (The hearty imam was shot five times but did not die from his wounds until 1962.) His son Muhammad al-Badr succeeded him as the Zaydi imam. If the revolutionaries had any hope that Imam al-Badr would reform Yemen, he quickly set the picture straight. In his first speech as imam, he warned the people of Ta'iz that harsh consequences would befall anyone who even thought of opposing the regime. The revolution that would finally overthrow the 1,000-year-old imamate broke out within a week.

Following the start of the revolution, northern Yemen endured nearly eight years of civil war as the republic forces were assisted by Egypt and the royalists by Saudi Arabia and Britain. The civil war ended in 1970 with the victory of the newly formed Yemen Arab Republic ('YAR').

Just as the Free Yemenis and other movements had been working toward independence in the north, the National Liberation Front ('NLF') and the Front for the Liberation of Occupied South Yemen ('FLOSY') fought the British in the south. The NLF was a leftist-leaning guerrilla movement and FLOSY an Egyptian-encouraged movement that grew out of the British–Egyptian conflict playing itself out in northern Yemen. British forces began to engage with the NLF guerrillas in the Radfan Mountains in late 1963. Fierce fighting and harsh tactics were used by both sides as the 'Aden Emergency' wore on. In 1966, the British announced their intention to remove all military installations east of Suez, and the last British forces withdrew from the country on 30 November 1967.

North and South Yemen Following its independence from the British, South Yemen was dominated by the NLF, and in three years the country became the

People's Democratic Republic of Yemen ('PDRY') – the only Arab Marxist state in world history. Relations between the two states were tense, even as initial exploratory committees were formed as early as 1972 to consider unification. Border disputes flared into a brief war in the same year.

The 1970s was not a good decade to be president of the YAR. President Iryani was sent into exile in 1974, Ibrahim al-Hamdi was murdered in 1977, and his successor Ahmad al-Gashmi was assassinated when a 'secret message' briefcase exploded in 1978. Ali Abdullah Saleh became president in 1978, and, managing to make it through the rest of the decade unscathed, has held the position to the present day.

Following the collapse of the Soviet Union in 1989, North and South Yemen renewed their discussions to unify the country, and by 1990 the process of unification began. Growing pains were expected, but in 1994 the country fell into complete civil war. With the eager support of the northern tribes, the conflict had ended within the year.

Following the attacks of 11 September 2001, Yemen became a staunch supporter of the United States in the war on terror. Given that the *USS Cole* had been attacked by al-Qaeda members the year before off the coast of Aden, President Saleh may have felt the need to prove Yemen's commitment. Several months after a late-2001 visit to the United States, the Yemeni government began an intense crackdown on suspected Islamic militants, eventually expelling more than 100 foreign Islamic scholars – including citizens of Britain and France.

In 2004, Yemen and Saudi Arabia at last finalised their mutual border. An impromptu and undemarcated border had existed between the two countries since the signing of the Treaty of Taif that had ended a short conflict between them in 1934. The new border agreement restores some, but not all, of the land that Yemen had lost to Saudi Arabia in that conflict.

In the same year that the border agreement was executed, a new conflict arose in the north. From 2004 to the present, the government has been involved in attempts to quell the al-Houthi rebellion in the northern governorate of Sa'ada. The conflict has died down several times, only to reignite again at a moment's notice. The most recent development at the time of this writing was a cease-fire agreement in mid-June 2007.

GOVERNMENT AND POLITICS

Yemen is a constitutional democracy with three branches of government specified by the constitution: executive, legislative and judicial. The executive branch is headed by a president, but also includes the lesser position of prime minister. The legislative branch contains a 301-seat elected parliament and a 111-seat president-appointed Shura Council.

There is a multitude of political and independent parties in Yemen, but the long-ruling al-Mu'tammer Party ('the General People's Congress') is the only one with any real authority. Al-Mu'tammer is the party of President Ali Abdullah Saleh and of 228 of the 301 members of parliament. Next in line in importance behind al-Mu'tammer is the Islah Party ('the Reform Party'), the Islamic reform party founded and headed by Sheikh Abdullah al-Ahmar. The Islah Party holds 47 seats in parliament. A third party that has decreased in importance over the last two decades is the Yemen Socialist Party. It currently holds seven seats in parliament, down from the 69 seats it held in the pre-civil war elections of 1993. Currently, only one woman holds a seat in parliament.

Yemenis tend to show their support of political parties mostly by displaying the party's symbol. Thus, as you travel across the country, you are likely to see rearing horses (*al-mu'tammer*) and shining suns (*islah*) spray painted on countless building walls. Perhaps it is these icons, which relate back to pre-Islamic symbols, which explain why these two parties have fared so well. Independent parties that use symbols like umbrellas or mobile phones do not do as well at the polls.

The latest presidential election was held in 2006. Ali Abdullah Saleh ran for the Mu'tammer Party, despite repeated assertions that he would not seek office for another term, and Faisal bin Shamlan was the candidate of the Islah and Socialist party. The elections were not completely fair – bin Shamlan in no way had the resources or media time that Saleh wielded – but they were given surprisingly good reviews by a European Union monitoring committee. Saleh won 77.2% of the vote and bin Shamlan 21.8%. In the 1999 elections, Saleh had prevailed with 96%.

ECONOMY

Yemen is the poorest country in the Arab world, especially in comparison with its significantly richer neighbours. Yemen's GDP per capita rests at US$900, a far cry from the US$14,000 of Saudi Arabia and Oman. Yemen's economy relies on a delicate balance of exploiting its small oil wealth, exporting goods from fisheries and the agricultural sector, and receiving a large amount of foreign aid and remittances from Yemenis working overseas.

PEOPLE

The Arabs of Yemen are divided into different ethnic and socially ordered groups, although it is not correct to refer to the latter in terms of castes. Ethnically, people are distinguished as coastal inhabitants, mountain dwellers or Bedouin.

The social distinctions in the north of the country in order of importance are as follows: first, the upper level is the Sayyids, descendants of the Prophet Muhammad; second, there are the tribesmen; and third, there are the muzayyin, the working servant class, including the occupations of barbers, butchers, musicians, and even restaurant owners. Needless to say, the social orderings do not necessarily correspond with economic status – a wealthy muzayyin restaurant owner will be better off financially than a poor tribesman, for instance. These social distinctions have come to have less importance in recent history, but they still affect certain ways of life. As an example, people rarely marry outside their social class.

Tribal culture is one of the main cornerstones of society in Yemen, and how people act on a day-to-day basis is affected largely by notions of tribal honour. A tribesman loses honour by committing 'ayb – shame or disgrace. The word is often used playfully, or at least half-jokingly, with the accompanying signal of grabbing your chin with your thumb and index finger (as if pulling on a beard). When used in all seriousness, however, the word is a serious challenge that questions the appropriateness of another's behaviour.

There are hundreds of tribes in the country, but most belong to one of three major tribal federations. The most powerful of these are the Hashid tribes, who are not the largest grouping, but who contain such important members as President Ali Abdullah Saleh and Sheikh Abdullah al-Ahmar (leader of parliament and president of the Islah opposition party).

There is also a small Jewish population in Yemen, mostly centred in the cities of Sa'ada and Raydah.

LANGUAGE

The official language of Yemen is Arabic, although English is spoken to a small extent in some of the larger cities. Yemeni Arabic is reputed to be the closest to the original classical dialect – presumably this refers to the dialect of Bedouins, who are generally regarded to speak the purest Arabic. Different areas of the country have regional variations of the language.

Several languages of the Modern South Arabian language family exist in the governorate of al-Mahra and Socotra. Native speakers of Mahri number 70,000 and speakers of Socotri 50,000. A third language, Bathari, is spoken by only 200 people or so in eastern parts of the country. Needless to say, all three of the languages are in danger of extinction.

RELIGION

The religion of Islam is based on the belief that the Angel Gabriel (of Old and New Testament fame) revealed the words of the Koran to Muhammad, the last in a long line of prophets. According to Islamic belief, there have been many messengers and prophets sent to various groups of people throughout history. In some cases, God sends prophets to deliver messages to the larger human community. As time passed, the words of the prophets were changed and the message became distorted; God found it necessary to send a new prophet to bring mankind back to the path of the true religion.

For this reason, Muslims believe that the Angel Gabriel revealed the Koran to Muhammad over a period of 23 years. The religions of Judaism and Christianity had been sent true prophets (such as Abraham, Moses and Jesus), but the message that the prophets had delivered had been distorted over time. (So just as Christianity views itself as the continuation of Judaism, so Islam views itself as the continuation of the Judeo-Christian line.) To prevent the problems that had occurred with previous messages, the Koran was revealed in Arabic – a language that would allow the entire message to remain unchanged throughout the rest of history. According to Muslim belief then, the Koran has remained absolutely unchanged since it was revealed to Muhammad, and only the original Arabic version of the text is authentic.

Muslims today are divided into two major groups – Sunni and Shi'a – the former comprising about 90% of Muslims worldwide. The schism between these two groups originates from the appointment of the first imam following Muhammad's death. The Shi'a believe that Muhammad appointed 'Ali to be his successor, but the Sunni do not believe that Muhammad made any such claim. After the prophet's death, Abu Bakr became the first caliph of the Islamic world. While the Sunni regard Abu Bakr as having been rightfully elected, most Shi'a regard him and his two successors ('Omar and 'Uthman) as usurpers. According to the Shi'a the imam must be a member of the *Ahl al-Bayt* – the family of the house – a descendant of 'Ali and Muhammad's daughter Fatima. For the Sunni, the only familial requirement of an imam is that he belong to Muhammad's tribe, the Quraysh.

There are other differences between the two groups, and the dissimilarity between them often resembles the differences between Orthodox and Gnostic Christianity. The Shi'a represent the more mystical side of the debate, often attributing divine nature or powers to the imams. Many Shi'a also believe in a 'hidden' imam – that one of the previous imams had not really died, but that he had gone into hiding and would return later in time as the Mahdi. The Shi'a place a great importance on esoteric knowledge, the hidden meaning of the Koran. The Sunni, on the other hand, base their faith more on rationalism than mysticism. The founding tenets of Sunni law are based on the Koran and the Hadith, the later recorded sayings and actions of Muhammad. The Sunni reject the notion of occultation, and they do not believe that imams have been imbued with divine power.

Within each branch, there are further subdivisions. The Sunni are divided into four major schools of law: Malaki, Hanafi, Hanbali, and Shafi'i, the last being prevalent in Yemen. The major subdivisions of the Shi'a branch are the Twelvers, the Isma'ilis, and the Zaydis, of which the two last are found in Yemen. Among both branches of Islam are found orders of Sufism, a more mystical side of Islam that emphasises oneness with God.

ISLAM IN YEMEN In Yemen, there are three distinct Islamic sects. In the mountain areas of the north, the Zaydis are prominent, but there are small pockets of Isma'ilis. In the rest of the country, the Yemenis primarily belong to the Shafi'i school of Sunni Islam, and they constitute the largest religious group in the country.

The Shafi'is Among Sunni Muslims today the meaning of what religious school you belong to is of little importance. In essence, the meaning of one's being Shafi'i means that when questions of Islamic law arise, you will have them resolved by a Shafi'i legal scholar. Thus, there is little impact resulting from the choice of one of the four schools in a Muslim's day-to-day affairs, and a general description of Sunni Islam suffices to explain the practices of Shafi'i Muslims.

The word 'Islam' in Arabic means 'submission' – as in submission to the will of God. The 'Muslim', therefore, is the one who submits to the will of God. The traditional view is that the religion is based on 'five pillars', which constitute the primary commands to which the true believer must submit. These five pillars are the profession of faith, praying, the charity tax, fasting, and the pilgrimage.

The first of these pillars, the profession of faith, is the most important and is required to be said to become a Muslim. The transliterated Arabic text of the profession is *ashadu an la ellahu illa Allah, wa ashadu Muhammadan rasul Allah*, which translated means 'I bear witness that there is no deity but God and that Muhammad is His messenger'. The second pillar requires Muslims to pray five-times daily. You will often hear the words of the profession of faith announced from the speakers of the minarets during any one of the five calls to prayer, at dawn, noon, afternoon, sunset, and evening. Third, Muslims are required to pay a charity tax known as *zakat* that is similar to the notion of tithing. The charity tax is normally calculated at 2.5% of a Muslim's income and is paid each lunar year. Fourth, during the month of Ramadan, Muslims are required to fast during daylight hours, abstaining from food, drink, smoking and sex. The Koran is believed to have been first revealed to Muhammad during this month. Last, every Muslim that is capable of doing so is required to make a pilgrimage to Mecca once in his lifetime.

In addition to the five pillars, there are six traditionally recognised articles of faith within mainstream Islam. These articles are belief in God, His angels, His prophets and their scriptures, the final judgement and predestination.

One peculiarity of the Shafi'i school is its traditional acceptance of and relationship with the mystical practice of Sufi schools. In Yemen this connection is quite close, and many Shafi'is also combine a version of Sufi mysticism into their faith. One outcrop of this combination is the prominence many Shafi'i place on visiting the graves of Muslim saints.

The Zaydis The branch of Islam most adhered to in the highland regions of the country is the school of Zaydiyya, which traces its origin back to Zayd bin 'Ali. Zayd and his brother Muhammad were sons of the fourth Shi'a Imam 'Ali bin al-Hussayn and the grandsons of the 'founding father' 'Ali. Towards the end of the Umayyad Caliphate's reign in AD740, Zayd made plans for an uprising in Kufa against the rulers. Although Zayd was successful in garnering support from most Shi'ites initially, many abandoned his planned revolt after his refusal to renounce totally the previous three caliphs that had preceded 'Ali. Among those who withdrew their support for the revolt was his elder brother Muhammad.

The massive army that Zayd had prepared before for the revolt dwindled to some 300 men. Nevertheless he proceeded with the attack and was well known throughout the Muslim world for his subsequent martyrdom. Supposedly after his body was found, his head was sent to Syria and rest of his corpse hung in Egypt for several years before the next caliph burned it, scattering the ashes to the wind. While Zayd earned the nickname 'the martyr', his brother Muhammad is known as being one of the least persecuted Shi'a imams by a reigning caliph.

Zayd's followers were displeased that Muhammad had not taken part in the revolt. They believed that armed rebellion against illegitimate or corrupt governments was a religious duty, and this belief has remained an important part of Zaydi thought to this day. (The recent skirmishes between al-Houthi's 'believing youth' and government forces in the northern governorate of Sa'ada, for example, seem to be based on this principle.)

The Zaydis stem from the group of Shi'a that recognised Zayd as their fifth imam. For this reason they have been known in the West also as 'Fivers', although the term is misleading. Whereas the largest Shi'a branch, the 'Twelvers', strictly believe that there were only 12 visible imams, the 'Fivers' have recognised many more imams throughout their history. The term merely denotes that the initial source of the Zaydis' disagreement with the mainstream Shi'a schools, such as the Twelvers and the Isma'ilis, was over the position of the fifth Imam. Contrary to the Zaydis, most Shi'a recognise Zayd's brother Muhammad as the fifth imam.

Zaydi beliefs Zaydi thought and culture is far removed from that of other Shi'a branches. The Zaydis take a more rationalist approach to religion, and they are often described as the 'fifth school' of Sunni Islam. The Zaydis do not embrace the mystical and supernatural tenets of the other Shi'a sects. For example, there is no belief in the hidden imam or the divine nature of the imams. In choosing their Imam, Zaydis place primary emphasis on religious learning. Unlike the other Shi'a sects as well, there is no requirement that the imamate passes from father to son – any descendant of 'Ali may become the imam if he meets the Zaydi requirements. These beliefs create the interesting situation in Yemen of Zaydi–Shafi'i relations in which the Shi'a are more focused on a strict rationalist approach while the Sunnis accept a more mystical version of the religion.

The Zaydis do, however, use an extended version of the Shi'a call to prayer. Like the Shi'a, they add the phrase 'make haste toward the best deed', but unlike them, they do not use the phrase "Ali is the friend of God'. The voice booming over the minaret loudspeakers that you will hear as you walk through Sana'a calls out:

الله اكبر	(allahu akbar)	God is the Greatest
اشهد ان لا اله الا الله	(ashhadu ana la illaha illa allah)	I profess that there is no deity but God
اشهد ان محمد رسول الله	(ashhadu ana muhammadun rusul allah)	and that Muhammad is God's prophet
حي على الصلاة	(Hay 'ala as-Salah)	Make haste toward prayer
حي على الفلاح	(Hay 'ala al-falah)	Make haste toward welfare
حي على خير العمل	(Hay 'ala khayr al-'amal)	Make haste toward the best deed
الله اكبر	(allahu akbar)	God is the greatest
لا اله الا الله	(la illaha illa allah)	There is no deity but God

The Zaydi movement in Yemen was founded in AD897 by Imam al-Hadi ila al-Haqq, who established his capital in the city of Sa'ada. Al-Hadi and his two sons (both of whom were recognised as imams) were buried in the al-Hadi Mosque in Sa'ada, and the city has remained the centre of Zaydi thought to this day. Zaydi imams ruled parts of northern Yemen on and off from the arrival of al-Hadi until the revolution in 1967.

The Isma'ilis Around the area of the Haraz Mountains there is a number of pockets of Da'udi and Sulaymani Isma'ilis. The religion is an esoteric faith that resembles Gnosticism in many ways. Because of harsh persecution by Zaydi rulers throughout their tenure in Yemen, the Isma'ilis maintain a level of secrecy about their beliefs that is hard to breach. Below I have tried to outline the somewhat confusing history that has led to the creation of the Isma'ili sects in Yemen today as well as a short discussion of their very intriguing beliefs.

The beginnings of Isma'ili history The Isma'ilis separated from the major branch of Shi'a over the appointment of the seventh imam. While the Isma'ilis agreed with the Twelvers in favouring Muhammad bin 'Ali over his brother Zayd as the fifth imam, the schism between the two groups manifested shortly thereafter. The problem arose during the reign of Muhammad's son, Jafar as-Sadik. Although Jafar had appointed his eldest son Isma'il bin Jafar as the heir to the imamate, Isma'il died before the position could be passed down. Following Jafar's death, the Shi'a disagreed over the issue of succession. The majority of the Shi'a rallied around Isma'il's brother Musa al-Kazim and claimed that the imamate be passed to him.

A small group of 'strict legitimists' argued that the imamate could only pass down to the eldest son of the reigning imam. These adherents believed that Isma'il had not actually died but had gone into occultation as the hidden imam, a figure who would rule in secret and return later in time as the Mahdi to rule the entire world in peace and justice. Other members of the faith believed that the imamate had passed to Isma'il's son, Muhammad ibn Isma'il, and that it was Muhammad who later disappeared and who would return as the Mahdi.

From these two groups emerged the branch of Islam known as the Isma'ilis. In the west, particularly, this religious group came to be known as the 'Seveners' for their initial belief that the seventh Imam had been the last. Changes over the religion within the next century (as we shall see) caused the name to no longer apply to Isma'ili beliefs. As with the term 'Fivers' for the Zaydis, the appellation is not quite correct. Isma'ilis themselves prefer the term 'Fatimids', an allusion to Muhammad's daughter Fatima who was married to 'Ali.

The Isma'ilis as a political power By the end of the 9th century AD, the Isma'ilis had emerged as a well organised religious movement intent on challenging the rule of the Abbasid Caliphate. Missionaries were sent to various parts of the Islamic world to bring Muslims under the sway of the Isma'ili leader Ubayd Allah. In Yemen, Mansur al-Yemen ibn Hawsab and 'Ali bin Fadl had great success in bringing much of the country under their control.

Going against prior doctrine, Ubayd Allah then claimed that he was both the imam and the returning Mahdi. Moreover, he stated that all of his predecessors up to Muhammad ibn Isma'il had also been imams and that they had only concealed their true identity as a means of protection against the Abbasid Caliphate. (Thus, there are more than seven imams.) Many of the missionaries who had been sent out rebelled against the news, but the sects in Yemen remained faithful. (While 'Ali bin Fadl later repudiated Ubayd Allah, it was for different reasons.) Ubayd Allah's claim to the imamate eventually dominated all Isma'ili belief.

Some 200 years later the death of Imam al-Mutansir – the seventh imam after Ubayd Allah – created another schism. While al-Mutansir's son Nizar was appointed by his father as the rightful successor, most sources state that vizier al-Afdal installed Nizar's brother al-Musta'li in an attempt to rule the kingdom by proxy. Supposedly, Nizar was imprisoned for protesting and eventually killed. Those who followed Nizar formed the larger Isma'ili contingent known as the Nizaris, while those who supported the imamate of the younger brother, such as the communities in Yemen, formed the Musta'lis. Naturally, the Musta'lis deny any foul play in the instalment of al-Musta'li as the 19th imam, claiming that al-Mutansir had designated al-Musta'il as the new imam on his deathbed.

New imam, same occultation When al-Musta'li's son and appointed heir died after a short reign as the imam, the imamate was due to fall to al-Musta'li's grandson, the newborn at-Tayyib. Instead, at-Tayyib's uncle took the throne as regent, but later claimed the imamate for himself. The infant heir apparent was never heard from again; he likely met an untimely end to suit the political appetite of his uncle. Although there was a movement supporting the evil uncle, it eventually died out. The majority of Musta'lis believed that at-Tayyib had not disappeared, but that he had gone into hiding as the Mahdi, as the Isma'ilis had originally believed of Muhammad bin Isma'il. Accordingly, Musta'lis are known more commonly today as Tayyibis. (Thank God they are not known as the 'Nineteeners' or the 'Twenty Oners!')

Since the worldly concealment of Imam at-Tayyib each new leader of the Tayyibi faith has held the title of *di'a al-mutlak*, meaning that he has absolute authority to conduct religious matters on behalf of the hidden imam at-Tayyib. After the headquarters of the Tayyibi faith had moved from Yemen to India, a disagreement over who should succeed the 26th *di'a* led to another rift of the religion. The differences were irreconcilable and led to the creation of the Da'udi Branch – which recognised Da'udi bin Kutbshah – and the Sulaymani Branch – which recognised Sulayman bin Hasan. (The 'Twenty One plus Twenty Seveners' doesn't have a good ring to it either.) Both of these branches of the Tayyibis are present in Yemen.

Tayyibi Isma'ili beliefs Interestingly enough, even though the name 'Seveners' is often misapplied to the Isma'ilis, the number seven figures predominantly in the sect's religious beliefs. Unlike the Sunni description of belief, the Isma'ilis hold that there are seven pillars of Islam: love of God, the prophets, the imam and the *di'a*; purity and cleanliness; seven daily prayers; charity tax; fasting; the pilgrimage to Mecca; and jihad, a holy struggle.

In the beginning God created ten intellects. The third intellect, known as the spiritual Adam, tried to rise above his place just as the Adam of the Garden of Eden ate the fruit to become like God. The spiritual Adam's punishment was his fall – he plummeted below the other intellects along with other spiritual bodies that had tried to recognise his ascendancy to a higher intellect, thus creating the physical world. Following his repentance, the spiritual Adam rose to the rank of the tenth intellect.

There are seven major cycles, each heralded by a prophet and his interpreter or by the return of the Mahdi. Accordingly the first six prophets were Adam, Noah, Abraham, Moses, Jesus and Muhammad. It is believed that each of these prophets delivered a message from God, but that there was also a hidden meaning contained within that could be expounded by the prophet's appointed interpreter. For Muhammad this man was 'Ali. For the Tayyibis, this interplay between the prophets and their interpreters is very important. Religious law and the esoteric meaning are weighed equally on the scale, and compliance with each is expected.

Alan George

The Arabic countries, particularly the countries of the Near and Middle East, are mostly perceived in the West as conflict-prone areas. In the Arab world, Western economic and technological superiority, as well as the intervention of the US and its allies, have led to increasing feelings of humiliation and inferiority. Wide parts of Arabic societies are suspicious of Western ideas and concepts. At the same time Western lifestyles are taking hold of the cities and the elites. However, on a cultural and societal level, Islam has a special meaning for the cultural identity and civil society of the Muslim people in the Middle East, yet Islam as a political concept comes up in conflict situations. Ironically the political incidents of the last decade could prove that religion is becoming more relevant as a cultural connecting point between east and west.

There are differences between western and Yemeni understanding of conflict management, and between Islamic and tribal methods, approaches and rules. Local traditions and pre-Islamic customs are integrated into everyday life, but traditional perceptions hit upon new ideas and modern attitudes. Globalisation and migration have altered the way of life in Yemen, and lead to feelings of insecurity and a threat to accustomed behaviour. This has fuelled extremist views fostered by societal change processes, economic backwardness, extremely difficult local premises and historical conflicts.

One of the most important conflict lines in Yemen is the relationship between state and tribes and between the tribes themselves. The reasons for conflicts usually stem from the distribution of resources (water, oil, land), which result in violent clashes, particularly in rural areas. However, there are also alliances between the conflict actors, which suit the purpose of political power in the country. Perhaps a second conflict line is the relationship between the former north and south of Yemen. Since reunification of the two Yemeni states in 1990, the southern political elites lack a sense of participation in political power. This results in tensions at a governmental level and in grievances of the population in the south.

Another conflict line is the clash between tradition and modernity. The Yemeni urban and rural elites increasingly question their own culture and adopt Western life concepts due to the influence of globalisation. Furthermore, the urban centres are affected by migration from rural parts of the country. Cities become more influenced by the rural population which causes a tribalisation and ruralisation of urban areas and sharpens the conflict between traditional and modern behaviour.

The Islamic belief is considered as a moral guideline and is deeply rooted in the Yemeni society. Furthermore, honour and reputation of a family are part of the basic elements of Yemeni culture since pre-Islamic times. An essential characteristic of identity is ancestry, respectively origin of a family. Collective interests are much more important than individual needs. This leads to decisions in conflict cases that are not always concordant with individual justice, but serve the common welfare.

In difficult situations, the Koran calls for patient and calm behaviour. Public holding of personal conflicts is not desired, as confrontational behaviour leads to the loss of face. From the religious as well as the societal point of view it is desired to face conflicts rather in a passive and expectant way than with confrontation.

In severe cases that have a violent impact on society (eg: murder) and which can cause a potential threat of perpetuating revenge, there are different possibilities of conflict resolution, one of which being the acknowledgement of debt by the perpetrator. This situation allows for the debt to be admitted and to accept the sentence – which once initiated, cannot be debated – of his opponent. According to tribal tradition, it is expected that the remorseful delinquent receives a diminished punishment or is set free. The reason behind it is the importance of the common welfare (by stopping escalation of the conflict) and the demonstration of one's own honour and dignity. Another possibility for conflict resolution is by paying blood money by way of compensation for murder. The sum is fixed according to the way the murder has been carried out and the persons that were involved. If the murder took place under unfair conditions, eg: by shooting the victim in the back, or if it is regarded as a shameful act like killing a guest, the sum rises and the delinquent can even be expelled from the tribe. Returning to the tribe is only possible by performing a great deed. If the blood money is for whatever reason not paid by the accused, the other tribesmen have to contribute to it.

If a solution for such a conflict case cannot be found, the murder is avenged by another murder. In many cases the retaliation for the murder continues, causing further violent clashes.

There is a clear structure of responsibilities and competences in conflict resolution. The 'Aqil' is the head of a tribal branch and responsible for arbitration of conflicts in everyday life. If he is not competent enough to solve the case, the persons involved in the conflict can address a sheikh of another tribal branch or tribe.

The sheikh is responsible for difficult and serious cases. His judgement is legally effective for the whole tribe. The sheikh has to be male, of considerable age, and authorised for his function with the required knowledge and wisdom. It is his duty to make sure that unwilling conflict parties negotiate with each other. Usually he would sacrifice an animal of his own and get it slaughtered in front of the houses of the opponents, obligating them to hand over their weapons and negotiate under his supervision. Complicated cases of conflicts between different tribes demand an expert, who is called a *maragha* and is specialised in complex tribal conflicts. He is firm with the specific coherences and the history of a tribal conflict and is the highest judicial authority. Although it is desirable and possible that every tribe has its own maragha, he is not brought out by every tribe. If the tribe does not have its own maragha, the maragha of another tribe can be asked for advice and support.

Internationally, Yemen is perceived as a country where conflicts are mostly solved with weapons; however, non-violent methods of conflict resolution are rooted and used in Islamic as well as in tribal tradition. Conflict management in Yemen follows certain rules that have been tried out for centuries and are predominantly accepted by the local population. Problems in implementing these rules and methods of conflict management result from the parallel existence of tribal tradition and the attempts of modern state to enforce state power and rule of law.

The following differences emerge when comparing Western and Yemeni methods of conflict management. While the Western focus lies on the individual right, the traditional Yemeni legislation strongly underlines the maintaining of common welfare. It is not the issue to accomplish the legal claim of the victim against the offender or to punish the perpetrator, but the rebuilding and preservation of the community to which both actors belong. Remarkably, this principle has been changing due to the impact of modern and Western judicial approaches.

State legislation on the other hand is strongly influenced by religion and tradition. Partly, state jurisdiction legitimises subsequent decisions that were made according to traditional rules. This is a huge problem for foreign investors as the legal position in the country is not reliable.

The concept of remorse is, from the Western point of view, essential for the relationship between victim and perpetrator as well as for the determination of the punishment. In contrast, conflict management in Yemen puts emphasis on retaining honour and reputation of the actors. Where the conflict case, ie: the crime, is of such a dimension that it is not possible to retain reputation, the community separates from the person, who is then expelled from the tribe.

At the end of each cycle, the spiritual Adam moves up one rank in the ordering of intellects. The start of the seventh and final cycle that will allow the spiritual Adam to take its rightful place as the third intellect will begin with the return of the Mahdi at-Tayyib, who instead of delivering a new message will reveal the entirety of all hidden wisdom. (And thus, the claim that Muhammad is the last prophet remains valid.)

EDUCATION

Although education indicators have been steadily improving over the last few decades, Yemen still faces problems. Roughly half the adult population is literate – comprising approximately 70% men but only 30% women. More schools have been built in some of the rural and remote areas of the country, but the educational system is still largely driven toward providing urban males with schooling needs.

Over the last two decades, the percentage of children enrolled in primary education has risen, but the percentage of youths enrolled in secondary and higher education has not seen as large a change. Currently over 87% of primary-aged children are enrolled in primary schools, although only 60% or so actually finish the initial six-year education – up from a 65% enrolment figure in the early 1990s. Nearly half of appropriately aged children are enrolled in secondary school, and 9% pursue higher education.

CULTURE

QAT To fully understand Yemen and its people, you need to know what is important to Yemenis. These aspects vary among different Yemenis and could include knowledge of tribal life or the historical skills of local workers, or perhaps the importance of religious education or the yearning to embrace mysticism.

In almost all areas of Yemen, a basic understanding of *qat* is necessary to understand the people. Hardly anyone in the country has ambivalent feelings about the drug, a leaf that is chewed and stored in the side of the cheek over a period of several hours. Opponents of the drug argue that it is ruining society, but most chewers sing its praises, relishing the opportunity to spend their Fridays (or every day, as the case often is) chewing away the hours in conversation and looking out from their sitting room windows at the spectacular landscape unfolded before them. The World Health Organisation estimates that qat is chewed by 80% of adult males, 40% of adult females and 15% of children under 12.

The effects of qat The qat shrub is known by its scientific name as *Catha edulis*, and is often described as a 'mild stimulant'. The main chemical stimulant in the leaf is cathinone, which is closely related to amphetamines and which produces a similar effect: qat chewers often say the drug increases concentration and mental acuity, reduces feelings of tiredness, and suppresses the appetite. Some scientific studies have shown that qat, like amphetamines, may produce feelings of euphoria or aggressiveness. Qat leaves are only effective within several days of being severed from the tree, and best chewed on the same day. Once the branches are cut down, the cathinone in the plant begins to convert to the less potent cathine.

Primarily, qat is used as a social lubricant – Yemenis will gather in a *mafraj* (the intimate sitting room on the top floor of a house overlooking the city or on the ground level facing a garden) after lunch and spend the rest of the daylight hours chewing and conversing with their friends. Because of the variety of effects the drug can produce, different Yemenis chew the leaf for different reasons. Because

THE ORIGINS OF QAT

The exact origin of qat is shrouded in mystery and mythology. The leaf is also chewed in several east African countries, and like coffee the plant probably originated in Ethiopia. After being transported across the Red Sea, the leaf thrived in the highlands of southern Arabia.

There are several legends concerning how the stimulant effects of the leaf were discovered. One story finds a local Yemeni shepherd tending his flocks in the northern highlands. As the goats moved through the mountains, they indulged themselves in the variety of shrubbery the countryside offered. One night, the shepherd noticed that the animals were not going to sleep as usual, but were trotting about and jumping from terrace to terrace with goatly ebullience.

To discover the source of his goats' energy, the shepherd took his flock the next morning and retraced his steps from the previous day. Soon, the goats began to pick leaves from a small tree glistening in the sunlight. Like a concerned parent reading his schoolchild's novel, the shepherd began to chew on the leaves himself. Discovering the leaves to have the same effect upon him, he rushed to the village to spread the good news. The age of chewing had begun.

A separate story is that of the sleepy Sufi mystic, who chewed the leaf by chance and discovered that it enabled him to stay up late into the night and complete his devotions. It should be noted that both of these tales are told with regard to the origin of coffee as well.

If the Sufis did not discover qat, they at least propagated its popularity. Like coffee, the Sufis in Yemen chewed qat to help them stay awake and worship longer – and they encouraged others to do so. The early rise in the popularity of coffee, for instance, was largely due to travelling Sufi mystics who carried the beans with them. Because qat stays good for only two days after being picked from the tree, the Sufis were not able to travel far with it. But for that fact, qat might have enjoyed the same popularity as coffee, and you would have been able to stroll down to your local Starbucks and order a *decath grande lowfat qat bundle*.

qat increases mental acuity and fights fatigue, students often partake of the leaf to concentrate on their work, especially during exam periods when extra help is needed to keep the midnight oil burning. Because the drug acts as an appetite suppressant, some Yemenis (especially women) chew the leaf when dieting. After a hard day of work (well, half-day of work), qat is said to rest your body and energise your mind to prepare you for the rest of the day. And in a familiar refrain, parents may let their older children chew because 'it keeps them off the streets' and away from harder drugs or alcohol.

Although nearly all Yemenis chew qat, they are torn as to whether the leaf is good or bad for society. Some say qat is bad for your health, while others claim that it gives you the strength of many men. Some say that it causes tooth decay, while some somehow cling to the assertion that it makes the teeth stronger. In a half-hour debate over whether qat was good for diabetics, both sides of the argument finally agreed that 'at least qat has no sugar in it'. The best qat, it is claimed, can make you 'strong as a bull', particularly in the bedroom. Most Yemeni women claim that the opposite is true.

Undeniably, the mass production and marketing of qat does produce social and economic problems in the country. Many Yemenis spend too much of their income on the drug, at times up to 50% of their income when the money is crucial otherwise for basic family needs. Nearly 60% of arable, cultivated land that could be used for growing exportable crops is devoted to the support of qat trees, and because of the vast amounts of water such crops require, estimates state that nearly 90% of new wells are used for qat fields.

Non-Yemeni sources vary in their descriptions of the effects of qat. The *Handbook of Medicinal Herbs* cites a variety of herbalists who claim qat cures such maladies as anorexia, boils, depression, headaches, and the plague. The World Health Organisation describes inactivity as one of the primary effects, noting that chewing the leaf leads to an average of 1,460 wasted hours a year. Authors such as Shelagh Weir give a more unbiased discussion of qat, while Timothy Mackintosh-Smith is more inclined to give a romantic description.

For Mackintosh-Smith, chewing qat is about achieving a state of *kayf*, the particular state of mind that in part 'stretches the attention span, so that you can watch the same view for hours, the only change being the movement of the sun'. Somewhat absurdly, Jose Ortega y Gasset suggests that one of the 'endless ways of producing delightful visions or conveying intense bodily pleasures' can by achieved by chewing the leaf, 'which affects the prostate and thereby makes walking increasingly gratifying the longer it is done'. This may explain why most Yemeni men are content to spend the majority of the waking day away from the company of their wives, but it is hardly equivalent with Mackintosh-Smith's description of *kayf*.

Most Yemenis describe the qat-chewing experience in terms of stages. At first, the chewer gains a sense of heightened awareness and mental acuity. In the setting of a group chew, this stage manifests itself in playful conversation, high energies, and quick-fire jokes. In the second stage of the qat journey, the chewer becomes more relaxed, the quick banter of the group dies down, and conversation turns to more serious topics. Light-hearted jokes become pointedly inappropriate. Religion, politics, and the problems the group, country or world faces: these are the weighty topics of the qat chewer.

Later, group conversation finally ceases, and the evening is occupied with monologues and lengths of silence. This third stage typically coincides with the fall of night. In Sana'a, the period of dusk into twilight is known as *sa'a Sulaymia*, the hour of Solomon. Lights are left off as long as can be maintained, and a period of silence is appropriate. Men may get up periodically to perform the sunset prayer. Having qat in the cheek while praying is not strictly *haram* (forbidden), but nevertheless before performing ablutions the chewers will empty their cheeks in a plastic bag or cellophane wrapper and tie it up. Respect for prayer and wasting perfectly good qat, however, are two entirely different matters. The chewer will reinsert the wad after his religious obligations have ceased.

Finally, if still rolling the leaves around in his cheek, the chewer's thoughts often will turn to his own issues and problems. At this point, things can go one of two ways. On the one hand, if he has been chewing qat that had been stolen or that which had grown over someone's grave, he may find himself overcome with sadness too great to bear and retire in solitude for a private weep.

On the other hand, he may find that no problem is too big to be solved by the genius of the qat-enhanced mind. One of the most common descriptions Yemenis give about the effects of qat runs thus: 'When you chew qat, you will walk to America!' The explanation of the description is an exaggeration of qat's effect to help you plan things to fix your problems. So if you miss your homeland of America (or elsewhere), qat will make you think you can walk there.

Hence, many authors have often described qat as producing 'feelings of invincibility', but the description is not quite right. It is better described as being able to see the means to realise your potential. While under the influence of this feeling, for instance, my friend Ahmed notes that his thoughts always turn to his enlarging family and his need to build another storey to his house. Meticulously, he goes over the steps in his mind to complete such a task, and resolves to begin work in the morning. Ali, his companion during the chew, countered that he never made any decisions while chewing qat, doubting the ingenuity of qat-inspired plans. Ahmed, like most Yemenis, makes plenty of lofty decisions and plans; also, like most Yemenis, he hardly ever acts on them.

In any event, qat in Yemen is more about a way of life than a means to achieve some drug-induced effect. The Yemenis seem quite content to lounge away the afternoon hours, chewing the leaves in good company and good conversation as the sun moves across the scenic countryside. Alfred Lord Tennyson's *The Lotus Eaters* is often quoted when speaking about qat, and it is highly appropriate to do so. The poet seems to have written the work with Yemenis in mind:

> Let us swear an oath, and keep it with an equal mind,
> In the hollow Lotus-land to live and lie reclined
> On the hills like Gods together, careless of mankind.

Attending a qat chew The key to having a successful qat chew is first to have a large, hot lunch that will prevent juice from the qat leaves from adversely affecting your stomach. *Saltah* is recommended – the whipped *helba* froth made from fenugreek is said to give you the taste for qat.

Although qat chewers are typically expected to bring their own leaves, if you are going to chew qat for the first time, you will not be expected to bring your own bundle. On the contrary, you may have a hard time refusing the generous supply of qat that will be passed your way.

At some point, you may want to purchase your own qat, and the logical place to do so is the qat souk. You may be overwhelmed by the selection. A tried and true method of finding decent qat at a good price is to wander over to one of the stalls with the most customers and see what they are paying for their qat. As a novice, avoid unpopulated stalls where a merchant whistles you to come over: you will likely pay too much for poor-quality qat.

Besides the price, there are three things to keep in mind when buying qat. First, where does the qat come from? Just as different grapes and different vineyards give rise to a vast variety of wines, so do different areas of the country and different fields give rise to a large diversity of qat. The best and most expensive qat is *shami*. Other good regions for qat are Hamdan, Erhab, Jabal Saber, and Wadi Dhahr. Particularly potent versions of qat are Sawti and Yafi'.

Second, what kind of leaves are you buying? Broadly speaking there are three categories. The best and most expensive is known as *rūs* – asparagus-like stems and leaves from the tops of the trees. Nearly every piece will be entirely chewable. Next is *baladi*, the long branches from which you will pick off your own qat. Third, there is *qatal*, the pickings from the lower parts. Keep in mind that you will only chew the fresh shoots and leaves.

Third, what kind of condition is the qat in? Qat connoisseurs caution on buying qat that is too green (it won't bunch in your cheek), too shiny (possible use of pesticides) or too limp (it has sat in the sun for too long).

For the actual qat chew itself, there are several key ingredients. First, a good room with a good view. Typically chewing sessions are held in the *mafraj*. For larger and more formal occasions, the chews will be held in *diwans*, large sitting rooms. Second, good company is a must. Conversation is a key ingredient to an enjoyable qat session. Last, you will need drinks – qat causes you to become quite parched, and water or a raisin drink is recommended.

Before entering the mafraj or diwan, remember to remove your shoes. Recite the following greeting ritual listed below and you will impress everyone in the

Anisa George

Ladies, if you're invited to a wedding during your time in Yemen, definitely accept the invite and definitely arrive wearing the most glamorous getup you can muster. Weddings are one of only a few opportunities women have to strut their stuff in Yemen, and you'll be flabbergasted at some of the ensembles they concoct. With the traditional *baltos* and *abbayas* cast aside, Yemeni women emerge in see-through red beaded sequin evening gowns, long skirts that turn at mid thigh to transparent black lace, clinging leopard-print holster tops – and painted, hennaed, and permed to the last eyelash.

I'd like to show you a picture, but cameras were *mamnoo'a* (forbidden, along with men). A gruff female guard checked mine at the door to the *khama* (a very large tent/hall rented especially for weddings) and later I learned mobile phones were banned as well (so don't even try it). The only guests permitted to wield a camera were the female relatives of the bride, who back-stepped at snail's pace down the marathon runway, waving their digital devices to catch the bride's promenade at the end of the night.

She came very late, in a glistening white dress, ballooned about her, and trailing such a long veil in her wake that two young boys were recruited to hold it aloft as she moved, step by delicate step, towards the sea of cheering guests gathered around the end of the walkway.

There wasn't much food besides the bagged gifts of cake and Fanta we were handed at the door, and not any gift giving to speak of, but the music was non-stop, and the women, though tentative at first, were packing the dance floor by the end of the night.

If you're a Westerner and the DJ starts playing Usher they'll probably start looking in your direction. You may not be Shakira, but don't be shy, show them some of your moves, and learn some of theirs. If you're not an Arabic student, it'll be one of the few occasions you'll have to interact with Yemenis, when language won't get in the way. So take advantage of it.

room. Remember too the Yemeni maxim: greet one, greet all. After the greetings below, you should work your way around the room counter-clockwise, shaking the hand of every person in the room. If you would rather not do this, or the room is too large, simply say *Salam Tahīyya* ('greetings to everyone'). You cannot now shake anyone's hand. If another person says *Salam Tahīyya* while you are sitting in the room, the traditional response is *ablaght* ('we have received your greeting'). A more humorous response that can be made is the rhyming *aslamātena āladhīa*, meaning roughly 'you have saved us the trouble of greeting you'.

Greeting ritual

1 Peace be upon you.   *salām 'alaykum*
  (And also on you.)   *wa 'alaykum as-salām*
2 How are you?   *kayf Hāllikum?*
  (Thanks be to God.)   *al-Hamdu li-llāh*
3 God grant you rest.   *wa rīHūm*
  (And you as well.)   *wa Ho*

WEDDINGS During your stay in Yemen it is likely that you could be invited to a wedding celebration. Weddings offer you a great opportunity to experience Yemeni culture, including qat chews, music and dancing. Like most things in Yemen, weddings are segregated according to sex.

The men gather for a large lunch and afternoon qat chew, and the evening usually ends with poetry competitions, dancing, and local music being played on the *oud* (a large lute) the *mizmar* (a double-reed screeching wind instrument), and drums. For women, the event is one of the few opportunities for the locals to put on their finest dress and enjoy a night of dancing.

There are other reasons for the women to look their best – matchmaking in Yemen is typically done by the mother of the man. After she picks out a potential mate for her son, the two potential lovebirds may each decide whether they want to proceed with the union. Weddings offer the best opportunities for mothers to scout around and find potential daughters-in-law. In Yemen, if you're not kind to your mother, it could haunt you for the rest of your life.

MUSIC AND POETRY The only truly recognised art form in Yemen is poetry, and it is used to great extent. Leaders who can issue statements or challenges in verse are well respected among the people. Every Yemeni secretly believes himself to be a poet, especially after an hour or two of qat chewing.

Music in Yemen is deeply connected with poetry, and purely instrumental music is a rarity, unless when used for dancing. Put otherwise, Yemenis rarely ever sit and listen to music unless it is accompanied by poetry. Yemeni music differs according to the area, and certain regions in particular are known for their styles. In Hadhramawt, for instance, the Hadhrami Dan style of music and song combines poetry and music that establish a feeling of genuineness and sincerity, while the Sana'ani Muwashaha put poetry to music with an emphasis on rhythm.

Music without accompanying singing is used for dances, and both the music and types of dances also vary by region. Finally, the drums can be used alone to provide the background beat for the *bara'* – a type of tribal step performed in a circle while brandishing a traditional dagger or *jambiyya*. Technically speaking, the bara' is not considered a dance, but rather a distinct set of movements, and each tribe has their own unique bara'. The easiest place to view the bara' dance is in Wadi Dhahr and the nearby Dar al-Hajar on Fridays.

NATURAL HISTORY AND CONSERVATION

with Dominic Ashby, Kate Reimer and David Scoville

GEOLOGICAL HISTORY Tectonic activity formed the major geological features of the southwestern Arabian Peninsula, making present-day Yemen a country rich in diverse geological features. The separation of the Arabian Peninsula from the African continent resulted in the formation of the Red Sea and Gulf of Aden. As shifting plates pressed the landmass upward and out from the developing bodies of water, mountain ranges were also formed: the dominating Sarat range that stretches the entire distance of the Tihama sedimentary plains before turning eastward to run along the southern coast and the virtually uninhabitable limestone cliffs of the Jol in the east that sandwich Wadi Hadhramawt. Between these mountain ranges lie the central deserts of Ramlat as-Sabatayn and part of the Empty Quarter. Tectonic plate movement is also responsible for the Socotran Archipelago and some of the islands in the Red Sea. Other Red Sea islands are of volcanic origin.

Yemen's varied terrain, as well as varied precipitation (50–500cm annually, falling primarily in the highlands), have produced a stunning variety of habitats. In addition to Tihama's dry plains, the coastal areas include mangrove swamps, marshes, and wetlands. Inland there are scrub lands, deserts, and even a few swamps near major watercourses. Because Yemen is affected by seasonal monsoons, the highland regions contain many *wadis*, dry riverbeds that flow with water during periods of high precipitation, creating small areas of flora in greater density than other, more arid areas of the country.

FLORA Most of Yemen's plant life, both wild and cultivated, is adapted for an arid environment.

Having been an agricultural region for millennia, the majority of Yemen's arable land, about 2.9% of its surface, has been cultivated. Even so, there are areas where the natural vegetation still thrives. Most of these natural 'forests' consist of scrub, thickets, and dwarf shrubs. Some of the richest concentrations of flora in Yemen are found in the western mountainous region. There, altitude stratifies the plant life into bands. The lowland slopes (below 2,000m) produce a bushland thicket where acacias (*Acacia commiphora*) thrive. From 2,000–2,500m the camphor bush is predominant. This medium-sized, hardy bush can be identified by its grey-green leaves. Its small, fragrant fruit is covered in a light fluffy coating. These trees are prized for their medicinal purposes and have been used to treat headaches, sinus pressure, bronchitis and even toothaches. Between 2,500m and 3,200m there lies a dwarf-shrub forest. The Abyssinian rose (*Rosa abyssinica*) is found in this region. These thorny bushes produce small, fragrant, pale yellow flowers. The small orange fruits of this bush are edible and enjoyed by children and baboons alike. Be careful not to eat too many, though, as this can lead to stomach ache. Above 2,500m one can find such species as junipers (*Juniperus procera*), and high-altitude shrubs such as *Euryops arabicus*. At these elevations, particularly on the southern slopes, succulents are quite common. Euphorbias and aloes abound. While there is a variety of flowering plants in Yemen, the majority of the blooming is restricted to seasons of heavy rainfall (April through May and August through September).

Because of Yemen's agricultural history, crops make up a sizeable amount of the vegetation. In the Hadhramawt region date palms are plentiful. Also grown in the area are wheat, millet, and coconut. On the Tihama plains and lowlands, which are heavily irrigated to maintain productivity, there are date palms, citrus fruits, bananas, cotton, and millet along with the acacia and euphorbias. In the mid elevations grow fig trees, wheat, barley, and sorghum. The higher elevations are dedicated to qat and coffee. Yemen is also a producer of both frankincense and myrrh. Frankincense is produced by *Boswellia sacra*, a tree grown in the Hadhramawt region. The trees are small with smooth bark; the incense is produced from the trees' resin. Myrrh is produced from *Commiphora myrrha*. The myrrh tree is small (no taller than 3m) with rough bark and thorny branches. These trees are grown in the western highlands of the country. Once again, the incense is produced from the resin of the tree.

FAUNA Yemen holds a unique location in the world. It has proximity to three distinct ecological regions: Africa, Europe, and Asia. This proximity is represented in its unique assortment of wildlife. In Yemen leopards, hyrax, and baboons can be found, originally native to Africa. Asian wildlife is represented by mongoose and Indian monitors. The adaptable fox and wolf, which range across Eurasia, have representatives in Yemen as well.

Birds Lying as it does at the intersection of major migration routes for birds heading from Europe to Africa and from Africa to Asia, Yemen boasts a diverse bird population. Nevertheless, the natural features (mountains, deserts, seas) isolate Yemen enough for a large number of endemic species to have developed. Thus, of the 370 known bird species in the region, 25 are considered endemic.

Endemics The majority of the endemic species can be found in the highlands where they take advantage of the denser vegetation. One of the most common endemics is the Arabian Wheatear (*Oenanthe lugentoides*). This black-winged bird can be identified by its white belly and a white strip on the top of its head. These lovely little birds are quite common in the highlands. Two species of endemic partridges can be found in number in the highlands as well. They are Philby's rock partridge (*Alectoris philbyi*) and the Arabian partridge (*Alectoris melanocephala*). Both are round, grey birds with striking black-and-white facial markings. When startled they will fly off quite noisily and vocally. Another bird to look for is the Arabian woodpecker (*Dendrocopos dorae*). The males of the species are particularly identifiable by the patch of bright red on the tops of their heads. In the slightly lower elevations, among the euphorbias, one can find the gold-winged grosbeak. These heavy-beaked relatives of finches can be identified by their namesake golden wing markings. On the Tihama plains, typically in millet and sorghum fields, one can find flocks of Arabian golden sparrows (*Passer euchlorus*), as well as the occasional Arabian bustard (*Ardeotis arabs*). The bustard is Yemen's largest bird, standing as tall as 1m, with a correspondingly large wingspan.

Migratory birds Yemen plays host to several bird species that are of cultural significance to the people of Yemen and their neighbours. One such bird is the hoopoe (*Upupa epops*). This charming bird is easily identified by sight or sound. It vocalises with a loud 'oop-oop' call as its name would suggest. The bird is small, about a foot long, with very distinct plumage. It is pink or reddish with black-and-white banded wings, and black tufts on its crest. Its beak is long with a gentle curve. The hoopoe is significant to several cultures, and is found in Greek mythology, Chinese artwork, the Old Testament (the Hoopoe is the messenger who makes King Solomon aware of the Queen of Sheba) and Koran, as well as *The Conference of Birds*, a prominent piece of Sufi literature.

Falcons, which are of cultural significance to the peoples of the Arabian Peninsula, are fairly common in Yemen. Of the ten species of falcon in Yemen, only one is endangered, the Saker falcon (*Falco sherrug*). These brown and grey falcons are among the largest of their family. The striking red-footed falcon (*Falco vespertinus*) can also be found in Yemen. These grey birds can be identified by their striking red or orange belly and underwings. Also in the area is the ever popular Peregrine falcon (*Falco peregrinus*). The Peregrine is the fastest animal in the world, capable of achieving speeds of up to 300km/h when in a dive.

Of the countless species of migratory birds that visit Yemen, several are endangered. Yemen is a stopping point in the migratory path of two types of endangered eagle: the greater spotted eagle (*Aquila clanga*) and the imperial eagle (*Aquila heliaca*). The coasts of Yemen are breeding grounds to the endangered white-eyed gull (*Larus levophthalmus*). The masked booby (*Sula doctylatra*) also comes to the shores of Yemen to mate and breed. Though not endangered, this large white and black seabird only ever comes to land in order to raise its young. One noteworthy bird on the plains is the Abyssinian roller (*Coracias abyssinica*). With its bright blue plumage and streaming tail feathers, this bird can be quite striking. Even in the wetlands, Yemen plays host to handsome avians. Among them, the endangered ferruginous pochard (*Aythya nyroc*) is quite a sight to behold. These little ducks sport lovely deep chestnut plumage, and can be seen among various other waders and divers. One rare, though extremely significant, bird is the bald ibis (*Geronticus eremita*). These large black birds can be distinguished by their pink bald heads, and long, gently curving beaks. It is estimated that the total worldwide population of these birds is as low as 200. Though most can be found in Morocco, a small number of bald ibises have been sighted in the wetlands near the city of Ta'iz.

Mammals Though by no means as numerous as the birds, Yemen's mammal population is still a diverse one, with upwards of 70 land mammal species. Hamadryas baboons (*Papio Hamadryas hamadryas*) and rock hyrax (*Procavia capensis* ssp *jayakari*) live on the lower slopes of the western mountains. The Arabian red fox (*Vulpes vulpes arabica*) is found throughout the country and Blandford's foxes (*Vulpes cana*) can be found in the highlands. Other mammals include the caracal (*Caracal caracal*), the crested porcupine (*Hystrix indica*), Aden gerbil (*Gerbillus poecilops*), Egyptian fruit bat (*Rousettus aegyptiacus*), and Dorcas gazelle (*Gazella dorcas*). There are even still small populations of Arabian leopards (*Panthera pardus nimr*) and Arabian wolves (*Canus lupus arabs*). These large predators are confined to remote regions of the country.

Turtles and reptiles Yemen is home to some 103 species of reptiles. These include an endemic species of monitor lizard (*Varanus yemenensis*), and numerous other lizards such as the Agama lizard (*Agame adranitana*), geckos (*Pristurus flavipunktatus*), and the popular veiled chameleon (*Chamaeleo calyptratus*) There is at least one species of freshwater terrapin, the helmeted turtle (*Pelomedusa subrufa*), as well as one species of land turtle (*Geochelon sulcata*). Several species of sea turtles are known to nest on Yemen's coasts (see below).

Yemen is home to several species of venomous snakes. Among these, the Egyptian cobra (*Naja haje*) is perhaps the most dangerous. Other snakes include the horned viper (*Aspis cerastes*) with its characteristic 'horns' above the eyes, and the puff adder (*Bitis arietans*). Off the coast, there are a few species of sea snake, including the lovely yellow-bellied sea snake (*Anguis platura*). Though quite venomous, the sea snake is not very aggressive and will not often strike unless cornered, captured, or threatened.

YEMEN'S MARINE LIFE The waters off the coast of Yemen are teeming with life. The Red Sea is separated from the Gulf of Aden (and thus the Arabian Sea) by the Bab al-Mandab Channel. This watercourse, which is narrow and shallow, serves to isolate many species from the Indian Ocean. Likewise, water currents in the Gulf of Aden serve as a barrier from the rest of the ocean. The result is a beautiful and unique aquatic ecosystem. It is estimated that of the over 1,000 species in these waters, 10–20% are endemic.

The coast of Yemen is a breeding ground for several species of sea turtles. These include the leatherback turtle (*Dermochelys coriacea*), hawksbill turtle (*Eretmochelys imbricata*), loggerhead turtle (*Caretta caretta*), green turtle (*Chelonia mydas*), and Olive Ridley turtle (*Lepidochelys olivacea*). All of these species are endangered.

Commercial fishing in Yemen's waters brings in primarily sardines, tuna, kingfish, and mackerel. Other open water fish include dolphin (not to be confused with the mammal; they are also known as *mahi mahi*), billfish, and sharks. One of the most striking of the resident shark species is the whale shark (*Rhincodon typus*). These gentle giants can reach lengths of 12m or more and are quite safe around divers.

The waters in the Red Sea are particularly rich, and provide a home to over 400 types of corals. The area is known particularly for its soft corals, though hard corals occur in great variety as well. The fish that occur with these coral are no less noteworthy. Some endemics include the masked puffer fish (*Arothron diadematus*). This lovely fish can be identified by its black fins and namesake black mask over the eyes. The golden butterfly fish (*Chaetodon aureofasciatus*) is also unique to the

Red Sea and the Gulf. This bright yellow fish can be identified by its white eye patch. The raccoon butterfly fish (*Chaetodon lunul*) is also in these waters. It can be distinguished from its cousin by its black striping and black-and-white mask. Also in the area is the Arabian Picasso triggerfish (*Rhinecanthus assasi*). This interesting little fish can be identified by its small but distinct orange markings around the anus, eyes, and lips. Also in these waters one can find the beautiful but dangerous lionfish (*Pterois miles*). This brightly striped fish sports venomous dorsal spines and its sting can be fairly dangerous, so look but don't touch.

The waters of the Red Sea and the Gulf of Oman also play host to several well known but noteworthy species. Stingrays, such as the blue spotted stingray (*Taeniura lymma*), can be found along the sea floor, often hiding in the sand in order to ambush prey. Reef holes and caves provide shelter for the slender giant moray eel (*Strophidon sathete*). This great fish can grow up to 3m in length. The Red Sea is also home to the ocean's great chameleon: the cuttlefish (several species). These amazing cousins of the octopus can change not only the colour of their skin but the texture as well. They are true masters of camouflage, blending into their surroundings with surprising accuracy.

The waters off the coast of Yemen play host to a number of sea mammals as well. Among them is the rare dugong (*Dugong dugon*). This gentle herbivore is a close relative of the manatee. Several species of dolphin can be found, including the ever popular bottlenose dolphin (*Tursiops truncatus*). Also in the area is the rare short-finned pilot whale (*Globicephala macrorhynchus*). Whales such as blue whales (*Balaenoptera musculus*), sperm whales (*Physeter macrocephalus*), and humpback whales (*Megaptera novaeangliae*) can be found in the Gulf of Aden. Whales are rare in the Red Sea.

The waters around the Socotran Archipelago are equally abundant with life, in particular coral and kelp forests. Much like the mainland, life in these waters is only recently being explored.

CONSERVATION IN YEMEN As a small country with rapidly increasing development, conservation has become a key issue for Yemen. Areas of conservation effort include water conservation, prevention of overgrazing, soil erosion, deforestation, and desertification. Another area of conservation that receives a great deal of attention is the conservation of wildlife and their habitats.

At the centre of most conservation efforts and debates is water. Yemen has minimal water resources and water use exceeds the ability of the ecosystem to replace it. With rainfall so minimal, most water use relies on tapping groundwater collected in natural aquifers. While the shallow aquifers can be replenished over time by rainfall, the deep aquifers, which are now being tapped, cannot. With water needed for agriculture, industry, and urban and rural household use, Yemen's natural reserves of water are being depleted far faster than they can be replenished.

With limited water available, human and wildlife needs compete for the minimal viable terrain. Increasing concentrations of grazers can quickly lead to loss of pasturage through overgrazing. A great deal of water is also diverted to crop production and urban use, further increasing the strain on limited pasture land. Deforestation is another issue rooted in the competition for arable land. What limited forests exist are utilised for firewood, construction materials, and charcoal production. These factors of heavy land use lead to soil erosion as the ground loses protective cover, which can result in desertification.

As the land is affected by the aforementioned factors, limited habitat is lost for wildlife. Yemen is host to a number of threatened species including the Nubian ibex (*Capra nubiana*) and the Saker falcon (*Falco cherrug*), both of which are considered endangered; the critically endangered Arabian leopard (*Panthera pardus nimr*) and northern bald ibis (*Geronticus eremita*), whose population numbers in the mere hundreds; and over a dozen vulnerable species such as the dugong (*Dugong dugon*) the Dorcas gazelle (*Gazella dorcas*), and the sand bat (*Eptesicus nastus*).

Recent efforts have been made in animal conservation such as the declaration of the Socotran Archipelago as a biosphere reserve. Socotra is home to numerous endemic species including the dragon's blood tree (*Dracaena cinnabari*) and the Socotra bunting (*Emberiza socotrana*), both of which are considered vulnerable species. The Socotra Archipelago Biosphere Reserve aims to ensure better living conditions for inhabitants of Socotra based on sustainable use of natural resources. On mainland Yemen, several important wildlife reserves have been established. Among them are the Bara' protected area in the central mountains, the Hof protected area along the Omani border, and the 'Utmah protected area in the southern mountains. Conservation efforts are also being made in other key areas such as the Aden Coastal Wetlands, one of the most important breeding sites for migratory birds, other wetland areas and other environmentally important areas throughout the country. Two of these, the Sharma-Jethum, of great importance to several of the local sea turtle species, and the Belhaf-Burum reserves lie in the central coastal region of the country.

Arabian wolf

2

Practical Information

WHEN TO VISIT

The traditional high season in Yemen falls between October and April – right after the early autumn rainy season and before the heat of summer begins. The traditional wisdom makes sense here, especially if you have any inclination to visit the areas of Tihama or Aden, which are brutally hot in the summer months.

Additionally, while some visitors may try to travel to some countries during the 'low season' to avoid a gaggle of other tourists clogging up all the hot spots, the same rationale does not apply to a country that does not regularly receive those gaggles.

During the winter months, the mountain highlands and the desert can be quite chilly – particularly at night. Therefore, the best time to visit the country is October, when the end of the rainy season brings much of the country's greenery to life and before the winter months require an extra sweater.

HIGHLIGHTS AND SUGGESTED ITINERARIES

What you should see in Yemen depends largely upon what you are interested in. If you are an ancient civilisation and archaeology buff, tailor your trip around the sites of the old incense trade. Hiking and nature enthusiasts could easily fill up two weeks camping in the highlands of Yemen, and those interested in religious sites could also stuff an itinerary with satisfying locations. For those purely interested in the cultural aspects of the country, arranging a two-week stay with a highland tribe through one of the travel agencies could give you an unbelievable and different taste of the country. Conversely, of course, if any of those pursuits utterly bore you, you will want to avoid the associated sites when planning your trip.

HIGHLIGHTS Sana'a, one of the oldest continuously inhabited cities in the world, is one of the major highlights of any visit to the country. The concentration of culture, architecture, and Old-World souks make for an unbelievable experience. To the west, the town of **Manakha** in the **Haraz Mountains** offers fantastic hiking opportunities during the day and excellent food and tribal dancing in the hotels in the evening. To the south and the west lie the regions of the **Tihama** and the **Southern Mountains**. Driving across the country to the east, you will cross the desert of **Ramlat as-Sabatayn**, where you can careen through the dunes in a 4x4 or ride over them slowly on the back of a camel after spending the day in a Bedouin camp. On the other end of the desert is **Wadi Hadhramawt**, where you can see mud skyscrapers towering out of a sea of flat plains and listen to the renowned regional music and taste the local honey. If you have enough time, the island of **Socotra** offers a completely different picture of the country.

ITINERARIES As noted above, the itinerary you plan for your trip should be tailored to your specific interests. Even within different categories, there is a vast amount of iterations for any given trip. Personally, I prefer a trip that displays a large variety of the country, especially on your first trip. (You will want to take another one!) On this basis, a few suggested itineraries for one- and two-week trips are given below.

Option one The first trip takes you from Sana'a through the desert, where you will be able to explore both the sand dunes and the ancient temples of the Sabaean Kingdom, into the culturally rich region of Wadi Hadhramawt. Travelling south through the date-palmed valley of Wadi Do'an you will arrive at the southern port city of Mukalla, where you can spend your penultimate day swimming with dolphins off the ancient, biblical port of Qana near modern Bir 'Ali.

Day 1 Sana'a
Day 2 Marib, Sirwah
Day 3 Ramlat as-Sabatayn
Day 4 Shibam, Seiyun
Day 5 Wadi Do'an
Day 6 Mukalla, Bir 'Ali
Day 7 fly to Sana'a

Option two The second option brings you into the central mountains of Yemen for some great opportunities for trekking and experiencing tribal culture before descending rapidly from the highlands to the Tihama coast. The latter end of the trip brings you back into the mountains to see the cities of Ta'iz, Ibb and Jiblah, famous for their historical importance to the country and their local souks.

Day 1 Sana'a
Day 2 Shibam, Kawkaban, Hajjah
Day 3 Manakha
Day 4 Hudaydah
Day 5 Bayt al-Faqih, Zabid, Ta'iz
Day 6 Ibb, Jiblah
Day 7 Sana'a

Option three Two weeks is an ideal amount of time to travel about the country, affording you the opportunity to experience the treasures of both of the previous options as well as a trip to the biologically fascinating island of Socotra or a visit to the city of Aden and local hot springs.

Day 1 Sana'a
Day 2 Shibam, Kawkaban, Hajjah
Day 3 Haraz Mountains
Day 4 Hudaydah, Tihama/Haraz Mountains
Day 5 Ta'iz/Rada', Hammam Damt
Day 6 Sana'a/Ibb, Jiblah
Day 7 Socotra/Ta'iz
Day 8 Socotra/Yafrus, Aden
Day 9 Socotra/al-Bayda, Ataq, Azzan
Day 10 Mukalla, Bir Ali
Day 11 Wadi Do'an, Seiyun, Shibam
Day 12 the Empty Quarter, Ramlat as-Sabatayn
Day 13 Marib, Sirwah
Day 14 flight home

TOUR OPERATORS

UK Costs for two- to three-week packages range from £1,350–2,300, including flights.

Adventures Abroad Worldwide Travel Ltd Unit M, Staniforth Estates, Main St, Hackenthorpe, Sheffield S12 4LB; ☎ 0114 247 3400; e sales@adventures-abRd.com; www.adventures-abRd.com. Offers land tours of Yemen alone or in conjunction with other Gulf countries.

Explore Worldwide Ltd Nelson Hse, 55 Victoria Rd, Farnborough, Hampshire GU14 7PA; ☎ 0870 333 4001; f 01252 391 110; e res@explore.co.uk; www.explore.co.uk. Tours to Socotra & Sana'a.

High and Wild Ltd Compass Hse, Rowden's Rd, Wells, Somerset BA5 1TU; ☎ 01749 671 777; f 01749 670 888; e adventures@highandwild.co.uk; www.highandwild.co.uk. Package group tours to the mainland & Socotra.

Nomadic Thoughts Ltd 81 Brondesbury Rd, London NW6 6BB; ☎ 020 7604 4408; f 020 7604 4407; e travel@nomadicthoughts.com; www.nomadicthoughts.com. Personalised travel tours.

ResponsibleTravel.com 4th Floor, Pavilion Hse, 6 Old Steine, Brighton BN1 1EJ; ☎ 01273 600 030; e amelia@responsibletravel.com; www.responsibletravel.com. Offers an 18-day ecotourism trip of Socotra & the mainland.

The Traveller & Palanquin 92–93 Great Russell St, London WC1B 3PS; ☎ 020 7436 9343; www.the-traveller.co.uk. Two-week tours focusing on the archaeological aspects of the country.

CANADA

Adventures Abroad Worldwide Travel Ltd 2148-20800 Westminster Highway, Richmond, British Columbia V6V 2W3; ☎ +1 604 303 1099; e sales@adventures-abroad.com; www.adventures-abroad.com. Offers land tours of Yemen alone or in conjunction with other Gulf countries.

Arabian Horizons 2 Bloor St, West Suite #700, Toronto, Ontario M4W 3RI; ☎ +1 416 972 5086;

f +1 416 972 5087; www.arabianhorizons.com. Offers a wide range of tours, including birdwatching, trekking & diving.

Bestway Tours and Safaris Suite #206, 8678 Greenall Av, Burnaby, British Columbia V5J 3M6; ☎ +1 800 663 0844; f +1 604 264 7774; e bestway@bestway.com; www.bestway.com. Offers cultural tours to Yemen & Oman

US

Adventure Center 1311 63rd St, Suite 200, Emeryville, CA 94608; ☎ +1 800 228 8747; f +1 510 654 4200; www.adventurecenter.com. Group tours of Sana'a & Socotra.

Adventures Abroad Worldwide Travel Ltd 1124 Fir Av, #101, Blaine, WA 98230; ☎ +1 800 665 3998; e sales@adventures-abroad.com; www.adventures-abroad.com. Offers land tours of Yemen alone or in conjunction with other Gulf countries.

Arabian Horizons 203 Court St, Brooklyn, NY 11201; ☎ +1 718 797 0906; f +1 718 797 0917; www.arabianhorizons.com. Offers a wide range of tours, including birdwatching, trekking, & diving.

Caravan-Serai Tours 3806 Whitman Av North, Seattle, WA 98103; ☎ +1 800 451 8097; f +1 206 547 8607; e info@caravan-serai.com; www.caravan-serai.com. Offers a number of different tours, including diving in the Red Sea.

Geographic Expeditions 1008 General Kennedy Av, PO Box 29902, San Francisco, CA 94129; ☎ +1 800 777 8183; f +1 415 346 5535; e info@geoex.com; www.geoex.com. Offers 19-day tours of mainland Yemen.

Spiekermann Travel, Inc 18400 East Nine Mile Rd, Eastpointe, MI 48021; ☎ +1 800 645 3233; f +1 586 775 9556; e info@mideasttrvl.com; www.mideasttrvl.com. Group tours led by an archaeological professor.

LOCAL TOUR OPERATORS The cheapest way to travel in Yemen is to arrange tours through a local travel agency – after all, that's what most of the tour agencies listed above do. The agencies listed below, all located in Sana'a, are reliable and should prove for a great tour of the country:

Abu Taleb Group Hadda St; ☎ 01 441620; e info@atg-yemen.com; www.atg-yemen.com

Al-Mamoon International Tours Zubayri St; ☎ 01 242008; e info@al-mamoon-group.com;

www.al-mamoon-group.com. The pharmacy turned travel agency has proven very popular with the Dutch crowd.
Arabian Horizons Travel & Tourism Hadda St; ✆ 01 506010; e horizon-tours@y.net.ye; www.arabianhorizons.com. With offices in the US & Canada, Arabian Horizons is a good choice for North Americans who would like a home agent before setting out.
Ashtal Global Tours Hadda St, PO Box 1501; ✆ 01 440917; e sales@ashtal.com; www.ashtal.com. Offers a variety of programmes focusing on north or south Yemen.
Bazara Travel & Tourism Zubayri St; 01 285925; e bazara@y.net.ye; www.bazaratravel.com
Cameleers Tours Nouakchott St 12, PO Box 20372; ✆ 01 464793; e info@cameleerstours.com; www.cameleerstours.com
Future Tours Industries al-Qiada St, PO Box 1203; ✆ 01 253216; e info@ftiyemen.com; www.ftiyemen.com. Operates Red Sea cruises & dives on the Yemeni yacht *Katharina Maha* that is normally anchored off Kamaran Island.
Marib Travel & Tourism Hadda St; ✆ 01 272432; e info@marib-tours.com; www.marib-tours.com. In the business since 1973, Marib Travel offers a wide range of programs, including scuba diving & ecotourism.
Murjan Travel Hadda St, PO Box 19354; ✆ 01 400722; e murjan@griffin-ltd.com; www.griffin-ltd.com/murjan. Focuses on meeting the needs of business travellers.
Summer Tours & Travel Hadda St, PO Box 16820; ✆ 01 413416; e summer@y.net.ye; www.summer-yemen.com. Offers eco-friendly tours such as snorkelling & birdwatching on Socotra & biking or hiking tours on the mainland.
Universal Travel & Tourism 60 Metre Rd; ✆ 01 272861; e touring@utcyemen.com; www.utcyemen.com. The largest & most frequently used of Yemen's local tour agencies, Universal can tailor a package to suit your specific needs.
Yamanat Tours PO Box 1977; ✆ 01 256086; e info@yamanat.com; www.yamanat.com. Offers hiking, diving & fishing tours.
Yemeni Dreams al-Khortoom St; ✆ 01 514028; e info@yemeni-dreams.com; www.yemeni-dreams.com. Yemeni Dreams specialises in adventure travel, including visits with desert Bedouins & mountain tribes. Truly unique & exciting, however, are its 1- or 2-week tribal-immersion programmes.
Yemen Explorer Tours PO Box 23091; ✆ 01 404838; e yescom@y.net.ye; www.yemen-explorers.com
Yemen Old Splendour Tours Al Yaheri Commercial Center; ✆ 01 261755; e yostours@y.net.ye; www.yostours.com.ye. In addition to offering standard tours of the country, Yemen Old Splendour also offers combined tours of Yemen & Ethiopia or Dubai.

RED TAPE

VISAS Citizens of Jordan, Iraq, Syria, and the Gulf Co-operation Council (GCC) states may enter Yemen without a visa, and nationals of Hong Kong are permitted to stay in the country for up to 30 days without a visa. Passport holders of all other states are required to have a visa. For nationals of most countries, it is possible to purchase a visa at the airport or the Omani border crossings, although this changes from time to time. (For the latest information and list of countries, view the Ministry of Tourism's website at www.yementourism.com/.)

Holders of Israeli passports will not be admitted to Yemen. Officially, if you have an Israeli stamp in your passport, you will not be allowed to enter the country either. Most often, the official at the airport will not search through your passport for a potential stamp (I have entered the country nearly ten times, and my Israeli stamp has never been a problem). Nevertheless, that isn't to say that a surly border guard might not refuse your entrance if he hasn't had his qat for the day. If you want to be certain, get a clean passport.

You can purchase a three-month tourist or visitor visa or three-month, six-month, or one-year business visa from your local Yemeni consular office. It is important to know that each of these visas allow you to stay in Yemen for only one month at a time. The time length given on the visa states how long the visa is valid after it has been issued. Thus, with a one-year multiple-entrance business visa, you can enter Yemen as often as you like over the course of the year, but no single visit may be longer than one month in duration.

To stay longer than one month in Yemen, you will need to renew your visa, acquire a residency visa, or simply pay a fine at the airport for overstaying your visa when you attempt to leave. To renew your visa, you can take your passport to any of the Passport and Immigration offices in Sana'a or Aden. Officially you are allowed to renew your visa twice, although it is unlikely that the Passport and Immigration officials will be keeping a close count.

A residency visa will allow you to stay in the country for up to one year, but you will need to be sponsored by a Yemeni employer or educational institution to get one. If you have a residency visa, you will need to obtain an exit visa at the Passport and Immigration office before leaving the country. Without an exit visa, you will be turned back at the airport. Visitors travelling with tourist or business visas do not need to get an exit visa prior to departure.

CUSTOMS REGULATIONS Firearms, narcotics, obscene literature and pornographic materials are banned. If you have magazines or books they may be examined to determine whether or not they are pornographic. There is also an official ban on all products of Israeli origin. Alcohol is allowed in certain quantities – non-Muslims are allowed to bring two litres of alcohol into the country.

ⓔ YEMENI EMBASSIES AND CONSULATES

ABROAD
Australia 11 West St, North Sydney, NSW 2060; ☎ +61 2 8920 9111; f +61 2 9923 1053; e yemconsyd@hotmail.com
Austria Wasagasse 6/10, Vienna; ☎ +43 1 503 2930; f +43 1 505 3159; e yemenembassy.vienna@aon.at
Canada 54 Chamberlain Av, Ottawa, Ontario, KIS 1V9; ☎ +1 613 729 6627; f +1 613 729 8915; e consular@yemenincanada.ca; www.yemenembassy.ca
Djibouti PO Box 194, Djibouti Ville, Djibouti; ☎ +253 352975
France 25, Rue Georges Bizet 75016 Paris; ☎ +33 1 53 23 87 87; f +33 1 47 23 69 41; e ambyemenparis@easynet.fr
Germany Budapester Strasse 37, 10787 Berlin; ☎ +49 30 8322 5901; f +49 30 8322 5902; e Konsulat@Botschaft-Jemen.de; www.botschaft-jemen.de
Ireland The Irish Embassy to the United Nations handles diplomatic representation to Yemen. 1 Dag Hammarskjold Plaza, 885 Second Av, 19th Flr, New York NY 10017, USA; ☎ +1 212 421 6934; f +1 212 752 4726; e irlun@undp.org; www.un.int/ireland

Italy Via Antonio Bosio, 10, 00161 Rome; ☎ +39 06 4423 4299; f +39 06 4423 4763; e info@yemenembassy.it; www.yemenembassy.it
Netherlands Surinamestraat 9, 2585 GG The Hague; ☎ +31 0 70 365 3936; f +31 0 70 356 3312; e consular@yemenembassy.nl; www.yemenembassy.nl
Oman Shati al-Qurum, Way 2840, Hse 2981, Medinat al-Qaboos 115, PO Box 105, Muscat; ☎ +968 24 600 815; f +968 24 605 008
Saudi Arabia Omar bin Aumia ath-Thumary Rd (Diplomatic Quarter), PO Box 94356, Riyadh 11693; ☎ +966 1 4881 731; f +966 1 4881 562
South Africa 329 Main St, Waterkloof 0181, PO Box 13343, Hatfield, 0028 Pretoria; ☎ +27 12 425 0760; f +27 12 425 0762; e info@yemenembassy.org.za; www.yemenembassy.org.za
UAE 7B St, Bur Dubai, (PO Box 1947) Dubai; ☎ +971 4 397 0213; f +971 4 397 2901
UK 57 Cromwell Rd, London SW7 2ED; ☎ +44 0207 581 4039; f +44 0207 589 3350; e yemen.emb.consul@btconnect.com; www.yemenembassy.org.uk
USA 2319 Wyoming Av NW, Washington, DC 20008; ☎ +1 202 965 4760; f 202 337 2017; e consul@yemenembassy.org; www.yemenembassy.org

IN YEMEN
Australia The Australian Embassy to Saudi Arabia handles diplomatic representation to and services for citizens in Yemen. Abdullah bin Hozafa Al-Sahmi Av

(Diplomatic Quarter), PO Box 94400, Riyadh 11693, Saudi Arabia; ☎ +966 1 488 7788; f +966 1 488 7973

Austria Baghdad St, PO Box 1465, Sana'a; ☎ 01 445491; f 01 445489

Canada St 11 off of Hadda St), PO Box 340, Sana'a; ☎ 01 208814; f 01 209523; e canconsulye@hotmail.com

Djibouti St 6 (off Amman St in the Diplomatic District), PO Box 10377, Sana'a; ☎ 01 445236; f 01 445237

France Mujahed St (off Khartoum St), PO Box 1286, Sana'a; ☎ 01 268888; f 01 269160; e hicham.baba-ali@diplomatie.gouv.fr; www.ambafrance-ye.org

Germany Hadda Zone 37 (off Hadda St and Ring Rd), PO Box 2562, Sana'a; ☎ 01 413174; f 01 413179; e info@sanaa.diplo.de; www.sanaa.diplo.de

Ireland The Irish Embassy to the United Nations handles diplomatic representation to Yemen. 1 Dag Hammarskjold Plaza, 885 Second Av, 19th Floor, New York NY 10017, USA; ☎ +1 212 421 6934; f +1 212 752 4726; e irlun@undp.org; www.un.int/ireland

Italy Safiah Janubia St, PO Box 1152, Sana'a; ☎ 01 269164; f 01 266137; e ambasciata.sanaa@esteri.it; www.ambsanaa.esteri.it

Netherlands Off 14th October St (Hadda District) PO Box 463, Sana'a; ☎ 01 421800; f 01 421035; e holland@y.net.ye; www.holland.com.ye

New Zealand New Zealand is not accredited to Yemen; New Zealanders who need embassy services should visit the British Embassy (listed below)

Oman Al-Hoboob Corporation St (off Baghdad St), PO Box 105, Sana'a; ☎ 01 208875; f 01 204586; e omanembassy@y.net.ye

Saudi Arabia Al-Quds St (off Hadda St); PO Box 1184; ☎ 01 240429; f 01 240427

South Africa Al-Qiyadah St, PO Box 353; ☎ 01 224051; f 01 221611; e zubieri@ynet.ye

UAE Ring Rd, PO Box 2250; ☎ 01 266058; f 01 248779

UK 938 Thaher Himiyar St (East Ring Rd), PO Box 1287, Sana'a; ☎ 01 302450; f 01 302454; e britishembassysanaa@fco.gov.uk; www.britishembassy.gov.uk

USA Sa'awan St (Dhahr Himyar Zone), PO Box 22347, Sana'a; ☎ 01 755 2000 ext 2153; f 01 303182; e consularsanaa@state.gov; www.usembassy.state.gov/yemen

GETTING THERE AND AWAY

✈ **BY AIR** While Sana'a International Airport is the main entry point for air travellers, it is also possible to fly into the country to Aden International Airport. Yemenia Airways flights arrive in Aden from a number of neighbouring points, including Abu Dhabi (2hrs), Dubai (2hrs), Amman (7hrs), Damascus (6hrs), Djibouti (1hr) and Mumbai (4hrs). (Yemenia also flies directly from Abu Dhabi and Dubai to the airports of Seiyun and Mukalla.) The other airlines that service Aden are Djibouti Airlines (daily flights to Djibouti) and Royal Jordanian (daily flights to Amman).

From the UK and Europe Yemenia Airways has direct flights to Sana'a from London (9½hrs), Paris (8hrs), Frankfurt (7½hrs), and Rome (7hrs). Lufthansa also flies directly to Sana'a from Frankfurt (7½hrs). It is also possible to travel from major European cities to Sana'a with a stopover on the Arabian Peninsula by flying with airlines such as Emirates, Gulf Air, Qatar Air or Royal Jordanian.

With a little time searching, it is possible to find good deals on airfares to Yemen. Bargain websites on the internet (*www.cheapflights.co.uk, www.travelocity.co.uk*) have posted roundtrip fares as low as £319.

Emirates ☎ 0870 243 2222; www.emirates.com/uk
Gulf Air ☎ 0870 777 1717; www.gulfair.co.uk
Lufthansa ☎ 0870 837 7747; www.lufthansa.co.uk. Flies roundtrip to Sana'a via Frankfurt for about £410.

Qatar Airways ☎ 0870 770 4215; www.qatarairways.com
Royal Jordanian ☎ 020 7878 6300; www.rj.com
Yemenia Airways ☎ 020 8759 0385; e sales@yemenairways.co.uk; www.yemenairways.co.uk

In Yemen
Yemenia Airways Aden Airport ☎ 02 240838
Yemenia Airways Hudaydah Airport ☎ 03 231797

Yemenia Airways Mukalla (Riyan) Airport ☎ 05 385228

Yemenia Airways Sanaa ☎ 01 201822;
www.yemenia.com
Yemenia Airways Seiyun Airport ☎ 05 402145
Yemenia Airways Socotra ☎ 05 660123

Yemenia Holidays ☎ 01 211699;
e y_holidays@yahoo.com;
www.yemenia.com/new2/holydays/holydays.htm

Other airlines

Air Arabia ☎ 01 440001; www.airarabia.com
Egypt Air ☎ 01 275061; www.egyptair.com
Emirates ☎ 01 444442; www.emirates.com
Gulf Air ☎ 01 440922; www.gulfair.com
Lufthansa ☎ 01 213400; www.lufthansa.com
Qatar Airways ☎ 01 506030; www.qatarairways.com

Royal Jordanian ☎ 01 446064; www.rj.com
Saudi Arabian Airlines ☎ 01 506574;
www.saudiairlines.com
Syrian Air ☎ 01 506020; www.syriaair.com
Turkish Airlines ☎ 01 445970; www.thy.com

 BY SEA Yemen has six sea ports: Aden, Hudaydah, al-Khawkha, al-Mokha, Nashtoon, and Mukalla. Most of these ports are purely for cargo ships, and arriving by sea to Yemen is not easy. Boats carrying passengers and cargo sail from al-Khawkha to Djibouti. A limited number of cruise lines, such as Costa Cruise (e *info@us.costa.it; www.costacruise.com*), offer two- to three-week cruises from Europe to Dubai with stops at the ports of Aden and Hudaydah for around US$1,700.

 BY LAND Yemen borders Saudi Arabia and Oman, and it is possible to enter or exit the country through any of the six border points it shares with these neighbours with some restrictions.

The border crossings with Oman are at Serfayt in the south (east of Hof) and Shahan in the north. You may acquire a Yemeni visa from either border crossing, and you can easily acquire an Omani visa if you are travelling in the opposite direction. If you are travelling by private car, you will need proof of ownership and papers documenting insurance coverage in Oman and Yemen.

The border crossings with Saudi Arabia (from east to west) are Haradh (near the coast, east of Midi), Alab (north of Sa'ada), al-Buqa' (in the eastern part of the Sa'ada governorate) and al-Wadee'ah (in the desert of the Shabwa governorate). The easiest crossing point is at Haradh, where there are fewer security concerns. Still, you may be required to be accompanied by government security for some length of your drive into Yemen. It is possible to enter over the desert at al-Wadee'ah, but you must have Bedouin security guards waiting for you at or accompanying you across the border. The border crossings at Alab and al-Buqa' are a little trickier because of security concerns in the Sa'ada governorate. To be allowed to cross, you should make arrangements through a tour agency in Yemen before you make the trip. You will likely be met by (or only have to wait an hour or two for) a small Yemeni army that will escort you straight to Sa'ada. Getting permission to take detours is unlikely.

When travelling from Saudi Arabia into Yemen, you should acquire your visa before arriving at the border crossing. If you attempt to enter Yemen with a private vehicle, you will need to provide papers demonstrating ownership and insurance. Additionally, you may be required to pay a hefty deposit (around US$1,000) to ensure you leave Yemen with the same car. A receipt will be provided, and you can collect the deposit when you exit the country. You will need to secure a visa for Saudi Arabia beforehand if you want to exit Yemen along the northern border. Note that it is not possible to get a tourist visa to Saudi Arabia – the only visas that are issued are for business, transit and the pilgrimage to Mecca.

Yemen is a developing country and does not have the medical facilities of industrial countries. Outside the major cities, the facilities that are available to travellers drop dramatically. The most common ailments that a visitor is likely to experience are altitude sickness, traveller's diarrhoea or sunburn.

It is not safe to drink tap water in Yemen, but safe bottled water is available cheaply throughout the country. To help remain healthy, you should drink several bottles of water per day.

VACCINATIONS To help ensure more serious conditions do not occur, you should be up to date on routine vaccinations for hepatitis A, typhoid, diphtheria, tetanus and polio. The last comes as an all-in-one vaccine (Revaxis) and lasts for ten years. Hepatitis B vaccines are recommended for healthcare workers, those working with children and other individuals who foresee that they could be exposed to blood or bodily fluids. Travellers may also want to consider a series of prophylactic rabies vaccines, as potentially infected dogs and bats can be found even in major cities.

MALARIA While Yemen has made great progress in fighting the malaria epidemic, the disease remains prevalent. The World Heath Organisation estimated that there are 800,000 cases per year (that boils down to about 1 out of every 27 people in the country). Travellers are at risk of infection – particularly those who plan to be travelling in the coastal areas between February and September. There is no risk of infection in Sana'a or other locations in the highlands above 2,000m (6,500ft). There is also very little risk in Aden city and the airport perimeter.

While visiting areas under 2,000m, and especially along the coast, travellers should take care to guard against mosquito bites. Malaria mosquitoes bite from dusk till dawn and therefore it is essential to prevent bites as much as possible. Cover your arms and legs with clothing – you may even wish to impregnate clothing with permethrin. Also apply an insect repellent containing around 50% DEET to exposed areas of skin and make your accommodation as mosquito-proof as possible by sleeping under an impregnated bed net, using plug-in mosquito killers. The malaria most common in Yemen (*Plasmodium falciparum*) has developed strands that are resistant to chloroquine. Thus, travellers who wish to take preventative measures should consult with their health physicians about atovaquone/proguanil, doxycycline and mefloquine. In speaking with your physician, be sure to detail all of the drugs that you currently are or soon will be taking, as these may hinder the efficacy of either treatment or result in unwanted side effects.

If mefloquine (Lariam) is suggested, start this two-and-a-half weeks (three doses) before departure to check that it suits you; stop it immediately if it seems to cause depression or anxiety, visual or hearing disturbances, severe headaches, fits or changes in heart rhythm. Side effects such as nightmares or dizziness are not medical reasons for stopping unless they are sufficiently debilitating or annoying. Anyone who has been treated for depression or psychiatric problems, has diabetes controlled by oral therapy or who is epileptic (or who has suffered fits in the past) or has a close blood relative who is epileptic, should probably avoid mefloquine.

In the past doctors were nervous about prescribing mefloquine to pregnant women, but experience has shown that it is relatively safe and certainly safer than the risk of malaria. That said, there are other issues, so if you are travelling to Yemen whilst pregnant, seek expert advice before departure.

Malarone (proguanil and atovaquone) is as effective as mefloquine. It has the advantage of having few side effects and need only be continued for one week after returning. However, it is expensive and because of this tends to be reserved for shorter trips. Malarone may not be suitable for everybody, so advice should be taken from a doctor. The licence in the UK has been extended for up to three months' use and a paediatric form of tablet is also available, prescribed on a weight basis.

Another alternative is the antibiotic doxycycline (100mg daily). Like Malarone it can be started just one day before arrival. Unlike mefloquine, it may also be used in travellers with epilepsy, although certain anti-epileptic medication may make it less effective. In perhaps 1–3% of people there is the possibility of allergic skin reactions developing in sunlight; the drug should be stopped if this happens. Women using the oral contraceptive should use an additional method of protection for the first four weeks when using doxycycline. It is also unsuitable in pregnancy or for children under 12 years.

Remember even if you take your tablets exactly as instructed and do everything you can not to get bitten, it is still possible to contract malaria. Any high unexplained fever over 38°C anything from 1 week into your trip up to one year thereafter should precipitate an immediate visit to the doctor.

RABIES Rabies is carried by all mammals (especially dogs and bats) and is passed on to man through a bite, scratch or a lick over an open wound. You must always assume any animal is rabid, and seek medical help as soon as possible. Meanwhile, scrub the wound with soap under a running tap or while pouring water from a jug. Find a reasonably clear-looking source of water (but at this stage the quality of the water is not important), then pour on a strong iodine or alcohol solution of gin, whisky or rum. This helps stop the rabies virus entering the body and will guard against wound infections, including tetanus.

Pre-exposure vaccinations for rabies is ideally advised for everyone, but is particularly important if you intend to have contact with animals and/or are likely to be more than 24 hours away from medical help. Ideally three doses should be taken over a minimum of 21 days, though even taking one or two doses of vaccine is better than none at all. Contrary to popular belief these vaccinations are relatively painless.

If you are bitten, scratched or licked over an open wound by a sick animal, then post-exposure prophylaxis should be given as soon as possible, though it is never too late to seek help, as the incubation period for rabies can be very long. Those who have not been immunised will need a full course of injections. The vast majority of travel health advisors including the World Health Organisation recommend rabies immunoglobulin (RIG), but this product is expensive (around US$800) and may be hard to come by – another reason why pre-exposure vaccination should be encouraged.

Tell the doctor if you have had pre-exposure vaccine, as this should change the treatment you receive. And remember that, if you do contract rabies, mortality is 100% and death from rabies is probably one of the worst ways to go.

OTHER ISSUES In early 2005 there was an outbreak of **dengue fever** in the southern Tihama region. Dengue fever is a haemorrhagic fever spread by day-biting mosquitoes. Symptoms of the disease include fever, headaches, muscle pain, and a bright rash. Typically the fever will end within a week or so, but there can be more serious consequences with repeated infections. There is no vaccine for dengue fever, but taking normal preventative measures against mosquito bites (ie: wearing clothing that adequately covers your arms and legs and using an insect repellent with DEET) will go a long way.

In 2000, Yemen experienced a problem with **Rift Valley fever**, another infectious fever spread by mosquitoes or by handling infected animals. The fever typically lasts for several days and in rare cases results in some level of vision loss. Since the 2000 incidents, there have not been any other reported outbreaks. The risk of a visitor contracting Rift Valley fever is low. Again, basic protection against mosquito bites will be helpful.

In the governorate of al-Jawf, there was an outbreak of **cholera** in early 2006 in which 14 children died. Cholera infections are spread most frequently by drinking contaminated water, and the risk of infection to visitors of Yemen is very low. Cholera vaccines are not recommended except for high-risk visitors, such as those travelling to the country to work in clinics in regions where cholera is currently a problem. An oral cholera vaccine (Dukoral) is available in the UK. Two doses are required to be taken 1–6 weeks apart and at least one week before entering Yemen to be effective.

TRAVEL CLINICS AND HEALTH INFORMATION A full list of current travel clinic websites worldwide is available from the International Society of Travel Medicine on www.istm.org. For other journey preparation information, consult www.tripprep.com. Information about various medications may be found on www.emedicine.com. For information on malaria prevention, see www.preventingmalaria.info.

UK

Berkeley Travel Clinic 32 Berkeley St, London W1J 8EL (near Green Park tube station); ☎ 020 7629 6233

Cambridge Travel Clinic 48a Mill Rd, Cambridge CB1 2AS; ☎ 01223 367362; e enquiries@ travelcliniccambridge.co.uk; www.travelcliniccambridge.co.uk; ⏰ 12.00–19.00 Tue–Fri, 10.00–16.00 Sat.

Edinburgh Travel Clinic Regional Infectious Diseases Unit, Ward 41 OPD, Western General Hospital, Crewe Rd South, Edinburgh EH4 2UX; ☎ 0131 537 2822; www.link.med.ed.ac.uk/ridu. Travel helpline (☎ 0906 589 0380) ⏰ 09.00–12.00 weekdays. Provides inoculations & antimalarial prophylaxis, & advises on travel-related health risks.

Fleet Street Travel Clinic 29 Fleet St, London EC4Y 1AA; ☎ 020 7353 5678; www.fleetstreetclinic.com. Vaccinations, travel products & latest advice.

Hospital for Tropical Diseases Travel Clinic Mortimer Market Bldg, Capper St (off Tottenham Ct Rd), London WC1E 6AU; ☎ 020 7388 9600; www.thehtd.org. Offers consultations & advice, & is able to provide all necessary drugs & vaccines for travellers. Runs a healthline (☎ 0906 133 7733) for

country-specific information & health hazards. Also stocks nets, water-purification equipment & personal protection measures.

Interhealth Worldwide Partnership Hse, 157 Waterloo Rd, London SE1 8US; ☎ 020 7902 9000; www.interhealth.org.uk. Competitively priced, one-stop travel health service. All profits go to their affiliated company, InterHealth, which provides healthcare for overseas workers on Christian projects.

Liverpool School of Medicine Pembroke Pl, Liverpool L3 5QA; ☎ 051 708 9393; f 0151 705 3370; www.liv.ac.uk/lstm

MASTA (Medical Advisory Service for Travellers Abroad) Moorfield Rd, Yeadon LS19 7BN; ☎ 0870 606 2782; www.masta-travel-health.com. Provides travel health advice, antimalarials & vaccinations. There are over 25 MASTA pre-travel clinics in Britain; call or check online for the nearest. Clinics also sell mosquito nets, medical kits, insect protection & travel-hygiene products.

NHS travel website www.fitfortravel.scot.nhs.uk. Provides country-by-country advice on immunisation & malaria, plus details of recent developments, & a list of relevant health organisations.

Nomad Travel Store/Clinic 3–4 Wellington Terrace, Turnpike Lane, London N8 0PX; ☎ 020 8889 7014; travel-health line (office hours only) ☎ 0906 863 3414; e sales@nomadtravel.co.uk; www.nomadtravel.co.uk. Also at 40 Bernard St, London WC1N 1LJ; ☎ 020 7833 4114; 52 Grosvenor Gardens, London SW1W 0AG; ☎ 020 7823 5823; & 43 Queens Rd, Bristol BS8 1QH; ☎ 0117 922 6567. For health advice, equipment such as mosquito nets

& other anti-bug devices, & an excellent range of adventure travel gear.
Trailfinders Travel Clinic 194 Kensington High St, London W8 7RG; ☎ 020 7938 3999; www.trailfinders.com/clinic.htm
Travelpharm The Travelpharm website, www.travelpharm.com, offers up-to-date guidance on travel-related health & has a range of medications available through their online mini-pharmacy.

Irish Republic
Tropical Medical Bureau Grafton St Medical Centre, Grafton Bldgs, 34 Grafton St, Dublin 2; ☎ 1 671 9200; www.tmb.ie. A useful website specific to

tropical destinations. Also check website for other bureaux locations throughout Ireland.

US
Centers for Disease Control 1600 Clifton Rd, Atlanta, GA 30333; ☎ 800 311 3435; travellers' health hotline; ☎ 888 232 3299; www.cdc.gov/travel. The central source of travel information in the USA. The invaluable *Health Information for International Travel*, published annually, is available from the Division of Quarantine at this address.
Connaught Laboratories PO Box 187, Swiftwater, PA 18370; ☎ 800 822 2463. They will send a free list

of specialist tropical-medicine physicians in your state.
IAMAT (International Association for Medical Assistance to Travelers) 1623 Military Rd, 279, Niagara Falls, NY14304-1745; ☎ 716 754 4883; e info@iamat.org; www.iamat.org. A non-profit organisation that provides lists of English-speaking doctors abroad.
International Medicine Center 920 Frostwood Drive, Suite 670, Houston, TX 77024; ☎ 713 550 2000; www.traveldoc.com

Canada
IAMAT Suite 1, 1287 St Clair Av W, Toronto, Ontario M6E 1B8; ☎ 416 652 0137; www.iamat.org
TMVC Suite 314, 1030 W Georgia St, Vancouver BC

V6E 2Y3; ☎ 888 288 8682; www.tmvc.com. Private clinic with several outlets in Canada.

Australia, New Zealand, Singapore
IAMAT PO Box 5049, Christchurch 5, New Zealand; www.iamat.org
TMVC ☎ 1300 65 88 44; www.tmvc.com.au. Clinics in Australia, New Zealand & Singapore, including:
Auckland Canterbury Arcade, 170 Queen St, Auckland; ☎ 9 373 3531

Brisbane 6th floor, 247 Adelaide St, Brisbane, QLD 4000; ☎ 7 3221 9066
Melbourne 393 Little Bourke St, 2nd floor, Melbourne, VIC 3000; ☎ 3 9602 5788
Sydney Dymocks Bldg, 7th floor, 428 George St, Sydney, NSW 2000; ☎ 2 9221 7133

South Africa and Namibia
SAA-Netcare Travel Clinics P Bag X34, Benmore 2010; www.travelclinic.co.za. Clinics throughout South Africa.

TMVC 113 D F Malan Drive, Roosevelt Park, Johannesburg; ☎ 011 888 7488; www.tmvc.com.au. Consult website for details of other clinics in South Africa & Namibia.

Switzerland
IAMAT 57 Chemin des Voirets, 1212 Grand Lancy, Geneva; www.iamat.org

FURTHER READING
Wilson-Howarth, Dr Jane, and Ellis, Dr Matthew *Your Child Abroad: A Travel Health Guide* Bradt Travel Guides, 2005
Wilson-Howarth, Dr Jane, *Bugs, Bites & Bowels* Cadogan, 2006

Yemen is a land of wonder and amazing landscapes, of religious scholarship and family relations, of the Queen of Sheba and the birthplace of the coffee trade. Ask your average Westerner about the country, and invariably you will get something related to tribal kidnappings, the bombing of the USS *Cole*, or an episode of *Friends* in which Chandler was trying to avoid Janice – each of which is painfully damaging to the country's image.

CRIME The crime rate in Yemen is very low, and incidents of pickpocketing, mugging and theft are virtually unheard of. Although most Yemenis today complain that the crime rate is rising in the country – particularly in Sana'a – any increase in criminal activity has been minimal and has not been felt by the visiting tourist population. The biggest risk you will face here is losing belongings that have been left unattended; a minimal level of diligence should suffice.

WOMEN TRAVELLERS Women travelling to the region should dress appropriately – loose-fitting clothing that covers both the arms and legs. While it is mandatory for Yemeni women to wear a *balto* (a full-length black robe) and headscarf, foreign women are not required to do so. Note, however, that you may be scolded infrequently by passers-by for not wearing the proper Islamic clothing. If you would feel more comfortable wearing either the balto or the headscarf, you should feel free to do so. It is not viewed as strange or condescending for a foreign woman to do so. Again though, there is no requirement to don the Yemeni articles of clothing. Additionally, about 80% of women in Yemen also wear a veil to cover their faces. Wearing a veil is not mandated in Islam, and foreign women should feel no pressure to wear one.

Whether you are wearing loose-fitting Western clothing or a balto, you are likely to be subjected to various catcalls in the streets of various cities, especially if you are alone or in a group of women. If the Neanderthal's behaviour continues or you feel uncomfortable, feel free to make a scene. It is considered shameful in Yemeni culture for men to treat women in this fashion, and demonstrating your harsh displeasure with the comments is typically enough to bring the episode to a close.

Other than these annoyances, female travellers are unlikely to face any other specific dangers. Sensible precautions will go a long way.

TERRORISM There have been very few attacks against tourists in Yemen, but travellers should be advised that there is a threat of terrorist activity in the country, particularly against British and American targets. Events that have occurred in conjunction with al-Qaeda's threats to carry out attacks on the Arabian Peninsula present significant factors of concern. Travellers should be alert to any suspect behaviour.

In October 2000, the USS *Cole* was attacked off of the port at Aden – an incident in which 17 US sailors were killed. A similar attack was carried out against a French oil tanker near Mukalla in 2002. In early 2006, some 23 convicts escaped from a prison in Sana'a; among the fugitives were known al-Qaeda affiliates and individuals involved with the two previous ship attacks. Two of the escaped men died in failed attempts to attack oil installations in Marib and Mukalla later that year. While others voluntarily turned themselves in, some of the escaped convicts remain at large. The 2006 escape marked the second time men involved with the USS *Cole* bombing had escaped from prison.

Other terrorist attacks in Yemen include the murder of three American doctors at the Jiblah Baptist Hospital in 2002. That same year, there was an attack against a helicopter of the US oil company Hunt, and a cache of explosives likely planned for an attack against Western targets was seized in Sana'a. Since then other explosives and weapons have been seized at various points, although it is hard to tell for certain whether in each incident the weapons had been meant for merely increasing a tribe's supply of firepower or for something more sinister.

In July 2007, seven Spanish tourists and two Yemeni tour guides were killed when a suicide bomber drove an explosive-laden 4x4 into the tour group's vehicle convoy at an ancient site in Marib. The attacks followed on the heels of unspecific threats against Western interests in the country if jailed members of al-Qaeda in Yemen were not released.

Travellers headed to the region are advised to stay up to date on the latest security situation in the country. Two particularly good resources are the Foreign & Commonwealth Office (*www.fco.gov.uk*) and the consular information sheet of the US State Department (*http://travel.state.gov*).

KIDNAPPINGS One of the darkest blotches of Yemen's reputation has been the country's frequent kidnappings. There is reason to believe that kidnappings may decrease significantly, but travellers should be aware of the threat. Nearly all kidnappings occur while travellers are in transit between cities.

Historically, kidnappings have had little to do with any animus toward foreigners. Tribal forces would take Western tourists and hold them out as hostages, releasing them when the government agreed to the tribe's demand for improved infrastructure, such as water access, roads, schools and electricity. While kidnapped, the foreigners are often treated as honoured guests and have been well taken care of until their release has been negotiated.

Not all kidnappings have ended peacefully. In 1998, members of the 'Islamic Army' captured 16 Western tourists. The aims of the kidnappers were unclear, but the kidnapping was clearly unlike the other 'guest' kidnappings. The incident ended with an ill-executed rescue attempt by the Yemeni government in which four tourists were killed. Another tourist was killed in 2000 following another shootout between the government and the kidnappers.

Following 9/11 the government enacted stricter laws against kidnapping to help its international image, but unfortunately kidnappings continued until a greater effort was exerted by the government to provide areas of the country with better infrastructure.

From late 2005 to mid 2006 there was another string of kidnappings – these incidents stemming from a tribe's desire to see some of its tribesmen released from prison. The kidnappings were quickly ended and, for the first time, the government enforced harsh penalties. Many of the kidnappers were sentenced to 15–20 years' imprisonment. The resurgence of kidnappings quickly stopped, and it is likely that harsher sentences, together with a general improvement of the infrastructure, will help end kidnappings in the country altogether.

OTHER SECURITY CONCERNS From time to time the Yemeni government will decide that various regions of the country are off limits due to the local security situation there. In general, regions that often find themselves on the list include Sa'ada, Marib, al-Jawf, and Shabwa. If your proposed tour includes any of these regions, there is a chance that a last-minute decision by the government will force you to adopt a new itinerary. Lucky for you there is always plenty to see.

Since 2004 there has been a conflict in the northern Sa'ada governorate between the Yemeni government and the followers of Hussayn al-Houthi. The situation had calmed by late 2006, and the region was reopened to tourists before fighting re-emerged several weeks later. Check with your embassy or travel agency to get the latest information on the conflict.

Finally, travellers should be wary of sailing in the waters off Yemen. The seas around the country have been populated historically by pirates, and the waters remain dangerous today. There were reports of pirate attacks in both 2004 and 2005 against private yachts sailing off the southern coast of Yemen. In 2005, a cruise ship escaped a separate attack while travelling through nearby Somali waters.

WHAT TO TAKE

You will likely do a good deal of walking outside in Yemen. You should bring comfortable walking or hiking shoes, comfortable clothes, and a good sunscreen. If you do forget the sunscreen, you won't be able to find it easily. The best bets for purchasing some are Shamaila Hari in Sana'a or the Aden Mall in Aden.

You will want to tailor your clothing to the time you visit as well. Keep in mind that the periods of March–April and July–August are the rainy seasons in the country – bring your raincoat and umbrella. If you are planning on staying in Sana'a during that time, you will want a good pair of waterproof boots. During the winter months it can get surprisingly cold at night, especially in the mountains and in the desert: sweaters and coats may seem like an odd choice for a suitcase to the Arabian Peninsula, but better your friends thinking you strange than you shivering away sleepless nights. Along the coast it is hot all year round; you will want light, breathable clothing that satisfies modesty requirements.

ELECTRICITY

Yemen's electrical current is 220V/50Hz. In most of the country electricity is accessible by the British three-prong plug, although the European two-pin outlet is also widely used. In eastern Yemen, the old Soviet-style outlets – similar to those used for the German two-pin plugs – are prevalent. Multi-plug converters are available in most stores.

$ MONEY AND BANKING

CURRENCY The official unit of currency is the Yemeni rial. Notes are issued in denominations of 10, 20, 50, 100, 200, 500, and 1,000, and coins come in values of 5, 10, and 20. Because the largest note is only 1,000YR, people often are required to carry around large amounts of money. This is especially true because Yemen remains a cash society. It is not uncommon to see businessmen carrying bags of notes to the banks to make weekly deposits. Nevertheless, because issuing larger notes supposedly would give the appearance of a weakening economy, 1,000YR is as high as it comes. Wear trousers with big pockets.

The current exchange rate (October 2007) is: £1=406.44YR, US$1=199.14YR, €1=281.32YR.

EXCHANGING CURRENCY The easiest way to exchange currency is by stopping in at an exchange shop. All the shops normally offer roughly the same rates, although some will offer a low figure. The US dollar is the preferred currency of exchange, and new US$100 bills will fetch the best returns. Smaller denominations of any currency will not be given as good a rate. Exchanging money with individuals on the street is not recommended, and with the proliferation of exchange shops offering good rates, there is little need to do so.

Increasingly, ATMs have begun to spring up around the country, much to the delight of travellers. The machines can be found easily in all of the major cities, and even some smaller towns now boast their own ATM.

The acceptance of credit cards, however, is still not widespread. You will be able to use them in major hotels, some souvenir shops in the Old City, and at a few travel agencies, but little else.

BANKING There are several decent banks in Yemen:

Cooperative & Agricultural Credit Bank ('CAC Bank')
✆ 01 220110; www.cacbank.com.ye
International Bank of Yemen ✆ 01 407035;
www.ibyemen.com

National Bank of Yemen ✆ 02 253753;
www.nbyemen.com

Foreigners are permitted to open local accounts at any of the three banks in either Yemeni rials, US dollars, British pounds or the euro. Local ATM cards may be issued that work internationally or only domestically. To open an account you will need to visit one of the offices with your passport and photos.

BUDGETING

It is very easy to visit Yemen without spending a lot of money. Most hotels are inexpensive and food in local restaurants is even cheaper. The most expensive part of your visit will be the transportation. You will have to pay for the airfare of course (unless you want to hitchhike to Djibouti and take a boat across the Red Sea).

Hiring a 4x4 vehicle through a local tour agency costs about US$60–70/day, so if you are looking to travel on a very tight budget, you will need to rely on other means of transportation. Because of security reasons, the government limits the destinations within the country that tourists are allowed to visit without going through a tour agency. Thus, for example, you would not be able to visit Marib, the desert, much of the highlands north of Sana'a, or parts of the southeast of Aden. But that still leaves a lot to see!

Daily costs for touring the Yemeni countryside can run to less than 2,000YR. This will include hotels (but assumes two people sharing accommodation), meals and transportation. Double rooms in most cities can be acquired for less than 1,000YR per person. You will need to spend money on water, but not much. Bottled water goes for only 30–35YR. You can spend less than 400YR per day by eating modestly at local restaurants. Transportation by bus or shared taxi in between near destinations will cost less than 400YR. You will even have enough left over to try some inexpensive qat (200YR).

Travelling around Yemen in a more comfortable fashion will not cost an arm and a leg either. A daily budget of about 11,000YR (£28/US$56/€43) will enable you to travel the countryside in a private 4x4 vehicle with an English-speaking guide, stay in decent hotels, and enjoy a nice spread of Yemeni and Western dishes.

By budgeting a daily allowance of 25,000YR (£65/US$128/€99), you can afford to have a private 4x4 vehicle with an English-speaking guide take you from the top hotel of one city to the next, as well as pay for flights to cover some of the longer travelling distances.

GETTING AROUND

There are four major ways to travel in Yemen – bus, shared taxi, private car, and by air. Most major and medium-sized cities have bus and shared taxi access.

There are several different bus companies in Yemen, but the only ones worth riding on are Yemitco and Al-Esayi. Both companies have comparable air-conditioned buses, and each play an interesting mix of Arabic movies during the journey. Prices are rarely more than 2,000YR for a ticket. The cheaper companies are not significantly less expensive (perhaps 500YR less per ticket), but the buses are extremely uncomfortable, old and prone to breakdown. Buses normally gather at the place where you purchase your ticket.

A slightly less comfortable but quicker way to travel in between cities is to use the shared taxi system. Shared taxis, or *bijous*, gather at certain points in each city known as *furzat*. (Thus, if you wanted to take a taxi from Sana'a to Aden, for instance, you would ask for 'furzat Aden'.) The bijous are station wagons that fill up with nine–ten passengers (two in the front seat with the driver, four in the middle seat, and three–four in the back) before departing. Seats typically fill quickly, but sometimes you may be required to sit and wait for a long time before the last customer arrives. The driver will under no condition leave without a full load unless the other passengers split the costs of the missing traveller. If you are travelling in a tour group of five or six, it might be a good idea to hire a 'full' bijou – you won't have to wait for other passengers and you will have much more room for comfort.

The most convenient way to travel the country is by hired car – typically a Toyota Landcruiser. The most popular model, which came out during the President Clinton scandal in the US, is fondly known as 'the Monica', in part because of the large boot. If you are planning your trip with a local tour agency, this is most likely how you will do the majority of your travelling. The cost for a car and driver ranges from US$60–70.

Finally, it is possible to see a large portion of the country by plane – Yemen has a number of airports throughout the country, and Air Yemenia operates domestic flights connecting them. There are operational airports at Sana'a, Aden, Ta'iz, Hudaydah, Seiyun, Mukalla, al-Ghayda, and Socotra. (There are also airports but no current service to the cities of Sa'ada and Ataq.) Air Yemenia is a pleasant enough airline, and the eclectic music selection at least will keep you entertained – from Vivaldi's *Spring* on takeoff to *The Godfather* theme on landing.

 ## ACCOMMODATION

Yemen is beginning to get a wider variety of hotels that will allow for greater flexibility in the type of travel visitors can enjoy. Many of Yemen's hotels are very basic, and they include Yemeni-style 'squat holes' in the bathroom. Nearly every town that has a hotel will typically also have more accommodating rooms with private Western-style toilets – and still at a very cheap price. In the larger cities, more luxury hotels have begun to spring up.

Hotels throughout this guide will be given a price code based on the following prices for double rooms:

$$$$$	**Exclusive**	– Rooms that cost over 25,000YR
$$$$	**Upmarket**	– Rooms that cost between 12,000YR and 25,000YR
$$$	**Mid-range**	– Rooms that cost between 6,000YR and 12,000YR
$$	**Budget**	– Rooms that cost between 2,500YR and 6,000YR
$	**Cheap**	– Rooms that cost up to 2,500YR

Some hotels include continental or Arabic breakfasts within the price of the room. Hotels which do so are noted within.

Yemeni cuisine is both unique and delectable – a great combination for those looking to try new types of food. Breakfast and dinner are typically smaller affairs, with lunch ranking as the largest and most important meal of the day. In addition to your standard Middle Eastern fare (kebab, shawarma and falafel), there is a number of Yemen-specific dishes to delight your palate. Most dishes include rice and variations on goat or chicken. A number of other Yemeni dishes are listed below.

MAIN DISHES *Saltah* is Yemeni-style stew made with vegetables and meat broth served piping hot in a stone bowl. The most important ingredient of the dish is *helba* – a greenish froth made by soaking fenugreek powder in water. The dish is said to give you the taste for qat. If you take a bowl of *saltah* and cook it with shredded meat you will get *fahsah*. The meat gives the broth a great flavour and balances nicely against the *helba*. Trying either *saltah* or *fahsah* while in Yemen is virtually mandatory.

Other dishes include *fasoolia*, a white bean dish that can be served by itself, as a soup, or with eggs, *ful*, a mashed bean porridge, and *brayk*, a pastry-style flat bread filled with minced meat and eggs.

APPETISERS The first dish consumed during lunch is normally *marag*, a small bowl of meat broth. Another excellent dish (and one of my favourites) is *shafoot*, a cold dish in which yoghurt, *zahawag* (see below) and vegetables are poured over several layers of pancake-like bread similar to Ethiopian *injira*. The dish is normally served mostly in Yemeni homes, but makes an appearance at restaurants during Ramadan.

SIDE DISHES *Zahawag*, diced tomatoes mixed with spices, is similar to salsa and is served with almost any meal. It is sometimes mixed with cheese. *Aseet*, a large mountain of cornmeal surrounded by a sea of meat broth, is tasty but difficult to find in restaurants. *Hareesh* is a similar dish made with wheat flour.

DESSERTS One of the tastiest Yemeni dishes is *bint as-Sahn* ('the girl of the plate'), an oven-cooked flat pastry-style bread covered in a mixture of oil and honey. *Fattah* (bread) may also be served as a dessert, mixed with either *tammer* (dates), *mawz* (bananas) or *'asal* (honey).

DRINKS Although Yemen was famous for the coffee trade during the 16th and 17th centuries, Yemenis do not drink much *bunn* (coffee) themselves. More popular is *qishr*, a weaker drink made from the husks of the coffee bean and mixed with ginger and cardamom. The other drinks most common (besides soda) is *shay* (tea) and *'aseer* (juice). 'Aseer is made from all variety of fruit, but a particularly popular variety is *sharab al-zabeeb*, made from raisins.

ALCOHOL Yemen is a strict Islamic country, and the drinking of alcohol is forbidden to Yemenis in most locations. These rules do not apply to foreigners, who are allowed to bring alcohol into the country and to consume it in private. There are some restaurants in Sana'a and Aden that will allow you to purchase or bring in your own alcohol. Drinks may also be purchased in the nightclubs of Sana'a or Aden and in many of the top-end hotels.

RESTAURANT PRICE CODES Restaurants throughout this guide will be given a price code based on the average cost of main dishes as follows:

Practical Information **EATING AND DRINKING**

2

$$$$	**Expensive** – Above 2,000YR
$$$	**Above average** – Between 1,000–2,000YR
$$	**Mid-range** – Between 500–1,000YR
$	**Inexpensive** – Up to 500YR

PUBLIC HOLIDAYS AND FESTIVALS

Like most Middle Eastern countries, Yemen celebrates a combination of religious and secular holidays. The secular holidays are always celebrated on specific dates of the Gregorian calendar. The religious holidays, however, are fixed to dates in the Islamic calendar, which is lunar based. Thus, every year the date on the Gregorian calendar that corresponds to the Islamic holiday moves back about 11 days.

National Unity Day celebrates the day in 1990 on which the Yemen Arab Republic of the north and the People's Democratic Republic of Yemen in the south merged to form the Republic of Yemen. The date marks the ratification of the constitution and the election of Ali Abdullah Saleh as the president of the newly formed republic. **Revolution Day** commemorates the 1962 overthrow of the Zaydi imam that marked the beginning of the Yemen Arab Republic. South Yemen's equivalent to Revolution Day is **National Day**, observing the date the revolution began against the British and the states of the Aden Protectorate. The date the British actually turned over authority of the south to the National Liberation Front is celebrated on **Independence Day**.

During the month of **Ramadan** Muslims fast during daylight hours, observing the month that Muhammad received the first revelation of the Koran from the Angel Gabriel, and, most notably, abstain from food, water, sex and smoking. The end of Ramadan marks the celebration of **Eid al-Fitr** (literally 'the festival of breaking the fast'). Parents indulge in new fineries and sweets for their children, families go on holiday, and family members visit each other with gifts.

Eid al-Adha is a holiday that occurs at the end of the pilgrimage, when the pilgrims are descending from Mount Arafat. The four-day festival commemorates Abraham's willingness to sacrifice his son – Isaac in the Judeo-Christian literature and Ishmael in Islamic tradition (see Genesis 22; Koran 37: 99–111). Because Abraham sacrificed a ram instead of his son, Muslim families also sacrifice an animal (usually a goat or sheep), and the streets literally run with blood. The meat is divided into thirds: one for the slaughtering family, one for relatives, and one for the needy. With so many animals killed on the same day, people are eager to find people to whom they can give the meat. If you are in Yemen during the festival, you will probably be offered some on several occasions. In some parts of Yemen, particularly in the south, Eid al-Fitr is referred to as Eid as-Sagheer ('the little festival') and Eid al-Adha as Eid al-Kabeer ('the big festival').

SECULAR HOLIDAYS

Labour Day	1 May
National Unity Day	22 May
Revolution Day	26 September
National Day	14 October
Independence Day	30 November

ISLAMIC HOLIDAYS

Islamic New Year	1 Muharram
	10 January 2008; 29 December 2009;
	18 December 2010

Birth of the Prophet	12 Rabi' al-Awwal
	20 March 2008; 9 March 2009; 26 February 2010
Ramadan	The month of Ramadan
	2 September 2008; 22 August 2009; 11 August 2010
Eid al-Fitr	1 Shawwal
	2 October 2008; 21 September 2009;
	10 September 2010
Eid al-Adha	10–13 Dhu al-Hijja
	20–23 December 2007; 9–12 December 2008;
	28 November–1 December 2009;
	17–20 November 2010

🛒 SHOPPING

With the exception of a couple of shopping malls in Sana'a and Aden, Yemen does not have many modern shopping centres. The lack of these modern conglomerations is, nevertheless, more than made up for by the presence of the souk – old open-air markets that have persisted to this day since antiquity. It is in these souks that you will buy your best souvenirs to provide you with memories of your trip to Yemen.

One of the most common souvenirs is the *jambiyya*, the large curved dagger worn on a wide belt by nearly every tribesman in the country. These large knives serve many functions. For the most part they are ceremonial, used most frequently as an extension of the arm during the *bara'* tribal 'dance'. The knives also serve as status symbols, and the more expensive jambiyya you can afford reflects a lot about you to those around you – and there are vast differences in jambiyya quality. The knives can easily run into the tens of thousands of US dollars. The jambiyya can also be used as a weapon, but it should not be used lightly. Pulling out a jambiyya, even if not to attack someone, is a serious challenge. There is a custom in the country that a jambiyya pulled in anger may not be resheathed before drawing blood.

The most important and expensive part of the jambiyya is the hilt, and often fairly little attention is paid to the construction of the blade itself – another indication that the curved knives are meant to serve a more ceremonial purpose. Unfortunately, the most prestigious jambiyyas have their hilts made from the horns of the black rhinoceros. The consuming demand for the rhino's horn in Yemen has been a major cause for the plight of the animal. As of July 2006, the World Conservation Union announced that the west African Black Rhinoceros, one of the four subdivisions of the black rhinoceros, is believed to be extinct.

Jambiyyas made from black rhino horn are known as *sayfani*, and because of conservation and legal issues you should not attempt to purchase one. Other varieties of the dagger exist, and, because you are not a mountain tribesman who needs a rhino dagger to maintain your status, they should work just fine. Less expensive than the rhino-horn jambiyyas, but with the potential to look just as attractive, are those made from giraffe horn (*az-zaraf*) and ibex horn (*al-wa'al*). Cheaper versions of the jambiyya are made from cow horn (*al-baggara*) or plastic (*blastik*). A different style of jambiyya, common of the old Jewish artisanship, is a silver jambiyya (*al-fidda*) – although not many pieces of genuine Jewish artistry exist any longer in the country.

In addition to the jambiyya, another cultural souvenir is the *futa*, the wrap-around 'man skirt' worn by many Yemenis that is somewhat more informal than the long, white *thob*. Other souvenirs include elaborate pieces of silver or coral jewellery. In the area of Wadi Hadhramawt you may want to consider some carved

2

Ariadne Van Zandbergen

EQUIPMENT Although with some thought and an eye for composition you can take reasonable photos with a 'point-and-shoot' camera, you need an SLR camera if you are at all serious about photography. Modern SLRs tend to be very clever, with automatic programs for almost every possible situation, but remember that these programs are limited in the sense that the camera cannot think, but only make calculations. Every starting amateur photographer should read a photographic manual for beginners and get to grips with such basics as the relationship between aperture and shutter speed.

Always buy the best lens you can afford. The lens determines the quality of your photo more than the camera body. Fixed fast lenses are ideal, but very costly. A zoom lens makes it easier to change composition without changing lenses the whole time. If you carry only one lens, a 28–70mm (digital 17–55mm) or similar zoom should be ideal. For a second lens, a lightweight 80–200mm or 70–300mm (digital 55–200mm) or similar will be excellent for candid shots and varying your composition. Wildlife photography will be very frustrating if you don't have at least a 300mm lens. For a small loss of quality, tele-converters are a cheap and compact way to increase magnification: a 300 lens with a 1.4x converter becomes 420mm, and with a 2x it becomes 600mm. Note, however, that 1.4x and 2x tele-converters reduce the speed of your lens by 1.4 and 2 stops respectively.

For wildlife photography from a safari vehicle, a solid beanbag, which you can make yourself very cheaply, will be necessary to avoid blurred images, and is more useful than a tripod. A clamp with a tripod head screwed onto it can be attached to the vehicle as well. Modern dedicated flash units are easy to use; aside from the obvious need to flash when you photograph at night, you can improve a lot of photos in difficult 'high contrast' or very dull light with some fill-in flash. It pays to have a proper flash unit as opposed to a built-in camera flash.

DIGITAL/FILM Digital photography is now the preference of most amateur and professional photographers, with the resolution of digital cameras improving all the time. For ordinary prints a 6 megapixel camera is fine. For better results and the possibility to enlarge images and for professional reproduction, higher resolution is available up to 16 megapixels.

Memory space is important. The number of pictures you can fit on a memory card depends on the quality you choose. Calculate in advance how many pictures you can fit on a card and either take enough cards to last for your trip, or take a storage drive onto which you can download the content. A laptop gives the advantage that you can see your pictures properly at the end of each day and edit and delete rejects, but a storage device is lighter and less bulky. These drives come in different capacities up to 80GB.

Bear in mind that digital camera batteries, computers and other storage devices need charging, so make sure you have all the chargers, cables and converters with you; a spare battery is invaluable. If you're flying around to small safari camps, then most camps will

woodwork. There are also various local handicrafts, from handmade rugs to painted incense burners – in some places, such as the Hope in Their Hands store in Sana'a, it is possible to buy some of these items and help the marginalised artisans make a living and pass on their craft. Of course, you can also purchase frankincense and coffee, the two items that put Yemen on the map economically in different eras of the country's long history. Food items that would make particularly good gifts include dates, raisins and the amazing Yemeni honey (sometimes as expensive as US$100 per kilo!).

have some form of power, even though there is no socket in your tent. (Even the smallest bushcamp will normally have a fridge and a radio, and both will require some power.) If you bring a few sets of spare batteries, and a charger, most camps will usually be able to charge your batteries given 24 hours. Ideally, and crucially if you're camping, also bring an adaptor for a vehicle's cigarette lighter, as batteries can then be charged while you're on the road or during a game-viewing drive.

If you are shooting film, 100 to 200 ISO print film and 50 to 100 ISO slide film are ideal. Low ISO film is slow but fine grained and gives the best colour saturation, but will need more light, so support in the form of a tripod or monopod is important. You can also bring a few 'fast' 400 ISO films for low-light situations where a tripod or flash is no option. Film is difficult to find in Zambia, so bring anything you need from home.

DUST AND HEAT Dust and heat are often a problem. Keep your equipment in a sealed bag, stow films in an airtight container (eg: a small cooler bag) and avoid exposing equipment and film to the sun. Digital cameras are prone to collecting dust particles on the sensor which results in spots on the image. The dirt mostly enters the camera when changing lenses, so be careful when doing this. To some extent photos can be 'cleaned' up afterwards in Photoshop, but this is time-consuming. You can have your camera sensor professionally cleaned, or you can do this yourself with special brushes and swabs made for the purpose, but note that touching the sensor might cause damage and should only be done with the greatest care.

LIGHT The most striking outdoor photographs are often taken during the hour or two of 'golden light' after dawn and before sunset. Shooting in low light may enforce the use of very low shutter speeds, in which case a tripod will be required to avoid camera shake.

With careful handling, side lighting and back lighting can produce stunning effects, especially in soft light and at sunrise or sunset. Generally, however, it is best to shoot with the sun behind you. When photographing animals or people in the harsh midday sun, images taken in light but even shade are likely to be more effective than those taken in direct sunlight or patchy shade, since the latter conditions create too much contrast.

PROTOCOL In Zambia, as elsewhere, it is unacceptable to photograph local people without permission, and many people will refuse to pose or will ask for a donation. In such circumstances, don't try to sneak photographs as you might get yourself into trouble. Even the most willing subject will often pose stiffly when a camera is pointed at them; relax them by making a joke, and take a few shots in quick succession to improve the odds of capturing a natural pose.

Ariadne Van Zandbergen is a professional travel and wildlife photographer specialising in Africa. She runs the Africa Image Library. For photo requests, visit www.africaimagelibrary.co.za or contact her on ariadne@hixnet.co.za.

PHOTOGRAPHY

Photography in Yemen is one of the most exciting aspects of visiting the country. Amazing subjects are constantly appearing before you, and often you will be asked to take a picture before you can ask permission. Indeed, the repeated cry of *Sura! Sura!* ('Picture! Picture!') will bubble out incessantly from the mouths of children throughout the entirety of your journey. If they aren't posing for pictures before you reach for your camera, you should ask permission before snapping off a shot (*mumkin sura?*). Taking pictures of women is generally off-limits, as is photographing military installations or sites of 'strategic interest'. While not forbidden, Yemenis will find it insulting if you photograph areas of rubbish. See box on pages 58–9 for more information.

(MEDIA AND COMMUNICATIONS

Yemen has come under continued attack for the lack of freedom it affords its press. Both Yemeni and Western journalists have reported incidents of abuse and equipment being confiscated. The Yemeni government is often willing to seize work and edit it for mistakes.

The 1990 Law on Press & Publications guaranteed that the press 'shall be independent and shall have full freedom to practise its vocation'. The law also noted that prison sentences could be handed down to any member of the press who published anything that belittled the principles of Islam, that led 'to the spread of ideas contrary to the principles of the Yemeni Revolution', or that criticised the president in any way (although the penalties would 'not necessary apply to constructive criticism'). Under the law, journalists have been jailed for defaming the president, and Muhammad Al-Asadi, the editor of the *Yemen Observer*, was sentenced to imprisonment and was fined 500,000YR for reprinting the Danish cartoons of Muhammad in an article discussing reactions of the Arab world.

At the same time, Yemen does enjoy more press freedoms than many developing countries. The 1990 law does give newspapers a good deal of leeway, allowing them to criticise many aspects of Yemeni laws, protest incidents of jailing journalists, and report on the negative aspects of Yemeni life. Many of the political cartoons drawn by the *Yemen Times*'s Samer would not be printed in states with stricter press laws. Additionally, there has been some recent debate in Yemen's parliament to revise the 1990 law to allow for greater press freedoms. During the presidential elections of 2006, opposition candidate Faisal bin Shamlan was given great freedom in levelling charges of corruption and incompetence at the incumbent party – something that is not likely to be seen any time soon in elections elsewhere on the Arabian Peninsula.

NEWSPAPERS

Arabic press Al Thawra (*www.althawranews.net*) is the main government-owned daily newspaper. An online edition is available.

Al Motamar (*www.almotamar.net/en*) is the daily newspaper of the ruling political party. The online site is available in both Arabic and English.

English press The **Yemen Times** (*www.yementimes.com*) is an independent newspaper published twice a week. The **Yemen Observer** (*www.yobserver.com*) is an English newspaper published several times a week. Although the Observer's license was revoked after the Danish cartoon scandal, the revocation was overturned (conveniently) the day before the UN World Press Freedom Day. An online edition is also available.

After al-Asadi was released from prison for his involvement in the *Yemen Observer* Danish cartoon scandal, he founded the **Yemen Mirror** (*www.yemenmirror.com*), an online newspaper that can speak more freely about situations in Yemen, and the **Watchdog**, a site dedicated to monitoring human rights and freedom of the press abuses in Yemen. It remains to be seen whether the site will remain in existence.

Shahab Yemeni (*www.shahabyemeni.com*) is an English youth newsletter founded in 2004. Interesting polls include questions such as 'would you marry someone from the lowest caste?'

MAGAZINES Arabia Felix (*www.arabia-felix.com*) is a great source of articles about various tourist sites in Yemen and interesting points of culture by the same folks at the *Yemen Observer*. Some editions even come with CDs of Yemeni Music.

INTERNET Affordable internet cafes have begun to appear with some prevalence in larger cities, typically charging less than 3YR/min. Connections are also available at a higher rate in some of the more major hotels, and it is also possible to purchase cards for a set number of minutes of dial-up connection.

MOBILE PHONES In addition to a tribal jambiyya and an AK-47, nothing establishes a Yemeni's status quite like a trendy mobile phone. The phones are widely used throughout the country. There are three local providers: Sabafon, Spacetel, and Yemen Mobile. Sabafon seems to have the best coverage out of the three.

BUSINESS

When conducting business with Yemenis, Westerners are generally expected to wear suits; approaching a (especially new) Yemeni business contact while donning local, traditional clothing will likely make you come off as not seriously committed to the project. Handshakes are the established greeting, although women may want to wait for an invitation to shake hands from men. As in much of the Middle East, business cards are prevalent – having a large supply of flashy business cards and brochures will go a long way to help establish credibility.

Depending on the type of business being conducted, major decisions may be made over a qat-chewing session. It is important here to not rush headlong into discussions as soon as qat is being chewed, but rather to ease into talks once introductory and welcoming talks have died down.

Yemenis will rarely burst out with flat-out refusals (unless of course it is used merely as a negotiation tactic). More often, Yemenis prefer more subtle ways of declining offers. As one director of a local institute in Sana'a said: 'There are a hundred ways to say "no" in Yemen, and one of them is to say "yes".'

One phrase, heard in every aspect of Yemeni life and especially in regard to business is *in sha Allah* (God willing). The phrase is used as a marker to discuss any event which has not yet happened. Depending on its context, the phrase could mean 'yes', 'maybe', or even 'no'.

CULTURAL ETIQUETTE

CLOTHING Men and women both should make an effort to dress moderately. For women, this means loose fitting clothing that hides the shape of the body and covers the arms and legs completely. Men should avoid wearing shorts.

WOMEN One of the quickest ways to get in trouble in Yemen is making comments about local women to Yemenis. Western men who have spent time with or spoken with Yemeni women publicly have reported long interviews with secret police afterwards. Take care.

GREETING A good rule to keep in mind in Yemen is: 'Greet one, greet all'. Whether you are walking into a *majlis* or just approaching a table at a restaurant, if you shake only one person's hand, you will insult all of those whose hands you didn't shake. It does not matter whether you knew just the one person you greeted.

MOSQUES With a few exceptions non-Muslims are not allowed to enter most mosques. Strictly speaking, this is not an Islamic prohibition, but it has often come to be interpreted that way and has been propagated by some of the local imams. Some tour groups may have arrangements to enter certain mosques. Otherwise, feel free to ask politely whether you might enter, but be ready to respect the usual negative answer and under no circumstances should you walk into a mosque without permission. Remember that, if you do visit a mosque, you will need to remove your shoes.

GIVING SOMETHING BACK/LOCAL CHARITIES

SANA'A

Al-Aman Association for Blind Females Television St, PO Box 1509; ↘ 01 334005; e al-amanorg@ hotmail.com. Local charity that trains, finds employment for & defends the rights of blind women.

Care International Mujahid St, PO Box 11101; ↘ 01 243379 (Sana'a), +61 2 6279 0200 (Australia); e care@careaustralia.org.au; www.careaustralia.org.au. Supports a number or programmes including literacy projects, agricultural construction & institutional capacity building.

CHF International Iran St, PO Box 18407; ↘ 01 427426 (Sana'a), +1 301 587 4700 (US); e mailbox@chfhq.org; www.chfhq.org. Through its programme ACCESS-MENA, CHF targets the root causes of child labour while providing fees for child labourers to return to school.

Dar al-Salaam Organisation Sheraton St, PO Box 20871; ↘ 01 255971; f 01 341160; e peace@ peace-yemen.org.ye; www.peace-yemen.org.ye. Actively works to help resolve & prevent issues of revenge killing, & to decrease the number of guns in the country. You will see their logo of an AK-47 with a red circle & slash through it at most border crossings & on some bottles of water.

Hope in Their Hands Samsarat al-Halaqah, Old City; ↘ 01 482455. A small non-profit store located in the Old City of Sana'a that sells handicrafts made by women throughout the country.

House of Folklore Bab al-Balaka Zone; ↘ 01 481360; e housefolk@gmail.com. Small privately operated museum in Sana'a that seeks to preserve the folkloric traditions of the marginalised members of society.

International Community Services St 33, Kholani Bldg (Agricultural District), PO Box 45186; ↘ 01 217700 (Sana'a), +1 225 665 4444 (US); e info@ics-yemen.org; www.ics-yemen.org. Provides vocational training to the poor & physically handicapped in Ta'iz, Hajjah & Hadhramawt.

International Cooperation for Development Ste 20,

Hse 9 in the Diplomatic Quarter, PO Box 4039; ↘ 01 440359 (Sana'a), 020 7354 0883 (UK); e icdyem@y.net.ye; www.ciir.org. British NGO focusing on capacity building & the prevention of HIV.

Islamic Relief Worldwide Amman St, PO Box 15088; ↘ 01 207880 (Sana'a), 0121 605 5555 (UK), +1 888 479 4968 (US); e hq@islamic-relief.org.uk; www.alyateem.com. Website enables you to sponsor Yemeni orphans online for a monthly fee.

Islamic World League Ta'iz St, PO Box 14839; ↘ 01 615908; e mmc@y.net.ye. Runs orphanages & digs for water wells throughout the country.

Marie Stopes International 14 October St, PO Box 16160; ↘ 01 426169 (Sana'a), 020 7574 7400 (UK); e africa@mariestopes.org.uk; www.mariestopes.org.uk. Provides maternal & child health, reproductive health & health awareness services throughout the country.

Millennium Relief and Development Services Djibouti St, near the Modern American Language Institute (MALI), PO Box 19128; ↘ 01 442220 (Sana'a), +1 713 961 5645 (US), +1 604 533 0767 (Canada), +61 8 8178 0532 (Australia); e millennium@ mrds.org; www.mrds.org. Works in a number of important areas, including hospital services, education, & providing free healthcare to street cleaners.

Missionaries of Charity al-Jamhuria Hospital, PO Box 2148; ↘ 01 274292; e gilynn@y.net.ye. Yemen's branch of the order originally founded by Mother Theresa in India.

Oxfam St 22, Hse 11 in the Diplomatic Quarter, near the Modern American Language Institute (MALI), PO Box 1045; ↘ 01 444568 (Sana'a), 01865 313313 (UK); e oxfam@oxfam.org.uk; www.oxfram.org.uk. Large international organisation whose branch in Yemen addresses issues such as early marriage, poverty & disaster preparedness.

Save the Children Hadda St, PO Box 11391; ↘ 01 417899; e info.yemen@scsmena.org; www.scsmena.org. Swedish-based NGO that has been operating in Yemen since 1963 that bases its work on the UN Convention on the Rights of the Child.

Sisters Arab Forum for Human Rights Western Ring Rd, Hashidi Bldg, PO Box 14446; ☎/f 01 231686; e saf@y.net.ye. Conducts training seminars & workshops to further legal awareness about violence against women.

Socotra Conservation Fund PO Box 16559; ☎ 01 245310 (Sana'a), 05 660577 (Socotra); e scf@socotraisland.org; www.socotraisland.org. Join the membership in this UK-based not-for-profit organisation to support & have a say in conservation & ecotourism issues.

The Arab Corporation For Human Rights St 18 (off Mujahid St), PO Box 11181; ☎ 01 554698; f 01 241501; e rajna20002000@y.net.ye. Disseminates information on the rights of women & children, &

encourages women to participate in more social & political aspects of life.

The Yemeni Union for Protecting Journalists *al-Wahdawi* newspaper, PO Box 12482; ☎ 01 240930; f 01 416506; e Rapita-yemen@yahoo.com. Outspoken organisation monitoring press violations in the country.

Yemen Smile St 20, Hse 18 (Hadda), PO Box 2002; ☎ 01 429339; e info@yemensmiletrust.org; www.yemensmiletrust.org. Dr Bona S Lotha works in conjunction with a UK charity & the Smile Train to perform cleft-lip surgeries.

Yemen Women Union PO Box 3541; ☎ 01 219944. A large & internationally respected local organisation of women working to improve the social & economic status of women in the country.

TA'IZ

DIA al-Mugalia St, PO Box Ta'iz 244; ☎ 04 225707 (Ta'iz), +33 4 91 90 78 00 (France); e dia-taiz@yemen.net.ye. Runs development projects to address the problems of poverty in Ta'iz.

The Child Forum Society PO Box 5765; ☎ 04 228606; m 73 225815; f 04 215665; e childrentaiz@maktoob.com. With a medical centre, a library, & a summer centre, the CFS provides many layers of care to sick or disabled children.

The Coordination Council for Societies Fighting Poverty Osifra St; m 73 877965; f 04 253676;

e nagebsps2002@maktoob.com. Provides education & qualification programmes to the poor.

The Human Rights Information & Training Centre PO Box 4535; ☎ 04 216277; f 04 216279; e hritc@y.net.ye. Provides training seminars to police & prison officials, provides legal assistance to female prisoners, & conducts workshops to raise female political participation.

The Saba'a Society to Care & Protect Child Rights Jamal St; ☎ 04 257405. Lobbies for the passage of favourable child labour laws.

ADEN

Cooperazion Internazional at-Tawahi, PO Box Aden 1248; ☎ 02 204776 (Aden), +39 02 308 5057 (Italy); e aden@coopi.org; www.coopi.org. Italian-based organisation that provides healthcare projects, including reproductive services for women in refugee camps.

Handicap International Belgium Ras Marbat, at-Tawahi, PO Box Aden 6166; ☎ 02 205001 (Aden), +32 2 280 1601 (Belgium); www.handicapinternational.be. Provides rehabilitation services to the disabled in Aden & Ta'iz.

The Society For Fighting Children Labour Kuwait St; ☎ 02 386238. Conducts research to show the dangers of child labour.

The Society of Yemeni Child Rights Sheikh Othman, PO Box 2355; ☎ 02 386003. Runs a medical clinic & provides cultural activities for children in need.

Triangle Génération Humanitaire Agency al-Sa'ada Zone, Khormakser, PO Box Aden 6213; ☎ 02 236567 (Aden), +33 4 72 20 50 (France); www.trianglegh.org. Undertakes a number of agricultural & water projects in eastern Yemen & Socotra.

Alternatively, before you leave home check www.stuffyourrucksack.com, which contains lists of charities and small items that you can carry in your backpack and drop off before starting your travels.

2

Caracal

Part Two

THE GUIDE

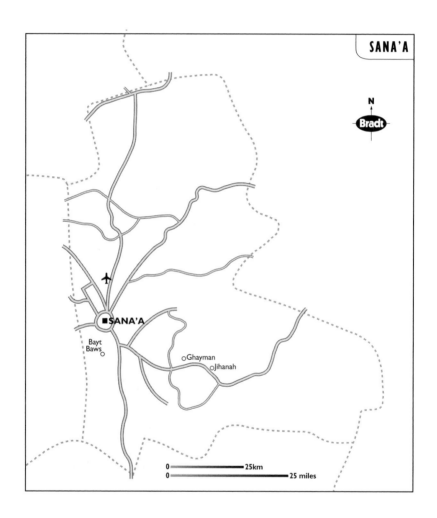

N

Bradt

SANA'A

Bayt
Baws

oGhayman
oJihanah

0 ____ 25km
0 ____ 25 miles

3

Sana'a

Telephone code 01

There is an old saying in Yemen that 'Sana'a must be seen, however long the journey takes or low the camel droops on knotted knee'. The city, sitting 2,300m (7,500ft) above sea level, hosts a large open-air souk with a history that stretches back into antiquity. The city is typically the beginning and end point of every traveller's journey here – and not just because this is where the main airport is. Sana'a is one of the most magical cities on the planet, and as the quotation runs, it simply must be seen.

HISTORY

PRE-ISLAMIC HISTORY According to tradition, the city of Sana'a was founded by Noah's son Shem after the flood subsided. The legend states that after Noah died, Shem decided to head southward and seek out a fertile region with a pleasant climate. When he finally settled on a spot, a bird swooped down and took off with his measuring rope. Perhaps in gratitude to Shem and his family for their assistance during the deluge, the bird guided Shem to the ideal location at the base of Jabal Nuqum. It was here that Shem built the city of Sana'a. The great Yemeni ancestor Qahtan was a fourth-generation ancestor of Shem, and one of his sons – Uzal – was also an ancient name for Sana'a.

Regardless of the veracity of the foundation story, Sana'a has long laid claim to being the oldest inhabited city in the world. The truth of this claim is also debated, but the history of the city does stretch back into antiquity.

During the era of the Sabaean Kingdom, Sana'a lay on one of two major caravan routes. The preferred route passed along the edge of the desert and could be controlled with some ease from the Sabaean capital of Marib. The second route passed through the mountains, far enough away from Marib to require additional support. Thus, Sana'a was likely built up early on as a fortified post to protect the overland incense trade. Many scholars have suggested that the name 'Sana'a' itself means 'fortified city'.

Throughout the tenure of the Sabaeans, Sana'a gained in importance. Beginning in the 2nd century AD the city served as a second capital to Marib. When the control of Sabaean's primary capital fell to the Himyarites, the Sabaeans would regroup in Sana'a and use it as their base for executing a counter-attack.

In the 3rd century, Ilsharah Yahdub, one of the last great Sabaean rulers, constructed the Ghumdan Palace in Sana'a – a palace claimed by al-Hamdani to have reached 20 storeys in height. Ilsharah Yahdub was successful in launching attacks against the Himyarites and capturing much of their territory. It would be the last great drive of the Sabaean Kingdom, however, as within 25 years of these conquests, the Sabaean Kingdom came to an end.

As the Himyarites rose as the sole power in southern Arabia, the political importance of Sana'a waned. The Himyarite capital of Dhafar would be the capital

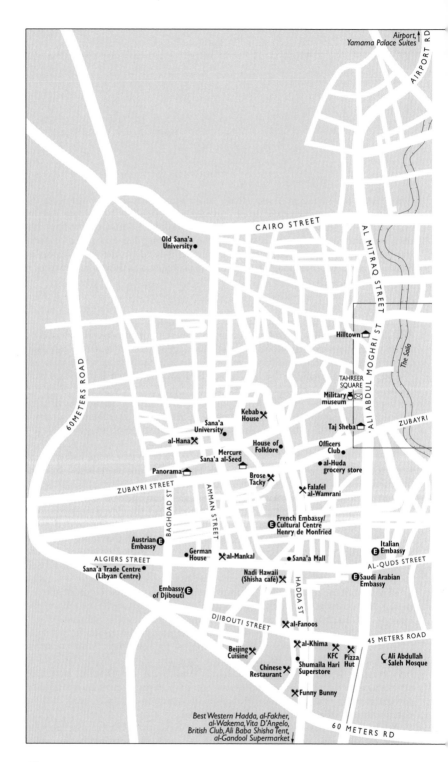

Airport,↑
Yamama Palace Suites

AIRPORT RD

CAIRO STREET

AL MITRAQ STREET

Old Sana'a
University ●

60 METERS ROAD

Hilltown ⌂

The Saila

TAHREER
SQUARE

Military ⌂ ✉
museum

ALI ABDUL MOGHRI ST

ZUBAYRI

Taj Sheba ⌂

Kebab ✕
House

Sana'a ●
University

al-Hana ✕

House of
Folklore ●

Officers ●
Club

Mercure
Sana'a al-Seed

● al-Huda
grocery store

Panorama ⌂

ZUBAYRI STREET

BAGHDAD ST

AMMAN STREET

Brose ✕
Tacky

✕ Falafel
al-Wamrani

French Embassy/
Ⓔ Cultural Centre
Henry de Monfried

Austrian Ⓔ
Embassy

● German
House

✕ al-Mankal

● Sana'a Mall

Italian
Ⓔ Embassy

ALGIERS STREET

Sana'a Trade Centre ●
(Libyan Centre)

AL-QUDS STREET

Nadi Hawaii
(Shisha café) ✕

HADDA ST

Ⓔ Saudi Arabian
Embassy

Embassy Ⓔ
of Djibouti

DJIBOUTI STREET

✕ al-Fanoos

45 METERS ROAD

Beijing ✕
Cuisine

✕ al-Khima

KFC ✕   ✕ Pizza
Hut

☾ Ali Abdullah
Saleh Mosque

Chinese ✕
Restaurant

Shumaila Hari ✕
Superstore

✕ Funny Bunny

Best Western Hadda, al-Fakher,
al-Wakema, Vita D'Angelo,
British Club, Ali Baba Shisha Tent,
al-Gandool Supermarket ↓

60 METERS RD

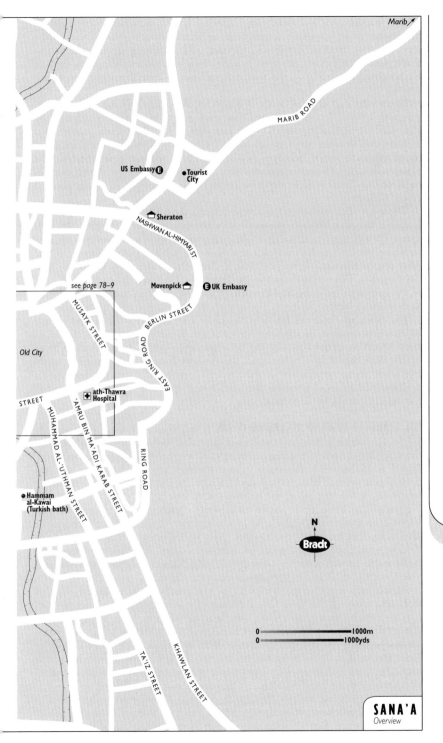

Marib ⬈

MARIB ROAD

US Embassy Ⓔ ● Tourist City

🏠 Sheraton

NASHWAN AL-HIMYARI ST

see page 78–9

Movenpick 🏠 Ⓔ UK Embassy

MUSAYK STREET

BERLIN STREET

Old City

EAST RING ROAD

STREET

🏥 ath-Thawra Hospital

'AMRU BIN MA'ADI KARAB STREET

MUHAMMAD AL-'UTHMAN STREET

RING ROAD

● Hammam al-Kawai (Turkish bath)

N

Bradt

0 ▬▬▬▬ 1000m
0 ▬▬▬▬ 1000yds

TA'IZ STREET

KHAWLAN STREET

SANA'A
Overview

Sana'a HISTORY

3

of the kingdom for the next two centuries. Sana'a, however, maintained its importance as an economic centre. Even as Dhafar rose in prominence, Sana'a maintained its status as *mahrab* – a sacred city where fighting was forbidden. The ability for rival tribes to enter the city and do business peacefully even in times of war contributed greatly to the rise of Sana'a as the central marketplace of the region.

Toward the end of the Himyarite Kingdom, the state oscillated between state religions in rapid succession: polytheism gave way to monotheism, followed by Christianity and then Judaism. The last Himyarite king, Dhu Nuwas, had adopted Judaism and began a harsh persecution of Christians – including a particularly brutal massacre in the northern city of Najran in modern Saudi Arabia. The massacre prompted an international outcry, and Aksumite forces were supported in their bid to overthrow the Himyarites in AD525. Sana'a was restored as the political capital of Yemen.

The reign of the Aksumites in Yemen lasted a short 50 years. During that time, however, the ruler Abrahah constructed a marvellous church in the city called the Qalis. With designs to thwart the pilgrimage from Mecca to his new religious structure, matters quickly came to a head between Abrahah and the Meccan tribes. After several Meccans defiled the temple, Abrahah led an attack against the holy city in AD570. The year is known as 'the Year of the Elephant' due to Abrahah's use of the animal in his army, and the date is also important as marking the year of Muhammad's birth.

The defeat of Abrahah's forces at Mecca paved the way for the removal of the Aksumite occupation by the joint forces of the Yemenis and Persians five years later. The Persians did not assist the Yemenis merely out of the goodness of their hearts. With the Aksumites removed, the Persians decided to stay in the country and made Yemen a province of the Sassanid Empire. The country remained a province for the next 50 years until the assassination of the Persian Emperor Khosrau II sent the empire into disarray.

THE STRUGGLE TOWARD ACCEPTING ISLAM When Khosrau II was assassinated in AD628, Badhan sat in Sana'a as the Persian governor. With the decade leading up to this time, Muhammad and Islam had been gaining in prominence in modern Saudi Arabia as Muhammad waged war against the Meccans for control of the city. Badhan converted to Islam, nominally making it the religion of Sana'a, although it would take some time before the religion finally took hold.

Around the same time several individuals claiming to be prophets began popping up around the Arabian Peninsula, and they challenged the authority of Muhammad. In Sana'a, it was the particularly skilled orator 'Abhalah bin Ka'b al-'Ansi who appeared shortly before Muhammad's death. After Badhan's death, he claimed that he was receiving messages directly from ar-Rahman ('the Merciful One') – one of the 99 names of God given in the Koran.

'Abhalah was a man of many nicknames. His vast supply of monikers included *al-Aswad* ('the black one') and *Dhu al-Khimar* ('the veiled man'), the latter given to him because he apparently always wore a mask when he gave his speeches in public. Yet another of 'Abhalah's nicknames was *Dhu al-Himar* ('the man of the donkey'), possibly a reference to Zechariah 9:9 – 'Rejoice greatly, O daughter of Zion, shout, O daughter of Jerusalem; behold, thy king cometh unto thee, he is triumphant, and victorious, lowly, and riding upon an ass' – an image also invoked by Jesus on his ride into Jerusalem. Or perhaps he was just stubborn.

'Abhalah's mission was probably mostly political. Adding the prophetic slant to acquire more followers, he campaigned to remove the Persian occupying power from the country. The Yemenis were eager to rid themselves of the Sassanid occupation, and even the local tribes that were sympathetic to Islam only put forward a modicum of resistance to 'Abhalah's rise to power.

'Abhalah attracted a large following, banished many of Muhammad's emissaries, and mounted a siege on Sana'a. He killed Badhan's son, who had followed his father as governor of the city, and took the dead governor's widow as his bride. 'Abhalah was successful in usurping power from the Persians, if only for a short period of time, and he established his capital in Sana'a.

When Muhammad learnt of 'Abhalah's rise to power, he was entering an illness that would ultimately claim his life. To prevent the new Yemeni ruler from undoing his life's work, he sent ten of his companions to speak with trusted Muslims still living in Yemen. The plan had been to capitalise on the bitterness of the overthrown (and conveniently Muslim) Persians to throw 'Abhalah from the throne. One such Muslim, Fayruz ad-Daylami, managed to gain entrance to 'Abhalah's sleeping chambers with some inside help from the ruler's unwilling newlywed and 'Abhalah's second-in-command, a young opportunist named Qays ibn 'Abd Yaghuth al-Makshur. Fayruz took to the task of killing 'Abhalah in his sleep, while the king's bride placated the guards nearby by telling them, 'Oh, he always screams like that when he's receiving revelations.' After four short months, 'Abhalah's reign came to an end.

Before the Persian forces could retake Sana'a, Qays ibn 'Abd Yaghuth al-Makshur, the young general who helped Fayruz assassinate 'Abhalah, made his own bid for power. Qays managed to muster his former troops from 'Abhalah's army, but they lost in battle to the Persians outside Sana'a. Fleeing to the mountains around the city, Qays continued guerrilla operations until Caliph Abu Bakr put an end to the matter by sending down a large army from Medina.

Reading the writing on the wall, Qays surrendered to al-Muhajir and was sent to Medina as a prisoner. Unlike most rebel leaders from the Ridda Wars, however, the wily general managed to spin events in his favour. Back in Medina, he got on the good side of Abu Bakr. The caliph sent Qays to Iraq as a military consultant, but he was intelligent enough to order his governor there never to put Qays in charge of any troops, lest the former general make yet another bid for the throne.

THE AGE OF ISLAM With Qays's rebellion quelled, Sana'a – along with most of the rest of the country – became staunchly Muslim, but power struggles within the religion often played themselves out in the city. Following the death of the third caliph, Sana'a took part in the debate between Mu'awiyah and 'Ali. While the city initially supported 'Ali, Mu'awiyah was able to gain support while 'Ali was preoccupied with other matters in Baghdad. Neither side was completely successful in securing the support of the city. In fact, it was not until after 'Ali died and Mu'awiyah took over as caliph that the matter was completely resolved.

The Umayyad dynasty (Mu'awiyah and his descendants) appointed governors to Yemen over the course of the next century from Damascus, but the Umayyads' grasp on the city was never completely firm. The Umayyads had never won the hearts nor the minds of the Sana'anis, and any opportunity to welcome the leader of a rebellion typically was seized. In one instance, power in Sana'a was completely taken away from the Umayyad dynasty as another self-proclaimed caliph in Medina appointed governors to the Yemeni city for over a decade. In another episode, an uprising by a group of Ibadhis (a moderate sect of Kharajite Islam) seized control of the city for several years.

When the Umayyad dynasty gave in to the Abbasids, Sana'a began to receive its governors from Baghdad. The Abbasids controlled the city much more effectively than their predecessors, appointing the city's leader for nearly a century. As with all things, Abbasid control of the city came to an end. In AD847, a young man named

Yu'fir al-Hiwali, claiming to be descended from the Himyarite kings, besieged Sana'a and defeated the Abbasid governor there.

The Yu'firid dynasty would govern from Sana'a for the next 150 years, although their control of the city was not continuous. A large family murder by the Yu'firid ruler in AD882 enraged the local tribes and citizens of Sana'a, and the Yu'firids were forced to retreat to their home in Shibam Kawkaban for a period of time. When the Yu'firids returned to Sana'a, confrontation lurked at every corner. Imam al-Hadi ila al-Haqq, the first Zaydi Imam of Yemen, threatened from the north, and the Fatimid forces of Mansur al-Yemen and 'Ali bin al-Fadl encroached from the south and west. In the span of one decade alone Sana'a was captured and lost 20 times.

Things finally settled down again when 'Ali al-Sulayhi founded the capital of his Sulayhid dynasty in Sana'a in 1047. 'Ali al-Sulayhi lived by the motto 'keep your friends close and your enemies closer'. Not wanting to leave his conquered rivals to their own devices in various parts of the country, he ensured that they all had tower houses in Sana'a where he could keep a close eye on them. When he travelled, he would often invite them along.

After 'Ali al-Sulayhi died, the crown eventually passed to Queen Arwa al-Sulayhi. The political intrigues of Sana'a were not her cup of tea, and she moved her capital away from Sana'a to the city of Jiblah – while the inhabitants of the latter carried goat tethers, those of the former brandished swords. Shortly after Queen Arwa left the city, al-Hamdani tribesmen took over Sana'a and proclaimed themselves sultans. Three separate tribal families ruled the city in succession until the arrival of the Ayyubids in 1173.

Despite the relative calm that the introduction of the Kurdish forces of the Ayyubids brought to much of Yemen, Sana'a was in a zone contested by the Zaydi imams and Hamdanid sultans. It was not until the Rasulids came to power and signed a peace treaty with the Zaydis that Sana'a began to enjoy the peace and prosperity that was beginning to set in across the rest of the country. Under the governance of 'Alam ash-Sha'bi, Sana'a underwent its first major development, and the city began to expand west of the Sailah riverbed.

Following the death of 'Alam ash-Sha'bi, Sana'a lived up to its reputation yet again of a city of conflict while much of the country continued to enjoy the benefits of Rasulid rule. The Rasulids battled for control of the city with local tribal forces and the Zaydi imams. After the Rasulid dynasty ended, the Tahirids took their place in occasionally attempting to capture the city. For the most part, the imams were able to maintain their hold on Sana'a throughout the 15th century.

In 1515, the Egyptian Mamluks landed in Yemen and captured Sana'a. When the Ottomans succeeded in capturing Egypt two years later, the disruption lasted long enough for the Zaydi imams to take control of the city. Twenty years later, the Ottomans arrived to take up where the Mamluks had left off, and the imams were expelled from Sana'a again. The Ottoman occupation lasted until 1636, during which time the city of Sana'a expanded again to accommodate the influx of Turkish soldiers – many new residential buildings popped up in the appropriately named Turkish Quarter of the Old City.

Yemenis did not take well to the Ottoman occupation, and rebellions and attacks were as frequent as the Turks' harsh retaliation. This state of affairs led to famine and plague breaking out across the country. Much of Yemen's large Jewish population was so affected by the calamities that it moved to Sana'a *en masse* to find a means of livelihood.

In 1623, after two decades of gathering support by the great Zaydi Imam al-Qasim 'the Great' and a three-year siege of Sana'a by his son, the Ottomans were forced to withdraw from the city. For the first time, the Zaydi imams finally had a

As the imams took control of the city, they began to enact harsher laws for the large Jewish population that had accumulated there during the Ottoman occupation. Much of the Jewish population was forced to convert to Islam, and the Jews were forbidden to build synagogues. Under the increased pressures of the imamate, many of the Jews were quick to cling to the claims of the Kabbalist Sabbatai Zvi, who rose to prominence in Turkey after claiming to be the Messiah in 1648 – the year that, according to the mystical Jewish text *Zohar*, would be the year of redemption and resurrection of the dead.

Convinced that the Messiah had come and that redemption was nigh, the Sana'ani Jews danced and sang in the streets before rebelling against the strict rules of the Zaydi imams. The rebellion took an unfortunate twist, however, when Sabbatai Zvi converted to Islam in 1666 – the vast majority of Sana'ani Jews suddenly found themselves Rebbes without a cause.

The imam, of course, took Sabbatai's conversion as a sign that all of Yemen's Jewry should convert. The Jews did not agree, and he banished them from Sana'a to the area of Mawza on the Red Sea coast. After realising that there was no-one left in Sana'a who knew how to make jewellery or even basic utensils, the imam quickly asked the Jews to return from exile. Of course, in the meantime all of the Jewish houses had been taken over by Muslims, so the returning Jewish population settled instead in the area of Bir al-'Azab.

firm grip on Sana'a. The imams would maintain their grip on the city until the Ottomans returned over 200 years later.

MODERN SANA'A In 1852, the Ottomans returned to Sana'a, ending nearly 150 years of continuous residence in the city by the Zaydi imams. The Sana'anis were not eager to see a return of the brutal Turkish occupation, particularly after enjoying so long a period of prosperity under the Zaydi imams. In the 20th century Imam Yahya said, 'I would rather that my people and I eat straw than let foreigners in'. The sentiment was shared at the time by the Sana'anis. When the first contingent of 1,000 Turkish troops arrived in Sana'a, the city's inhabitants arose in revolt, and by the next day nearly every single Turkish soldier had been killed. The Ottomans, not known to turn the other cheek, reacted strongly, and the city of Sana'a was forced to endure several dark decades of crime, plague and famine.

By 1872, the idea of eating straw no longer seemed as appealing, and the Ottomans were requested to settle down in Sana'a and help put an end to the city's problems. The Ottomans happily obliged and held the city until the new Zaydi Imam al-Mansur Hamid ad-Din took it from them two decades later. The fighting between the imamate and the Ottomans continued until the two powers agreed to a truce in 1911. Under the terms of the Treaty of Da'in, the Ottomans would retain complete control of the Tihama while the imamate would rule the highlands. Following the signing of the treaty, Imam Yahya ruled from Sana'a until his assassination in 1948.

The 1948 assassination was part of an attempted coup by the al-Wazir family, who proclaimed Abdullah al-Wazir the new imam after Yahya's death. The revolutionaries were unable to kill Yahya's son Ahmed, and the new Zaydi imam quickly laid siege to Sana'a. Capturing the city with the help of the northern tribes, Imam Ahmed opened the doors of the city to the tribesmen, telling them they could take or destroy anything they pleased. The destruction and pillaging that followed were devastating to the city. Imam Ahmad moved his capital to Ta'iz.

Alan George

When a person is holding together a happy family, a steady job, somewhere to live, and can surround himself with a few material possessions, then his next concern is living long enough to enjoy these pleasures. So the eternal struggle for an ordinary solvent man approaching half a century is that never-ending battle of removing the excess weight from around the waist and replacing it as muscle around once youthful shoulders. Or perhaps settling for not getting out of breath when leaving one's bed in the morning! That is why I cycle to work.

I teach at a school about 12km from where I live. Shortly before dawn I set off on my bike with headlight shining onto the deserted suburban roads of Sana'a. Soon starlight fades into dawn which blazes into another Yemeni morning. My Yemeni neighbours will puzzle why the 'Chelsea tractor' remains crouching on the driveway snoozing and later work colleagues wonder why recklessly I risk my life on Yemeni roads.

But cycling in the early morning is a time for meditation and later observation. The steady rhythm of the wheels revolving on their slightly buckled axis soothes a new day. At this early hour by the petrol station a handful of the many labourers soon to assemble with pickaxe, shovel, or bucket and paint roller in hand, sit sipping their piping-hot Lipton's tea whilst waiting patiently for the arrival of their friends and the chance of some casual work. On my US$100 Yemeni bike, I quietly and conspicuously cycle on, gliding downhill to Sixtieth Street, weaving around the patches of broken glass or plastic on the road.

I am indecisive while waiting at the junction at Haddah Street and Sixtieth Street. Do I go, like a skater venturing out onto thin ice, even though there is a red light which is always ignored by drivers at this time of the morning? Or do I wait patiently for the green, and be a Westerner doing what he thinks is the right thing regardless of where he finds himself to be? When a policeman is present the drivers do wait for his wave, albeit impatiently – their cars seem to be continuously in motion, reminding me of cows straining to get through a narrow gate at milking time.

I can see men wrapped in scarves to shield off the crisp morning air; they are crammed in the backs of Toyota and Suzuki pick-ups on their way to the fields. I look to my left and right and realise how much I will miss the surrounding mountains, their peaks dotted with motionless animals silhouetted against the powder-blue sky. About half an hour away from school I can pick out the faces of people in cafés or waiting along street gathering points. A polite nod of the head, or an acknowledging smile and beam of the eyes provides the necessary contact, human interconnectedness, all so important in daily life.

There is a different feel to early mornings in sleepy southwest England – perhaps a feeling of claustrophobia, being enclosed between the houses and shops while pedalling along narrow, viewless roads. Though English roads are safer with their dedicated cycle lanes, the pollution is always the same as rush-hour Sana'a owing to the greater density of traffic crawling from traffic light to traffic light.

Though the morning journey is an opportunity for reflection and observation, the trip home calls for tolerance and restraint. I can see all sorts of mind-blowing stuff, enough to make your toes curl. There are no safe crossings for pedestrians on Sixtieth Street,

Following the beginning of the revolution in 1962, Sana'a became the new capital of North Yemen and was one of the focal points of conflict during the extended civil war. As late as 1968, after the withdrawal of Egyptian reinforcements, Sana'a was besieged for 70 days. Under great hardships, the citizens of Sana'a and republican forces were able to win the battle, ending the last chance for the return of the imamate.

however women drift nonchalantly across the road as if they were on wheels, pretending that they are composed from an indestructible substance able to withstand the impact of speeding oncoming traffic. Men are more likely to jog across as if they were ducks in a fairground shooting gallery. Both get frighteningly close to passing traffic which makes my hair stand on end (what little I have these days!).

Sixtieth Street at about 16.00 is an opportunity to sharpen up those Formula One driving reflexes and experience the excitement of Arabia Felix on the road. One interesting phenomenon is the function of the car horn. Its use in Great Britain is regulated by the Highway Code. There, it should not be sounded between eleven at night and seven in the morning. Commonly it's mostly used for frightening away parading pigeons or the stray cat that ventures absentmindedly onto the road. Are Yemeni car horns louder than those of Great Britain? When I am cycling home the horns of Sana'a sound like a klaxon, blasted to alert me of anything ranging from imminent collision, neighbourly presence, kind acknowledgement, a forthcoming wedding or local rubbish collection (the last of which is always carried out as though the fate of the world hung in the balance).

Horns aren't the only nuisance. I find it particularly disconcerting to look up suddenly and see a laughing motorist on the wrong side of the street heading straight for me. Without a doubt, the debub drivers have a secret vendetta against cyclists! These gentlemen of the road are a law unto themselves. They swerve onto the pavement, usually without looking, at the drop of a hat. This is a definite risk for the cyclist, as I am either forced off the road or bike close enough to open the door handle of the debub and hop inside.

But the most serious threat to the lives of road users along Sixtieth Street is a vehicle turning into the path of other vehicles travelling at speed. You certainly need your wits about you because it's a road-made recipe for disaster. Though I reliably understand there is a reason: if a vehicle is being pursued by a police or army vehicle and the pursued car suddenly turns left between the central reservation and goes in the opposite direction then the pursuit car can fire off some bullets at the car as it goes by.

What makes road use worse are the non-existent give-way road markings at junctions and the roundabouts with occasional oil spills that can transform an ungraceful car into a mechanical ice skater. The water trucks look as if they have not seen water for eons, chugging along the central lane at about 35km/h (20km/h if going uphill), causing enough exhaust fumes to form a London pea-soup fog. Let's face it, in Sana'a many of the cars have bodywork to die for. They look as if they have been in a no-holds-barred demolition derby. Brake lights are non-existent and you can forget about turning indicator lights – everyone knows the indicator lever on the steering column was only made for suspending plastic bags full of qat, which slowly transforms healthy, chestnut-brown eyes into sagging, thick-lidded, lifeless ones hidden above stretched out, squirrel-like cheeks.

But I can't get enough. The next morning, I'm back on the road with my bike, looking forward to hours of cycling meditation. *In sha' Allah*, I will reach my next birthday. You should definitely give driving or cycling on the roads of Sana'a a try, but folks, look after yourselves. It's Wacky Races out there!

As the Yemen Arab Republic opened up in the 1970s, the city of Sana'a quickly expanded. As late as 1962 the complete city of Sana'a comprised solely the walled-in Old City. Development outside the walls grew quickly, and the population of Sana'a grew from 90,000 to 200,000 in the course of a decade. Today the population of the city has grown to nearly two million, and the city's area has expanded enormously.

GETTING THERE AND AWAY

BY AIR For details on international flights to and from Sana'a see *Chapter 2*, page 44. Yemenia Airways operates a number of domestic flights to the following destinations from the airport: Aden (seven days a week; flight duration: ¹/₂hr), al-Ghayda (Sunday; flight duration: 2¹/₂hrs), Hudaydah (Tuesday, Wednesday, Saturday and Sunday; flight duration: ¹/₂hr), Mukalla (at Riyan Airport) (every day except Wednesday; flight duration: 1hr), Seiyun (Monday, Wednesday and Thursday; flight duration: 1hr), Socotra (Friday; flight duration: 2¹/₂hrs) and Ta'iz (every day except Monday and Friday; flight duration: ¹/₂hr). Round-trip domestic flights should cost between US$100 and US$200. Better bargains can be had by combining the airfare with a hotel stay through Yemenia Holidays. Transfers from the airport to any point in the city are set at the fixed rate of 2,000YR.

BY BUS Most destinations can be reached by bus, although there may be some difficulty travelling to certain regions of the country in this manner (for example, across the desert to Seiyun). Check with a local travel agency before you make your plans to see what the current status of travel is.

Common destinations include: Aden (1,400YR, 6hrs), Mukalla (2,250YR, 10hrs), Ta'iz (1,150YR, 4hrs), Ibb (900YR, 3hrs), Seiyun (1,750YR, 7hrs), Hudaydah (1,050YR, 3hrs), and Hammam Damt (700YR, 3¹/₂hrs). Buses leave daily for each destination, but times of departure change frequently. Stop in at the local ticketing office for a timetable.

BY SHARED TAXI Shared taxis, or *bijous*, leave for the same destinations as the buses for roughly the same price. Departure points (*furzat*) for different destinations are located in various parts of the city. See the map on pages 68–9 for details.

GETTING AROUND

BY TAXI There are two different taxi systems currently operating in Sana'a. First, there are the traditional unmarked cars with yellow licence plates – they are the cheaper option if you are familiar with how much you should pay. Because there are no meters, tourists typically end up paying much more than they otherwise would. Fares run as low as 100YR and as high as 2,000YR (a trip to the airport). Second, there is the newer system of yellow marked cabs operated by Raha Transport Co (❂ *01 441177*). The Raha cabs are a bit more expensive, but the meters ensure you won't waste any time haggling over the price. As an added bonus, you can call a taxi to pick you up at any location or time.

DEBUB *Debubs* are small minivans that run certain circuits of the city. You can get to any area of town by using the right combination. For those of you planning on staying in the city for an extended period of time, the debubs are a very cheap and convenient way to navigate the city. To ask the driver to stop at any point, shout out *'ala jamb* ('to the side'). Trips cost 15–30YR.

WHERE TO STAY

EXCLUSIVE $$$$$
⌂ **Moevenpick Hotel Sana'a** (338 rooms) Berlin St; ❂ 01 546666; **f** 01 546000; **e** hotel.sanaa@ moevenpick-hotels.com; www.moevenpick-hotels.com.

Hands down the best hotel in Sana'a, although it is located a bit far away from any of the city's sights. High-speed internet in the rooms makes the hotel a good choice for business travellers as well. Evening string ensembles at the coffee shop make for a relaxing evening after walking around the Old City. There are two restaurants (Moroccan & Buffet) & a nightclub.

⌂ **Sheraton Sana'a Hotel** (276 rooms) Nashwan al-Himyari St; ☎ 01 237500; f 01 251521; e reservations.sanaa.yemen@sheraton.com; www.sheraton.com/sanaa. A decent hotel, but not as good as the Taj Sheba for location or the Moevenpick for quality. Planned upgrades may help

UPMARKET $$$$

⌂ **Mercure Sana'a Al Saeed** (70 rooms) Zubayri St; ☎ 01 212544; f 01 212487; e mercuresanaa@accoryemen.com; www.accoryemen.com. Very decent hotel with a number of amenities, including internet

MID-RANGE $$$

⌂ **Al-Yamama Palace Suites** (30 rooms) Tunis St; ☎ 01 236230; e alyamama.com@y.net.ye; www.yamama-palace.com. Located near the airport, all rooms are suites, with a bedroom, kitchen & relaxing *mufraj*.

⌂ **Best Western Hadda Hotel** (70 rooms) Hadda St; ☎ 01 415212; f 01 412543. Located far from the city centre, the hotel offers a good degree of privacy & tranquillity. In addition to the health club & swimming pool, there are good locations for smoking the *shisha* (water pipe).

BUDGET $$

⌂ **Arabia Felix Hotel** (20 rooms) As-Sailah St; ☎ 01 287330; f 01 287426; e arabia-felix@y.net.ye; http://arabiafelix.free.fr/index.php. Long recognised as one of the best budget hotels in Sana'a, the tower house structure is located in the heart of the Old City, a short walk from both Tahreer Sq & the Souk al-Milh. Shared bathrooms.

⌂ **Asia Hotel Sana'a** (53 rooms) Ali Abdul Moghni St; ☎ 01 272312; f 01 272324. Located near Taj Sheba Hotel, this hotel is one of the better options in its price bracket.

⌂ **Golden Daar Tourism Hotel** (11 rooms) Ta'iz St; ☎ 01 287220; f 01 287293. Acceptable rooms with shared Yemeni bathrooms.

CHEAP $

⌂ **Sinbad Hotel** (36 rooms) Zubayri St; ☎ 01 272539; f 01 261001. It's the cheapest option around, so do not expect anything glamorous. For

it compete with the other high-end hotels. Contains a number of good restaurants though, inc Chinese & Indian cuisine.

⌂ **Taj Sheba Hotel** (187 rooms) Ali Abdul Moghni St; ☎ 01 272372; f 01 274129; e sheba.sanaa@tajhotels.com; www.tajshebahotel.com. Located at the western edge of the Old City near Tahreer Sq, the Taj Sheba is the perfect hotel for the traveller who wants to be comfortable but stay in the heart of the action.

access & several restaurants. The Mercure is not as nice as the Moevenpick or the Taj Sheba, but it is a little cheaper.

⌂ **Hilltown** (65 rooms) Tahreer Sq; ☎ 01 278426; f 01 278427. Spacious rooms with private Western-style bathrooms. Located directly off Tahreer Sq.

⌂ **Sana'a International Hotel** (79 rooms) 60th Western St; ☎ 01 408201; f 01 219931; e info@sanaainterhotel.com; www.sanaainterhotel.com/en/. Sana'a International Hotel occupies the top two stories above Azal hospital. While the location might seem a bit odd, the hotel itself is surprisingly nice.

⌂ **Panorama Hotel** (36 rooms) al-Riyadh St; ☎ 01 218972; f 01 201492. A decent hotel, but most rooms were not available at the time of publication due to ongoing renovations.

⌂ **Sam City Hotel** (72 rooms) Tahreer Sq; ☎ 01 270752; f 01 275168. A decent style hotel with clean, private bathrooms.

⌂ **Sultan Palace** (9 rooms) Golden St; ☎ 01 273766; f 01 276175; e sultanpalacehotel@yahoo.com; www.al-bab.com/sultanpalace. One of the lower end hotels – better options are available nearby for the same price.

⌂ **Taj Talha** (36 rooms) ☎ 01 287130; f 01 287121. Yemeni-style rooms with private bathrooms located in the Old City.

travellers on the tightest of budgets, however, this hotel fits the bill.

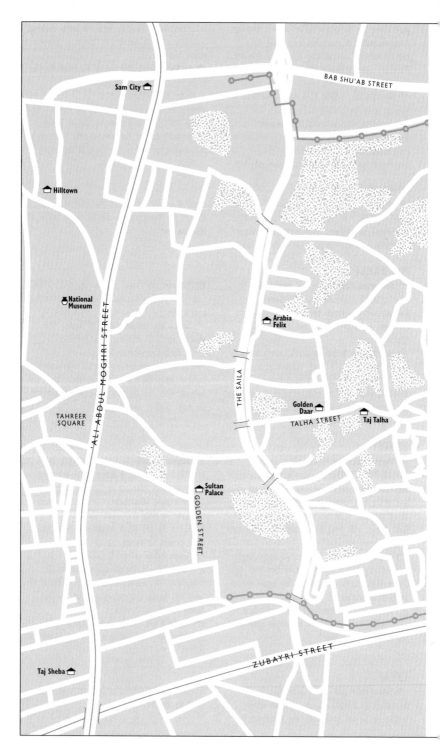

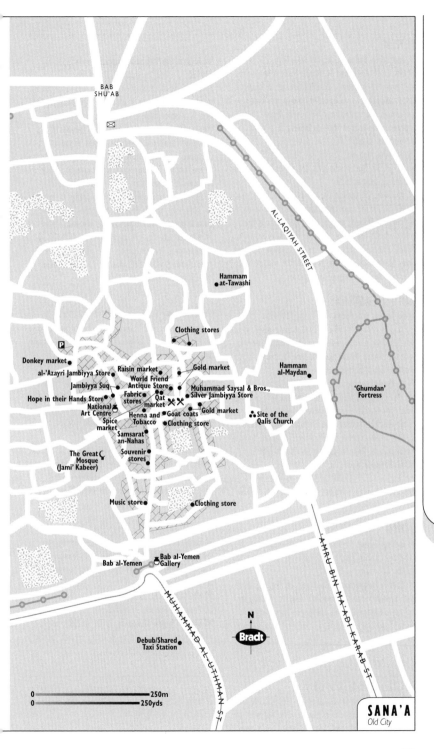

BAB
SHU'AB

AL-LAQIYAH STREET

Hammam
at-Tawashi

Clothing stores

P

Donkey market
al-'Azayri Jambiyya Store
Raisin market
Gold market
Hammam
al-Maydan

World Friend
Antique Store
Jambiyya Suq
Muhammad Saysal & Bros.,
Silver Jambiyya Store

Hope in their Hands Store
Fabric
stores
Qat
market

'Ghumdan'
Fortress

National
Art Centre
Henna and
Tobacco
Goat coats
Gold market
Spice
market
Clothing store
Site of the
Qalis Church

Samsarat
an-Nahas

The Great
Mosque
(Jami' Kabeer)
Souvenir
stores

Music store
Clothing store

Bab al-Yemen
Gallery
Bab al-Yemen

MUHAMMAD AL-UTHMAN ST.

'AMRU BIN MA'ADI KARAB ST.

N

Bradt

Debub/Shared
Taxi Station

0 ————— 250m
0 ————— 250yds

SANA'A
Old City

YEMENI

✖ **Al-Fakher** Hadda St, ⏱ 11.30–15.30, 19.00–22.30. Described in *Arabia Felix* magazine as the choice of statesmen & politicians for a 'power lunch', al-Fakher is an excellent choice for Yemeni specialities. The prices may be a little higher, but you are compensated with cleanliness & a great atmosphere. $$$

✖ **Al-Hana** Ring Rd, ⏱ 06.00–10.30, 11.30–15.30, 19.00–22.30. One of the best places for Yemeni-style seafood in Sana'a. $$

✖ **Al-Khima** Off Djibouti St, ⏱ 11.30–15.30, 19.00–22.30. The tent restaurant is near the junction of Hadda & Djibouti streets, near the Shamaila Hari grocery store. The menu hosts an impressive array of Yemeni dishes. Outside & private tent seating available. Every lunch hour, you get to watch the waiters battle several sneaky, scavenging cats. $$$

✖ **Al-Shaibani Modern Restaurant** Hadda St; ☎ 01 440920; ⏱ 06.00–10.30, 11.30–15.30, 19.00–22.30. Al-Shaibani is the best-known restaurant in all of Yemen. There is no menu, but the speciality here is a spicy fillet of fish, & the *zahawag* with cheese makes an excellent side dish. Bananas & honey are usually brought for dessert if you sit in the more exclusive 'tourist' section in the back. Tours of the kitchen are permitted & encouraged. $$$

✖ **Ash-sha'asaani** 60m St, ⏱ 11.30–15.30, 19.00–22.30. One of the best restaurants in town for *saltah* & *fahsah*. You can purchase fresh bread from a female seller right outside the door. $$

✖ **Hameed** 60m St, ⏱ 11.30–15.30, 19.00–22.30. Another good *fahsah* joint – the meaty soup is so good rumours abounded that the chef was adding hashish to the mix. $$

MIDDLE EASTERN

✖ **Al-Fanoos** Off Hadda St; ☎ 01 441042; ⏱ 11.30–15.30, 19.00–23.00. Lebanese restaurant with outdoor garden seating in the political district. Serves standard Middle Eastern fare, & *shisha* is available for a post-dinner treat. $$

✖ **Al-Mankal** Amman Rd; ☎ 01 207343; ⏱ 11.30–15.30, 19.00–22.30. Located near Das Deutschehaus, the German Cultural Centre, the restaurant has an extensive English menu, & seems to only be frequented by Westerners or locals looking for discretion. There is singing on Thu. $$$

✖ **Al-Waleema** Hadda St; ☎ 01 414786; ⏱ 11.30–15.30, 19.00–22.30. Large tent-style restaurant serving Lebanese food & *shishas*. $$$

✖ **Brose Tacky** al-Zubayri St; ⏱ 11.30–15.30. An appropriately named restaurant – the 'brose' refers to the main dishes of chicken, while the 'tacky' could only refer to the water fountain that spurts out through bendy straws. Food is solid though. $$

✖ **Falafel al-Wamrani** Hadda St, ⏱ 19.00–23.00. The best place for falafel in Sana'a is located here on Hadda St about a block before the intersection with Zubayri St. The tables are always packed, so expect to sit with some locals. $

✖ **Kebab House** ⏱ 06.00–10.30. Located in the old Jewish Quarter of the Old City, this restaurant serves up breakfasts of kebabs & only kebabs – which here means fried balls of ground meat & onions. A surprisingly excellent b/kfast. $

OTHER

✖ **Beijing Cuisine** Off Hadda St; ☎ 01 440203. Excellent Chinese cuisine, although the restaurant is usually quite empty. $$$$

✖ **Chinese Restaurant** Located next to the Shamaila Hari Superstore, the restaurant's food is terrible, but the establishment is well known for quenching your thirst. $$$

✖ **Funny Bunny** Hadda St. A fast-food hamburger restaurant modelled after Burger King. Rumour has it that Bluetooth technology is used here to facilitate meeting people. $$$

✖ **KFC** Djibouti St. $$

✖ **Pizza Hut** Djibouti St. $$$

✖ **Villa di Angelo** Hadda St; ☎ 01 412581. Serves an array of Chinese, Indian, & Italian dishes. $$$

ENTERTAINMENT AND NIGHTLIFE

RECREATIONAL CLUBS

British Club Hadda St (membership fees: US$100/six months/family). Sports & recreation club operated by the British Embassy (but open to other nationalities as well). Facilities include a swimming pool, tennis courts, darts & billiards.

Officers Club Zubayri St (membership fees: 8,000YR/month). Excellent sports club with an extensive gym, large swimming pool, sauna, & facilities for basketball & tennis.

BARS AND NIGHTCLUBS

☆ **Horseshoe Nightclub & Bar** Movenpick Hotel; ⊕ 17.00–02.30 Sat–Tue; entrance fee: 3,000YR; 17.00–02.30 Wed & Thu; entrance fee: 4,000YR; 16.00–23.00 Fri; no entrance fee. The nightclub at the Movenpick Hotel is more respectable than the Russia Club, & the drinks are more expensive. The bar is open on Fri, but there is no music.

☆ **Russia Club** Tourist city (across from the US Embassy) ⊕ 20.00–03.00 Thu; entrance fee: 3,000YR. Located in 'Tourist City' – the walled-in village (across from the American Embassy) which forbids any Yemeni from entering. The club caters to some of the city's seedier elements, but you can have a good time at the bar & dance floor if you go in large numbers.

SHISHA CAFES There are several relaxing cafes (⊕ 18.00–02.00) located throughout Sana'a where you can sit back with a cup of *Yementon* tea and smoke the flavoured tobacco of a *shisha* after a hard day of sightseeing. **Nadi Hawaii**, located in the political district off Hadda Street, has enclosed outdoor seating and access to table tennis and billiards tables. For a more serious and local haunt, Sana'anis gather at **'Ali Baba** (also known locally as *al-khaima*, 'the tent') on Hadda Street for cards and dominoes. For a more upscale *shisha* experience, try the lounge at **Best Western Hadda** on Hadda Street.

CULTURAL CENTRES

Cultural Centre Henry de Monfreid ☎ 01 269472; www.ccclsanaa.com. The French Cultural Centre, newly named after the drugs & arms smuggler whom the British banned from Aden during World War I. Later, he wrote down many of his adventures, publishing some 70 books during his life. One of the novels that has been translated into English, *Secrets of the Red Sea*, offers an interesting picture of Yemen (as well as gun running during the colonial days). Although the centre doesn't seem to offer any activities based on guns or drugs, it does offer classes in French, Arabic, & judo. Additionally, there are large monthly film screenings & musical concerts showcasing traditional music of Yemen. There is also a large library with an assorted array of works. **German House** (Das Deutsche Haus) Algiers St; ☎ 01 442486; e info@dasdeutschehaus-jemen.org; www.dasdeutschehaus-jemen.org. Like the French Cultural Centre, the German House offers film screenings & musical concerts as well as other cultural events. In addition to language classes, the German House also has offered such intriguing classes as bara' dancing – the local dances of tribesmen.

SHOPPING

MALLS If walking through malls filled with designer *baltos* and knock-off Italian clothing suits your fancy better than wandering through the narrow streets of the Souk al-Milh, you may get along with the trendy elite of the city. The malls do offer items you can't find in the souk, and if you are living in the city, you may find you need to stop at them from time to time. Two particularly good malls are the **Sana'a Mall** on the Ring Road, off Hadda Street and the **Libyan Centre** on al-Jazaar Street. Happy shopping!

GROCERY STORES For fruits, vegetables and spices, you can get better deals by shopping at smaller specialised shops throughout the city. The large one-stop grocery stores, however, are popular with the expat crowd, particularly the two-storey **Shumaila Hari Super Store** (*Hadda St;* ☎ *01 446001*). The lower floor contains all of your grocery and cosmetic needs, and the upper floor is dedicated to an eclectic assortment of clothing. Two other decent grocery stores are the **Al-Gandool Supermarket** (*Hadda St;* ☎ *01 422861*) and the **Al-Huda Supermarket** (*Zubayri St;* ☎ *01 240921*).

OTHER PRACTICALITIES

HOSPITALS If you are going to get sick in Yemen, Sana'a would be the best city to do it in. The city has the best hospitals in the country.

✚ **Ath-Thawra Hospital** Al-Khoulan St (near Bab al-Yemen); ☎ 01 246966
✚ **Saudi German Hospital** 60m St; ☎ 01 329882

✚ **Yemen German Hospital** Hadda St (near 60m St); ☎ 01 418000

POST OFFICE There are several post offices in Sana'a. The most frequented post office by tourists is the one in Tahreer Square. Another post office in the political district off Hadda Street serves the diplomatic corps. If you are living in Yemen and expect a package, you will receive a slip when the package arrives, and you will need to head to the post office on Airport Road, where your package will be searched in front of you before being handed over.

BANKS
$ **CAC Bank** Hadda St; ☎ 01 562994
$ **International Bank of Yemen** Zubayri St; ☎ 01 407000
$ **National Bank of Yemen** Zubayri St; ☎ 01 273311

ATMs are widely available in Sana'a. You can find them in any of the major bank buildings as well as at various points along Hadda Street and Zubayri Street.

WHAT TO SEE

OLD CITY The featured attraction of Sana'a is the Old City. As hard as it is to believe, the Old City comprised the entire area of Sana'a as late as 1962. At that time the city resembled an oblong figure of eight, with the smaller, western side of the city containing the Turkish Quarter and Jewish Quarter comprising one end, and the older and larger eastern circle comprising the other. The Sailah, the dry riverbed, ran from north to south and cut between them.

The city wall no longer stands outside the western circle of the town, which now flows rather seamlessly into Tahreer Square and on to the modern parts of the city through the area where the old door of **Bab as-Sabah** used to lie. The wall still stands around much of the eastern side of the city though, and it is in this section that most of the attractions of the Old City are found. The city's main gate, **Bab al-Yemen**, lies along Zubayri Street.

Tower houses The Old City has approximately 14,000 **tower houses** located in the eastern part of the city. The unique architecture and height of the tower houses, which loom over narrow stone streets, gives the Old City a very distinctive personality. The upper levels of the tower houses are constructed of exposed red bricks, with lighter-coloured bricks used to create designs in the houses – typically zig-zag and criss-cross patterns in between the floors, but also myriad geometric shapes and sometimes pictures of animals or Koranic verses.

Windows also employ intricate designs using plaster and stained glass, a more affordable version of the translucent alabaster windows known as *qamariya* which were prevalent in older times. Windows that are covered by protruding, carved wooden enclosures are designed to allow the women of the house to look upon the city or to see who is knocking at the door without exposing themselves to being seen by unwanted eyes.

The houses vary in height; most are five storeys or higher, and some rise as high as nine floors. These large houses are structurally dependant on the main pillar and circling staircase that extends from the ground to the top floor. Walking up these staircases from bottom to top is a quick litmus test for determining how fit you currently are.

The ground floor of a typical Sana'ani tower house is traditionally used for storing animals, although at times it may also include a mill for grinding grain or seeds. One tower house located to the left on the road leading northwest from the Bab al-Yemen has a camel-powered mill on the ground level. (The doors are usually kept open to the delight of tourists.)

The mill may also be placed on the first floor of the tower house, which is typically used for storing grain, fruit, vegetables and other food items. The next highest floor normally contains the *diwan*, a large sitting room used to host sizeable gatherings during the formal occasions that mark the major points of the life cycle: births, weddings and funerals. The floors above the diwan hold the basic living areas, such as the kitchen and bedroom, while the highest level is reserved for the *mafraj* – a more intimate sitting room that affords groups of qat chewers the opportunity to survey the scenery of the city while talking away the afternoon during a qat session. Appearances are very important – the most expensive furniture and rugs will be placed in the diwan and the mafraj, the two areas seen by visitors but used least by the family as a whole.

The tower houses enclose large numbers of *bustans*, private gardens throughout the Old City that are blocked from sight by the looming tower houses or large walls. The gardens contain fruit orchards and vegetables, and they are often held in trust as *waqf* by the local mosque. The gardens provide food for the local families, and the proceeds help support the families as well as the local mosque.

Sailah The dry riverbed that runs from the northern end to southern of the city separates the main eastern half from the Turkish and Jewish quarters. If you happen to be in Sana'a during the rainy season, stop on the bridge that runs over the Sailah on Zubayri St to see a river quickly spring up in the city. You can wager with your friends whether the brave debubs trying to ford the current will make it to the other side or if they should have caulked the wagon and attempted to float it across.

Souk al-Milh The crowning jewel to any visit to Sana'a is the Old City's main market, the **Souk al-Milh** ('Salt Market'). Spending a day wandering the back alleys and perusing the wares is quite possibly the single best way to spend a day in Yemen. The market dates back to antiquity, when Sana'a was given the status of a protected city, and tribesmen could trade freely with one another at the market while fighting outside the city walls. Today, the souk contains a large number of souvenir shops, but an even larger amount of stores that sell wares to the locals. Because the souk is used primarily by locals, it has a much more authentic feel than the souks of Istanbul or Khan al-Khalili in Cairo.

The main entrance to the Souk al-Milh is through the Bab al-Yemen, and the market extends northward towards the other end of Old City. Originally, the souk was divided into over 50 smaller, specialised markets each based around one caravanserai, or *samsara*, where merchants would come and unload their wares. The Souk al-Milh was originally one of these areas – referring specifically to the spice market – but the name has come to be applied to the market as a whole. A walk through the city reveals that the markets no longer necessarily adhere to the labelled area of the market. There are some exceptions: the Souk al-Zabeeb ('Raisin Market') sells all types of raisins, all the time; the Souk al-Henna still has a few henna stalls, and the Souk al-Janabi ('Jambiyya Market') still makes and sells a large number of knives.

The samsara of the Souk al-Milh were looted and destroyed in the tribal attack on Sana'a after the assassination of Imam Yahya in 1948, and many of the buildings have never been repaired. Several have reopened with tourist shops, such as the **Samsarat al-Mansurah**, the **Samsarat an-Nahas**, and the **Samsarat al-Halaqah**. Other buildings have been converted into storage facilities. To get a good idea how the samsara originally functioned, head over to the Samsarat al-Jumluk in the Raisin Market.

There is a number of stores in the souk that are worth mentioning:

Hope in Their Hands (✆ *01 482455*) This non-profit handicraft store is nestled into the back corner of Samsarat al-Halaqah. The store sells handicrafts made by women throughout the country and passes the proceeds directly on to the workers, helping to improve their livelihood. If that weren't enough, the wares for sale are quite good! Items include hand-painted incense burners, clothing, purses and other odds and ends.

Goat coats Right off the main north–south road from the Bab al-Yemen there is a small workshop for making attractive coats and blankets lined with goatskin and fur, to help keep customers 'as warm as the animals'. The family who operates the store has been in the goat coat business for three generations. Asked why the fur lined the inside of the coat while animals wore theirs on the outside, the store owner responded, 'we are smarter than the animals'. A quality coat will cost around 10,000YR.

Al-'Azayri There is a multitude of jambiyya shops in the Old City, but none of them compares to **Al-'Azayri**. The family-owned store has established itself as *the* place to buy the knives after several generations of quality work. Keep in mind that the hilts of the most expensive jambiyyas (known as *Sayfani*) are made from black rhinoceros horn, and that not only does the trade threaten the existence of the animal, but there are likely restrictions about bringing any such item back to your home country. It's possible to buy a good jambiyya that doesn't use rhinoceros horn though, and al-'Azayri has plenty of them. Other jambiyya hilts are made from giraffe horn (*az-zaraf*), ibex horn (*al-wa'al*), cow horn (*al-baggarah*) and plastic (*blastīk*).

Souvenirs There are plenty of good souvenir shops in the souk that offer silver, jewellery, jambiyyas, incense burners, spices and antiques. If you prefer to make your souvenir purchases by credit card, visit **World Friend**, **Caravanserai**, or **Muhammad Saysal & Bros**.

Great Mosque The centrepiece of the Old City is the Great Mosque, one of the first mosques constructed in Yemen. The request to build and the choosing of the

---

YOU WILL SEE GOATS; LUCKY NUMBERS: 4, 6, 17

Sana'anis have always been a particularly superstitious people, and nearly a millennium and a half of Islam has not been able to stamp out completely the interest in astrology or seers. There is a number of people in the city, typically old women, who claim to be able to tell fortunes by reading palms or tossing shells. While they have no specific and permanent location, you may be able to find some of these women and have your future told for a small fee. All inclusive oracles are known as '*arāfa*, palm readers as *gāriat al-fanjān*, and shell readers as *dāribat al-wada'*. In the Sana'ani dialect these women are known collectively as *mubashim*.

site for the mosque was supposedly made by Muhammad himself in AD630, only two years after the Persian governor Badhan converted to the religion. The construction of the mosque utilised stone from the Qalis Church, and possibly later from Ghumdan Palace.

Not much remains of the mosque as originally built. Extensive reconstruction efforts were undertaken in AD705. The mosque was damaged by several floods, and with rebuilding and repair work occurring in AD878 and AD911. The eastern wing was expanded during Queen Arwa's reign.

Non-Muslims will not be allowed to enter, but you may be afforded a peek through the doorway.

The Qalis Church In one square of the Old City souk lies the site of the **Qalis** (from the Greek word for 'church'), an elaborate Christian church built during the reign of Aksumite ruler Abrahah. With the assistance of artists and building supplies sent by the Byzantine Emperor Justinian, he constructed a large, elaborate cathedral the grandeur of which, according to his letter to the Aksumite king, no other builder had ever matched. With a bit of flair, one source reported that on the centrepiece altar of the cathedral sat a radiant pearl that shone like moonlight, enabling objects to be seen within the church throughout the night.

The Qalis was built on the site where, according to local legend at the time, Jesus had stopped to pray during his 40 days in the wilderness. Sure, a month and a half seems like a short amount of time to traverse the 4,000km round trip between Galilee and Sana'a, but covering long distances in short amounts of time is what prophets do. (Muhammad too is believed to have made a journey from Mecca to Jerusalem and back in a single night.) In the book of Matthew, the Bible relates that Satan took Jesus to a high mountain for his last temptation, showing Jesus the kingdoms and glories of the world that could be his. What could be more tempting than a bird's-eye view from Mount Nuqum of the walled city of Sana'a and the kingdoms of the Sabaeans and Himyarites? The Bible states that Satan left Jesus there – perhaps the rationale of the legend is that Jesus then walked down to Sana'a for a quick prayer before the angels took him back to Galilee.

Of course, there could be another explanation for the legend. The purpose of building such a grand cathedral in Sana'a was twofold. No doubt Abrahah had an interest in seeing Christianity spread throughout Arabia, and erecting a monolithic altar to the religion on the site where its founding figure had visited would facilitate that goal. More pragmatically, however, Abrahah also wanted to cash in on the trading widely prevalent in Mecca during the annual pilgrimage to that city. By diverting the pilgrims to the Qalis, the market that blossomed during the pilgrimage would be moved to Sana'a. For the more sceptical readers, the visiting Jesus legend might have been created post hoc as an added incentive for pilgrimage. After all, the Kaaba is reputed to have been built by Abraham and Ishmael – the Qalis would need similar religious celebrity connections if it wanted to compete properly.

Thinking about the vast amount of money that moves through Mecca and its environs today, several Yemenis looked at the ruins of the church and half-jokingly told me, 'Abrahah was a clever man. Imagine how much better our economy would be today if the pilgrimage were held in Sana'a!' But with people dying in Yemeni stampedes in both 2005 and 2006 without the oft-deadly stoning ritual of the hajj, perhaps it's best the pilgrimage stayed in Mecca.

Of course, the pilgrimage was not diverted. Having failed to persuade the Arab pilgrims by use of grandeur and legend alone, Abrahah is said to have issued an edict ordering the pilgrimage to be held in Sana'a. At some point, the indignity became too much for the ruling Meccan Quraysh tribe. One of the Quraysh tribesmen, having succeeded in gaining entrance to the Qalis, defecated therein so as to defile the temple. Enraged, Abrahah led his unsuccessful attack on Mecca where he met his untimely end.

The Qalis was later dismantled, and much of the stone and artistry was used in building the nearby Great Mosque. Today, nothing remains of the church but a walled-in, sunken pit where children sometime play. The memory of the Qalis still lingers in the city, and any local will be able to point you toward the site.

Ghumdan Palace Directly to the east of the Old City is the fortress named Ghumdan, reputed to be built on the site of the famed Ghumdan Palace. (Another site claimed to have been the location of the palace is located directly west of the Great Mosque.) Ghumdan Palace was built in the 3rd century AD by the last great Sabaean King Ilsharah Yahdub. The palace towered above its surroundings with ten storeys of height – an amazing accomplishment at the time. (Al-Hamdani claims that the palace had 20 storeys!) The sleek four walls of the palace were each painted a different colour, and hollowed, holed bronze lions on the ceiling were said to roar when the wind passed through them. The entire ceiling is said to have been made of *qamariya* alabaster so transparent that one could make out the shape of birds flying overhead. The building was so beloved by the Sana'anis that they began to model all of their houses after it.

According to tradition the palace was destroyed in the 7th century by Caliph 'Uthman to prevent the fortification from being used as a base for rebellion. Pieces of the palace were taken and used in construction of the Great Mosque. Today, the Ghumdan Fortress houses barracks and a prison that was constructed during the Ottoman occupation, and thus, going inside for a visit is off limits. Nothing remains at the site of the original palace anyway.

Hammams (*entrance fee: 500–1,000YR*) There are multiple Turkish baths, or *hammams*, in Sana'a that steam with natural hot springs. The most well-known and oft-used of the hammams is **Hammam al-Maydan**, located outside the Ghumdan Fortress. Other recommended bathhouses are **Hammam at-Tawashi** in the Old City and **Hammam al-Kawai** in the area of Hay as-Safiyah. Hammams are open all day long, many open late into the night, but alternate on days between men and women.

Art galleries There are two major art galleries in the Old City, and both offer prints and originals of artwork ranging from US$20–1,000. These places function more as stores than museums, and provide a central location where tourists can see the works of local artists. Unlike most shops in Sana'a, bargaining here seems to be frowned upon.

National Art Centre (⏰ *09.00–12.30, 16.00–20.00*) Located in Samsarat al-Mansurah, not far from the Great Mosque, the National Art Gallery features the work of Yemen's prominent artist Fuad al-Futaih. The ground floor mainly displays a large selection of prints, while there are originals hung on the second and third floors. Everything is for sale. There is a great view of the city from the top floor.

Al-Bab Gallery (⏰ *09.00–12.30, 16.00–20.00*) This smaller gallery is located directly to the right of the Bab al-Yemen. Even if you have no interest in viewing or purchasing any art, a trip to the gallery is worth a visit – the stairway inside leads up onto the top of the Bab al-Yemen.

THE LEGENDARY WOMEN OF SANA'A

Ask any Sana'ani and he will tell you that the women of Sana'a are of the most beautiful in Yemen. (Of course, Yemenis from Dhamar or Jabal Saber may have their own biases.) Al-Hamdani described them thus: 'No women in the world ever surpass in appearance the beautiful belles of Sana'a, and none ever excel them in elegance or charm.' In the classic epic of *1,001 Arabian Nights*, Scheherazade tells the story of 'The Ebony Horse', in which a young Persian prince finds the women of the city equally appealing. In the story the prince travels the world on a flying mechanical horse (having been duped into doing so by an ugly Persian trickster, of course), and he alights on the roof of the Sana'a palace. Tiptoeing through the palace to find his way out, he stumbles across the sleeping chambers of the Sana'ani princess, who was 'chemised with her hair as she were the full moon rising over the eastern horizon, with flower-white brow and shining hair parting and cheeks like blood-red anemones, and dainty moles thereon.' He fell in love instantly. Although the prince faced multiple trials, several trips back and forth to Sana'a, and a long search for the princess following her abduction (that blasted Persian trickster!), the two lovers were eventually joined in marriage with the Sana'ani king giving his blessing.

TAHREER SQUARE The area around Tahreer Square is the focal point of modern Sana'a. The area contains most of the city's museums as well as being a large shopping centre. Stores seem to mainly sell shoes, clothing and luggage, but there is a store for musical instruments and two bookstores that sell English books on nearby Jamal abdul Nasser Street.

MUSEUMS
Military Museum (⊕ *09.00–12.30 Sat–Thu; entrance fee: 500YR*) The interesting military museum contains an eclectic display of materials from the Neolithic period, the ancient kingdoms, and recent military periods of the country, with an emphasis on the time surrounding the revolution. In the back there is a small library with an eclectic English section – you'll have to ask for it.

National Museum (⊕ *09.00–12.30 Sat–Thu; entrance fee: 500YR*) If you only make it to one museum during your stay in Yemen, this one should be it. The museum has some of the best pieces displayed in the country covering a multitude of aspects of Yemen. The prized possessions of the museum are two (larger than) life-size bronze statues of Dhamar 'Ali Yuhabirr and his son. The statues are not the originals, but were constructed in Germany by carefully making replicas of the complete set of pieces that had been found. There are plans to devote a new room to some recently found mummies.

House of Folklore (*Bab al-Balaka Zone; next to 'Laundry Light of City';* ✆ *01 481360;* e *housefolk@gmail.com;* ⊕ *08.00–15.00 Sat–Thu; entrance fee: 500YR*) A small, privately run museum in a former private residence dedicated to preserving the folkloric heritage of Yemen, especially those of the more marginalised members of society. Displays detailing the traditions of female society feature prominently.

Arwa, the owner of the museum, is a gem. Having dedicated her life to the preservation of cultural heritage, she sold what land she had in order to fund the opening of the museum. Since then, she has been able to carry on through embassy grants and private donations.

Old University Museum (⏲ *09.00–12.30 Sat–Thu; entrance fee: 500YR*) A decent enough museum that contains a room of local mummies found in the area.

OUTSIDE SANA'A

BAYT BAWS Directly outside the city of Sana'a toward the direction of Hadda is the old, mostly abandoned mountaintop village of Bayt Baws. The small village dates back to the Sabaean Kingdom, and there are some inscriptions on the side of the mountain along the track to the top. At the bottom of the mountain stands the small residential district where the Jewish inhabitants used to live until 1949. The synagogue is still in place.

Bayt Baws was an inhabited village in its own right until the early 1990s, housing mainly families of farmers who tilled the land at the base of the mountain. After the unification of North and South Yemen, the city of Sana'a began a quick process of urban sprawl and eventually made its way to the region of Bayt Baws. The meeting of the two regions increased the land value of the farms considerably. The inhabitants of the mountain village promptly sold their property, and most of them moved out to avoid a now unnecessary steep climb every day.

WADI DHAHR A mere 15km outside Sana'a stands the five-storey palace of **Dar al-Hajar** ('the Palace of the Rock') (*entrance fee: 500YR*). The mansion, built in the 1930s as a summer retreat for Imam Yahya, is constructed atop a large boulder in the middle of the wadi. The boulder has a longer history – there are deep wells and prehistoric cave burial rooms that show settlement long before the imam wanted a big house to while away his summer days.

Together the boulder and palace dominate the surrounding scenery, and the picture is just as amazing from afar as it is close up. Today, the palace is an open museum of sorts, and a very popular place to visit, not only for tourists but also for local Yemeni families. Different rooms have descriptive labels in English and Arabic. Sometimes there is a photo exhibit as well.

The palace is located near the village of Qaryat al-Qabil, and the road down to the palace is lined with fruit and qat vendors hawking their wares. Just as popular as the palace is a clearing that overlooks the wadi. Turn off onto a dirt road on the right before the descent of the main road begins. Here on Fridays from 09.00–12.00 Yemenis gather for wedding celebrations. Although gunfire is no longer allowed, you can still see large crowds brandishing their jambiyyas as they participate in the tribal bara'.

Undoubtedly, you will be approached by the 'falcon man' – one of several men and boys with a live falcon on their shoulders. The idea is that the friendly falcon man will put the bird on your shoulder, you will get a picture with a bird of prey, and he will get a few rials for his trouble. Politely refuse the bird if you are not interested.

GHAYMAN Ghayman is a short 13km away from Sana'a, and makes for a great day trip. The small village has a great feel to it, and it is the closest place to Sana'a that served as a Himyar heavyweight. Ghayman is believed to have been something of a summer retreat during parts of Sabaean and Himyarite rule, acting as a place of solitude for the kings. Locals claim that the legendary Himyarite ruler and national hero Asa'ad al-Kamil spent time here when not at the Raydan Fortress of Dhafar.

One of the best qualities of the town is its abundance of stone archways and doorframes. The large arches of Ghayman's two ancient entrances, the eastern Bab al-Balad ('the country gate') and the western Bab al-Qudmah ('the gate of submission') both remain. You can still see part of the foundation of the palace of the legendary Himyarite ruler and national hero Asa'ad al-Kamil, complete with one 4m-long stone (now broken in two).

The cistern in the village also bears the ancient ruler's name. An old secret tunnel in one of the abandoned houses (now blocked) winds underground and exits on the other side of the wall, halfway down the hill at the 'the well of the dog' – it proved a useful way of entering and exiting the city when it was under siege. Throughout the town, three or four different buildings have incorporated old stones bearing Himyarite reliefs. One oft-shown stone is that of Asa'ad al-Kamil's foot.

The ground of the area is reputed to be rich with gold, and many Yemenis have sought their fortunes in the town or the environs (sometimes by digging up the tombs of the holy men buried within the mosques). Al-Hamdani relates a poem supposedly written by the Himyarite king abu Karib As'ad:

Should e'er the vandal's hand our shrouds unfold,
Our tombs will yield precious silver and gold.

It's unlikely that Himyarite royalty actually penned the above words; more improbable still is the truth of al-Hamdani's description that a buried vault was uncovered in the area that contained 'a ruby which equalled in value the income of the world'. Regardless, local tales hold that an individual named Mansoor al-Hamdani recently dug and struck gold in the small cave at the top of the road leading to the village. Perhaps to protect the loss of any further treasures, the children have been told that the cave is inhabited by evil jinn spirits.

One rogue villager, not able to make his fortune by digging for gold, absconded with an old Himyarite bull sticking out from the outer wall leading to the main gate, presumably to sell it on the black market. The hole in the wall remains, and the villagers are not quick to forget the theft. You may be asked, if you press the subject, whether you have seen the individual in question while in Sana'a. Luckily the incident has not spoiled the tradition of hospitality in the town; the villagers are very friendly and very amenable to posing for pictures.

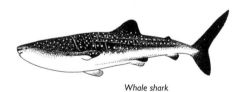

Whale shark

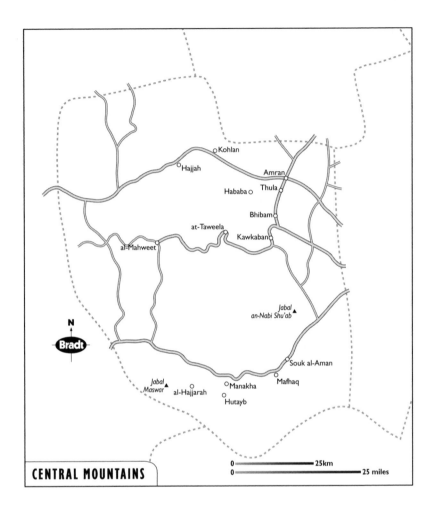

Kohlan

Hajjah

Amran

Hababa   Thula

Bhibam

at-Taweela
al-Mahweet   Kawkaban

*Jabal
an-Nabi Shu'ab* ▲

Souk al-Aman

*Jabal
Maswar* ▲   al-Hajjarah   Manakha   Mafhaq

Hutayb

| 0 | 25km |
| 0 | 25 miles |

CENTRAL MOUNTAINS

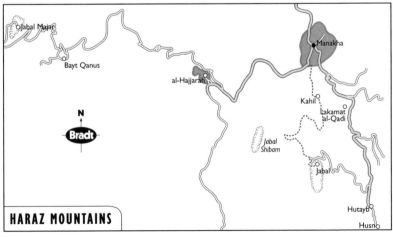

○Jabal Majar

Bayt Qanus

Manakha

al-Hajjarah

Kahil

Lakamat
al-Qadi

*Jabal
Shibam*

Jabal

Hutayb

Husn

HARAZ MOUNTAINS

4

The Central Mountains

THE HARAZ MOUNTAINS

The Haraz Mountains remain one of the best locations for trekking and experiencing Yemeni culture. The mountain scenery is absolutely breathtaking and the food and dancing provided by the local hotels ensure that your nights are no less memorable. You can easily spend several days in the area – the first for taking in the centres of Manakha and al-Hajjarah, the second for hiking through the Isma'ili pilgrimage site of Hutayb and the smaller mountain villages around the area, and the third for exploring the environs of the Sulayhid fortification of Jabal Masar. If you are lucky enough to have a fourth day in the region, head out and camp at the remote and deeply tranquil site of Jabal Shugraf, where the mountains give way to views of the plains heading out to the Tihama.

MANAKHA *(2,250m/7,380ft)* In the past, Manakha served as the regional centre in a different respect. During the 17th and 18th centuries, all the coffee grown in Haraz region would be gathered at Manakha before being carted down to the port of Mokha. From there, the coffee was shipped to Europe. During the Turkish occupation, control of Manakha and the surrounding Haraz region was key to maintaining and protecting the Turkish road from Hudaydah to Sana'a.

Getting there The road from Sana'a heads to the west toward the region, and you'll go through two checkpoints before leaving the Sana'a environs. After you pass the market village of Mettina, the next paved road that branches to the right (across from the Sana'a Retread Factory) heads toward **Jabal an-Nabi Shu'ayb** ('Mountain of the Prophet Shu'ayb'), the highest mountain on the Arabian Peninsula with an altitude of 3,760m (12,333ft).

The mountain is named after the Prophet Shu'ayb, who was believed to have served as the messenger to the Hadhoor tribe in the modern region of Bani Matar, although he is often confused with Jethro, the father of Moses, whose Arabicised name is also Shu'ayb. As in the tales of most prophets, the mountain messenger's words were not heeded and disaster followed shortly thereafter – an earthquake ended the days of the heathen tribes dwelling there. The prophet's grave is believed to be located at the top of the mountain along with an accompanying mosque. Owing to the high altitude, the water of the hammam is said to freeze frequently during the nights of the winter months.

Many of the tribesmen of the region believe that the holiness of Prophet Shu'ayb's tomb will enhance the chances that their supplications are heard. (The fact that it is so high up and presumably closer to heaven can't hurt either.) In this way, it exists as an interesting Zaydi counterpart to the Sufi mosque of bin Alwan in Yafrus. While the Zaydis don't stab themselves with their jambiyyas here, the tribesmen and women will come often to make donations or perform animal sacrifices in order to curry favour with God by their proximity to Shu'ayb. In particular, women yearning for pregnancy will frequent the mosque, hoping that the sacrifices and donations offered at the foot of the prophet's tomb will better their chances of conceiving a child.

Unfortunately, due to its 'strategic location', foreigners are not allowed to visit the mosque and tomb at the top. There is a checkpoint around the 3,450m mark (11,315ft), and without duly authorised permission from the proper governmental agency (one from the tourist agency won't suffice), you will be asked to enjoy the views offered on your drive back down the mountain. Hopefully the site will become accessible once the government realises that the views from the peak reveal much less about the countryside than can be gleaned from 30 seconds of playing with Google Earth.

If you are driving through on a Thursday, you might want to stop in at the town of **Bo'an** (perhaps 'The Two Foot Bones'?), which has a weekly market that day. The next turn-off to the right following that village leads to the area known as **al-Haima**, a green region of the area famous for its coffee, enormous qat trees (up to 15m!) and smoking hot red peppers.

The names of the next two villages, Souk al-Aman ('the Market of Safety') and Souk as-Sameel ('the Market of the Whip'), seem to be at odds with one another. Perhaps when the two villages work in tandem, the whip is used to provide safety. There is a market on Thursday at the former and one daily at the latter. A larger daily market is held a little farther down the road at the town of Mafhaq. There are also several local restaurants there. The left turn-off at the town of Maghrabat Manakha leads to the final 5km leg of the trip to Manakha.

Where to stay

Al-Hajjarah Tourist Hotel & Restaurant (15 rooms; 10 with private Western bath) \ 01 460124; f 01 460211; e alhajjarahotel@hotmail.com. To get there, turn right past the Manakha Tourist Hotel (or take the stairs right next to it). With a well-deserved reputation for outstanding dancing, the lunchtime and evening festivities are reason enough to stay. Like the Manakha Tourist Hotel, there is an extensive lunchtime spread for 1,000YR. Local tour guides 3,000YR/day; 1,500YR/half day. $. HB.

Al-Tawfiq Tourist Hotel (10 rooms) The first hotel on your left coming from Maghrabat Manakha.

Sleeping rooms are similar to the other 2 hotels (read: mattress on a floor), but the evening entertainment is not as grand. Local tour guides 2,000–3,000YR/day. $. HB.

Manakha Tourist Hotel (26 rooms) \ 01 460365. The hotel is on your right just as you enter town from Maghrabat Manakha. It's a bit more subdued, so it's your place to stay if you prefer the quieter 'oud stylings to the beat of the bara' drum at the neighbouring al-Hajjarah Hotel. The restaurant offers an extensive Yemeni lunch for 1,000YR. Local tour guides 3,000YR/day; 1,500YR/half day. $. HB.

Where to eat The hotels in town have the best spread of food available. They can generally pack you a lunch as well if you would like to take something with you on the hike. If you decide to eat outside the hotels, there are two local restaurants just beyond the souk in the direction of al-Hajjarah that serve *fasulia* and one of the best-tasting bowls of *ful* in the country (200YR) during the breakfast hours and offer chicken, vegetables and rice during the lunch hour. They are closed in the evenings.

Other practicalities You can buy postcards and stamps at any of the local hotels. There are also several silver and 'antique' shops in town. The prices won't be any cheaper than what you'll find in the Old City of Sana'a, but you may see something that catches your eye. Also, the silver shops are one of the few places where you can exchange money in the region. There are no banks in the Haraz Mountains.

For centuries, Yemen was known as having the widest range of crops of any country in the Middle East. The trick of course was simply to turn the slopes of mountains into arable land. These terraces, going up the mountainsides like stairs for giants, are one of the more interesting aspects about the Haraz countryside. By levelling off the fields to provide for deep saturation and by directing the rainwater falling down the mountainside toward the terraces, not only can the Yemeni farmers harvest crops in terrain that would otherwise be unarable, they can also grow crops in areas where the limited annual rainfall typically would not be sufficient to produce a harvest in a normal field.

Even steep mountains pose no obstacle. You can often see terraces with a width of less than 1m – wide enough for only one row of crops! Only 3% of land in Yemen is arable, but over 25% of that land is composed of these mountain terraces.

What to see The city of Manakha is the centre of activity in the Haraz Mountains for both tourists and locals alike. For most of the residents of the region, Manakha offers the best chance for employment – many of the neighbouring villages are near deserted. If the villagers haven't gone to Sana'a, there's a good chance they probably came here. In a more positive light, Manakha also serves the entire region as the main market place. There is a daily morning souk (⊕ *08.00–12.00*) that is frequented by residents of the surrounding region.

In the centre of the town there is a small dirt football field, used for afternoon matches by the youth. If you'd like to try your best against them, they would be happy to have you join in on the fun. Where the souk meets the football field, you'll find the Manakha Post Office.

OUTSIDE MANAKHA

Al-Hajjarah (*2,370m/7,775ft*) Al-Hajjarah was founded during the Sulayhid period and served as an important fortification both at that time and during the Turkish occupation. More than any other village in the area, al-Hajjarah still very much has the feel of a fortified city. There is only one entrance into the town, through the large gate called Bab al-Husn ('the Fortress Gate'), at the end of a set of stone stairs leading up away from the road. The buildings of al-Hajjarah have obviously been built with defence in mind. The lower floors facing the outside contain no windows.

Outside the fortified area of the town is the old Jewish quarter – today, just an extension of the town. To get there, simply turn right before the stone stairs that lead up to the Bab al-Husn. As has happened in several other towns, the old synagogue has been transformed into a building for housing animals. This is not necessarily a slight – even in al-Hajjarah the first floor of most Muslim residences is used for animals as well. The path down to the old Jewish quarter continues down to Wadi Mo'inah below (approx 90mins).

Like Manakha, al-Hajjarah serves as a great base for hiking in the region. It's not as busy as its sister Manakha, but that might be what you're looking for. There is a couple of stores to buy water and various food supplies, but there are no restaurants outside the single hotel.

🏠 **Where to stay**

🏠 **Husn al-Hajjarah Tourism Hotel** (14 rooms) 📞 01 460210; 📠 01 460559. Clean & pleasant rooms, with lively dancing & entertainment in the evenings. The hodgepodge of Yemeni tourism bumper stickers in the lobby can be quite mesmerising. $. HB.

Below is a list of distances between some of the mountain villages and of several of the better itineraries. Estimated travel times are given as well, but you should remember to tack on time for sightseeing when planning your trip. Always remember to have plenty of water bottles in your backpack; you'll drink a lot. You'll be able to pick up supplies at many of the villages, but not all of them.

Don't worry too much about getting lost. After all, most of the beauty of the region comes from the journeying. If you need help with directions, a simple '*wayn al-tareeq ila* (destination name)?' should win a smile and a finger point in the right direction from one of the locals. You're going to have a great time!

FROM MANAKHA AND AL-HAJJARAH

Manakha (2,250m/7,380ft)	Al-Hajjarah (2,370m/7,775ft)	3km/45mins
	via al-'Ayn (2,690m/8,825ft)	4km/2hrs
	Kahil (2,600m/8,530ft)	1.5km/1hr
	Lakamat al-Qadi (2,440m/8,000ft)	1.5km/45mins
	al-'Ayn (2,690m/8,825ft)	2km/1hr
Al-Hajjarah (2,370m/7,775ft)	Manakha (2,250m/7,380ft)	3km/45mins
	via al-'Ayn (2,690m/8,825ft)	4km/2hrs
	al-'Ayn (2,690m/8,825ft)	2km/1hr

ROUTES

1	Manakha (2,250m/7,380ft) — Kahil (2,600m/8,530ft) — Jabal (2,780m/9,120ft) — Hutayb (2,450m/8,350ft)	7.5km/3¹/₂hrs
2	Manakhah (2,250m/7,380ft) — Lakamat al-Miq'ab (2,190m/7,175ft) — Lakamat as-Sawda (2,100m/6,890ft) — az-Zayyah (2,050m/6,735ft) — ash-Shariqah (2,100m/6,890ft) — az-Zahiah (2,270m/7,445ft) — Manakha (2,250m/7,380ft)	17km/6hrs
3	Al-Hajjarah (2,370m/7,775ft) — al-'Ayn (2690m/8,825ft) — Jabal (2,780m/9,120ft) — Hutayb (2,450m/8,350ft)	8.5km/4hrs
4	Al-Hajjarah (2,370m/7,775ft) — al-Hatab (2,390m/7,840ft) — Bayt Awmas (2,370m/7,775ft) — Jabal Masar (2,760m/9,055ft)	11km/5¹/₂hrs
5	Al-Hajjarah (2,370m/7,775ft) — Wadi as-Serif (2,080m/6,820ft) — al-Hadud (2,280m/7,480ft) — Bayt al-Qanus (2,290m/7,510ft) — Bayt Awmas (2,370m/7,775ft) — Jabal Masar (2,760m/9,055ft)	16km/7hrs
6	Jabal Masar (2,760m/9,055ft) — Wadi Mo'ena (1,200m/3,935ft) — Souk ath-Thalouth (1,380m/4,525ft)	7km/3¹/₂hrs
7	Al-Hajjarah (2,370m/7,775ft) — Maghrabat al-Gashami (2,360m/7,740ft) — 'Arjaz (2,340m/7,675ft) — al-'Urr (2,320m/7,610ft) — Bani Shubati (2,280m/7,480ft) — Jethuwa (2,190m/7,180ft) — as-Sunsel (2,100m/6,890ft) — Shugraf (2,000m/6,560ft)	18km/8hrs

Kahil (*2,600m/8,530ft*) Other than the walk between Manakha and al-Hajjarah, the climb to the village of Kahil is one of the shortest walks available and is the one most frequented by tourists. But that's not to downplay the trip – the one-hour hike from Manakha to the village is amazing, and it will definitely give you a taste for the kind of scenery you are in store for if you plan to do some more trekking in the region.

Kahil is a good example of how the struggling economy of the area has affected the smaller towns. You're unlikely to meet many people in the often-abandoned streets of the area. Most of the population has left to live in cities like Sana'a in order to earn money. Because the town is so empty, there is not much to see (other than the scenery, of course) and nowhere to buy supplies. There is a small clearing on top of one of the buildings that offers panoramic views of the countryside. Most tourists typically stop here to take in the sights and catch their breath. The main entrance to the town is called Bab al-Husn ('the Fortress Gate').

Getting there To get there from Manakha, head from the hotels over to the souk. Pass the stores and then find the road that cuts back to the left up the hill before turning back to the right after about another 100 yards. You'll find the path that leads up to Kahil from here. Ask around if you need some assistance. From al-Hajjarah, the hike is slightly longer (about three hours) and takes you first through the village of al-'Ayn.

On the opposite side of town, a road heads down the mountain toward the village of Lakamat al-Qadi (20–30mins) and Hutayb (1hr). Taking the short-cut down the slope to catch the road early on will save you a lot of time if you are headed to the former. To reach Hutayb, follow the path straight before the road curves back around. Turning off to the right off the road just outside of the town, a path leads to the village of Jabal (1hr).

Jabal (*2,780m/9,120ft*) Jabal ('The Mountain') sits about 200m above Kahil, and the walk between the two villages takes about an hour. The views get better and better as you go. The village is not very large, and like Kahil there are not many residents remaining. It is, nevertheless, a very good example of the small Isma'ili villages that dot the surrounding mountains.

During the pilgrimage time to Hutayb, Jabal teems with the overflow of pilgrims. Even aside from the pilgrimage, you may see a few Isma'ilis looking around. Not far from the citadel door – 'Bab al-Husn', of course – lies the grave of Ali bin Mas'oud 'Ulwi, who was a minister in the government of the Isma'ili Di'a Idris Imad al-Din bin Husan. 'Ulwi had been sent to the neighbouring town of Jabal from Hutayb in the late 15th century, and he built the mosque here. After his death, his contemporaries built his small tomb structure next to the mosque.

On the northern part of town next to a small door called Bab al-Gafla are the remains of an old synagogue – a reminder of the large Jewish presence that once inhabited the Haraz Mountains. All that survives is a couple of triangular-shaped designs on one of the walls.

Outside the main village gate of Bab al-Husn there are some great flat areas of land perfect for camping. The road heading out from the main gate leads down to Hutayb (1hr). Pathways branch off in various directions toward the village of Bayt Hamidi in the west and al-'Ayyana in the south. Nearby to the west lies the peak of Jabal Shibam with the old Turkish fort of Si'dan. The fort is used by the military now, which means trekking to the location or snapping pictures of it are off-limits.

Hutayb (*2,450m/8,350ft*) Not long after the death of Queen Arwa in Jiblah, her Isma'ili Sulayhid dynasty crumbled. Luckily for the Isma'ilis, they had managed to separate themselves from the ruling party before it collapsed. By the time Hatem al-Hamidi was appointed as the third *di'a* of the Tayyibi Isma'ilis, the title of the highest-ranking religious leader who is authorised to act on behalf of the hidden imam, the Hamdanid sultans had taken over power in Sana'a. The ruler in Sana'a at the time, 'Ali bin Hatem, would prove to be a bitter rival of Hatem al-Hamidi. Although Hatem al-Hamidi had originally secured the fortress of Kawkaban, early battles with 'Ali bin Hatem forced him to abandon the site.

After a short period, Di'a Hatem al-Hamidi turned to the Haraz Mountains. This was the area, after all, where the founder of the Sulayhid dynasty, 'Ali bin

Muhammad al-Sulayhi, had grown up. Initially there was resistance from the Hafizi Isma'ilis (who did not recognise the imamate of the infant at-Tayyib). With the help of the local military leader Saba' al-Ya'buri, al-Hamidi managed to conquer much of the area of Haraz and centred his headquarters in Hutayb. From his base in the mountains, the Isma'ili di'a continued his war with 'Ali bin Hatem in Sana'a. Al-Hamidi made another attempt at securing the fortress of Kawkaban, but was repelled.

When his friend and strategic advisor Saba' al-Ya'buri was assassinated, al-Hamidi could no longer compete against the sultan in Sana'a. He spent the rest of his days teaching the faith in Hutayb and writing a massive collection of literature spanning the subjects of ethics, Isma'ili literature and esoteric knowledge. In AD1199, al-Hamidi died and was buried in Hutayb. He is remembered among the Tayyibi Isma'ilis as a great teacher, poet and warrior.

After al-Hamidi's death, Hutayb remained the centre of the Tayyibi Isma'ili faith for several centuries, hosting a number of important *di'as*. Most prominent among the Hutayb leaders was the 19th Di'a al-Mutlak Idris Imad al-Din bin Husan, who led the Isma'ili community from 1428 until his death in 1468. In addition to bringing the Hutayb Isma'ilis to the height of their power, Di'a Idris was an important historian and scholar. His work is the principal source of much of the world's knowledge of the history of the Isma'ilis in Yemen.

Overall, the religious believers were able to maintain peace and stability with most of the surrounding dynasties but often fought with the Zaydis. Even today, Zaydi–Isma'ili relations can be quite fragile. In the 16th century, however, on the eve of the Zaydi Qasimi imamates' rule of northern Yemen, religious persecution by the Zaydis was at its height. In response, the Tayyibis relocated their headquarters in 1539 to Gujarat, India – the residence of a large Tayyibi community that had been founded by Yemeni missionaries over 500 years earlier. While small pockets of Isma'ilis remained in the country, many left for destinations on the Indian subcontinent.

Toward the end of the imamate rule in Yemen the 52nd di'a of the Da'udi Tayyibi Isma'ilis, Syedna Muhammad Burhanuddin, re-established links with the community in Yemen. As a result of his efforts, Hutayb was beautified – new brick streets were added, buildings were improved, and small gardens were planted. A paved road was laid also to connect the town to Manakha. Over the past 15 years, Burhanuddin has returned to Yemen on many occasions to continue projects in the Haraz area, such as the uprooting of qat trees while providing subsidies to farmers to grow other products. A hefty donation to 'Ali Abdullah Saleh's election campaign fund in 1999 has helped ensure that his access to the sites remains unhindered.

Today, Hutayb remains an important pilgrimage location for the Tayyibi sect of the Isma'ilis, a Shi'a branch of Islam. Every year, thousands of Tayyibi pilgrims from the Indian subcontinent gather in Hutayb on the anniversary of Hatem al-Hamidi's death, 16 Muharram (25 January 2008, 13 January 2009, 2 January 2010). The town's two hotels, which are said only to cater to pilgrims, fill to the brim, as do temporary hotels that open up for the occasion in the neighbouring mountaintop villages. There are also yearly celebrations of Eid al-Ghadir on 18 Dhu al-Hajja (28 December 2007, 17 December 2008, 6 December 2009), the anniversary of Muhammad's farewell speech at Ghadir Khumm in Saudi Arabia in which the Shi'a believe Muhammad designated 'Ali as his successor.

Additionally, in recent years the town has become a popular location for Isma'ilis to group together for mass weddings. By getting married at the same time as others, expenses are defrayed considerably. The town even has a 'Marriage-Easing

Society', a charity that fronts money to would-be bridegrooms who otherwise could not afford to pay the hefty bride prices required. (For information on the Tayyibi Isma'ilis, see *Chapter 2*, pages 25–8.)

Getting there Hutayb is connected by a paved road from Manakha. Unless you are driving or taking a taxi, you may want to consider the mountain pathways instead to make the journey a little more interesting. Paths or dirt roads connect with the town from Kahil, Jabal and al-'Ayyana (via Naweet).

Where to stay Although there are two hotels in town, they are said to cater only to Ismaili pilgrims. It is better to stay in nearby Manakha and come to Hutayb to visit.

Where to eat There is a small restaurant in the first building past the gate where cars park. The menu isn't too extensive, but you can order a couple of Yemeni standards such as *salta* (200YR). While the diner can't cook up a plate of *fahsah*, try buying a can of tuna from the store next door and have the restaurant use it as a substitute for the meat. It cooks up a tasty dish.

What to see The **tomb of Hatem bin Ibrahim al-Hamidi** is located in the main part of the town, surrounded by a small courtyard. Non-Muslims will not be allowed to enter. Opposite the mausoleum is a large fellowship hall and small mosque that was erected as part of Syedna Burhanuddin's revival of the town. Catering to so many visitors from the Indian subcontinent, Hutayb is the only city in Yemen which advertises STD phones. With the stone walkways underneath, the inscribed marble of the tomb and the impeccable cleanliness of the town, it feels a bit as though you are entering a different world as you walk through the town's main gate. Posted signs throughout the town ask you to 'Help keep Hutayb Mubarak clean and green'. It definitely has a completely different vibe from neighbouring Manakha.

The **mosque of al-Hamidi** is located on the top of the mountain – a climb of 180 stone stairs. As long as you are respectful, it should not be a problem for you to climb the stairs. Non-Muslim men and women both may be allowed to enter the small mosque, which is usually full of singing Indian and Pakistani visitors even outside the pilgrimage month. A random old man at the base of the stairs may charge you a small fee of 100YR at the bottom of the stairs on your return. It is unlikely that he is actually officially sanctioned to collect the money.

Jabal Masar (*2,760m/9,055ft*) If you have time while you are trekking about the Haraz Mountains, you should make the trip to Jabal Masar. The site is rich with history, the views are stunning, and the area is a good base if you would like to make some longer hikes. There are no hotels around, so you will need to bring camping supplies. Besides the shops located at the old fort, there are a few other places on the mountain where you can get supplies. Bayt al-Qanus (2,260m), at the foot of the mountain, has some extensive farmland, and you can probably buy some fresh corn and tomatoes if they are in season, as well as the two Yemeni standards: coffee and qat. Two other villages with stores are Bayt Shamran (2,185m) and Lakamat Hezb (2,080m).

History 'Ali bin Muhammad al-Sulayhi, father-in-law of the famous Queen Arwa of Jiblah, grew up in the mountain village of Jabal adjacent to Manakha. His father was a prominent local jurist who instructed 'Ali al-Sulayhi in the laws of the Sunni school of Shafi'i. Al-Sulayhi was befriended as a boy by 'Amir bin Abdullah az-Zawahi, the Isma'ili Fatimid *di'a* in the country, who instructed him secretly about the Isma'ili Fatimid position.

The Yemeni historians note that az-Zawahi had with him a prized book of Aristotleian treatises, occult sciences and prophesies that had been written down by the sixth Shi'a imam Jafar as-Sadik. Az-Zawahi told the young al-Sulayhi that the boy's name was contained within the book and that he was preordained to have a great and noble future. What youngster wouldn't like to hear that he was destined to be the ruler of the country? Al-Sulayhi became committed to the Fatimid cause. At az-Zawahi's death, al-Sulayhi was appointed as the next *di'a*. Like a good Isma'ili, he committed himself to studying the two subjects of Shari'a law and the hidden meanings of the Koran.

After marrying the notably beautiful and generous Asma, al-Sulayhi took up residence on Jabal Masar with 60 fiercely committed members of his tribe. The local historians state that the day after al-Sulayhi raised his banner on the peak of the mountain, his group of merry men was surrounded by over 20,000 swordsmen. The demand was simple: leave Jabal Masar or die. Al-Sulayhi responded that he had come for their safety, under a mission from God, but that he would leave if they wanted him to. His speech was effective, and he was permitted to remain on Masar.

He built a large and impressive fort on the mountain peak, but soon he had visitors again. Seeing how the last confrontation hadn't stopped al-Sulayhi, one of his rivals marched toward the fortress with an army some 30,000-men strong, looking to put an end to al-Sulayhi's rising power and popularity. By this time, however, al-Sulayhi had amassed a considerably larger force, and the rival's attack was not successful. Al-Sulayhi led a surprise offensive against the enemy while they were encamped at the base of the mountain. The generals were killed, the army scattered, and al-Sulayhi's dominance secured. Once much of the country was brought under his power, Al-Sulayhi moved his residence to Sana'a but continued to maintain the fortress at Jabal Masar.

After al-Sulayhi's assassination by a rival prince, the fortress at Jabal Masar would see more battles. The death of al-Sulayhi led to several insurrections within the Sulayhid state, and Jabal Masar was besieged by the locals of the Haraz area. It took an army sent by al-Sulayhi's son to calm the area and restore it to the Sulayhid fold. Many years later, the mountain fortification figured predominantly in the Turkish strategy to maintain their occupation.

What to see The peak of Jabal Masar hosts the **small fort** that was built and used by 'Ali al-Sulayhi at the beginning of his rise to power. Centuries later, the fort was occupied during the Turkish occupation, and it proved to be an important holding ground for their power. The Turks are no longer present, but the fort is no less occupied. Today's colonisers are SpaceTel, Yemen Mobile and a Yemeni television station, each of which have constructed large antennas adjacent to the site to take advantage of the peak's high altitude.

There is one entrance to the citadel, known today as Bab al-Maktab ('the office door'). The gate's name was not always so innocuous. During al-Sulayhi's reign, the gate had the rather unoriginal name of Bab al-Husn ('the door of the citadel'). But leave it to the Turks to spice things up: during their occupation of the country, the fort was besieged frequently. As the only entrance to the inner grounds, the gate became the prominent site of most of the massive battles. People fought, and people died. The villagers today still talk about the blood that would flow outward from the door as a result of the concentrated violence. The gate was renamed Bab al-Magtal ('the door of killing'). After the occupation ended, the kind-hearted villagers didn't like the gruesome appellation, and they gave it the current, more professional designation, despite the fact that there's hardly anything office-like about the place.

Outside the gate stands one of the three remaining guard towers. All are currently being used residentially, so you'll have to content yourself with viewing them from an attacker's rather than a defender's viewpoint. To the right of the tower along the wall are some other vestiges of the Sulayhid period – four large stones in the fort are carved with various reliefs. The one with Arabic calligraphy on the far left reads, 'Muhammad is the prophet of God'. There are some other smaller and less impressive stones with relief work throughout the village.

The top of Jabal Masar provides some lovely views of the countryside. On the southeast side, Jabal Shibam dominates the immediate landscape, and you can get a good view of the old Turkish fort of Si'dan at its peak (currently occupied by the military – so be careful about taking photographs in that direction). To the west lies Wadi Mo'ena and Jabal Sa'fan after that. Over the peak and down the other side of Jabal Sa'fan sits the village of Souk ath-Thulouth ('the Thursday Market'), which has a daily market and a considerably bigger one on Thursday. (Walking to the small village to catch the afternoon market would make for a great trip.) In the far distance in the west, you can see the rising peak of Jabal Bura. The mountain to the north is known as Jabal Bani Hajaaj.

Shugraf *(2,000m/6,560ft)* The village of Shugraf has a great 'edge of the world' feeling to it. The landscape is dramatic – the mountains drop off with sharp cliffs that lead down to the plains below. The entire place is imbued with a feeling of quietude. Even the children seem different; while the young boys usually produce quite a ruckus with their requests for pictures and pens, the young inhabitants here were content to sit by the campsite and quietly take in the scenery with me.

Located to the west is the village of Mahalat Himlat. The locals here seem a bit more suspicious of outsiders than the other villages of the region, but they are still friendly. Interestingly, the men in the town are fast to complain about the number of children they have – a conversation that will soon end in queries about whether you brought any birth control with you.

If it has rained within the past week or so, you will find a small stream running between the two villages, heading off over the cliffside. It is a much-welcomed place to freshen up after days of hiking!

The hike to Shugraf from al-Hajjarah will take a full eight hours, bringing you through the villages of Maghrabat al-Gashami, 'Arjaz, al-'Urr, Bani Shubati, Jethuwa, as-Sunsel and Ma'azib. At the top of the mountain near the village of al-'Urr, there are the remains of an old Turkish fort. It takes a brisk 30 minutes to climb to the peak (2,560m/8,400ft), and you'll pass a small, natural pool that may be used for swimming or washing up along the way. The fort at the top, known as Husn al-Hajjarah, is completely overrun by wild cacti, making many areas of the ruins inaccessible. Perhaps if the Turks had used the plant as their first line of defence they would still be running the country today. In any event, the large swath of cacti provides an abundance of prickly pear fruit, which are absolutely invigorating after the climb up. You can see the remains of another fort, Husn Now'eet, to the northeast.

THE MOUNTAIN CIRCLE OF HAJJAH, AL-MAHWEET AND AMRAN

SHIBAM The village of Shibam (one of four such named towns in the country!) is located about 35km northwest of Sana'a. Although it was distinguished during the time of the Himyarite Kingdom as Shibam Aqyan, today it is often referred to as Shibam Kawkaban, on account of its neighbour perched on the adjacent mountain.

History The village's location has been used as a settlement for a long time. Even before the Himyarite days, the Sabaeans had inhabited the area, when the city had gone by the name of Yahblis. The present village dates back to the 9th century, when it served as the capital of the Yu'firid dynasty for a brief period of time.

Yu'fir bin Abd al-Rahman al-Hiwali, the founder of the Yu'firid dynasty, grew up in the village here. He used the town as a base to raise supporters and eventually led an assault against the weakened Abbasid-appointed governor in Sana'a. He defeated the governor and took control of Sana'a, moving the capital of his dynasty to the newly conquered city. From there his dynasty ruled mostly independently, although they continued nominally to accept the authority of the Abbasid Caliphate.

A little less than 40 years later, Yu'fir's grandson Ibrahim bin Muhammad would return to Shibam after a series of events that resemble the plot of a failing soap opera. After a reign of 30 years Yu'fir abdicated power in favour of his son Muhammad bin Yu'fir, complaining that old age had caught up with him and that he needed to retire. Muhammad took the reins, but soon afterwards he also released his grip on power. Muhammad's reasoning was not based on failing health like his father; a trip to Mecca had inspired him to take up an eremitic devotion to Islam. He gave up the political life of Sana'a and moved back to Shibam, where he constructed **the Great Mosque** – built from the stones of old Himyarite palaces and temples – that still stands today. Back in Sana'a power passed over to his son Ibrahim bin Muhammad.

Here's where things get strange. Ibrahim bin Muhammad and the old, failing Yu'fir conspired together to end the life of Muhammad bin Yu'fir – perhaps they didn't want him to take back the throne, or perhaps they didn't like his new passion for religion. In either event, Ibrahim decided that one murder would be a waste of time if he were already holding the knife, so while his father and uncle were worshipping in the newly constructed mosque in Shibam, Ibrahim assassinated them both. From there, he also went out and killed his cousin and even his poor grandmother!

The tribes of the area would not submit to Yu'firid rule after the outrage, and insurrections broke out among all the tribes. Ibrahim was forced to leave Sana'a. Oddly enough, his fellow tribesmen in Shibam were willing to take him back in and protect him. Tribal loyalty can be quite strong. Eventually, with a little help from the Abbasids years later, the Yu'firids were able to recapture Sana'a under the rule of Ibrahim's son Asa'ad bin Ibrahim.

Getting there and away The easiest way to get to and from Shibam (other than by using a private vehicle, of course) is by taking one of the shared taxis. The proximity to the neighbouring towns and frequency with which the locals travel back and forth should ensure that you don't have to wait too long for the bijou to fill up. Destinations and prices: Sana'a (100YR; 1hr), Thula (50YR ½hr) and al-Mahweet (300YR; 1½hrs). Private taxis climb the road up to Kawkaban or back down for about 500YR.

Where to stay

🏠 **Hamida Tourist Hotel** (20 rooms) ☎ 07 450458. The hotel is located outside the city, right before the road to Kawkaban. It has small, basic rooms with Western bathrooms but seatless toilets. Most visitors opt to stay at one of the hotels in Kawkaban, & for good reason. Staying the night, however, does include b/fast & dinner at the famous Hamida Restaurant, located farther down the street. Even if you don't stay here, you should make it to the restaurant for lunch. ⑤

Where to eat

✗ **Hamida Restaurant** ☎ 450480; ⏰ 11.00–14.30. The Hamida Restaurant is the culinary wing of the hotel bearing the same name, but it is located farther down the road toward the centre of town. While there may not be many reasons to spend a night at the hotel, there's a number of good reasons to eat lunch at the restaurant. For only 1,000YR pp you can enjoy a huge smorgasbord of Yemeni dishes in a (frequently private) mafraj-style sitting room. Dishes of *salta*, *bint as-sahn*, *shafoot*, vegetables & meat from the restaurant's own goats are laid out before you in massive quantities. Just try & finish it all.

The restaurant is operated by Madame Hamida, a friendly & eccentric character who has been in the tourism business for over 30 years. She & her daughters run the entire restaurant, & she has been featured on an al-Jazeera television special about the country of Yemen as the quintessential Yemeni working woman — a hard worker who must maintain the household while the traditional 'breadwinner' only strives to transform the family's 'bread' into his own supply of qat.

Do not be deterred by the front entrance restaurant (you won't eat there). Cross the yard & enter the next building, where Hamida's daughter will take you up to your room & you can begin gorging yourself on all the Yemeni delights. $$

What to see Today the glory of the Himyarite settlement and Yu'firid military base is long gone. Unfortunately, most initial impressions of the town are darkened by the large amounts of rubbish strewn about the streets and fields with reckless abandon. It is sincerely hoped that the Yemeni government will take a proactive stance soon toward cleaning up the country. Measures have been taken in some of the larger cities, but some of the smaller towns – even ones that are major tourist attractions – continue to be neglected.

There is a couple of things to see and do in Shibam. The town is popular among the tourist crowd for the tasty lunch at the Hamida Restaurant and for the path that leads up the mountain to Kawkaban. As far as sites go, there is the great mosque, which was built by Muhammad bin Yu'fir and which, after the mosque in al-Janad and the Great Mosque in Sana'a, is one of the oldest Muslim religious structures in the country. Non-Muslims probably won't be allowed to enter, but if you are with a guide have him ask one of the local villagers; they may let you go in to look around.

There are also many caves against the mountainside that the locals claim were used as burial tombs in the past. They were probably also used for food storage (though not at the same time). During the 1967 revolution the villagers used the caves to escape the bombs that rained down from the sky, as the revolutionary forces pelted the previously unconquerable Kawkaban into submission. Today, the caves are used by villagers or by others passing through the town to escape the heat of the noon sun.

Shibam's importance today stems from its role as the regional market town. On Fridays, Yemenis from all around the area come to the souk to sell or buy goods at the weekly market. The majority of the souk occurs on the main street entering the town, just outside the old part of the city, but some vendors do set up their carts within the old city wall.

KAWKABAN The fortress of Kawkaban is built on the Jabal ad-Dila', overlooking the town of Shibam. Al-Hamdani claims that the town got its name, which means 'the Two Planets', because 'it was externally girdled with silver band above which were white stones'. Luckily, al-Hamdani's explanation is supplemented by Yemeni legend: the mountaintop of Jabal ad-Dila' was the site of two large castles that were both ornately decorated with precious gemstones. From the plains below, these rocks produced such a glimmer from the reflection of the sun while it was setting that they looked like two planets in the sky.

Traces of these two castles are nowhere to be seen, so perhaps the origin of the name lies elsewhere. Old historical records indicate that the city was used as a granary during the Himyarite period. Along those lines, another legend indicates that the village takes its names from a Himyarite king, but that's not really as romantic as two bejewelled palaces glimmering in the twilight. The Yemenis seem to like their castle story best, and that's what we're going to go with too.

History Throughout most of its history, Kawkaban has been a Zaydi stronghold. What that means in practice is that the leaders have fought against foreign invaders and persecuted the smaller Muslim faiths that challenged Zaydi beliefs. The first famous ruler to use the site for these dual purposes was Imam al-Mansur Billah Abdullah bin Hamza (b1166). Like most Zaydi imams, al-Mansur bin Hamza was based in Sa'ada. Kawkaban and other surrounding cities of the high mountains, however, became an important staging ground for his struggle against the Ayyubids, the Kurdish dynasty led by the famous Saladin. The Ayyubids were the first foreign occupying power in Yemen since the age of Islam, and the mountain tribes did not plan to give in without a fight. In addition to the fortress at Kawkaban, al-Mansur bin Hamza had a major base at Dhafar Dhi Bin, and his brother had erected the fortress at Kohlan. During the 50 years of the Ayyubid occupation, the Zaydis were in constant rebellion.

In addition to his struggle with the Ayyubids, al-Mansur bin Hamza spent a significant amount of effort trying to stamp out the Zaydi branch of the Mutarrifiyyas, a more scientific than mystical religion. When the Ayyubids confined him to the mountain regions of the country during the end of his tenure, fighting the 'heretic' Zaydis became his preoccupation, and the sect no longer exists. Al-Mansur bin Hamza was more than just a destroyer – he also built a number of mosques in the area, including the one in Kawkaban and the more famous one in Dhafar Dhi Bin. Although the latter site houses his tomb, al-Mansur bin Hamza actually died while in Kawkaban.

The second leader to take up the nationalist Zaydi cause here was a native of Kawkaban named Mutahar Sharaf ad-Din. Mutahar ad-Din had become the Zaydi imam while the Tahirids were ruling much of Yemen. From his hometown and the neighbouring village of Thula he mounted the strongest defence against the Tahirids in the country. To his initial pleasure, the Egyptian Mamluks landed in Yemen around 1515. When the foreigners began their campaign by fighting the Tahirids, they received much encouragement from Sharaf ad-Din. After the Tahirids were defeated, the Mamluks kept expanding, and the tentative alliance between the Zaydi imam and the foreign occupiers quickly ended. The Mamluks besieged both of Sharaf ad-Din's fortresses in Kawkaban and Thula, but the Zaydis were able to withstand the attacks at each location. Within two years, however, the Ottoman Empire had engulfed Egypt, and Mamluk soldiers in Yemen soon changed their Egyptian uniforms for Turkish garbs. Some things didn't change: the foreign forces and Sharaf ad-Din's followers were still at odds with each other.

Throughout the Ottoman occupation, the Turkish soldiers repeatedly tried to take over the Kawkaban fortress. The villagers were so secure that they formed their own state in defiance of Ottoman rule. Although the name of the small country – Kawkabaniyya – sounds like a kid's cereal, the people were stalwart enough to hold off the Turks during the entirety of their occupation.

Like al-Mansur bin Hamza, Sharaf ad-Din spent much of his time hunting down minority religions. The object of his distaste was not rogue Zaydis but the growing Ismai'li community in the Haraz Mountains and surrounding regions. Although the Isma'ilis had been established in the Hutayb environs for nearly 400 years, the heavy persecution they faced during this time forced them to move their religious centre to India.

In addition to its great successes, the city of Kawkaban also has its share of defeats. During the last Turkish occupation, the city was not able to hold out, and the high settlement was used by the Turks to maintain rule there. The city was also one of the major holdouts of the Zaydi Imamate after the 1967 revolution, but modern warfare ultimately demonstrated that steep paths and stone walls would no longer be sufficient to provide protection in the years to come. Bombarded from the air, Kawkaban soon submitted to the republican revolutionaries.

Getting there The best means of getting between Shibam and Kawkaban is the twisting path and stone stair walkway that connects the two villages. It takes about an hour to walk from the bottom to the village at the peak. There is also a new paved road that connects the two villages. Private taxis can be hired to cover the distance for about 500YR.

Where to stay

Al-Taj Tourist Hotel (11 rooms) \ 07 450170. The hotel is respectable enough, but not used as often as either of the other 2. Rooms are a mixture of shared Western or private Yemeni bathrooms. $. HB.

Hotel Gabal Kawkaban (4 rooms) \ 07 451427. While not as clean as its counterparts, the hotel has a much homier feel to it, & those who stay there seem to love it. The owner of the establishment is a friendly man named Yahya, & he & his family will provide you with some excellent Yemeni meals during your stay. There are shared Yemeni bathrooms. $. HB.

Kawkaban Hotel (11 rooms) \ 07 450154. As the most popular of the 3 hotels in Kawkaban, the hotel brochure boasts that it is 'lasting the best'. Rooms vary greatly, however, so make sure you get one that is suitable (eg: has a bed). Half the rooms have private, Western bathrooms. The remainder have shared Yemeni bathrooms. $. B&B.

What to see The large mosque in Kawkaban was built by Imam al-Mansur Billah Abdullah bin Hamza in the late 13th century. Although he is not buried here, the tomb of the other great Kawkabani imam, Mutahar Sharaf ad-Din, is contained within. The city wall and gate through which you will enter the town were built by the Turks. The sole entrance to the fortified city is known as Bab al-Hadeed ('the Iron Gate'). Inside the city, there are usually children wandering around, playing a variety of games. When they spot you, they usually give up what they are doing to stand with you. They may have goods to sell, or they may initially be interested in getting some pens or having their pictures taken. They are naturally cordial though, and after a few laughs they'll treat you more like a good friend than as a fount of pens.

Beyond taking in the great views of Shibam and the surrounding plains, Kawkaban is a great location to do some birdwatching. There are 13 endemic birds

If you're planning on doing some hiking in the region, Kawkaban is a great place to base yourself. Below are listed some common trekking destinations and how long it takes to reach them from Kawkaban.

HUSN ZAKATI (3hrs) A small village with a fortress that has a population of two. The fortress is now used to house animals and seeds. An old man with the key (who is a little hard of hearing) will vouchsafe your entrance to the fortress for a fee of 200YR.

BAKOUR (4hrs) An old and lovely abandoned village fortress, from where you can see houses built into the cliffside. A small dirt and wood bridge spans the small ravine that leads to the broken-down door of the old settlement. Most buildings have collapsed, but there is a guard tower still standing, and you can climb to the top of it. There are also several old cisterns. (Distance via Husn Zakati: 4½hrs.)

HUSN BAYT 'UZ (½hr) Large set of ruins on a mountain, overlooking an impressively built *samsara*. From the ruins, you can see Hababa in the distance.

AHJAR (2hrs) Fertile area located at the end of Wadi Ahjar. The town is famous for its inordinate number of springs. When Yemeni families take a holiday they love to go where there is water, and areas with springs or rivers excite them to no end. Thus, you'll always see a large crowd here in the town, as large family groups move about together to find a good place to set up their picnic and enjoy the lovely greenery.

AT-TAWEELA (8½hrs) See below (via Bakour: 9½hrs).

on the Yemeni mainland, and most of them spend their time in the highland areas such as Kawkaban. The area is particularly good for finding the endemic species of Philby's partridge, the Arabian partridge, the south Arabian wheatear, and the Arabian accentor. The south Arabian wheatear is the most common of the endemics; it is a black bird with a white underbelly and stripe on its head. Both of the partridges are larger birds with grey feathers and a striped stomach. Philby's partridge has a swath of black from eye to eye under the chin. The last of the four endemics found in Kawkaban, the Arabian accentor, is a small but plump bird with two very distinguishable white eyebrows. The bird is believed to live in only a couple of areas in Yemen.

THULA Thula is the best preserved fortified town in the region. Even with modern updates such as paved or stone roads, the old town has managed to keep its antique appearance and feel. The streets are narrow and lined with innumerable antiquities stores, a sure sign that Thula has been a popular tourist destination. With fewer visitors to Yemen than in previous years, the shop owners may plead with you as best they can to get you to 'just come and take a look'. The town is surrounded by the old city wall that has four entrances – the main one is quite large. Towers built of stones taken from the local mountain dot the various edges of the wall. The houses are built in much the same style – local stones provide the structural walls of the buildings, but are also used in various ways to decorate the houses. Since 2002, Thula has been on the UNESCO tentative list for inclusion as a World Heritage Site.

Like many of the fortified towns in the area, Thula used to be a Himyarite settlement. According to the inscriptions on the nearby cliffside, the defensive settlement that existed at the time was known as at-Talah. Throughout Yemen's history Husn Thula ('Thula Fortress'), on the top of the mountain overlooking the city, has served as a last stand of defence. During the 16th-century reign of the Rasulids, the city was used as a base of operations by the Zaydi Imam Mutahar Sharaf ad-Din to fight the dynasty in Sana'a. In the following century it withstood the invasions of both the Egyptian Mamluks and the Turkish Ottomans.

Getting there and away Shared taxis run to and from both Sana'a (170YR) and Shibam (50YR).

Where to stay

🏠 **Thula Tourist Hotel** (25 rooms) Thula Main Sq; ☎ 07 665005. The guesthouse has a number of large rooms that hold up to 10 people. The rooms are divided & categorised by what floor they are on, & the ones on the upper level have better beds. Each of the 2 floors has 1 bathroom for all the guests to share. After a day of walking around, relax on the high roof of the hotel, enjoying your view of the city with a hot glass of tea. The cook can whip up an impressive Yemeni spread of chicken, potatoes, & *bint as-sahn*. ⑤.

✗ **Where to eat** Your best bet on getting a good meal is going to be at the **Thula Tourist Hotel** (*complete meal:* **$$$$**). If you'd like to branch out, there is a small restaurant right across from the hotel in the main square. Both the price & the quality of the food will be significantly cheaper.

Other practicalities There is a **post office** in the main town square right next to the hotel.

What to see
Husn Thula (*2,835m/9,300ft*) The walk to the castle from the base of the mountain takes about 30 minutes on the path carved into the side of the mountain. At the top, there are great views of the surrounding countryside. If you are planning doing any long hiking in the region, you could plot out your entire trip by taking in the positions of the nearby cities. To the south, you can see Hababa, and visible beyond that are the villages of Shibam and Kawkaban. In the far distance, you can just discern Bait 'Uz, barely visible in the distance. The northern side of the fortress looks down on the city of Thula. With a bird's-eye view, you can see the complete gate and towers that surround the city.

The true glory of the fortress disappeared with extensive destruction by the Turks during the last holdout against the Ottoman Empire. Despite this, the western side towers are still intact. In the centre of the grounds there is a large narrow building erected by President Ibrahim al-Hamdi. Other interesting parts of the grounds include extensive tombs and the rooms carved into the rock on the southern side.

AT-TAWEELA The small town of at-Taweela is located on the slopes of Jabal al-Qarani'. Like Manakha in the Haraz Mountains, at-Taweela served as the central collection centre for coffee bound for the Red Sea ports. Today there is not much going on in the town. There is a small fortress on the top of the mountain and a weekly market on Sunday. At the edge of the town heading toward al-Mahweet there is a large boulder that has had its interior carved out to make a small room. It is often used by African immigrants that are passing through.

Getting there At-Taweela is located along the road from Sana'a to al-Mahweet, and shared taxis running to the latter can be found in Sana'a for 600YR.

Where to stay

🏠 **Hotel Rest al-Hana** (7 rooms) ☎ 07 456369. The small guesthouse doesn't see many visitors. If the main doors of the building are locked, try around the side. The blue & pink décor of the rooms give it a nursery feel, & mattresses are provided upon request. The hotel has shared Yemeni bathrooms. $. FB.

AL-MAHWEET

Al-Mahweet has the feel of a hard-working mountain village. The city is built on the mountainside, and only pedestrians may traverse its streets. The pathways are full of stairs, and the roads too narrow for any car to squeeze through them. One of the best aspects about a stroll through the town is the number of house doors you'll see done in the old woodcarving style. Unlike many of the nearby towns that have opted for brightly coloured aluminium doors on every house, al-Mahweet continues to use many of the old styles and it retains its quaint charm in the process.

Getting there Shared taxis from Sana'a to al-Mahweet cost 600YR.

Where to stay and eat

🏠 **Al-Mahweet** (24 rooms) ☎ 07 404076; 🖷 07 404591. The hotel maintains very clean rooms with Western bathrooms, & the receptionist speaks English. Interestingly enough, the suites are oddly reminiscent of 1970s' bachelor pads, & if you stick a cassette tape into the system built into the sofa, surround sound will permeate the room. There is also an open terrace restaurant with an extensive menu of Western & Yemeni dishes (b/fast buffet: 1,000YR; lunch/dinner buffet: 1,700YR) & a 'Bedouin Tent' where you can relax by smoking a *shisha* after a long day of hiking. There is also an ATM in the downstairs lobby. $$$

What to see The entrance to the old city of al-Mahweet is called **Bab al-Masna'**. There is an old house prominently featured in the old city known as **Bayt al-Imam**, which used to be the house of a prominent Jewish family before the imam converted it to his governor's estate. While it is used for other purposes now, you can still see the large archway and stairs leading up to the main doors.

Right outside of town is an area known as **ar-Riyyadi**, which has great flat areas for camping and provides amazing views of another mountain village. Down a path at the end of the road there is a large cave complex that locals claim is haunted by jinn. The putrid smell of bat guano and the cramped quarters makes you feel like you may have entered the **well of infidels**, a cave found to the east of Seiyun in which there was supposed to be much weeping and gnashing of teeth. Local rumour maintains that one of the passageways leads through the mountain to another village. Other locals tell of a villager who was lost in the cave for several days and who only found his way out by following the faint sound of drums being beaten by the villagers at the entrance. Once you find the main arm of the cave, the layout is rather labyrinth-like, so make sure you have plenty of caving supplies if you want to do some serious exploring.

AMRAN

Amran sits on a well-trodden path. In the days of the incense trade, it was one of the posts along the As'ad mountain incense road. Today, its proximity to Sana'a and surviving fortifications guarantee that nearly every tourist who visits Yemen makes at least a brief stop at the city. One of the excellent side effects of the town's popularity is that foreigners seem to have become less of an attraction here than in other small towns of the country. Unlike other cities, the children will not necessarily come flocking over to you to check out the strange creature with a camera (and possibly some pens) that has entered their territory. Rather, their aloofness allows you to get a good idea regarding how Yemeni children pass their time, either by playing a variety of interesting games in the street or by playing with the toys they have sculpted from everyday objects. It's quite a treat.

When the great Sabaean Kingdom was master of the environs, the city of Amran was known as the fortification of A'aran. Perhaps the later name change occurred because of a scribal error; it would only take one errant pen stroke to make the letter 'ayn of A'aran look like the *mim* of Amran. During the days of its earlier appellation, sometime around the 7th century BC, Amran sided with the Kingdom of Saba' during the wars against several local tribes. Remnants of the Sabaean Kingdom remain. Various houses throughout the old city have incorporated small pieces of old temples or palaces. The city wall, which completely surrounds the old city, has a large Sabaean inscription near the largest entrance to the town, Bab al-Kabeer ('The Big Gate').

During the 6th century AD, Amran was the political centre of the area for a short period of time, but served as an important trade nexus for the surrounding villages and tribes for much longer. In the first part of the 21st century, Amran regained some of its past importance when it became the administrative centre of a new governorate of the same name, which was carved out of the unwieldy Sana'a governorate landmass.

Getting there Located on the northern road toward Sa'ada, tourists are not permitted to travel to the city by buses or shared taxis. Contact a travel agency to make arrangements.

Where to stay

Golden Beach (18 rooms) Amran–Sa'adah St; 07 604407. The rooms are a nice escape from the heavily perfumed lobby. Rooms have private, Yemeni bathrooms, & come ready with hot water.

The prices of the dbl & trpl rooms depend on the day & the whim of the receptionist, but should be somewhere in the cheap range. $

What to see and do Conditions in Amran have improved a little more recently. The old medical centre was transformed into a small public hospital, and the old section of the city inside the wall has had its dirt streets transformed with the laying of local stones. The new stone roads have helped tremendously with the problems that would occur every time it rained. Unfortunately, problems persist in the dirt roads of the outer city, where the rainwater transforms the entire area into large pools of mud. Supposedly, Amran was once surrounded by marshes – a geographical feature that was altered by a large drainage project during the 2nd century BC by a local sheikh. When you're trying to navigate through the souk after a large rain, it's not hard to imagine what the area must have looked like over 2,000 years ago.

Come rain or shine, there is a weekly market on Saturday in the area outside the main gate. The region is said to be a particularly good locale for leather workers, and you can see the artisans' wares on display in the stalls of the market. As Amran sits on the southwest edge of Qa'a al-Bawn, a valley particularly suitable for growing a variety of crops, you will see vendors filling the spaces with carts of local fruits and vegetables as well (although much of the fruit is imported as well; nearly all the apples you'll find, for example, come from the US or China). During Monday and Tuesday, the town is particularly quiet – the local vendors have gone off with their goods for the weekly markets of other towns.

Bab al-Kabeer is one of only two entrances to the old city through the city wall, which has 15 strategically placed towers. The other, smaller gate is called Bab al-

'Ala ('The Door of Illness'). Exiting through the gate, you can continue down a small alley that leads back to the old Jewish quarter of the city.

KOHLAN Kohlan lies on the road from Amran to Hajjah. Coming from Amran, the Kohlan Citadel can be seen on the right once you pass the small village of **Halmlam**. Continuing onward, you leave the Amran governate and pass through the **Nagil al-Khodali** ('the Khodali Pass'), where a large portion of the mountain had to be hewn away to make way for the road. A pillar of rock remains on the left as a monument to how deep the construction workers had to dig.

Local stories regarding the pass claim that the engineer in charge of the project made a mistake in determining the path the road should take. As a result, the work became mired down in clearing away the rock, and many people died. The local legend claims that the engineer at fault met an unfortunate end by fire on returning to China. Right after the Khodali Pass, a road breaks away to the village of Kohlan. The road goes up the mountain, but you must exit the car at the top for a short walk through the village to reach the citadel.

What to see As you walk toward the citadel, you can see the old Jewish village below to your right, which used to be renowned for the production of agricultural tools. These tools were likely used to harvest the wheat and sorghum that were traded heavily in the village below. Today, the lower village hosts a weekly market on Mondays. During the other six days of the week the place is mostly deserted. From the fort it takes approximately 45 minutes to walk down the labyrinth-like paths, or a little over an hour to walk the more clearly demarcated long, winding path.

The grounds of the citadel begin once you enter through the Bab al-'Aredha ('the Door of Invitation'). The other two doors from which you could enter are known as the Bab al-Gharbi ('the Western Door') and the Bab al-Medina ('the City Door'). Through another door, past the old kitchen, and up the stairs you reach the citadel proper.

As the door here is locked you need to employ the services of an old gentleman by the name of Hezam al-Arashi. Several years after the 1967 revolution, Hezam, a Kohlani native, was stationed in the citadel along with a small police force. Around 1991, the government lost interest in maintaining a presence in the fort, and all the officers left. Hezam, however, stuck around and ever since has held the only key to the door. Retired now, he happily obliges tourists by opening the grounds for a small fee. Somewhere in the range of 200–500YR is appropriate.

The citadel itself resembles what Dar al-Hajar might have looked like before its recent restoration. It would definitely benefit from a little work, but no-one seems particularly interested in doing so. From the top of the citadel, one can see the older, smaller fort, Husn al-Ghufla, across the village, as well as views of the surrounding countryside along the Wadi Seres.

Looking around the surrounding land from the top of Husn Kohlan, it's easy to see why the city was chosen in the past as the administrative centre of the surrounding area. In 1216, Amir Yayha ibn Hamza, the brother of the imam Abdullah ibn Hamza, picked the location to govern the surrounding lands. Kohlan may have had some defensive structures existing at the time, making the choice even more agreeable. Regardless, Amir ibn Hamza had the citadel and city walls constructed during his governance. His tomb lies in the local al-Amir mosque, although, like most mosques in Yemen, non-Muslims are forbidden from entering.

The town remained the administrative centre of the district for over seven centuries. In 1924, Imam Yahya moved the provincial capital to Hajjah, where it remains today. The change did not come easily, as the residents were not eager to have the city lose its important status, and Imam Yahya was forced to send the army to enforce his order. This is apparently the only action Husn Kohlan has ever seen.

HAJJAH Located over 125km from Sana'a, Hajjah is situated within the Washha Mountains. It is the capital of the governorate that bears its name. Although the large citadel that presides over the city was originally built by the Turks during the Ottoman occupation, the city is most famous for the importance it played in the revolution. As a stronghold of the Zaydi Imamate, it was infamous for its prisons that held the enemies of the imam.

On the dawn of the revolution, the imam's governor in Hajjah tried to appease the locals by releasing many of the prisoners from the cells of the Nafi' Prison. Once the news of the revolution began to spread, the newly released prisoners led an attack against the governor and were able to capture his mansion and Cairo Castle.

All the surrounding area, however, was still loyal to the old Zaydi Kingdom. The fighting in the area was fierce and lasted for roughly five years. The republican soldiers managed to pacify the region only once the Egyptian reinforcements arrived. The Egyptians seemed happy to stay behind, and it looked like Yemen would be occupied yet again. Shortly afterwards the Egyptian–Israeli war broke out, all the foreign soldiers were called back home, and the days of the new Yemeni Republic could begin in earnest.

Getting there A shared taxi from Sana'a costs 600YR. Private taxis also run to Mabyan, the ruins of an old castle on the adjacent mountain for 1,500YR return.

What to see and do on the way The road from Kohlan to Hajjah passes through a number of villages. At the top of a small hill next to the village of **al-'Aridah**, there are the ruins of an old fort that is said to date back 'from before the time of the Turks', and no-one seems to have any information other than that. It is possible to climb up and have a look around. After passing by **Wadi Maor** – one of the biggest valleys in Yemen – you will pass through **Shallal Ain 'Ali**, a small town known for its coffee.

Getting around Hajjah has a unique taxi setup – you have your choice between motorbikes (30–50YR) and 4x4 Jeeps (150–200YR).

Where to stay

Babel Tourist Hotel (20 rooms) Hodaydah St; 07 222075. 15 of the rooms have private bathrooms, which vary in quality according to the room. Overall, the hotel is a bit drab. $$.

Ghamdan Haggah Hotel (52 rooms) 07 220420; f 07 220423. Situated at the top of one of Hajjah's peaks, the Ghamdan provides great views of the city. The decorations in the lobby have a certain Rococo flair, but the rooms are very pleasant & clean. Bathrooms have Western-style toilets & come supplied with toilet paper. Western tourists are usually given the nicer rooms on the fourth floor, but you may want to request one of the rooms with a balcony on the third floor. $$.

Funduq al-Jazeera (18 rooms) Sana'a St; 07 220800. Basic rooms with Western toilets. $.

Hotel Province Green (7 rooms) Off Hudaydah St. Not pleasant. $.

Qaser al-Hmra'a Tourism Hotel (13 rooms) Hodaydah St; 07 223310. If you can find some old bread from a local restaurant, the sgl rooms are perfect for pretending that you are a political prisoner in the time of the imam. Dbl rooms are a bit larger. Private Western bathrooms are clean though, but come without toilet seats. $

Where to eat
There is a number of local restaurants on the main street of Hajjah, including the slightly fancier **al-Nnil Restaurants Broast ($$)**. The restaurants serve Saltah, chicken, and other typical Yemeni dishes.

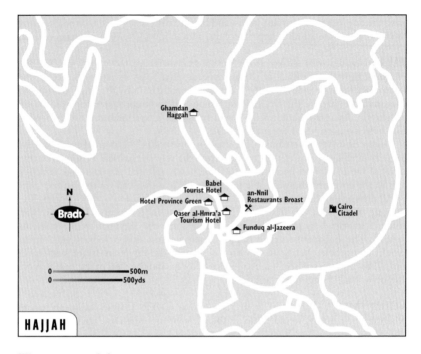

Ghamdan
Haggah

Babel
Tourist Hotel
Hotel Province Green
an-Nnil
Restaurants Broast
Qaser al-Hmra'a
Tourism Hotel
Cairo
Citadel
Funduq al-Jazeera

N

Bradt

0 ——————— 500m
0 ——————— 500yds

HAJJAH

What to see and do

Cairo Citadel (Gel'at al-Gaahera) (⊕ *07.00–17.00; entrance fee 200YR*) The Cairo Citadel sits atop a peak on the eastern side of Hajjah. It was built during the Turkish Occupation and later was used prominently by the imams. Imam Yahya used it as a prison to hold political prisoners, such as Hussan al-'Amri and Abdullah as-Sallal, the first prime minister and president of the new Republic of Yemen. The prison contained two chambers where the confined intellectuals were able to read, write poetry, and join together in study groups. Isma'il al-Akwa', a Yemeni cultural scholar who spent time in the prison, noted that: 'the time in prison was a little like time spent in a garden. We used to laugh and dance, even though our feet and hands were chained.' The garden was less rosy for other leaders of the revolution, such as members of the al-Wazeer family and Abbas, the brother of Imam Ahmed, who were both executed on the castle grounds.

Not all prisoners are high profile, of course. Those not fortunate enough to be held in the Cairo Citadel were incarcerated in the infamous Nafi' Prison, known for its instances of severe torture. Over 800 members of the Zaraniqs, a tribe located along the Tihama plain that fought violently against the rule of the Zaydi Imam, were cruelly put to death in the human slaughterhouse.

The main building of the citadel which previously housed the political prisoners is largely in disrepair. One of the rooms that was formerly closed off as the guard's quarters has been transformed into a small monument to the revolution and modern Yemen. Old firearms are attached to the walls, along with photocopies of news clippings from the revolution and pictures of President Ali Abdullah Saleh with various world leaders.

Hiking the road from Hajjah to Thula There are several long and exciting hikes you can make within the Hajjah and al-Mahweet province. One particularly good trek would be from Hajjah to Thula (see descriptions above). There is a mountain road that connects the two villages that is *nearly* impossible to cross by car, but plenty of natives walk along it. Thus, you would have a great path for walking and an excellent chance to interact with the people who live in the area. There are plenty of towns to stop and restock on your supplies; just make sure you always have plenty of water with you.

Distances in the regions are not measured by locals in terms of kilometres or miles. If you ask someone how far away something is, he'll give you an answer using the term *marhala*, which means 'a day's journey'. The trip between Hajjah and Thula will take *marhala wa nos* – a day and a half.

If you do decide to make the hike, start on a Wednesday, so you can purchase your initial supplies while experiencing one of the small mountain village weekly markets in the town of **Souk** ('Market') (⊕ *07.00–12.00*). The long hike will take you through the villages of Shamatha, Husn adh-Dhari on Jabal Maswar, and Bait adh-Dhaga.

JABAL MASWAR In the early 9th century AD, al-Haysam bin 'Abd al-Samad led an important revolt against the Abbasid governors from Jabal Maswar. The mountain terrain gave the Yemeni rebels a strong advantage, and the Abbasid governor's initial attempts to quell the rebellion failed. Even with reinforcements from Baghdad, the insurrection continued until the Abbasid forces were able to find and arrest al-Haysam.

Toward the end of the same century, Jabal Maswar was chosen as the home base of the Isma'ili missionary **Mansur al-Yemen ibn Hawshab**. Ibn Hawshab was sent to Yemen along with another missionary named **'Ali bin Fadl**. Together the two were very successful in bringing much of the country under the sphere of the north African Fatimid ruler Imam Ubayd Allah al-Mahdi.

After two decades of military conquests, the two missionaries' areas of rule began to overlap. At the same time Imam Mahdi was facing dissention in north Africa. 'Ali bin Fadl declared his independence from the imam and fought against ibn Hawshab, besieging his fort on Jabal Maswar for eight months. Neither side could secure a victory, and 'Ali bin Fadl eventually withdrew after ibn Hawshab agreed to the old Yemeni custom of giving up his son for imprisonment.

The area of Jabal Maswar provides some of the best hiking opportunities in Yemen. The mountain scenery, needless to say, is amazing. At the top of the mountain is the town of **Husn adh-Dhari**, which has the remains of an old fort.

Unfortunately, there are no places to stay or eat on the mountain.

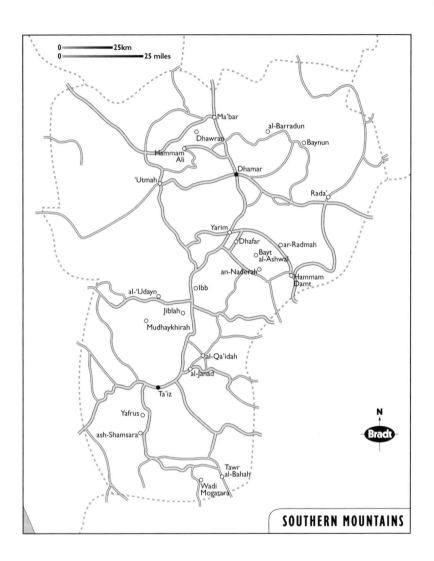

SOUTHERN MOUNTAINS

5

The Southern Mountains

RADA'

This moderately sized city is best known for the beautifully restored al-Amiriya mosque, originally built in the 15th century during the reign of the local Tahirid dynasty. Following the long and culturally active period of the Rasulids, the Tahirids established themselves as the ruling family in AD1454. Until they were defeated by the Egyptian Mamluks in 1517, the Tahirids used the city of Rada' as their summer capital.

GETTING THERE Shared taxis are located at the intersection of Sana'a and al-'Am streets. Taxis run toward Sana'a (650YR), al-Bayda (400YR) and Dhamar (200YR).

 WHERE TO STAY

🏠 **Al-Ahram** (18 rooms) Sana'a St; m 777 701045. $$.

🏠 **Al-Akhwah** (25 rooms) al-'Am St; ☎ 06 553466; f 06 553465. Al-Akhwah has been the sole hotel in Rada' in most of modern history, the hotel rooms maintain a fair quality despite having a certain dated feeling. $$

🏠 **Al-Obahi** (20 rooms) Sana'a St; ☎ 06 556530. $$. This new building offers some of the best hotel rooms in Rada'.

🏠 **Ash-Sha'er** (18 rooms) al-Souk al-Markazi; ☎ 06 550720. More often used by locals than foreigners, ash-Sha'er sacrifices cleanliness for low prices. $

✗ **WHERE TO EAT** There are several basic restaurants serving standard fare on al-'Am St, including al-Jazeera ($), al-Obahi ($), and the Palestine Restaurant ($).

EWE AND I HAVE UNFINISHED BUSINESS

In 1503, the Italian explorer Ludovico di Varthema visited Rada' before the construction of the great al-Amiriya Mosque. Even so, he found the city 'very beautiful and ancient, populous and rich'. As Ludovico arrived in Rada', the Tahirid Sultan az-Zafir 'Amir II was preparing for one of the dynasty's few battles against the city of Sana'a. Unfortunately for Ludovico, he was thrown into prison before the sultan left – it was not the first time he was imprisoned on his travels in the country.

Ludovico feigned madness in the hopes of being released. In one of his exploits, he cornered a sheep and demanded to know its faith. When the sheep could not repeat the words 'There is no deity but God and Muhammad is his prophet', Ludovico tore into the animal, much to the delight of his bemused onlookers. According to the Italian traveller, his madness enticed the queen, who became very interested in the imprisoned explorer while the sultan was away. The sensible Ludovico, not wanting to remain a prisoner of the sultan forever, thought it best not to yield to her advances.

The Southern Mountains RADA'

5

113

OTHER PRACTICALITIES There are three hospitals, a post office, and a CAC Bank with ATM located on Sana'a St.

WHAT TO SEE The **Al-Amiriya Mosque** was built by the Tahirid Sultan az-Zafir 'Amir ibn Abd al-Wahhab in the early 16th century. The large multi-domed building was recently restored after a long process of repairing the building with its original materials, such as *qadūd*. It is possible for tourists to go in and visit now, and it is rumoured the mosque will be turned into a museum in the near future.

HAMMAM DAMT

Hammam Damt is Yemen's premier mineral water resort. Renowned for its healing properties, the water draws many Yemenis throughout the year seeking to relieve their arthritis, rheumatism, or joint pain. Even if you are not suffering from any sort of ailments, a soak in a private bath filled with the naturally hot mineral water is the perfect end to a harried day of sightseeing.

GETTING THERE Shared taxis run regularly between Hammam Damt and several other cities in Yemen. The easiest destinations to travel from are Sana'a (700YR, 3½hrs), Dhamar (300YR, 2hrs), Ibb (400YR, 2½hrs), and Aden (1,400YR, 3hrs). (Bijous coming from Aden will charge a full fare to Sana'a, even if you are only going to Hammam Damt.)

WHERE TO STAY

⌂ **Babel Tourist Hotel** (36 rooms) ☎ 04 456942. Babel Tourist is the newest hotel to spring up in Hammam Damt. The private hammams are comparable with Damt Hot Spring Beach Hotel, & the rooms are preferable. Access to the private baths is included in the price. $$

⌂ **Damt Hot Spring Beach Hotel** (20 rooms) ☎ 04 455600; f 04 456254; e info@as-complex.com. Although there is not much to conjure up the image of a beach here, the hotel is one of the most popular in town, & rooms fill up quickly. During the day, locals pay a small fee to jump in the pool of hot water next to the manmade bubbling rock structure. If you care for a little more private bath setting, renting a room grants you 24hr access to the private hammams (limited by others' reservations, of course). $$

⌂ **Al-Nasser Tourism Hotel** (42 rooms) ☎ 04 556220; f 04 556224. Although it does not have a private hammam, the rooms are clean & sizeable with Western bathrooms. Because the price is about half that of a hotel with baths, it may be a good option to stay here if you are part of a larger party — you can rent a large swimming pool-sized hot bath for everyone with the money you'll save from 1 room. $

✕ WHERE TO EAT

Although you might expect a town that derives its wealth from a supply of visitors to have a few decent places to eat, that does not seem to be the case with Hammam Damt. There is a local restaurant on the main street of the town that serves standard fare, and another smaller café tucked away by the tiny souk where you can purchase tea, juice, and egg and cheese sandwiches.

WHAT TO SEE AND DO If you decide not to partake of the hotel hammams, there are plenty more **private baths** for rent. After all, the town is literally bubbling with them. You have a variety of options. Entrance to the large shared baths cost about 100YR. For small private baths large enough for two or three individuals, the cost is 1,000YR. A private, large bath the size of a swimming pool costs 1,500YR and can accommodate up to eight people.

The **Haradha Volcano** lies just to the south of the village, and is a favourite tourist attraction for Yemenis visiting Hammam Damt. To assist those climbing to the top, a metal staircase with over 100 steps has been installed. At the top of the volcano, a wide rim perfect for strolling wraps around the large crater that dips deep into the mountain. At the bottom of the crater is a large pool of water. Although there have been frequent attempts to clean up the crater, the bottom is filled with hundreds of empty plastic water bottles, giving the volcano the appearance of the world's largest rubbish bin.

DHAMAR

Dhamar is reputed to have been founded by its namesake, the late Himyarite ruler Dhamar 'Ali Yuhabirr. Statues of Dhamar 'Ali and his son were found in the nearby village of an-Nakhla, and the large statues now occupy the central position in the Sana'a National Museum. Modern Dhamar is linked to other Himyarite statues as well, such as the number of bronze horses – some found not far from the area – that were regularly sculpted at the time. The city's workers no longer engage in crafting bronze horses, but that is not to say that they have abandoned the equine business entirely. Dhamar has long enjoyed a good reputation for thoroughbreds.

For most of its early history, Dhamar was eclipsed by the Himyarite capital of Dhafar (located to the south of the city). This is evidenced by the fact that the first known historical document mentioning Dhamar dates from the late 12th century – nearly a millennium after the town was founded. These early documents, while also mentioning that Dhamar had some pretty buildings, noted the beauty of the town's women and their ability to draw men from miles away to engage in good old-fashioned licentiousness.

Dhamar quickly gained historical and moral stature after its first references in the history books. The town became an important centre for the Zaydi imams for several centuries afterwards. Although the imams ultimately withdrew from the town, they established a theological school that long outlasted their dominance of the town.

In 1982, a devastating earthquake that measured 6.0 on the Richter scale hit Dhamar, killing several thousand people and injuring several thousand more. The rebuilding effort took many years. The government quickly threw together makeshift houses of mud and brick for many residents of the governorate. Some 25 years later, many people are still living in these makeshift abodes, especially in the area around Ma'bar to the north.

GETTING THERE Shared taxis come to and from Dhamar. The most common destinations are Sana'a (250YR, 1½hrs), Ibb (400YR, 1½hrs), and Ta'iz (700YR, 3hrs).

WHERE TO STAY

Al-Ahram Tourism Hotel (32 rooms) Rada' St; 06 511616; f 06 505274. The only hotel to offer 'special' higher prices for tourists, the al-Ahram has small rooms & bathrooms, but they are pretty clean. There is a nice mufraj on the top floor. $$

Dhamar Palace Hotel (34 rooms) Main St; 06 507501; f 06 507504. Decent hotel. 10 of the rooms have private bathrooms, which are moderately clean. If travelling with 3 or more people, getting a 2-room suite with private shared bath makes for a nice stay. Rooms have TVs, some with desks. $

Yarmook Tourist Hotel (29 rooms) Rada' St; m 733 592246. Only the dbl rooms have private bathrooms, which are dirty & Yemeni style. There is no TV in the rooms, but if you're dying for some Yemeni sitcoms during your stay in Dhamar, you can retire to the upstairs diwan. $

WHERE TO EAT
There is a number of local restaurants along Main St and Rada' St. While you can get a number of local Yemeni dishes, you will be unlikely to find any *wazīf*, the small, dried fish that are sold in abundance in Ta'iz. A local story relates that a man from Dhamar choked while eating a piece of *wazīf* and then died. Consequently, it was banned from the town.

OTHER PRACTICALITIES
There is a **post office** and several **banks with ATMs** along Main Street.

WHAT TO SEE
The attraction of Dhamar lies mostly in its centrality to a number of surrounding sites: Baynun, Ma'bar, Dhawran, Hammam 'Ali, Yarim, Dhafar and Rada'. The features of the town itself include the **Great Mosque**, built during the time of the first Muslim Caliph Abu Bakr, and the small souk in the Old City.

While the small streets and stalls of the old souk are interesting in themselves, of peculiar attraction is the souk's **Arms Market**. The Dhamar market is not as large or extensive as the major weapons markets of Jehenem (in Marib) or Souk at-Talh (in Sa'ada), but while these two last are almost always off-limits to visitors, the Dhamar market is always open to them. Thus, the souk in Dhamar represents your best chance to see how and where the Yemenis buy their many, many guns. (Remember, there is a 3:1 ratio of guns to people!) The stalls carry a variety of goods, ranging from AK-47s to pistols to trendy, stylish holsters.

OUTSIDE DHAMAR

MA'BAR Located about 30km to the north of Dhamar, the city of **Ma'bar** ('Crossing Point') sits at a major junction point on the road going to Sana'a. The road to the east from Ma'bar heads toward Baynun, and to the west the road leads to Medinat ash-Sharq and ultimately to al-Hudaydah. In addition to being a stopping point for travellers heading to any of these directions, Ma'bar is known for its two-storey mud-brick buildings.

DHAWRAN About 10km to the west of Ma'bar, on the mountain of Jabal Dhamigh rest the abandoned ruins of **Dhawran**, the capital of the ruling Zaydi imams in the 17th century. In 1630, Dhawran had been visited by the Zaydi Imam al-Hasan bin al-Qasim – a religious scholar but also a fierce warrior; he had begun fighting against the Ottoman occupation at the tender age of 15. When he first arrived in Dhawran, he was taken by its defensive capabilities. Indeed, by that point the site had been used as a fortification for centuries – al-Hamdani noted in the 10th century that Dhawran contained three castles.

Imam al-Hasan's lasting contribution to the area was the construction of an elaborate mosque that was used from the 17th century until it was destroyed by the earthquake of 1982. The mosque, built in the style of Yemen's early great mosques, used a number of arch supports rather than columns. Even after the earthquake, evidence of the ornate designs is still readily apparent. In addition to the cisterns and old school, there is an elaborate tomb chamber on the northwest side of the complex which houses the grave of Imam al-Hasan.

In 1644, after the end of the first Turkish occupation, al-Hasan's more famous brother Imam al-Mutawakkil bin al-Qasim moved the capital out of the mountain stronghold of Shahara to Dhawran. Imam al-Mutawakkil reigned from Dhawran for over 30 years. Under his rule, the Zaydi Imamate grew to one of its greatest points of power. He expanded the imamate's territory to include Hadhramawt, and he corresponded with the rulers of Ethiopia and India. He is remembered as one of the country's greatest sovereigns.

HAMMAM 'ALI Another 10km southwest of Dhawran is the village of Hammam 'Ali, which together with Hammam Damt and as-Sukhnah comprise Yemen's three major mineral spring water resorts. Like that of the other two spring resorts, the water of Hammam 'Ali is reputed to have curing abilities.

'UTMAH PROTECTED DISTRICT The small, unassuming town of 'Utmah lies about 35km to the west of Dhamar. The city is the capital of the small 'Utmah district, recognised as one of Yemen's four Environmentally Protected Areas. (The other three are the island of Socotra, the region surrounding Hof in the southeast corner of the country, and Jabal Bura, located not too far away in the foothills of the Tihama.)

As far as the protected districts go, 'Utmah is the least exciting of the bunch. Still, the area offers some interesting sites, highlighted by the increased greenery. If you are going to try to go through the area, the direct road from Dhamar to 'Utmah may be your best bet.

There is another road that runs north to south through the region. At the southern end of the road is the village of **Rihāb**, a one-horse town with a weekly market on Thursday. On the northern end is the significantly busier town of **Medinat ash-Sharq** ('City of the East'). This market village used to be known as Medinat al-'Abd ('City of the Slaves'), but it had its name changed in the 1970s by then President Ibrahim al-Hamdi, who did not care for the appellation.

BAYNUN Although the ruins of Baynun date back to the ancient Himyarite kingdoms, the area is one of the least excavated or visited of all the archaeological sites. With newer roads making the trek somewhat easier, and with a new, decently setup museum nearby, that may change soon.

Getting there There are two paths you can take to get to Baynun. The first option is to take the mostly paved road from Dhamar – the trip to the village of an-Numāra will take about 45 minutes. If you have more time and would like to take in more of the countryside, try the route from Ma'bar. It takes approximately two–three hours on bumpy dirt roads. The trip will take you through the village of Bayt Bowsan, where the remains of a castle further ravaged by the earthquake are situated. Many of the villages you will pass, such as Bayt Akroush and al-Barradun, have multiple buildings riddled with bullet holes and rocket rubble – evidence of a previous tribal conflict. If tribal conflict proves to be inevitable, the conflict at Bayt Akroush would not be a bad model: the tribes resolved their problems without anyone getting killed.

What to see and do The ruins of the town of Baynun are located near Jabal Isbil. A 4x4-only dirt path leads up to the remains of the fortress and town from the

Although the evidence of previous conflicts in the area would give one the impression that all the villagers in the region are constantly looking for an excuse to pull out their weapons, at least one man from the area worked much more with the pen than the sword. The work of Yemeni poet Abdullah al-Barraduni, who hails from the village of the same name, is revered throughout the country. Al-Barraduni's bout with smallpox at the tender age of six left him permanently blind. Like Homer, the poet's work at times turns to a sojourner trying to make his way home. While Homer's subject was Odysseus, al-Barraduni's was his country – the glory of its past and the problems of its present decline.

In addition to poetry, al-Barraduni worked on promoting democracy and women's rights. From the 1950s to the 1970s he served several jail sentences for criticising both the imamate and the later revolutionaries through his poetry. Later, despite receiving multiple death threats from Muslim extremists, he refused to accept police protection. He died peacefully in 1999. His house in al-Barradun now houses a library bearing his name.

village of an-Numāra. On top of the mountain there are two sets of ruins, known as **ad-Dākhala** and **Mināra**. Locals call the entire ancient site by the name an-Nasla, which means 'the dagger of the jambiyya'. Although it's a very interesting and provocative name, the residents prefer to call it Baynun when tourists are around, so as to associate themselves with the ancient site.

Because Baynun has still not received a proper excavation, not much is known about the site. It is known to have been a Himyarite stronghold and al-Hamdani reports that King As'ad Tubba' used the fortress as well as his palace in Dhafar as a residence. Before the Himyarites, it likely served as a dwelling for the Sabaeans as well, and several of the inscriptions in the area may date back to that period. According to old legends, the older Sabaean fortification of Baynun was constructed for the Queen of Sheba by the jinn given to her by Solomon. The jinni-fortified walls could not withstand every assault though, and in AD525 the fortifications were destroyed by the Aksumites when they invaded from Ethiopia in order to overthrow Dhu Nuwas.

The ruins of ad-Dākhala contain the town and temple, and you'll find most of the goodies in this area. You can see the dark, finely cut squares used by the Himyarites in their building, coming out of the ground, forming small walls. One is able to observe them better in the adjacent town, where villagers as late as the mid 1990s were using the ruins as their personal quarry. Nearly 5m of every house has been constructed using Himyarite stone (and it doesn't hurt to have a nice inscription over the doorway). Only within the last decade have the villagers decided to stop carrying off the blocks.

Right before the road ends, you'll notice several large columns sticking vertically out of the mountain and continuing under the road. Supposedly, these columns once stood tall as the **Sun Temple**, a counterpart to the similar temple in Marib. Now, it provides good foundational support for the dirt road. Opposite ad-Dākhala lies Mināra, the area where the palace once stood. Some digging has revealed the foundation, but little else abounds to attract the eye.

Baynun has not been excavated to a large degree, and the land is still wonderfully rich with artefacts. After every rainfall, the locals collect the stone engravings, statues, and coins that have been freshly revealed. The villagers would not take kindly to would-be tourists turned freelance archaeologists attempting to dig up or purchase a fine piece of history for the mantelpiece, however, and you should under no means attempt to do so. Besides being strictly illegal to take antiquities out of the country, it would be a great *ayb* to rob the people of the artefacts that connect them to their ancient past.

Much more awe-inspiring than the ruins of Baynun are the **manmade tunnels** that were carved by hand through the nearby mountains. These tunnels were used for irrigation by bringing all the water that flowed down the mountain on one side gushing through the tunnel to the other. They are no longer used for that purpose, and have not been for some time. Even as early as the 10th century, al-Hamdani thought the tunnels were merely 'two great roads which are carved through two mountains and are therefore difficult to find'.

Of course, this wash of water carries with it a lot of debris that will cause the tunnel to disappear if not properly maintained. Such is the case with the tunnel connecting the villages of an-Numāra and Jelāhen. The walkthrough portion of the tunnel is completely submerged under dirt and rocks, although it is still possible to see where the large slit is carved into the mountain. With the road leading to Baynun on your left, continue through the village of an-Numāra, and you will see the carved entrance on the left-hand side.

Recently, there was a co-ordinated attempt to reopen the tunnel by the residents of several of the surrounding villages. Unfortunately, disagreements blossomed, bickering ensued, and work ceased. The final nail in the coffin was when one of the villagers turned soothsayer and prophesied that the work would not be completed without seven of the workers dying. Upon hearing this, the residents decided to busy themselves with other affairs.

The other tunnel, which connects Wadi Baynun and Wadi Hayyawa, is open, and the work of the Himyarites in cutting through the rock is truly marvellous. Walking towards the narrow opening the slices through the rock of the mountain high above the tunnel's entrance offers a similar experience to the narrow passageway that gives way to Petra. At the entrance on the Hayyawa side, a Himyarite inscription celebrates the opening of the tunnel. Residents are proud to note that President Ali Abdullah Saleh walked through the tunnel in 2004, and you can see a picture of him walking through the tunnel in the nearby museum.

The **Baynun Museum** (⊕ *09.00–12.00; entrance fee 500YR*) is located in the nearby village of al-Moga, directly adjacent to Baynun. For being a small and out-of-the-way place, the museum is surprisingly well built and well stocked. At the request of Sheikh Ahmed Aleezi, the museum was constructed in 2003, replacing the older museum that had been constructed in 1994. The museum contains several large rooms stocked with antiquities from the Sabaean–Himyarite kingdoms. Another room holds cultural treasures from the area, including several old Korans, swords, guns, and jewellery. Among the more interesting pieces are a relief that has the improbable claim of picturing the Queen of Sheba talking to a hoopoe, and a bronze lion with numerous holes throughout that would create a roaring noise as the wind blew threw it.

IBB

The city of Ibb is built on the mountain of Jabal Ba'adan, overlooking the lush green countryside of the rain-blessed governorate of the same name. The city likely was founded during the reign of the Himyarite Kingdom, when it was known as Thogha. The first historical document referring to the city of Ibb dates from the 10th century AD. Throughout most of its history, Ibb had sat on the caravan route from Aden to Sana'a as well as a pilgrimage route to Yemen, ensuring that it was never lacking in customers while maintaining its position as a trade centre.

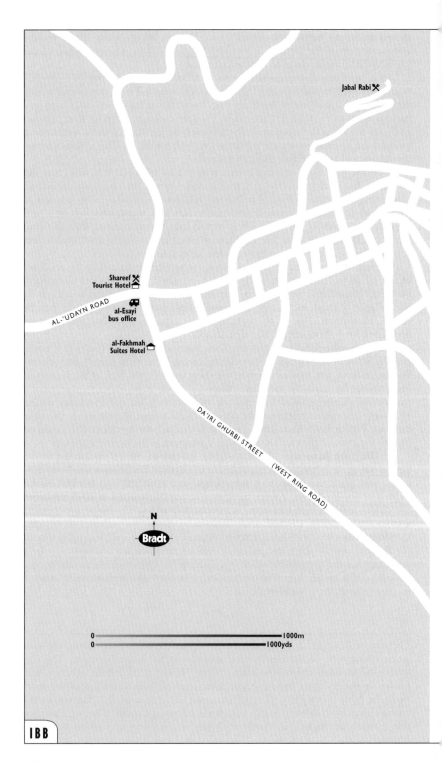

Jabal Rabi

Shareef
Tourist Hotel

AL.'UDAYN ROAD

al-Esayi
bus office

al-Fakhmah
Suites Hotel

DA'IRI GHURBI STREET   (WEST RING ROAD)

N

Bradt

0 _____ 1000m
0 _____ 1000yds

IBB

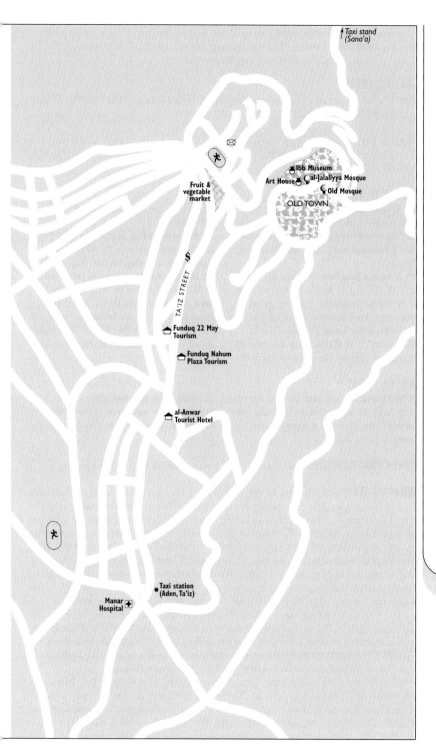

Taxi stand
(Sana'a)

Ibb Museum
Art House
al-Jalaliyya Mosque
Old Mosque
OLD TOWN

Fruit &
vegetable
market

TA'IZ STREET

$

Funduq 22 May
Tourism

Funduq Nahum
Plaza Tourism

al-Anwar
Tourist Hotel

Taxi station
(Aden, Ta'iz)

Manar
Hospital

Today, Ibb is the provincial capital of the governorate, and has kept its position as a regional trade centre, although it now derives its economic position chiefly from its well-placed position between Sana'a and Ta'iz.

GETTING THERE

Bus The Al-Esayi bus company runs two daily buses to both Ta'iz (300YR, 1½hrs) and Sana'a (900YR, 3hrs).

Shared taxi Bijous gather outside the city, waiting for seats to fill for the destinations of Sana'a (800YR, 3hrs), Dhamar (400YR 1½hrs), Ta'iz (300YR, 1½hrs) and Aden (850YR, 3½hrs).

WHERE TO STAY

⌂ **Al-Anwar Tourist Hotel** (27 rooms) Ta'iz St; ☎ 04 416841; f 04 416845. Rooms are fine; some have balconies & Western toilets. Small convenience store & restaurant (meals: 100–500YR) on the first floor. $$

⌂ **Al-Fakhmah Suites Hotel** (69 rooms) Da'iri Ghurbi St; ☎ 04 457755; f 04 457663. The hotel has some of the best dbl rooms in Ibb. Make sure you get a room with a decent bathroom. $$; apts $$$

⌂ **Funduq 22 May Tourism** (35 rooms) Ta'iz St; ☎ 04 407307; f 04 404108. Rooms are typical, but the staff are unfriendly. The attached restaurant is

not bad for a bite to eat (lunch/dinner: 200–1,000YR). $$

⌂ **Funduq Nahum Plaza Tourism** (also called Hotel Star) (48 rooms) Ta'iz St; ☎ 04 406802. Small rooms with Yemeni toilets, but very clean. $$

⌂ **Shareef Tourist Hotel** (30 rooms) Jalat al-'Adeen; ☎ 04 457126. This hotel has clean & spacious rooms, especially the apts. The old building has Yemeni bathrooms; the new building, due to be open soon, has Western ones. The restaurant below serves up tasty Ibb delights (meals: 200–1,000YR). $$; apts $$$

WHERE TO EAT

✕ **Jabal Rabi** Located atop Jabal Rabi ('the Mountain of My Lord'), the restaurant of the same name offers panoramic views of the city & countryside while serving up Yemeni dishes. $$$

✕ **Shareef Tourist Restaurant** Jalat al-'Adeen. Extensive outdoor seating next to the Shareef Tourist Hotel. Restaurant offers a number of Yemeni dishes. $$

OTHER PRACTICALITIES There are several banks with ATMs on Ta'iz Street.

WHAT TO SEE The **Old City** of Ibb makes for a pleasant stroll. Most of the roads cannot be navigated by cars, giving it a distinctly different feel from the rest of the city. The houses are built differently from those of other Yemeni cities by their use of stone blocks. Much of the woodwork you will see on the older doors was done by the population of Jewish artisans who lived in the city before 1948. The buildings are typically four-six storeys in height. There is a number of historically important buildings in the Old City, some of which date back before the advent of Islam. Ask one of the villagers to show you to the building of **al-BayāDa** ('the white one'), reputed to have been built for a fair-skinned Himyarite princess.

The Old City had five gates: Bab al-Kabeer ('the big gate'), Bab an-Naseer ('the defender's gate'), Bab ar-Rakeeza ('the gate of support'), Bab ar-Rayha ('the smelly gate'), and Bab Sunbul ('the gate of grain stalks'). Today, many of these gates are merely locations, and only portions of the fortified wall remain. Bab ar-Rakeeza and Bab al-Kabeer are the only gates that have survived in some form.

Next to the Old City's main gate, Bab al-Kabeer, is the small **Ibb Museum** (⏰ 08.00–12.30; entrance fee 500YR). The quaint building contains two small rooms with Himyarite antiquities and a model of the city, along with several slapdash English descriptions on some of the items. Although the museum's offerings are not that vast, they are impressive considering that the museum was created and is maintained by local Yemenis with some support from a German archaeological team – the museum itself receives no support from the Yemeni government.

There are several important mosques in the old city. The **Old Mosque** was built during the reign of the second Muslim caliph, 'Omar ibn al-Khatab. The more aesthetically appealing mosque and red-brick minaret of **al-Jalaliyya** dates to the 18th-century Ottoman occupation.

One of the more interesting locations in the Old City of Ibb is the local **Art House**. As opposed to the unique Yemeni-style adopted by the artists of the art houses of Sana'a, the Ibb artists for the most part imitate a Western style in their work. A few of the pieces envelop Arabic themes – such as modern takes on calligraphy. The Art House features the works of both male and female artists from Ibb. Many of the pieces are quite nice and would make a lovely souvenir. Paintings range in price from US$100–1,000.

The real treasure of the art house, however, is being able to watch the artists at work. From 16.00–21.00 you might catch the artists painting in the workshop rooms, although there is no set schedule for the days which they come. Contact the manager, Nabil al-Kahsah (m *711 719116*), who also does some of the painting, to learn what days the artists might show up. When you have had your fill of the creative process, stroll up to the roof to catch some lovely views of the Old City and overlooking mosque.

Outside the Old City, the small tourist facility on top of **Jabal Rabi** ('The Mountain of My Lord') offers panoramic views of the city and surrounding countryside. There is a swimming pool of questionable cleanliness in which you will be more than welcome to immerse yourself for a mere 100YR.

The fortress of **Husn al-Habb** ('Fortress of Grain') sits on the mountain of **Jabal Ba'adan**. It is inaccessible by car, but a 30-minute to one-hour walk on the path leads up to the ruined remains. Surrounded by three walls and a sharp cliff face, Husn al-Habb was noted by the medieval Yemeni historians as being one of the strongest fortresses in the country.

The fortress fell once to invaders, but not for lack of defences. In 1561, during the first Ottoman occupation of Yemen, the Turkish ruler Mahmoud Basha attacked the Husn al-Habb, then under the control of the Zaydi cleric 'Ali al-Nidhari. When Basha was unable to breach the fortress's defences, he launched a lengthy siege. Fearing that his forces' food and supplies would soon be exhausted, al-Nidhari agreed to discuss a truce. When an agreement had been reached through a mediator, al-Nidhari and his family went out to meet Basha, who had them all immediately slaughtered. The Ottoman forces then easily plundered the fortress, and it has not been used since.

There is a single-arched gateway into Husn al-Habb, and much of the buildings still remain. Inside the walled fortifications, there is a mosque, a three-storey palace, an old prison, a camel stable, four manmade cisterns, and (of course) multiple grain stores. The local guard is a pleasant and informative fellow (if you can speak some Arabic), and he will be happy to show you around the sites. A small tip (200–500YR) is appropriate.

In August, there is an **annual tourist festival** that takes place in a different location within the governorate each year. The exact dates of the festival seem impossible to determine with any certainty before a couple of months in advance. (The last four festivals have fallen on various dates of the second, third, or fourth week of August.) The festival begins on a Sunday and lasts the entire week; festivities typically include a variety of artistic, poetic and sporting events and competitions. If you are interested in attending, run a search on the *Yemen Times* website (*www.yementimes.com*) sometime around June to find an announcement for the dates.

OUTSIDE IBB

If you are interested in doing some trekking in the 'Green Country' outside of the main tourist spots, the area surrounding the villages of **al-'Udayn** and **Mudhaykhirah** is quite lovely. There is a paved road from Ibb to al-'Udayn, but the track becomes tougher to get to Mudhaykhirah. There are several small villages around the area, and you should be able to pick up water and a small snack relatively easily. Stock up just the same, however. Walking through the peaceful areas affords you with some of the best opportunities for spotting the large and interesting Yemeni chameleon.

JIBLAH The town of Jiblah is a small, quiet village tucked away between two wadis that is dominated by its larger neighbour, Ibb – only 8km away. In the past, Jiblah was the seat of power of one of Yemen's greatest and most fondly remembered rulers. Queen Sayyida Arwa bint Ahmed ruled most of Yemen from the town during one of the country's most brilliant periods.

History In the 11th century the future Queen Arwa was born in the Haraz Mountains as Sayyida bint Ahmed while 'Ali bin Sulayhi, her uncle and future father-in-law, had conquered and ruled most of Yemen. Arwa was educated within the royal palace at Sana'a under the tutelage of 'Ali al-Sulayhi's wife, Queen Asma. Like 'Ali, Arwa was taught at a young age about the Isma'ili Fatimid position. Also like her future father-in-law, there were reputed premonitions regarding her rise to power. Whereas 'Ali's name was said to have been written in a book of the occult, predictions about Arwa's future came from her dreams and from the presages of 'Ali.

Before 'Ali was killed at the hands of an old rival from Tihama, Arwa married 'Ali's son al-Mukarram Ahmed al-Sulayhi. As a dowry, she was given the yearly revenue of Aden – over £500,000 in today's market. Not a bad wedding gift when you get to marry the prince.

When 'Ali al-Sulayhi died, al-Mukarram succeeded him as head of state. He deferred often to the counsel of his mother, Queen Asma, and when she died he requested Queen Arwa rule the country. It is not exactly clear why the transfer of power took place – historical sources from the time disagree over whether al-Mukarram had been paralysed or had merely given himself over to the pleasures of music and wine.

Queen Arwa moved the state capital from Sana'a to Jiblah sometime after she assumed control in 1063. When she made the move, Jiblah was a small city that had been built 25 years prior – only slightly older than Arwa herself. The town was named after a Jewish potter who may have still been working there when Arwa transferred her seat of authority.

Tales from the time relate that prior to the move Arwa had asked al-Mukarram to look down at the people from their palace in Sana'a. Doing so, he saw the knife- and sword-wielding Sana'anis going about their business. Taking her husband to

Jiblah, she asked him to do the same. As they looked down on the inhabitants of the small town, they only saw farmers and merchants. The contrast was compelling. The royal couple moved to the town, converted the palace there to the Great Mosque, and built a new palace named Dar al-'Izz.

Arwa's choice in Jiblah reflected the style of her rule well. While the political intrigues of Sana'a suited the military style of her father-in-law, Arwa was known to rule for the most part by wit and diplomacy. She did, however, find it necessary to battle frequently with the Najahids, the rival power with whom 'Ali al-Sulayhi had fought before her.

For the most part though, Queen Arwa was concerned with public works, trade and religion. She is said to have used an entire year's budget on the construction of aqueducts, bridges, and roads. Her construction of aqueducts in places like Jiblah and neighbouring Yafrus earned her the enduring nickname 'Arwa' – *thirst quencher*. Under Arwa's rule, the Sulayhids maintained close contact with the Fatimids in Egypt, and Jiblah became a commercial and educational capital of the region. In religious affairs, although Arwa was never promoted to the position of *di'a*, the title of the highest-ranking religious leader short of the imam, she was promoted to the position of *hujja* – a role which had never been held by a woman before.

In addition to the mosque that bears her name, Queen Arwa also constructed a number of other mosques and schools in Jiblah. Taking after the tradition of the previous Sulayhids, Queen Arwa stressed sexual equality, and the number of mosques and schools were split equally for men and women. Of course, a look at the distribution today reveals how the importance of equality has fallen since Arwa's time – of the 37 mosques in Jiblah, only one is reserved for women.

After al-Mukarram died, the queen was sought in marriage by Saba' bin Ahmed, one of her advisors and military generals. When Arwa promptly refused his proposal, he decided to woo her by attacking her palace. Arwa was not amused by this display of machismo, and her rejection remained steadfast. Informed by Arwa's brother-in-law that nothing short of a command from the Fatimid Imam in Egypt would change her mind, Saba' sent messengers to fetch a decree from the imam. With a little creative fabrication regarding Arwa's standpoint, the messengers were able to convince the imam to order the marriage.

5

If Saba' had thought his plan through a little more carefully, he might have also requested that he and Arwa be married in more than anything but name. When he returned to Jiblah with the marriage decree, he was accepted into the town as Arwa's husband, but was refused entrance into the queen's palace. After a humiliating several-week stint waiting on the palace grounds, he begged Arwa to let him enter the palace for one evening to validate his position before the people. Arwa assented, but when night fell, she sent to his room a slave girl who bore a fair resemblance to her. Saba' understood her message perfectly, and consummation was not discussed again.

Toward the end of Arwa's reign there were several schisms among the Fatimids in Egypt. When the imam who had ordered her marriage died, the Isma'ili Fatimids split over the support of his two sons, Nizar and Musta'ili. After Musta'ili and his son died, his supporters were further split between his grandson, Tayyib, who mysteriously disappeared, and his other son, al-Hafiz, who was all too quick and eager to take the religious throne. Arwa supported the position of Tayyib, and Isma'ili tradition holds that Musta'ili's son had sent word to Arwa to appoint the *di'a al-mutlak* in the imam's absence. Arwa's stance did not go down well with the supporters of al-Hafiz in Egypt, but the Tayyibis ultimately carried the day.

It is very interesting, of course, to see the fond attachment Yemenis have to Queen Arwa – for a woman who ruled by diplomacy, she is revered as one of the greatest Yemeni leaders by conflict-prone, male-oriented Yemenis. The historian 'Omarah wrote that Arwa was: 'perfect in beauty, of a clear-sounding voice, well read and a skilful writer, her memory stored with history, with poetry, and with the chronology of past times.' Ask your average Yemeni about her today – you will probably get a similar response.

Getting there Shared taxis shuttle passengers to and from Ibb (50YR, ½hr).

Where to stay

🏠 **Funduq ar-Riyan** (25 rooms) al-'Am St; ☎ 04 451499. This standard Yemeni-style hotel is your only option in Jiblah. If you are dead set on staying in Jiblah, it should suit you fine. Otherwise, there are better options in neighbouring Ibb. $

What to see The **Queen Arwa Mosque** was converted into the current religious structure from the palace that existed on the spot in 1088, shortly after Arwa moved her state capital to Jiblah. Like the Fatimid architecture and designs of its time, the mosque is quite elaborate, although time has taken its toll. An extensive renovations project began in 2000, but given the pace of the work and the number of tasks remaining, the local villagers are under no illusion that the renovations will be finished any time soon.

With supervision, non-Muslims will be allowed to enter through one of the side gates to walk into the mosque's pillar-surrounded courtyard, where water carried from the mountains above fill a central pool. In the courtyard, you will be able to peer through the windows into the prayer hall, but it is unlikely that non-Muslims will be allowed to enter. Small groups or modestly dressed visitors who ask politely stand the best chance of acquiring permission to enter.

One of the mosque's four entrances, located on the northern side by the marketplace, still has the original wooden door carved with intricate designs and Koranic inscriptions. The tomb of Queen Arwa is situated near the northern wall of the mosque. There are two minarets – the one by the southwest corner dates back to the construction of the mosque, although there have been several renovations since then.

Since 1965 the Jiblah Hospital was operated by the Southern Baptist International Mission Board. In 2002, the IMB had decided to turn over the ownership and management of the hospital to a local Muslim charity at the end of December of that year. By that time, the hospital was treating roughly 40,000 patients per year. The day before the change in management took place, a man walked into the hospital carrying an AK-47 wrapped in swaddling cloths. Claiming that the semi-automatic rifle was a child in urgent need of medical attention, the man rushed into the hospital, unveiled the weapon, and shot four of the American workers. Only one survived. The shooter was immediately apprehended and given the death sentence a year later.

Several months later, a second armed man tried the same thing. Luckily, the newly installed metal detectors alerted security officials before anything happened. The attacks were widely criticised at both a local and governmental level throughout the country.

The hospital reopened under Yemeni management as originally planned early in 2003. Despite the 2002 killings, many of the American and other foreign staff who had worked there previously have remained, and the Jiblah Hospital continues to treat Yemenis from all over the country. The top floor of the Queen Arwa Museum now contains a room dedicated to the work of the hospital and the three Americans who died in the attack.

Queen Arwa's former palace, **Bayt al-'Izz** ('The House of Glory'), no longer lives up to its name. The old palace is in severe disrepair. Although there are plans to restore the palace in several years' time, the schedule and progress of the renovations on the Queen Arwa Mosque do not give any cause for hope. In any event, there is some debate about whether the ruins are of Arwa's original palace or merely another palace built at a later date. Even if it is the latter, the materials used to construct the building would have been those from the original palace.

Standing on the ruins of Bayt al-'Izz, it is possible to see the small village of as-Safā ('the Cleansed One') below. Local legend holds that the villagers of as-Safā led an attack on Jiblah several centuries prior, and that in retaliation Jiblah launched a counter-attack and expelled the troublesome inhabitants. Thus, the village derived its name from being 'cleansed' of its troublemakers.

The **Queen Arwa Museum** (⊕ *08.00–18.00; entrance fee 500YR*) is located near the site of Bayt al-'Izz. The layout of the building resembles more of a shrine to Queen Arwa than a museum, giving the building a distinct personality. There are several floors of items relating to the queen as well as some odd life-sized mock-ups of individuals engaged in everyday activities. The top floor of the museum has a room dedicated to the work of the Jiblah Baptist Hospital, but conspicuously there is no mention anywhere of the recent massacre (see box above).

Perhaps the most interesting part of the museum is a peculiar contrast between the first and second floors. On the upper floor, a plaque states that Queen Arwa 'had such a great deeds for the country and people that kings would be shame to stand up beside such woman'. President Ali Abdullah Saleh, of course, feels no such shame. On the first-floor entrance there is a larger-than-life portrait of the president with accompanying text comparing his tenure in office to the reign of the famous queen.

On a small winding path leading down from the museum, you will come across the **Sheikh Yakub Mosque** ('the mosque of Jacob'). The villagers claim that this mosque is the oldest one in Jiblah, having existed as the town's sole mosque before

Arwa arrived and transformed the old palace into the grander mosque bearing her name. The small mosque is built with a simple white dome. Non-Muslims who ask politely may be allowed to peek or step inside.

Below the Sheikh Yakub Mosque, in the lower part of the town, there are several stone-arched bridges, one of which is said to date back to the time of Queen Arwa. The new stone roads of the town, however, only date back to 2004, when they were built by the government to celebrate the 14th anniversary of the country's unification.

DHAFAR

With a new paved road from Dhamar, the trip to Dhafar now takes about 30 minutes, as opposed to the several-hour journey it once took to reach the village on then disastrous roads. Furthermore, thanks to the continuing work of the Universität Heidelberg Jemen-Expidition, more and more of the ancient Himyarite capital is opening up to observation.

HISTORY The early fortifications of Dhafar are believed to have been built early in the 1st century AD after the Kingdom of Himyar had made inroads in subduing parts of the Sabaean Kingdom, although the settlement was likely in existence for sometime before that. The city is mentioned in Pliny's *Natural History*, written in the 1st century and referred to as being the residence of the king. The city is also mentioned in the book of Genesis as the general area where the sons of Qahtan had settled.

After conquering the Sabaeans, the Himyarites still faced battles with the Abyssinians of the neighbouring Kingdom of Hadhramawt. In the 3rd century, the castle of Raydan was attacked by the Christian Abyssinians of Ethiopia – the main Himyarite rival for control of Yemen. The attack was repelled and the castle walls were refortified. The Himyarite Kingdom's other rival, the Kingdom of Hadhramawt, was finally conquered during the reign of the Himyarite King Shamar Yuhar'esh. He managed to bring much of Yemen under his power, and demonstrated the unity of the country by becoming the first king to take the title 'King of Saba', Dhu-Raydan, Hadhramawt and Yamanat'. Like many of the kings after him, he decided that a new palace was in order to celebrate his victories.

In the 4th century King Malikkarib Yuha'min built the castle of Shawhatan, sister fortress to Raydan Palace. Inscriptions in Dhafar during the king's reign state that the new palace was built under the power of ar-Rahman, the lord of heaven, showing that the Himyarite rulers were abandoning the polytheistic religions of the past. This acceptance of monotheism made the transition to accepting Judaism and Christianity in Dhafar easier. Within a decade of Malikkarib's rule, the first evidence of a Jewish presence in Yemen appeared – a converted member to the religion noted his affiliation in the dedication inscription of his newly constructed home. According to the 4th-century Christian scholar Philostorgius, Emperor Constantine II sent a Christian mission to the Himyarites. The embassy was sent under the command of Bishop Theophilus Indus of Socotra, who had been part of the Christian community on the island supposedly founded by Thomas, the disciple of Jesus. With over 200 horses and chests of treasures, Theophilus was successful in impressing the Himyarite ruler of the time and was permitted to begin construction on a church in the city. King Abu Karib As'ad – known in popular lore as As'ad al-Kamil ('the perfect one') – announced his official conversion to monotheism at the end of the 4th century. (Stories of As'ad al-Kamal abound in local legends; try to fish out some good ones from the clamouring congregation of people vying to be your guide through the ancient sites.)

Although the church in Dhafar had previously been destroyed during the reign of Jewish King Dhu Nuwas, Christianity revived in the region under the Aksumite ruler Abrahah. Early on, many Jewish public circles throughout the country still wielded considerable power. The political confrontation between the groups made religious discussions the fashion of the day. A large public debate was scheduled to be held at the citadel of Raydan in Dhafar in the 6th century AD. Two highly respected scholars stepped into the ring: in the left corner, with long flowing *simonem* (the Yemenite word for sidelocks) and holding the Torah was the learned Jewish doctor Herban; in the right corner, garbed in fashionable shorts from Milan and Alexandria and holding an icon of the Virgin Mary was the esteemed Bishop Gregentius.

OK, so the debate did not break down into fisticuffs, but it was a large event nonetheless. In attendance were Abrahah, a number of bishops and Jewish scholars, and the entire town of Dhafar. The debate is preserved by reproduction in a 16th-century work known as *Disputatio cum Herbano Iudaeo*, thought by some to have been originally authored by Gregentius. The story relayed in the *Disputatio* no doubt contains a bit of healthy exaggeration, eventually disintegrating into a surreal narrative of the miracles that took place at the end of the debate. The actual substance of the debate, however, is likely quite near the mark, and was probably written down by Gregentius's scribe, Palladius of Alexandria. The work details in relative fairness three days of debate between the two heavyweights, ranging from Old Testament interpretation to the nature of God.

When the two men had argued themselves into a virtual standstill, the text states that the debate ended with the miraculous appearance of Jesus in the sky. Like Saul on the road to Damascus, the Jewish observers are all said to have gone blind at the vision. After their conversion and baptism, their sight was restored. The text claims that the appearance of Jesus led to the conversion of over five million Jews to Christianity – impressive as the figure is likely larger than the entire Jewish population of the world at the time.

At the conclusion of the debate, Gregentius successfully persuaded Abrahah to enact measures that would help 'mingle' the two groups. Accordingly, a law was passed that on pain of death all Jewish boys and girls would need to marry Christians before their 13th birthday – an interesting break from the Justinian code, which forbade Christians and Jews to marry.

Continuing with the Saul/Paul allusion, Abrahah gave the newly Catholicised Herban the name of Leo and appointed him to his royal council. Gregentius, later canonised by the Church, is believed to have died in Dhafar and was buried at the church that was rebuilt there (and of course, later destroyed). His feast day is celebrated in other parts of the world on 19 December.

During the 5th century, Sharahbeel Ya'fur built another palace in Dhafar – you can never have too many in one town! The residents of Dhafar primarily speak of three kings when recalling the Himyarites: Sharahbeel Ya'fur, As'ad al-Kamil, and Shamar Yuhar'esh.

In the early 6th century, the Abyssinians had once again made their way to Dhafar, but this time they were not entirely unwelcome. By the time they returned, King Ma'adikarib had converted to Christianity, but Christianity's reign as the state religion of the Himyarites was short lived. The next king Yusuf As'ar Ya'tar, known as Dhu Nuwas, accepted Judaism and did not deal kindly with his Christian subjects. Accordingly, the church in Dhafar was destroyed, and the Abyssinians were expelled. Dhu Nuwas's treatment of Christian subjects throughout the country sparked an international outcry, prompting his overthrow by another Abyssinian invasion. The Himyarite Kingdom officially ended, and Dhafar began its slide into obscurity.

GETTING THERE Public transportation is not available to get to Dhafar. You will have to arrange travel with a tour agency or hire a local car in Yarim (5,000YR) for a round-trip journey.

WHAT TO SEE The **Dhafar Museum** (*open on request; entrance fee: 500YR*) is at the top of the road that leads to the village. Despite Dhafar's period as the capital of the Himyarite Kingdom, the museum is a little run down and not as impressive as the newer museum at Baynun. Still, there are some good artefacts to see, including displays on visual arts, finds from various archaeological sites, and information on the religion and history of Himyar. Large posters throughout the several rooms provide good discussion in both English and Arabic.

Around the side of the museum are several large fields that contain **cemeteries**. The gravesites aren't marked, so be sure to walk along the clearly indicated paths to avoid trampling over the tombs and upsetting the locals. The path continues down and around the hillside, where there are plenty of interesting rooms carved into the rocks. Before monotheism caught on in Dhafar, many of these rooms were used for soothsaying. Other rooms were used as storage containers or tombs. The stairs leading to a small chamber under the mosque may be the site of the original church.

On the nearby hill lie the remains of the old **castle of Raydan** (2,910m). Only the remnants of a few walls and ruined houses remain. Like most sites around, a majority of the blocks have been carried off for use in modern residences. Some of the sites are now fenced off. The top of the peak hosts the scattered remains of more recent abodes. Heading toward the remains from the village, there is a set of tombs on the right, down the slope, that were discovered in 2002 and that date back to the 2nd century AD. The locals claim that there were mummies found within.

Walking around and passing over the old stones and carved-out rooms, the words of the Nashwan al-Himyar's *Himyarite Epic* seem particularly relevant:

Where are the kings of Himyar? A thousand kings have sunk into the dust and now rest under the ground in vaults and in tombs.
But their monuments all through the land still tell of their deeds, and in books their true tales are proclaimed.

(Translated by Al-Qadi Isma'il bin 'Ali al-Akwa)

OUTSIDE DHAFAR

Just outside Dhafar, there is an old **Himyarite Dam** that is now used as the local swimming pool for the children of the area during the rainy season. For a larger collection of Himyarite stones and relief carvings, the small village of **Bayt al-Ashwal** has an excellent collection. Most of the buildings have been constructed out of the stones from the old palaces, and plenty of carvings have been added for flair.

Driving along the road from Dhafar to Hammam Damt, you will pass a small, roped-off section of ruins. The site of this old house was discovered during the construction of the road. From here, there is a path that leads up the mountain to the few remains of the **castle of King Shamar Yuhar'esh**, who was the first to use the title King of Saba', Dhu-Raydan, Hadhramawt and Yamanat. At the very top of the mountain, you can have the very peculiar sensation of receiving small electrical jolts from the rocks underneath you. While the water trapped by the porous rocks likely cause the slight shocks, I prefer the explanation of Radhwan: the jinn who built the palace haunt it still.

Farther down the road is the village of Kohall, known predominantly as the hometown of the late Yemeni Socialist Party leader Jar Allah Omar. In 2002, Jar Allah gave a speech condemning violence and revenge killing in Yemen at the general conference of the Islah Party. Shortly after he finished he was assassinated. His death was a great political shock to the country.

The area is well known for the lush **Wadi Bana**, which runs through the region, providing water and beautiful waterfalls that seem quite out of place on the Arabian Peninsula. The road continues to **Hammam Damt**, but the asphalt way has not yet been completed. From the town of **an-Naderah**, you will need a 4x4 vehicle to reach Hammam Damt.

TA'IZ

Capital of Yemen during one of the country's most brilliant periods, Ta'iz enjoys a position today as a major economic centre. Like Sana'a, the walled-in Old City hosts an open air market, where merchants sell items ranging from antique silver pieces to rounds of cheese and dried fish. The city offers an opportunity for a well-rounded visit: after exploring the 14th-century mosques you can relax over a glass of tea at a café overlooking the city.

HISTORY While Ta'iz maintains a position as one of Yemen's major cities today, its initial development came much later than the cities of Sana'a or Aden. The nearby town of al-Janad, one of the country's three main early Islamic centres along with Sana'a and Hadhramawt, acted as the region's unofficial capital from the beginning of the Islamic age through well into the Middle Ages.

Ta'iz is first mentioned in the late 12th century AD during the reign of the Ayyubids – the forces which had first been led by Saladin's brother Turanshah. At that time, the quarterly revenue of the port city of Aden was brought to Ta'iz. Previously, the money had been given to Queen Arwa in nearby Jiblah (as part of her dowry arrangement), and it is likely that the Ayyubids simply diverted the funds to Ta'iz as they came to power.

While these funds were used for a variety of projects, they also likely helped in the initial development of the city. The city's first major growth, however, took place during the time of the subsequent Rasulids, the dynasty which peacefully assumed the reigns from the Ayyubids in AD1229.

The Rasulids not only tremendously expanded the city during their tenure, but from their seat in governance in Ta'iz, they ushered in one of the most prosperous periods of Yemeni history. Construction was abundant, studies of the arts and sciences flourished, and a rare peace was maintained in much of the country for nearly 50 years.

The city was visited by the explorer Ibn Battutah in 1377. The geographer found the city to be 'one of the finest and largest' in the country, but found the people to be as 'overbearing, insolent and rude' as any who dwell 'in towns where kings reside.' While the city today is one of the largest and most populated of the country, luckily the people no longer have a reputation for surliness.

The city was used as a capital of the country one other time. In 1948, a group called the Free Yemeni Movement assassinated Imam Yahya but failed to kill his son Ahmed. With the assistance of tribal forces, Ahmed quickly ended the attempted coup, initiated a mass number of executions, devastated the city of Sana'a, and moved his capital to Ta'iz. The city remained the capital of North Yemen until the 1962 revolution.

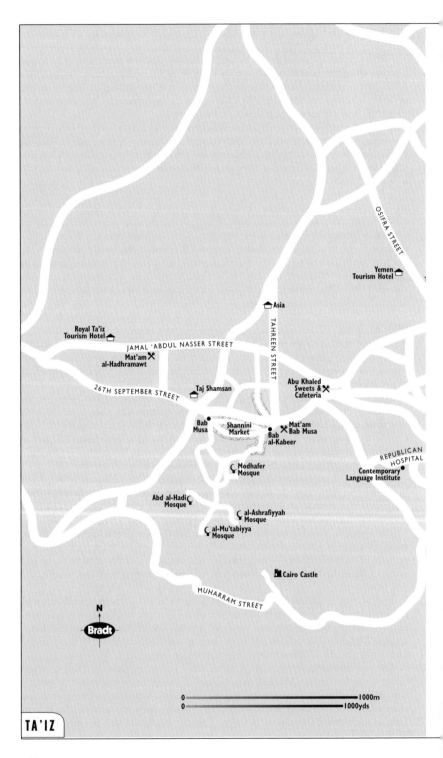

Yemen
Tourism Hotel

OSIFRA STREET

Asia

Royal Ta'iz
Tourism Hotel

JAMAL 'ABDUL NASSER STREET

Mat'am
al-Hadhramawt

TAHREEN STREET

26TH SEPTEMBER STREET

Taj Shamsan

Abu Khaled
Sweets &
Cafeteria

Bab
Musa

Shannini
Market

Mat'am
Bab Musa

Bab
al-Kabeer

REPUBLICAN
HOSPITAL

Modhafer
Mosque

Contemporary
Language Institute

Abd al-Hadi
Mosque

al-Ashrafiyyah
Mosque

al-Mu'tabiyya
Mosque

Cairo Castle

N

Bradt

MUHARRAM STREET

0   1000m
0   1000yds

TA'IZ

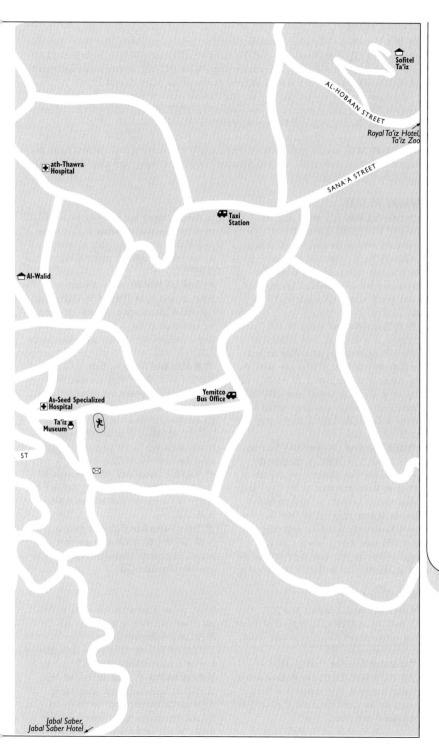

Sofitel
Ta'iz

AL-HOBAAN STREET

Royal Ta'iz Hotel,
Ta'iz Zoo

SANA'A STREET

ath-Thawra
Hospital

Taxi
Station

Al-Walid

As-Seed Specialized
Hospital

Yemitco
Bus Office

Ta'iz
Museum

ST

Jabal Saber,
Jabal Saber Hotel

GETTING THERE

By bus Yemitco (office located in front of the Republican Palace) has buses leaving for Sana'a (1,250YR, 5hrs), Ibb (600YR, 1½hrs), Dhamar (800YR, 3½hrs) at 11.00 and 18.00. Buses also head southward toward Aden (600YR, 2½hrs) and Hudaydah (1,000YR, 4hrs), leaving the road in front of the office at 09.00 and 16.30.

Al-Esayi buses (office located on the eastern side of the Ring Road, heading toward Sana'a) travel twice-daily to Sana'a (1,100YR, 5hrs), Ibb (300YR, 1½hrs), Aden (600YR, 2½hrs), and Hudaydah (900YR, 4hrs).

By shared taxi Bijous gather on the eastern side of the Ring Road across from al-Hayat Hospital. Full taxis head to Sana'a (1,000YR, 4½hrs), Ibb (350YR, 1½hrs), and Aden (650YR, 2hrs).

WHERE TO STAY

Sofitel Ta'iz Hotel (135 rooms) Jabal ad-Domaleh; ℄ 04 200311; f 04 200312; www.accoryemen.com. The hotel, perched on Jabal ad-Domaleh 'like an eagle's nest', is the cream of the Ta'izi crop. Facilities include a cosmopolitan restaurant (meals: 800–2,500YR), a swimming pool, sauna, gym, & business centre (internet: 35YR/min). $$$$$

Taj Shamsan Hotel (64 rooms) Off 26th September St by Bab Musa; ℄ 04 236514; f 04 236513; e tajshamsan@y.net.ye. While not as nice as either the Jabal Saber or Sofitel (see below), the Taj Shamsan is the best hotel in the vicinity of the city centre. There is an internet room (20YR/min) & fitness centre as well as a restaurant serving a variety of dishes (500–1,800YR). Accepts credit cards. $$$$. B&B.

Jabal Saber Hotel (24 rooms) Jabal Saber Rd; ℄ 04 261860; f 04 261861; e saberhotel@accoryemen.com; www.accoryemen.com. Originally a gift to the Yemeni government by UAE Sheikh Zayed whose ancestral home was in Yemen, the hotel is now run by Accor, along with the Sofitel Ta'iz. The rooms are wonderful, & with the suites being a mere US$5 more, there is no reason not to upgrade. There are great views of the city from the private balconies. Since the hotel is over halfway up

the mountain, staying here is very inconvenient if you do not have your own vehicle. If you're in the mood to throw a qat-chewing party to remember, you can rent the *majlis* with panoramic views for 35,000YR. $$$

Royal Ta'iz Hotel (49 rooms) al-Hobaan St. (before the zoo); ℄ 04 285994; f 04 285999. With very clean & spacious rooms, the hotel is one of the best-value places to stay in Ta'iz if you don't mind being a drive outside of the city centre. $$; suites $$$.

Al-Walid Hotel (61 rooms) Osifra St; ℄ 04 253000; f 04 253004. Al-Walid is a newer hotel that has quickly dilapidated. Opt instead for Yemen Tourism across the street. $$

Asia Hotel (30 rooms) Tahreer St; ℄ 04 254463; f 04 254508; e asiahotel@hotmail.com. Pleasant rooms with Western toilets, each equipped with either an AC unit or ceiling fan. $$

Royal Ta'iz Tourism Hotel (40 rooms) Jamal St (opposite Yemen National Bank); ℄ 04 250876; f 04 250875. Nice rooms with small balconies & Western toilets. $$

Yemen Tourism Hotel (52 rooms) Osifra St; ℄ 04 253999; f 04 253088. While the rooms are relatively standard, the attached restaurant serves up immensely tasty dishes. $$

WHERE TO EAT

Abu Khaled Sweets & Cafeteria Jamal St, ◷ 06.00–10.30, 12.00–15.30, 19.00–22.30. Popular local eatery that puts more effort into the dessert than the main course. $$

Al-Shaibani Restaurant ◷ 06.00–10.30, 12.00–15.30, 19.00–22.30. Serves the same kind of dishes that made its sister restaurants in Sana'a famous. The fish is the normal dish of choice. $$

Layalia al-'Arab ('Arabian Nights') ◷ 06.00–10.30, 12.00–15.30, 19.00–22.30.

Another popular restaurant located on the northern side of town, specializing in meat dishes. $$

Mat'am al-Hadhramawt Off Jamal St, ◷ 06.00–10.30, 12.00–15.30, 19.00–22.30. Serves a variety of standard Yemeni dishes. $$

Mat'am Bab Musa ◷ 06.00–10.30, 12.00–15.30, 19.00–22.30. Tiny restaurant with outside seating located outside the main entrance to the old city souk. Ask them to make the ful with the local Ta'izi cheese ('Ful ma'a juben Ta'izi'). $

OTHER PRACTICALITIES As one of the country's larger cities, Ta'iz offers more options for hospitals, banks, and learning opportunities than other nearby cities. The two best hospitals are reputed to be **ath-Thawra Hospital** (✆ *04 205500*) and **as-Saeed Specialized Hospital** (✆ *04 216219*). ATMs are available, and the **CAC Bank** (✆ *04 210480*) and the **International Bank of Yemen** (✆ *04 233646*) are both located on Jamal St. For shipping needs, you can find a DHL (*04 252455*) and a FedEx (*04 260500*) on Jamal St. as well.

The **Contemporary Language Institute** (*Republican Hospital St;* ✆ *04 216208; www.clarabic.com*) is given rave reviews by foreigners who are studying there. A variety of terms is available, and a complete course in Arabic for 77 weeks only costs US$3,640.

WHAT TO SEE AND DO

Ta'iz Museum (☉ *08.30–13.00, Sat–Wed; entrance fee 500YR*) The building was the former palace of Imam Ahmed. Ahmed died in the building in 1962, several weeks before the northern revolution began. Everything in the house has been exactly the way it was since the imam lived there, as a reminder of his lifestyle.

Old City/Shannini Market The Old City of Ta'iz has two entrances – Bab al-Kabeer ('the Great Gate') and Bab Musa ('the Gate of Moses'). The walled-in section of town contains a lovely souk that specialises in a delicious kind of Ta'iz cheese, dried fish ('*wazif*') and silver jewellery.

Cairo Castle The large fortification is currently being renovated using river stones and original building techniques. The interior of the building is currently being used as a military station, but the outer grounds are worth a walk anyway. The inside is planned to open with a small museum by late 2008.

Al-Ashrafiyyah Mosque The large al-Ashrafiyyah Mosque is one of the few mosques in Yemen that tourists are permitted to enter. Women should cover their hair, and both sexes should adorn moderate clothing. You will be able to walk around the grounds and see the tombs of al-Ashrafa, his wife, his father, his sons, and his primary security guard, as well as take one step into the mosque proper to admire the decorative work. The tomb markings signify the location of the actual graves in rooms below. There are many lovely reliefs inside.

A secret door was found in 2005 leading to an underground room. Supposedly, many of the local governmental officials flocked here when the rumours got out in the hope of unearthing large treasures that might be stored within. However, as Ahmed Abdullah, the mosque groundskeeper, explains, 'they were Muslims, not Pharoahs'. No treasures were found – only the tombs.

You should complete your tour of the mosque with a 300–400YR payment to the groundskeeper who shows you around.

Al-Mu'tabiyya Mosque The neighbouring al-Mu'tabiyya Mosque was built by al-Ashrafa in honour of his wife 23 years after the construction of his mosque. Both al-Ashrafa and his wife, Mu'tabia are buried in the al-Ashrafiyya Mosque. The two mosques were built with similar design, although the al-Mu'tabiyya is characterised by a large number of domes. Like its partner mosque, al-Mu'tabiyya is filled with designs and inscriptions. There are no tombs. The mosque used to be reserved for women to pray, but eventually the men decided they did not have enough space, and took it for themselves.

Abd al-Hadi Mosque The Abd al-Hadi mosque was built in 1618 in commemoration of a Sufi saint of the same name who had died a hundred years

On the road up to the top of Jabal Saber, you will pass the small town of al-'Aroos ('the Bride'), which is believed by some Yemenis as the location of one of the Koran's more interesting stories.

After Muhammad had made his claim to prophethood, several members of the Quraysh tribe in Mecca sought the advice of the Jewish Rabbis in Medina as to how they might know whether Muhammad was a true prophet. The rabbis gave a list of three things about which they should question Muhammad: the people of old, a great traveller, and the nature of the soul.

Two weeks after the Muhammad was asked the questions, he returned with the revelation of *Ahl al-Kahaf* ('the People of the Cave'), now the 18th chapter of the Koran. In answering the first question, Muhammad told the story of a small group of people who had been faithful to God despite the idolatry of all other people nearby. Fearful for their lives, the select few (and their pet dog) took refuge in a cave and entered a deep slumber, only waking much later in time.

Although not mentioned in the Koran, several flavourful details usually accompany the story. The cave dwellers are said to have slept for several hundred years. By the time they woke, the people of the surrounding villages had returned to the Islamic fold. Not knowing the time that had passed, however, one of the cave dwellers fearfully ventured into town to buy some food. When the man tried to pay for his bread, the villagers were astounded to see his antique coin in mint condition. After a bit of questioning by both sides, everyone gradually came to understand what had happened.

In the town of al-'Aroos on Jabal Saber there is a mosque above a small cavern that houses seven tombs. Many locals believe these tombs belonged to these 'People of the Cave'. In fact, the town sign has recently been altered to read *Ahl al-Kahaf* ('People of the Cave'), in an attempt to better advertise the town's connection with the legend.

earlier. There is a large grave monument to al-Hadi inside the structure. Scholars and others particularly interested in Sufi practices of the region may be able to attend the religious services on Mondays and Thursdays.

Modhafer Mosque The Modhafer Mosque is the oldest mosque in Ta'iz, built by and named after the great-grandfather of al-Ashrafa. It has a minaret with two, large white domes.

Ta'iz Zoo Ta'iz Zoo sits at the fringes of the city, and contains a number of sad-looking lions and baboons. If you come for a visit, keep your eye out for the mysterious **al-Hawban Tahesh**, a near-mythical lion-like beast said to have unnatural speed that haunts the hills of Ta'iz.

Jabal Saber The peak of Jabal Saber, the mountain which overlooks Ta'iz, tops out at over 3,000m. The villages dotting the mountainside are best known for their women, skilled bargainers who wear bright *baltos* and who are famed for their beauty. In the souks of Ta'iz below, it is they who are responsible for selling the qat.

OUTSIDE TA'IZ

AL-JANAD The small town of al-Janad was one of the earliest and most important Islamic centres in the country. Along with Sana'a and Hadhramawt, the city had its governors appointed from the ruling power at Medina, followed by the rulers of the Umayyad Caliphate.

During the Abbasid reign, a number of people from al-Janad killed the local governor's representative in a revolt against his cruel and callous method of ruling. The governor was not pleased, and responding with heavy military power, he had over 2,000 of al-Janad's inhabitants massacred.

Getting there To get to al-Janad, take the road between Ta'iz and Ibb and turn off on the road bearing out of the town of **Mafrag Mawwia**.

What to see The **al-Janad Mosque** was the first mosque constructed in Yemen, built during Muhammad's lifetime. Some features of the mosque grounds, such as the baths and minarets, were built by the Turkish later. Many of the pillars have carvings in old Kufic script. You may be able to enter and explore the mosque with a local guide if you are invited to do so. If you do, it is appropriate to give a small donation (300–500YR) to the mosque afterwards.

There is a small building in disrepair next to the mosque that may have been an old church from the time of Abrahah. It now houses two graves, one from about 900 years ago and another from the 20th century.

THE WESTERN ROAD TO ADEN

There are two ways to get to Aden from Ta'iz. The eastern road is quicker, but the western route has a number of interesting stopping points, including Yafrus, Wadi Mogatara and ash-Shamsara.

YAFRUS The small town of Yafrus is centred on the small but important **Sheikh Ahmed bin Alwan Mosque**. Sheikh bin Alwan was an important Sufi leader in Yemen who wrote many treatises and books of poetry and who is said to have died in 1142 at the age of 117. The mosque sprang up around his grave in the early 13th century, and it has served as an important pilgrimage site for members of the Sufi faith since then. Like most Sufi sites in Yemen, the mosque has had its share of hardships as well. The dome was destroyed by Imam Ahmed in 1929.

Besides the pilgrims who come to worship at the shrine, others come to benefit from the mythical properties associated with the area. In particular, some people perform animal sacrifices or deposit offerings of honey or incense in front of the mosque to honour bin Alwan and thus gain favour from God by proxy. The pool of water inside is said to help people recover from diseases.

ASH-SHAMSARA With its large quantity of local restaurants and food stores, the town is a good place to base yourself in if you want to do any hiking in the surrounding mountain areas, which are full of old fortifications and amazing views. There is also a weekly market on Friday, when the town serves as the gathering point for the surrounding mountain villages of al-Hajjarah.

Inside the town there is a huge **baobab tree** known as *Shajara ibn Ghareeb*, which roughly means 'the Tree of the Stranger.' (The name seems appropriate, given that the tree most likely originally came from Africa.)

WADI MOGATARA The zealous Ministry of Public Works and Roads has not completed the paved road from Ta'iz to Aden. There is a bumpy 19km section of the road running through **Wadi Mogatara** that can only be traversed with a 4x4 vehicle. Driving through the wadi, you'll pass a number of small villages, including **Souk ar-Rabu'** ('the Wednesday Market'), which, appropriately enough, has a market on Wednesday.

Well associated with the Sheikh Ahmed bin Alwan Mosque are a travelling group of mystics known as the majadheeb ('the charmed ones'). Similar to the 'holy fools' of the Russian tradition, the majadheeb exude a brand of holiness through insanity.

Although the majadheeb travel alone or in small numbers singing songs and reciting poetry, they are best known for their more mystical acts. Those who have seen the majadheeb perform state that, as their dancing intensifies, they stab themselves with their jambiyyas. Although they appear to be fatally wounding themselves, the knives leave no injuries whatsoever. In another attempt to demonstrate their questionable decision making skills and imperviousness to injury, the majadheeb also regularly eat shards of broken glass. Donations are welcome.

Even though many majadheeb may fall closer toward the psychic surgeon category than true Sufi mystic, they definitely are an interesting lot. According to local legend, the Yemeni majadheeb originated during the time of Sheikh bin Alwan's lifetime. In response to continued hardships the Sufi sheikh suffered at the hands of a nearby minister and his followers, bin Alwan prayed for God's protection. After the sheikh's supplication, bin Alwan's tormentors (and apparently their descendants) became divinely inflicted with holy madness. Since that time they have found it necessary to move throughout the country as beggars, regarding bin Alwan (who is supposedly responsible for their state) as their patron saint.

Coming from Aden to Ta'iz, the asphalt starts again once you leave the wadi at Najd al-Bared and begin the climb back into the mountains. Before you finish the ascent, there is a turn-off that takes you through a tunnel largely cleared by pickaxe. In 2002, after centuries of carrying seeds and flour over the mountaintop, the villagers decided that they had had enough. Twenty of the locals banded together with pickaxes and began to chisel their way through the stone. These few men did most of the tunneling by themselves, but government intervention with dynamite was needed for portions of the rock that were too hard to be picked away.

The tunnel leads to the area known as **Mogatara al-Gharbi**. Driving is not possible, as the road ends shortly after the tunnel's end (although there are plans to connect it to other roads in the region). The area has a very peaceful and secluded feel, and it could provide great trekking opportunities. A walking path leads down to the village of **Khizfar**, and another hour-and-a-half's trek takes you to **as-Swayt**, an old Turkish fortification on a mountaintop. Supposedly, on a clear day, you can look out from the fortress and see all the way to Aden.

TAWR AL-BAHAH This small agricultural town with its decent-sized souk lies 97km northwest of Aden. The few farms surrounding the town grow dates and various other vegetables. The larger, weekly souk takes place on Saturday. There are five local restaurants here, all serving up similar fare.

6

Central Desert

Telephone code 06

From the mountainous areas of the west extending to and north of Hadhramawt in the east, Yemen is comprised of an awful lot of sand. Nearest to Sana'a, beginning around the area of Marib is the area known as Ramlat as-Sabatayn ('the Sands of the Two Sevens'). This portion of the desert stretches eastward and eventually joins in the north with the large expanses of the Rub al-Khali ('The Empty Quarter'), which extends far north into Saudi Arabia. While it may not sound an ideal place to visit at first, the Yemeni deserts can be very attractive. Many of the country's oldest and most fascinating ruins are found in this area, including those at Marib, Baraqish and Shabwa.

The region is also home to the Bedouin, the oft-romanticised desert nomadic tribes known for their fierceness, their generosity, and their purity of language. Of their reputed ferocity, well-deserved or not, it must be recognised that life in the desert is not easy, even if Toyota Landcruisers now replace camels for most journeys. Of their generosity, the noted British traveller Freya Stark noted in an interview that 'the Bedouin will give their last drop of water' to a stranger who needs it. Finally, the Bedouin are often said to speak the 'purest' Arabic – the language which most closely resembles the original, classical language of the Koran. (A local travel agency may be able to arrange a visit with a Bedouin tribe.)

Lastly, the area has spectacular scenery and provides opportunities to take part in some interesting activities. Watching the sunrise over the dunes is well worth the grogginess that accompanies it and the massive sand dunes of Irq abu Dair and the Rub al-Khali are impressive (but out of the way). And of course, no trip from Marib to Seiyun or Shabwa would be truly complete without a slight diversion for dune driving or sand skiing.

Note, however, that any diversion from the Marib–Seiyun road, including a trip to the ancient town of Shabwa (see below) will require you to hire a Bedouin 'guide'. The Bedouin will not actually act as a guide, however, but he will serve as a visible sign to others that you have permission to be in the region, thus ensuring your safety. It's perhaps best to think of it as a really expensive visa stamp. The US$150/day cost is normally factored into tour programmes.

MARIB *Telephone code 06*

HISTORY The exact date when Marib rose to importance as the capital of the Sabaean Kingdom is uncertain. The chronology of the Sabaean Kingdom has long been disputed, although there has been more agreement recently toward the acceptance of the 'long chronology' – one of the two competing theories that dates the development of the Sabaean Kingdom to earlier in the 1st millennium BC than the other.

Irrigation settlements existed around the site of the city on a smaller scale as far back as the 3rd millennium BC, but Marib most likely rose in importance as the

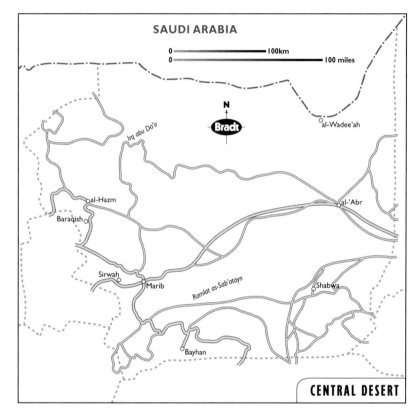

early caravan trade developed. Towards the end of the 2nd millennium BC the camel was domesticated, making the long journeys to carry incense across the desert possible. While there was a smaller route that took the caravans through the highlands, the most important road skirted the outside of the desert and through Marib. Over this road the caravans carried frankincense, myrrh, ivory and tortoiseshells – the trade provided a seemingly inexhaustible supply of funds to the Sabaeans.

In early Sabaean history the rulers took the title of *mukarrib* – a 'federator', who brought together and ruled over all the local tribes, and who as a result ranked higher than the local kings. (Although, of course, the mukarrib would often also be the local king of one of the tribes.)

The first known dates of the Sabaean 'Mukarrib Period' come from the annals of the Assyrian Kings Sargon II and Sennacherib, which noted that the Assyrians received tribute and gifts from the Sabaean mukarribs Yatha'amar Bayyin and Karib'il Watar in 715BC and 685BC respectively. The two have names similar to those used by rulers throughout the Sabaean Kingdom; for nearly 900 years the Sabaean mukarribs (and later the kings) chose from one of six names and four epithets. Needless to say, with only 24 possible iterations, there were multiple repetitions.

What Karib'il Watar lacked in moniker originality, he made up for in campaigns and construction. Lengthy inscriptions left by the ruler detail a series of eight military campaigns he carried out, including a great victory that ended the existence of the rival Awsan Kingdom. The inscriptions of the eight campaigns describe (with perhaps a small flair for exaggeration) that Karib'il Watar's forces killed over 25,000 people and took over 60,000 as prisoners. With his appetite for violence sated (and having now accumulated a massive workforce), Karib'il Watar turned to domestic construction. During his 50-year reign he completed construction on the royal Salhin Palace and undertook irrigation projects in the city's fields.

Karib'il Watar's successors were involved with building projects as well. Shortly after Karib'il Watar's reign, the mukarrib Yada'il Darih built three temples dedicated to the deity Almaqah, the patron god of Saba whom the Sabaeans viewed as their ancient ancestor. Almaqah was identified with the sun and symbolised by a bull. Yada'il Darih's temple, known popularly as Mahram Bilqis, is thus also referred to as the Sun Temple.

Several mukarribs after Yada'il Darih continued construction in the region – more temples were built and centuries of irrigation efforts led at last to the construction of the great Marib Dam, a large wall that would eventually stretch 650m and divert the rainfall flowing in from Wadi Dhana into two fields. These two oases produced crops twice a year, corresponding to the bi-annual rainy seasons of the highlands, and earning Marib the nickname 'the land of two paradises'. The fields supported barley, date palms, grapes, millet, sorghum, and wheat.

The 5th century BC saw the Sabaeans begin to lose their firm grip over southern Arabia. The mukarrib Yatha'amar Bayyin was forced to put down several rebellions as the Sabaean vassals of Ma'in, Hadhramawt and Qataban made bids for independence. As the vassals broke free and became Sabaean rivals, the mukarrib period of the kingdom came to an end. Sabaean rulers at some point around this time began using the title *Malik Saba'* – 'the King of Saba''.

For several centuries wars of supremacy between these kingdoms waged across the southern Arabian Peninsula. The Sabaeans in Marib were able to survive these wars without trouble, but the glory days of the mukarrib period had passed. Instead of Karib'il Watar's glorious campaigns, the Sabaeans had to content themselves with merely repelling the attacks of the other kingdoms.

In 24BC, the Sabaeans defended Marib from a new threat. Augustus Caesar had sent an expedition under the command of General Aelius Gallus to conquer the lands of southern Arabia. Having passed through and conquered the old fortification at Baraqish, the Roman expedition laid siege to the Sabaean capital. Only six days later, disease was rampant among the Roman soldiers, and the forces withdrew.

Around the same time the Himyarite Kingdom was rising to power, and the new kid on the block would prove a much fiercer foe than the disease-ridden Romans had been. From their palace of Raydan in Dhafar, the Himyarite kings quickly asserted linguistic control over the Sabaeans by giving themselves the titles of 'Kings of Saba' and Dhu Raydan'. The Sabaean rulers claimed the same title for themselves.

Over the next few centuries, wars continued between the Sabaeans, Himyarites, Hadhramis and Qatabanis. While the Sabaeans rebounded somewhat in the early 3rd century AD, the kingdom ceased to be independent in the year AD275 when control of Marib fell to the Himyarites.

As the new ruling power of Himyar converted to Judaism and later to Christianity, the temples dedicated to Almaqah ceased to maintain their importance. Inscriptions from the time mention a church and synagogue that existed in the area in the early 6th century, but, along with the famed Salhin Palace, they have remained lost under the dunes, awaiting discovery.

Over the years of Himyarite rule the city continued to dwindle in importance. Finally, after years of breaches and patchwork repairs, the Marib Dam collapsed for the final time in the mid to late 6th century. According to Islamic tradition, the final breach occurred in AD570 – the Year of the Elephant – the year in which Muhammad was born and Abrahah led his failed attack (with elephants, of course) from Sana'a on the city of Mecca.

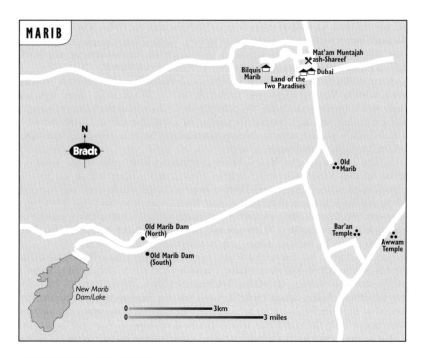

Mat'am Muntajah
ash-Shareef
Bilquis
Marib   Land of the
Two Paradises   Dubai

N

Bradt

Old
Marib

Old Marib Dam
(North)   Bar'an
Temple
Awwam
Temple

Old Marib Dam
(South)

New Marib
Dam/Lake

0   3km
0   3 miles

GETTING THERE AND AWAY Owing to the security situation in Marib, the only way to travel to and from the area, as well as traverse between the sites, has been to hire a private car and driver from a local travel agency. Cars heading to Marib gather at the checkpoint just outside Sana'a on the Marib Rd at 08.00. Once everyone has assembled and the army escort has arrived, the modern caravan will set out toward the ancient kingdom.

 WHERE TO STAY

Bilquis Marib Hotel (88 rooms) ☏ 06 302372; f 06 302371; e marib@universalyemen.com; http://universalyemen.com/hotels/bilquis.htm. The hotel, run by the Universal Group, may be a little expensive, but the tranquil settings, not to mention the large swimming pool, provide a much-needed place to relax after spending a day visiting the desert sites. The restaurant serves buffets for b/fast, lunch & dinner (above average: $$$). $$$$. FB.

Land of the Two Paradises ('Ard al-Janatayn') (26 rooms) ☏ 06 302310; f 06 302166. The rooms at the hotel are a bit small, but not that bad, & have Western bathrooms. The swimming pool & basketball court are no longer in working order. $$

Dubai Hotel (10 rooms) Although it is the cheapest option in town, the hotel managers have recently implemented a 'locals only' policy. If the security situation improves, this policy may change, as hotels are currently required to give free rooms to the local police who accompany those visiting this region.

WHERE TO EAT The Bilquis Marib Hotel in town serves as the main restaurant for tourists, but there are several good local restaurants in the new city that serve standard Yemeni fare. In particular, the Mat'am Muntajah ash-Shareef, located on main street toward Seiyun, is popular with locals and passers-through alike.

OTHER PRACTICALITIES At the time of writing there were no ATMs in Marib, although for a small fee the main currency-exchange store can produce the same effect by offering a cashback facility from your debit card.

WHAT TO SEE

Awwam Temple (Mahram Bilqis) The large temple structure situated about 3km southeast of Marib is known locally as Mahram Bilqis, 'the Sanctuary of Bilqis', but the connection with the Queen of Sheba is unlikely. The temple was constructed by the mukarrib Yada'il Darih sometime around the mid 7th century BC in honour of the national god of the Sabaean state, Almaqah. To archaeologists the structure is known as the Awwam Temple, and more colloquially to tour guides and tourists as the Sun Temple.

The eight columns of the temple stand outside a large oval wall that has been heavily damaged by the removal of its stones and hidden by covering sand dunes. The oval encompasses an area of some 6,000m². A large hall in the northeast section is clearly visible next to the pillars.

The temple was excavated by the American archaeologist Wendell Phillips and his team from the American Foundation for the Study of Man in the 1950s, although the team had to flee from tribal hostilities after they were suspected of taking away the antiquities. Since then the American Foundation for the Study of Man and the locals at Marib have been on better terms, and excavations at the site are now ongoing. Unlike the Arsh Bilqis Temple, this site has not been opened up for tourists, and a large fence encircles it entirely.

Bar'an Temple ('Arsh Bilqis) Like its sister site, the Awwam Temple, the Bar'an Temple goes by a number of names. Locally, it has come to be known as Arsh Bilqis – 'the Queen of Sheba's throne'; it is also called the Moon Temple and al-Ama'id. Also like the Awwam Temple, this structure was dedicated to the national deity Almaqah. Recent archaeological work at the site has uncovered a series of temples

HOOKED ON SABAEAN WORKED FOR ME

Inscriptions using the ancient south Arabian dialect date back to at least the 8th century BC. Like Arabic, the text is written only using consonants (except for the long vowels 'a', 'w' and 'y') and is written from right to left. The alphabet contains 29 signs – eight more than the Phoenician alphabet and one more than modern Arabic.

The south Arabian alphabet shares similarities with the Phoenician alphabet, although it is no longer conjectured that the former derived from the latter. Modern scholarship has shown that the south Arabian alphabet is just as old as its Phoenician counterpart, and that both alphabets derived from an older script known today as Proto-Canaanite.

The transliterations of the Sabaean alphabet to both Arabic and Roman script are given below. Please refrain from carving your name on temple walls.

		a			z			f
		b			s			q
		t			sh			k
		th			ś			l
		g			S			m
		H			D			n
		kh			T			h
		d			Z			w
		dh			'			y
		r			gh			

built on top of one another; construction of the first may have dated back to the time of the Queen of Sheba, although it is no longer present in its current form.

The temple is believed by some Mormon scholars to correspond with the site of Nahom – the place to which the Mormon prophet Lehi fled after leaving Jerusalem in the 6th century BC. According to the Mormon story, Lehi and his family came to the site and buried Ishmael at the temple before constructing a large vessel to sail to America. The story is interesting, especially given local tales that Noah's ark came to rest in the nearby mountains. Who would have ever thought the desert town of Marib would have been such an important port?

The Bar'an Temple has been exquisitely excavated. The five-and-a-half pillars rising from the temple altar have been reinforced at the base, and the entire site has been opened up to tourists, who can now walk through the site and inspect the engravings in close detail. The work that has been done here has transformed the Bar'an Temple into one of the most worthwhile archaeological sites to visit in Yemen.

However, it must unfortunately be noted that seven Spanish tourists and two Yemeni guides were killed here in July 2007 when a suicide bomber drove an explosive-laden 4x4 into the touring convoy. The attacks have been attributed to al-Qaeda and came after unspecific threats against various interests in the country if jailed members of the terrorist organisation in Yemen were not released. This was the first suicide bombing in Yemen to specifically target tourists. One hopes it is the last.

Old Marib Dam The Marib Dam was constructed some time during the second half of the 6th century BC, and inscriptions in the dam note that the mukarribs Sumhu'ali Yanuf and Yatha'amar Bayyin were responsible for the structure's completion. At that time, the dam existed largely as a long mound of dirt and stones, stretched across the riverbed of Wadi Dhana from the base of Jabal Balaq. Eventually, the stone wall of the dam would stretch 650m long and rise to a height of 16m.

Located about 7km away from the Old City, the dam was constructed to capture the water from the flash floods that rushed down Wadi Dhana – a riverbed that works its way toward the desert of Ramlat as-Sabatayn from the northern highlands. During the bi-annual rainy seasons of the highlands, large amounts of water and silt were brought from the mountains down the wadi. At times, the wadi could issue forth water at the staggering amount of over 1,700m³/second.

The purpose of the dam was not so much to capture and store this onslaught of water as to divert it into irrigation channels. Two large sluices on either side of the dam channelled water off to irrigate the fields of the northern and southern oases. Together, the two oases had a size of roughly 95km² – about the size of the city of Paris. The northern oasis was the larger, covering an area of over 5,700ha. Together, the two oases are said to have supported a population of 50,000 at its greatest point.

The large influx of water and silt meant that the dam had to be repaired often. Inscriptions on the dam walls note the dates of various reconstruction efforts, and the earliest-noted breach occurred in the year 100BC. Over the following centuries, more repairs were required, and in the century before its final collapse, there were four recorded efforts of patching breaches in the dam.

The Koran describes the collapse of the dam in AD570 in terms of divine retribution. In Sura 34 ('Saba'), the Koran states:

There was a sign for the Sabaeans in their homeland: two gardens, on the right and left. And they were told, 'Eat of what your lord has given you and be thankful, for fair is your land, and forgiving your lord.

But they turned away. So We released the flood from the dams, replacing their gardens with two others which bore only bitter fruit, and tamarisks and a few sparse lote-trees.

In addition to venerating a number of smaller, local deities, the Sabaeans worshipped a pantheon of five major gods and goddesses: Athtar, Hawbas, Almaqah, dhat-Himyam and dhat-Badanum. The first, Athtar, was the most important of the pantheon – a supreme universal god who controlled thunderstorms and rain. His name and position show a similarity to the Assyrian goddess Ishtar and the Semitic goddess Astarte.

Although he did not rank as high in the pantheon as Athtar, the god Almaqah was the most important god in the day-to-day lives of the Sabaeans. As the god of irrigation and agriculture, he was the national deity of the kingdom. All of the temples were dedicated to him, there was an annual pilgrimage, and his symbol, the bull, can be found in countless engravings and sculptures.

The purpose of the two goddesses dhat-Himyam and dhat-Badanum is unclear. It is possible that they were seasonal gods. Dhat-Himyam means 'she of the heat' and dhat-Badanum perhaps 'she of the winter months'.

The goddess Hawbas – at times depicted as male – may have been the counterpart to Athtar, based on the proximity the names of the two gods often share. In any event, the relationship between the gods was likely not a primary concern. Religion existed for the Sabaeans not as a way to explain the workings of the world, but as a means to ensure their livelihood through supplication. There have been found no myths describing the creation of the world, no stories of gods intermingling with one another, and no tales of moral dictates. The gods and goddesses were the ones who controlled that which was essential to life – rain, irrigation, agriculture, the sun, the seasons – and thus the most important aspect of religion was to ensure that the gods were pleased so that these necessities of life continued to flow. Temples were dedicated to Almaqah and ritual hunts to Athtar, all in the hope that the rains and subsequent harvest would follow without incident.

Other Arabic traditions note that there had been a prophecy that the dam would be destroyed by a rat. To prevent this foreboding premonition, the architects at Marib placed cats along the floodgates and the walls. (How the cats were induced to stand guard at their positions is not made clear in the legend.) In any event, the cats were no match for a large rat who possessed iron teeth and claws. Dispatching one of the feline sentinels, the rat began to gnaw away at the foundation of the dam. Luckily for the ruler of the time, the legend continues, the rat was spotted before any mischief could occur. Rather than take his chances with the metal-toothed monstrosity, the local sheikh sold the dam for a large bag of gold to several unsuspecting merchants. The ruler was long gone by the time the rat finished his ordained purpose and the dam suffered its final collapse.

There is a common belief in Yemen that the final destruction of the Marib Dam led to a mass exodus from the city, resulting in some accounts in the creation of the Bedouin tribes and in others in the widespread population of the entire Arabian Peninsula. This single, massive movement is unlikely – after all, Marib had already dwindled much in importance and population by the time the dam finally collapsed – but the story represents a simple way of explaining the fact that most Arabs in the Arabian Peninsula can trace their distant ancestry to Yemeni roots.

New Marib Dam Three kilometres away from the ruins of the old Marib Dam lies the large manmade lake of the new Marib Dam. The dam was constructed in 1986

6

by a Turkish company, and the US$70 million project was funded by the then UAE President Sheikh Zayed bin Sultan an-Nahyan. The late Emirati president, who could trace his own ancestry to family members who lived in the region before the collapse of the old dam in the 6th century, presented the new dam as a gift to the people of Yemen. An interesting video discussing the heritage of the region and the construction of the dam can be found online at the embassy of the UAE's website www.uaeembassy.org.au/cultural_video.htm.

The new dam is significantly smaller than its ancient counterpart. It is possible to climb up the stairs from the road below for a view of the dam and the lake. After lunch, there are usually some locals sitting off to the side for a qat chew.

The Old City The mud-brick buildings of the Old City of Marib do not date back to the Sabaean times. The city was used as late as the 1960s until Egyptian planes bombed the buildings, which housed royalist fighters, during the North Yemen revolution. After the bombing, the new city of Marib sprung up nearby.

Even so, there are plenty of Sabaean pieces and fragments of pillars strewn about, and a walk through the abandoned town and ruined buildings is interesting enough.

OUTSIDE MARIB

THE SIRWAH TEMPLE

History The town of Sirwah may have served as the first capital of the Sabaean Kingdom before the rise to dominance of neighbouring Marib. Even after the capital moved, the city continued to maintain its importance. The sanctuary here was one of the three temples dedicated to the god Almaqah that were built by the Sabaean mukarrib Yada'il Darih in the mid 7th century BC, and al-Hamdani notes (albeit improbably) that the Sabaeans used a palace in Sirwah as their winter residence.

Getting there Visitation to the site requires a somewhat large military convoy that can be arranged by your travel agency. The tribes in the region are known for their unruly nature, and an ever increasing military presence has attempted to rein them in. Coming to the site from Marib, you will see a large number of tanks (between 10 and 20) sitting near the checkpoint ready to be deployed at the slightest hint of any tribal disturbance. There have also been a number of kidnappings in the region, with the most recent in 2006.

What to see The Sirwah Temple is a large oval-shaped building whose walls once rose as high as 8m. Inside the structure, in the centre of the courtyard, is the large inscription detailing the military exploits and domestic construction of the great mukarrib Karib'il Watar – the largest Sabaean inscription ever discovered. Another large inscription describing the military campaigns of the 4th century BC ruler Yakrubmalik has been found here recently.

The German Institute of Archaeology is currently working on the temple's excavation and restoration. There is an abundance of inscriptions and enough ibex friezes to feed the Yemeni army (if the Yemenis could eat stone ibices). When the German team is not on the site, many of the pieces will be covered until the work is completed and the results are published.

Nevertheless, it is still possible to see much of the temple. Due in large part to the excellent restoration work of the German Institute of Archaeology, this is one of the best archaeological sites in Yemen. When finished, the sanctuary will rival the Bar'an Temple in Marib in terms of grandeur and beauty. Lucky for you the sites are relatively close to one another – located only 40km or so apart – and can both be visited easily in one day.

BARAQISH (YATHILL)

HISTORY The town of Baraqish (known in antiquity as Yathill) was originally a Sabaean stronghold, but eventually was eclipsed by the rising Minaean state, who established their political capital at the city for a short period of time. While the Minaeans eventually moved their capital northward to the city of Qarnaw, Baraqish remained the religious centre of the kingdom. By the time the Roman expedition of Aelius Gallus made it here in 24BC, the Minaean Kingdom had already faded away significantly, and there was not much remaining there to conquer.

GETTING THERE As with travel to Sirwah, accompaniment by an entourage of army guards is necessary to travel to Baraqish, located in the traditionally tribal stronghold governorate of al-Jawf. Baraqish is likely as far north into the governorate as you will be allowed to travel. The historically interesting ruins of the **Athtar Temple** at **Qarnaw**, 20km to the north, have been off-limits on a near-permanent basis, and it looks likely to stay that way for the foreseeable future.

WHAT TO SEE The large circular fortification of Baraqish is built on a small mound of earth that rises up from the surrounding wadi. The site is one of the few examples of an ancient city with its outer wall still to some degree intact – in some sections the walls are as high as 14m. The wall contains 55 tower houses and two gates. There are the ruins of several temples currently undergoing excavation as well as a more recent mosque inside. Near the main gate there is a large wall of ancient inscriptions, as well as carvings of snakes, which were considered to be sacred to the Minaean national god Wadd. The god, whose name means 'love', is mentioned in the Koran as one of the pagan gods whom the people worshipped during the life of Noah.

The army soldiers positioned at the site are very knowledgeable about the city's history and the ongoing excavation efforts. After showing you around, the guard will most likely offer a fossilised shell. Tips of 500–1,000YR are appropriate.

SHABWA

HISTORY Located in the middle of the desert governorate of the same name, the city of Shabwa was the ancient capital of the Hadhramawt Kingdom. According to Pliny the Elder's *Natural History*, large tithes were taken from the incense caravans, and this undoubtedly led to the early financial success of the city. To maintain this income, the rulers of the Hadhramawt Kingdom made circumvention of the city a crime punishable by death.

The city began as a settlement in the 2nd millennium BC, likely because of the salt mine that exists nearby. Sometime around the beginning of the 1st millennium BC, however, a tribal coalition formed that would become known as Hadhramawt Kingdom. The importance of the kingdom was recognized in the book of Genesis, which lists the Hebrew version of the name, 'Hazarmaveth', along side 'Saba' as sons of Joktan.

The Kingdom of Hadhramawt established itself at Shabwa early on, although for the first several centuries of its existence it served as vessel to the Sabaean Kingdom. Eventually, however, the kingdom broke away from Sabaean rule and reigned over varying portions of the country until its collapse in the 3rd century AD.

Shabwa suffered defeat first at the hand of the Sabaean ruler Sha'irum Awtar at the Battle of Shuwar'an, when the Hadhramite king was taken prisoner and the city was ransacked. And secondly, after a brief recovery, the city was crushed in battle again by the Himyarite king Shamar Yuhar'esh. Shibam to the northeast became the new capital of the region after the destruction of Shabwa. The unique architectural design of Shibam was probably modelled on the design and structure of Shaqir, the great palace of Shabwa.

GETTING THERE Travel to Shabwa can only be done through arrangements with a tour agency. Because of security concerns, travellers are required to be accompanied by government soldiers or Bedouin bodyguards.

WHAT TO SEE Although Pliny describes Shabwa as containing over 60 temples, little remains today. The old city wall and temple have been excavated somewhat by a French team previously, but the city would benefit from more archaeological love and tenderness. The ancient salt mine is still in use.

Bottlenose dolphin

7

The Northern Mountains

Telephone code 07

SHAHARA

With pictures of the city's bridge featured on the country's currency and advertisements, Shahara has become one of the icons of Yemen's tourism industry. The sheer remoteness and inaccessibility of the town has intrigued local and occupying forces throughout Yemen's history as much as has it has for the many travellers who make the journey each year. Even today, however, the villagers seem wary of allowing the town to become too well connected to the rest of the country. After all, you never know when a last bastion of resistance may come in handy.

HISTORY The small, remote village of Shahara has long been used as a Zaydi bastion of resistance. The sheer inaccessibility of the village, sitting atop a mountain at an elevation of nearly 2,500m, has provided the Zaydi imams with a final hiding place, or as a base to gather support, for nearly 1,000 years.

Interestingly, the first Zaydi group to use Shahara was the Husayniyyas – a splinter group deemed heretical by mainstream Zaydis. The sect's founder, Imam al-Husayn al-Iyani, succeeded to the imamate in AD1010 after the death of his father Imam al-Mansur al-Qasim al-Iyani. Zaydi Imams must typically meet a strict test of requirements to obtain their position, but al-Husayn may have snuck in through association with his very successful father, who had been recognized as a great scholar and who had restored the imamate after its first lapse major lapse in Yemen. Fearful of another lapse, the Zaydi community may have been willing to grant al-Husayn more leeway, but shortly after he rose to the position of imam many began to question his religious scholarship.

The imam decided that the best way to counter criticisms of his scholarship was to claim divine status. Who could argue with him then? He thus began claiming that he was the Mahdi, a messianic figure in Islam who will restore the religion worldwide before the Day of Judgment.

Imam al-Husayn was killed in battle four years later, but not before he had amassed a large following of believers who accepted his position as the Mahdi. The Husayniyyas, as they were called, claimed that Imam al-Husayn had not died but that he had gone into hiding and would return later. The idea of occultation is prevalent in the Isma'ili branch of Islam in Yemen as well, which had grown to power briefly in the previous century under the Fatimid conquests of Mansur al-Yemen and 'Ali bin Fadl.

The Husayniyyas fortified the village of Shahara, where it is claimed that Imam al-Husayn was seen walking with Jesus directly before his occultation. The vision is consistent with Imam al-Husayn's claim to be the Mahdi – one Hadith has Muhammad claiming that the Mahdi and Jesus will pray together. In any event, the Husayniyyas used the fortified town as their base of operations, and they became the main Zaydi opposition to the Sulayhids in the 11th and 12th centuries. At the

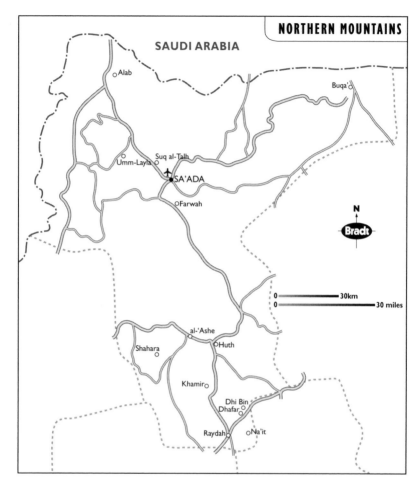

SAUDI ARABIA

Alab

Buqa'

Umm-Layla

Suq al-Talh

SA'ADA

Farwah

N

Bradt

0 ——— 30km
0 ——— 30 miles

al-'Ashe

Shahara

Huth

Khamir

Dhi Bin
Dhafar

Raydah   Na'it

end of the 12th century, the Husayniyya sect was declared heretical by Imam Ahmed al-Mutawakkil and his successor Imam al-Mansur Billah Abdullah bin Hamza. The sect completely died out several centuries later.

In 1587, the mountain stronghold was taken from the Zaydis for the first and only time by the Ottomans in the middle of the first occupation. The Turks only managed to rein in the mountain tribes here and hold Shahara for about a decade. Control of the city soon fell to Imam Qasim bin Muhammad 'the Great', who gathered support from Shahara to launch a major offensive that would ultimately end the Ottoman occupation in 1635.

During the second Ottoman occupation in the 19th and 20th centuries, the forces tried to recapture the mountain village again, but they were unsuccessful. The descendants of Imam Qasim the Great maintained control of the fortified town throughout the reign of the Zaydi Imamate.

During the 1960s' civil war following the republican revolution, Shahara again became one of the last strongholds of the imam. The remote town was not as well-suited to protect against air attacks. Although the Royalist forces of the Imam prepared for a long resistance from the mountain town, they were bombed from the skies by Egyptian planes.

GETTING THERE It is necessary to hire a private car when travelling to Shahara – there are no buses or bijous that reach the region and the security situation of the area will prevent you from travelling without an accompanying tour guide. Coming from Sana'a there are roughly six or seven checkpoints that you will have to cross. Early on you will pass by the city of **Raydah**, one of the most well-known cities for Jewish populations, with some adherents of the faith still living there.

Eventually you will turn off the main road from Raydah to Sa'ada to head toward Shahara at the village of **al-'Ashe**. From here the bumpy trek across the dirt road takes about an hour, until you reach the base of the mountain at **Funduq ash-Shirq**, where old 4x4 trucks wait to cart you to the top.

You will no doubt have hired your own Landcruiser to reach Shahara, but you will need to hire one of the local cars to take you to the top. The villagers of Shahara have instituted this practice for some time, and it is recognised by all travel agencies. Often, your travel agency will simply include the roundtrip costs in the estimate they give you.

The cost of a return journey to the village of Shahara is 7,000YR per person, and the trip takes about 30 minutes. Standing in the back of the old truck as it jostles up the bumpy mountainside or careens back downward on the return journey is a joy in itself – a bit like the frantic high you might get from riding a rollercoaster that you are not sure works correctly. Either way, you will most likely pick up a number of local passengers eager to avoid the long walk up or down. It is also possible for you to walk to Shahara from the base of the mountain. The four-hour hike would give you more time to enjoy the villages in between the two points, and you could pay for the return trip from the top at a cheaper price.

WHERE TO STAY AND EAT

⌂ **Funduq ash-Shirq** (12 rooms) m 711 416650. The small guesthouse is located at the foot of the mountain where the trucks transport people to the village of Shahara. The views are not as good, but the restaurant serves a great dinner. Shared Yemeni bathrooms. $. Dinner, B&B.

⌂ **Funduq Khaled** (10 rooms) ✆ 07 628133. The guesthouse at the top of the mountain offers larger rooms & cleaner shared bathrooms. The hotel also has a laundry machine if you find yourself in need of some clean clothing. $. Dinner, B&B.

The only places to eat in Shahara are at the two local hotels. A good Yemeni-style meal can be ordered at either even if you are not staying as a hotel guest. $

WHAT TO SEE People come to Shahara for one reason: to see **the Shahara Bridge**, which connects the village of Shahara to that of **Shaharat al-Faysh** on the adjacent mountain. The bridge was constructed in the 17th century by the architect Salah al-Yemen. The bridge, along with Dar al-Hajar and the walled city of Shibam, has become one of the main images of Yemeni tourism, and it appears on the 10YR coin.

The biggest problem with visiting Shahara has been its greatest asset throughout the centuries – its sheer inaccessibility. A trip to visit the village necessitates a good

ALSO, ELVIS SPOTTED AT ADEN NIGHTCLUB

The reputed witnessing of Imam al-Husayn and Jesus at Shahara marked the third Jesus-sighting in Yemen. Previously, Jesus is reputed to have prayed in Sana'a during his lifetime, and later to have appeared in clouds of glory at the Himyarite capital of Dhafar in the early 6th century AD. Each of these sightings has occurred roughly 500 years after the preceding one. Assuming that there was an undocumented appearance in the 1500s, the time is about right for another cameo. Cameras should be at the ready.

deal of time, and usually involves an overnight stay. If you are heading to Shahara simply to take a picture of the bridge, you may want to reconsider whether it is worth it. On the other hand, if you view the trip as a means to experience remote mountain villages and glimpse a peek at tribal culture, with the added bonus that you will be able to witness an amazing architectural masterpiece, the benefits will start to weigh in favour of a trip.

Even so, when you reach the bridge, try to refrain as long as you can from taking a picture. Far too many tourists simply snap a picture and then retreat to the safety of their hotels within five minutes. Sit down, take in the scenery, and enjoy it. (Granted, the view of the bridge may be too much for the camera finger to bear. Just remember to enjoy the trip while you are there, as well as vicariously through photos later.)

Before heading back to your hotel or back down the mountain, I recommend a walk over to Shaharat al-Faysh, the village on the neighbouring mountain. There is not much there, but the views are quite lovely. There is local talk of a tourist parachuting off the mountains here; it would be an exhilarating jump. If you are interested in chewing qat, you can buy a variety of the leaf called **Sawti**, which is particularly strong and reputed to ensure you stay awake late into the night.

Back in the village of Shahara, there are some 23 water cisterns.

DHAFAR/DHI BIN

Originally an ancient fortification, Dhi Bin became an important centre for a brief period of time during the 13th century under the patronage of Imam al-Mansur Billah. Today, the town is largely in ruins and mostly abandoned, but it provides a great opportunity to explore in some detail a mosque under repair, a crumbling minaret, and the tomb of the Imam.

top Handicraft workshop in Bayt al-Faqih (DM) page 170
above left Woman wearing traditional balto (EL)
right Bedouin kids playing football in the Ramlat as-Sabatayn (DM) page 139
below The camel-jumpers of al-Husayniyah are proud of their sporting traditions (DM) page 171

opposite	**Village carved into the mountainside** (EL)
top	**Yemeni house carved into the mountain, Wadi Dhahr** (JT) page 88
above left	**Egyptian vulture in front of a Dragon's Blood Tree, Socotra** (DM) page 35
above right	**The famous Shahara Bridge** (EL) page 151

above **The fertile plains near Hadhramawt cut a stark contrast to the dry mountain slopes** (EL) page 201

below **A local well** (EL)

above The rainbow-coloured
facade of the Khailah
Palace Tourist Hotel
(EL) page 195

centre Goat herds on the
move (HR)

right Sabaean engravings at
the Old Marib dam
(El) page 144

top Yemeni island, with extinct volcano and Red Sea in the background (EL)

left Bizarre-shaped 'bottle trees' on the coast, Socotra (DM) page 221

opposite Fishing boats fill the horizon at the coast, Bir 'Ali (JT) page 197

Early morning calls
to prayer (JT)

GETTING THERE Coming from Sana'a, take the north road toward Shahara. When you get to Raydah, bear right at the main fork and follow the road to the village of Dhafar. To reach Dhi Bin, take the right turn-off and follow the road a short distance until you see a dirt path that zigzags up the mountain on your left. (The main road continues all the way to the province of al-Jawf.) Bear off the dirt road and follow a small path from the right side of the road that starts at about the point where the heavy zigzag pattern ceases. From here, it's about a 20–30-minute walk to the mosque and ruins of Dhi Bin.

WHAT TO SEE Depending on who is at the door of the village, you may be charged an admission fee of 300–500YR, or you may be permitted to walk around the village for free. Either way, the inhabitants of the village will quickly warm up to you after a few brief friendly interactions.

Dhi Bin was an ancient site that was fortified in the early 13th century by the Zaydi Imam al-Mansur Billah Abdullah bin Hamza. He commissioned the mosque to be built that stands next to the fortress. The outer walls of the mosque are beautifully designed, with triple-curved arches in between each of the pillars. These walls are presently completely covered from sight by aluminium weatherproofing as part of a restoration project.

The mosque is no longer in use and therefore not considered to be holy ground. It is possible to enter the mosque for a thorough exploration. You do not need to take off your shoes; in fact, most Yemenis will light a cigarette within the walls and not think twice about it (not that you should, of course).

In the centre of the courtyard sits a small room that houses al-Mansur Billah's tomb. It is possible to enter the room, but you should take your shoes off beforehand – note that this area is still revered. As you enter the room, you will notice old Kufic writing on the wall to the right. The wooden sand- and dirt-filled container on the left shows the location of the tomb.

If you are feeling adventurous, you may want to take the opportunity to climb the minaret, as there will not be other chances for you to do so in Yemen. Entering the minaret requires a bit of (potentially dangerous) acrobatics, as the ground in front of the door has all given way. Some of the local inhabitants probably will be happy to assist you if your express interest is climbing to the top.

Outside the complex, on the eastern side of the mosque, there is also the smaller tomb of the imam's son. Much of the ground between the mountains is covered with old graveyards. Standing above the mosque is the fortress of **Husn al-Gahira**. There is a path leading up to the top.

From the old fortress, you can get a good view of your surroundings. On top of the large imposing cliff in front of you are the remains of the fortress of **Husn at-Taafa**. The ruins of **Husn Ta'iz** lies westward, the direction you most likely came from. To the northeast is the larger structure of **Galat Dar al-Hajar**, which has many water-storage tanks with arches and pillars.

OUTSIDE DHAFAR/DHI BIN

NA'IT The main site of Na'it is a **stone temple** reminiscent of the temples of Marib, but not so grand. Today only two pillars remain. Supposedly, the third pillar was taken to the Great Mosque in Sana'a by Imam Yahya. Near the temple lie the remains of a **stone quarry**, and the foundation of an old castle lies farther in toward the centre of town.

The village of Na'it serves as an interesting example of how villagers can incorporate ancient reliefs into their houses. The pieces are thrown into the building all higgledy-piggledy – pillars lie sideways or at an angle, with other reliefs crammed into odd spaces.

There are also several good pieces built into the mosque. While non-Muslims are not allowed to enter the mosque proper, you can probably take a walk around the outer grounds to see how the builders used the ancient pieces.

SA'ADA

The city of Sa'ada lies on the path of the old mountain incense road used during the days of the ancient caravan days, and pre-Islamic inscriptions from the area confirm the existence of Sa'ada in antiquity. During its early days, the city was known as Juma'a – likely named after one of the tribes in the area. According to local legend the name was changed to Sa'ada when a man from the Tihama, marvelling at the height of one of the palaces and the number of stairs one would need to reach the top, repeated the word three times. 'Sa'ada' literally means 'he has ascended'.

According to the 10th-century geographer al-Hamdani, Sa'ada was known during his visit as a region for tanning and acacia. Over the years the town and surrounding region also became a major supplier of iron ore and silver jewellery – the combination of which led to the highly prized Sa'ada silver jambiyyas. The region is also the main producer of *haradah*, the hardened-clay pots used to cook the national Yemeni dish of *saltah*.

In the late 9th century Sa'ada was the birthplace of the Zaydi Imamate. Following fierce tribal disputes in the region, the tribes requested Yahya ibn Hussayn ar-Rassi to come from Basra and conduct the tribe's mediations. Ar-Rassi's arbitration skills were successful, and in AD897 he returned to Sa'ada to serve as the first Zaydi Imam, taking the name al-Hadi ila al-Haqq. Over the next 1,000 years, the institution he founded would be an important part of Yemeni history, politics and culture. With the revolution in North Yemen in 1962, the 111th imam would be deposed and the imamate would finally come to an end.

During this period Sa'ada was used from time to time as an important centre for the Zaydi imams. Imam al-Hadi used the town as his capital, as did his two sons, Muhammad al-Murtada and Ahmed an-Nasser ad-Din Allah, who served as the second and third imams, respectively. All of the first three imams are buried at the Great Mosque in the city.

For a long period of time, Sa'ada served as an important area for a community of Yemenite Jews, who were well known as silver artisans. The Sa'ada Jews were able to avoid the 17th-century exile to al-Mawza, which many of their brethren in Sana'a faced. A significant community remained after Operation Magic Carpet, the massive exodus to the newly formed Israel in 1949, and have continued to live north of Sa'ada.

In early 2007, an anonymous letter, apparently written by Muslim fundamentalists, was sent to the Jewish inhabitants of the region. The letter directed the Jewish families to leave their homes within ten days, threatening the religious minority with murder, kidnapping and robbery should they attempt to stay. As a result of the letter, some 45 Jews sought refuge within one of the local town hotels for protection.

The origin of the letter is unclear, but it has been connected with the al-Houthi conflict that resurfaced in Sa'ada around the same time. In 2004, Zaydi cleric Hussein Al-Houthi led a rebellion of the 'Believing Youth' in the Sa'ada region that sought to re-establish the rule of the old imamate. After over two months of fighting al-Houthi was killed, but minor skirmishes continued.

In 2007, the conflict broke out again into a larger confrontation between the government and al-Houthi loyalists under the command of Sheikh Yahya Sa'ad Al-Khudhair. While it's likely that the letter was sent by al-Houthi supporters, the

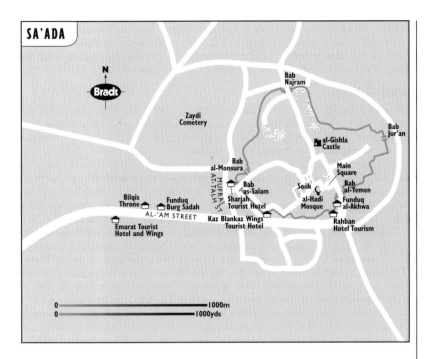

SA'ADA

Bradt

N

Bab Najram

Zaydi Cemetery

Bab Jur'an

al-Gishla Castle

Bab al-Monsura

Main Square

Bab as-Salam

Souk

Bab al-Yemen

MURAD AT-TALH ST

Sharjah Tourist Hotel

al-Hadi Mosque

Funduq al-Akhwa

Bilqis Throne

Funduq Burg Sadah

AL-'AM STREET

Kaz Blankaz Wings Tourist Hotel

Rahban Hotel Tourism

Emarat Tourist Hotel and Wings

0 — 1000m
0 — 1000yds

rebels have claimed that the Yemeni government sent the letter themselves to justify an attack against al-Houthi's supporters.

Because of the security situation at the time of writing, tourists were not allowed to travel to Sa'ada.

WHERE TO STAY
Budget $$

 **Emarat Tourist Hotel and Wings** (36 rooms) al-'Am St; ℡ 07 512203. The first establishment you cross coming up from the south & thus the farthest away from the city centre. While not the cleanest hotel in town, the rooms are spacious. Yemeni bathrooms, with no hot water.

Cheap $

Bilqis Throne Hotel (27 rooms) al-'Am St; ℡ 07 512973. The next hotel toward the city centre, its rooms are a bit cleaner & cheaper than the **Emarat**. The Western bathrooms have hot water but lack toilet seats.

Funduq al-Akhwa (12 rooms) al-'Am St (right before the gate entrance to the Old City); ℡ 07 511432. The hotel has shared Yemeni bathrooms, is in need of a good cleaning, & is a little skimpy on the sheets, but the price & location cannot be beaten. The sign is in Arabic only (فندق الاخوة), so if you have trouble finding it, ask for help around the city gate.

Rahban Hotel Tourism (50 rooms) al-'Am St; ℡ 07 512848; f 07 512856. With its clean rooms & Western toilets, Rahban is the preferred hotel in town by tourists. The rooms vary in quality; make sure you get one with a good view of the city.

Funduq Burg Sadah (6 rooms) al-'Am St; ℡ 07 513676. Although its basic rooms have showerless Yemeni bathrooms, the prices are pretty low, & it's a small step up from the **al-Akhwa**.

Kaz Blankaz Wings Tourist Hotel (60 rooms) al-'Am St; ℡ 07 514504; f 07 517419. Rooms are nice, & many have good views of the Old City & wall. Western toilets.

Sharjah Tourist Hotel (16 rooms) Mufraj at-Talh St; ℡ 07 512765. Typical rooms with shared Yemeni bathrooms.

✕ WHERE TO EAT There are three restaurants located on al-'Am Street outside the main gate of the Old City and around the area of the **Rahban Hotel Tourism**, with no real reason to differentiate between them. For atmosphere, although not better food, there is an outdoor café in the middle of the Old City.

WHAT TO SEE
Al-Gishla Castle
The tower and grounds are currently being renovated for tourism, but are open in the meantime. The field area gives off a *samsara* feel, although it was used in the past to house soldiers and prisoners. The best views of Sa'ada can be had from the roof of the tower.

Old City
The Old City of Sa'ada is surrounded by a **large wall**, at times reaching heights of 8m from the outside to the top. The wall includes over 50 defence towers, and several gates. Along many parts it is possible to stroll along the city wall, and it affords a great opportunity to see the people of Sa'ada going about their daily affairs.

There is a large **souk** through the main Bab al-Yemen gate. The market has a great distinctive feel to it, giving the impression of what the Sana'a souk might have been like 50 years ago. One of the interesting things still sold in the souk are the old **Maria Theresa Thalers**, the silver Austrian coins that were used as Yemen's main currency until the 1962 revolution. Regardless of the strike date, all Thalers bear the date of 1780 in commemoration of Empress Theresa's death. Although these coins are rare in most other parts of the country, they exist here in relatively abundant quantities. If you are interested, there is a small stand near the gate; if it is not staffed, you can ask around and someone will probably show up thereafter. The selling price is 2,000YR.

Zaydi Cemetery
To the west of the Old City gate is the vast Zaydi Cemetery. The cemetery contains hundreds of inscribed tombstones, many of which are quite nice. There are also crumbling dome structures over the families of more (wealthy) holy folk. Foreigners are not allowed in many Islamic cemeteries across Yemen, but here the prohibition seems to be lifted. That said, one should show the utmost respect while walking through the cemetery. In Islam, it is forbidden to sing or laugh in the cemetery; needless to say, you shouldn't walk over the graves.

Al-Hadi Mosque
The al-Hadi Mosque of Sa'ada contains the grave of Imam al-Hadi ila al-Haqq, the first Zaydi Imam of Yemen, and his two sons. The mosque is said to be built on the spot where Muhammad's camel once rested. Given the importance of the shrine and the natural distrust of foreigners in the area, it is highly unlikely that you would ever be granted permission to enter the building.

AROUND SA'ADA

SINARA CASTLE
Although there is a new road leading to the top of the mountain where Sinara Castle is located, a 4x4 vehicle is still necessary to make the climb. Once inside the fortress, your impromptu guides or the resident soldiers will be quick to take you to the well-known tourist destination of Sinara Castle – the *Sit*, and underground water chamber with nice acoustics. The castle has some great views of the countryside, and strolling around the grounds is pleasant.

SAMA' CASTLE
Although it is less visited than Sinara Castle, Sama' is a lovely fortress. There is less graffiti in the interior of the castle than at Sinara, although a couple of rooms are painted in odd styles that combine depictions of modern things like aircrafts with traditional Islamic designs. Although the exterior of Sinara Castle is a little more impressive, Sama' Castle is in slightly better shape, and it is

possible to climb the tower steps to the top and take in the wonderful views (including that impressive Sinara Castle). In any event, if you're out here, you'll probably visit both castles. The ten-minute drive between the two takes you through the quaint grape-growing town of 'Abdayn ('the two slaves').

UMM LAYLA The mountains of Umm Layla contains a Sabaean fortress used to guard the highland incense route, and there are several pre-Islamic inscriptions in the area.

SOUK AT-TALH The market town located to the north of Sa'ada hosts the largest market in the country and the biggest venue for the purchase and sale of guns.

FARWAH Located outside Sa'ada, the town of Farwah (meaning 'rich') takes its name from the fabled quality of the soil. The precious earth of the region is now used to grow grapes, and the distinct red colour is famous all over the country. Apart from the vines frothing over the walled-in fields, there are large multi-storeyed mud-brick buildings with wide foundations that narrow as your eyes rise upwards. The architecture of the buildings is very similar to that of Shabwa and Azzan.

With the region having been closed off for so long because of the al-Houthi scare, and because most tourists do not visit Farwah when travelling to Sa'ada, the children are very curious when tourists appear. You'll most likely have a large congregation gathered within 20 minutes, so have your camera ready for the inevitable cries of 'Sura! Sura!'. The children know how to whistle loudly here, and they will likely prove their ability to do so over and over again.

BUQA' The small town of Buqa' is one of the main border crossings into Saudi Arabia. The town has one main street, and you are given the impression that you are walking down a gauntlet of shack vendors who offer you the last opportunity to purchase their Yemeni wares. There was an airport built here, with grand plans to convert the small town into a larger city. In a familiar theme, however, tribal clashes ended those hopes and dreams. Now, the main source of its fame lies in its position in last place on the list of cities recited daily on the weather portion of the national news programme. ('And in Buqa', the temperature is a balmy 38°C.')

 Where to stay
⌂ **Funduq Buqa' Plaza** (9 rooms) Pretty basic, with shared Yemeni bathrooms. $

WWW.EGYPTAIR.BE

75 years of experience, 3 weekly flights from Brussels to Egypt, 2 direct to Cairo, 1direct to Luxor

And as everything is being done to please you ...

from November a 4th direct flight to Cairo from only

230 € return flight

EGYPTAIR PROMOTION

Return flights, prices ex taxes and according availability

NAIROBI :	565 €
DUBAI :	400 €
ENTEBBE :	500 €
KHARTOUM :	469 €
ASMARA :	500 €
PEKING :	650 €
BANGKOK :	650 €

" EGYPTAIR, MUCH MORE THAN A FLIGHT, SIMPLY A NEW WAY TO FLY "

Boulevard Emile Jacqumain 4 - 1000 Bruxelles

Phone : 02/ 219.16.14 - Fax : 02/ 219.36.81 - Email : sales.egyptair@skynet.be

158

8

The Tihama

Telephone code 03

The long coastal plain that runs down the western side of Yemen, from Midi in the north to the Bab al-Mandab in the south is distinctly different from its mountainous neighbours in terms of its people, culture, and architecture. In many ways, all of these have been influenced over the years by nearby Africa. Highlights of the region include snorkelling opportunities off Kamaran Island, camel-jumping events in the small town of al-Husayniyah, and a pleasant nature walk followed by a tough-love massage in the region of Jabal Bura. Try to avoid visiting the area in the summer, when the heat is nearly unbearable.

HISTORY

The word 'Tihama' likely traces its origin back to an old Semitic root meaning something along the lines of 'the deep of the sea' – possibly the same root which gave rise to the name of Tiamat, the Babylonian goddess who personified the saltwater ocean.

Recent discoveries of a few Palaeolithic and Bronze-Age settlements in the region indicate that the area of Tihama was settled long before previously thought. Little is known about what these civilisations were like, or what became of them. Trade existed between the Sabaeans and Ethiopians, which means there must have been more settlements along the Tihama to facilitate this exchange.

At some point the powerful 'Akk tribe arose in the Tihama. Although there had been a tribal delegation to Mecca to profess loyalty to Islam, the 'Akk tribe revolted against central Islamic control (as did several other regions of Yemen) shortly after the death of Muhammad. The rebellion was short lived, having been crushed by a large force sent to the region by the first Caliph Abu Bakr.

The tribes of the region were not easy to placate, and neither the Umayyads nor the Abbasids was able to get a firm hold on the region. Finally in the early 9th century the Abbasid Caliph al-Ma'mun sent Muhammad bin Ziyad to the region to put an end to a larger uprising that had broken out among the 'Akk and Asha'ir tribes. When Ziyad arrived in the region, he founded the city of Zabid, from where he and his descendants would rule much of the Tihama for about two centuries.

Following the end of the Ziyadid dynasty in the early 11th century, two former slaves of the kingdom founded the Najahid dynasty. Control of the Tihama swayed back and forth between the Najahid rulers and the Sulayhid power of the highlands. In the mid 12th century, 'Ali bin Mahdi finally brought about the end of the Najahid dynasty. His own dynasty did not last long, however.

The Ayyubid forces of Saladin that landed in and conquered the Tihama in the late 12th century marked the first of several foreign invasions to which the region would be subjected. There is an old Yemeni proverb that states: 'me against my cousin and my cousin and I against the stranger.' For much of the time leading up to the modern era, this generally was not the norm in the Tihama. Instead of the tribes banding together to fight off the foreign invaders, tribes often allied themselves with the foreigners to defeat other rival tribes.

That said, the time period beginning with the 50 years of Ayyubid's building-intensive reign, followed by the productive centuries of the Rasulid dynasty, is remembered as one of the finest periods in the Tihama, but it was not a time of perfect peace – opposition among rival leaders needed to be dealt with frequently.

When the reign of the Rasulids ended in the mid 15th century, the Tahirid dynasty inherited control at a time when the tribes of the Tihama were constantly feuding with one another. Around this time, the Portuguese were spotted off the coast of the Tihama, followed by the Mamluks, who actually landed and conquered the region. By default, the Mamluks became the Ottomans once the Turkish had captured Egypt. The Ottomans remained in the region until they were finally ousted from Zabid by the son of Zaydi Imam al-Qasim in 1635.

The 15th through the late 17th century marked another period of prosperity for the region as the coffee trade became increasingly important. Coffee was brought down from the highlands of Yemen into gathering points in the Tihama, and then shipped out to the ports of al-Luhayyah or al-Mokha. Once the coffee shrub was smuggled out of the country and successfully grown in European colonies, Yemen's wealth from the trade quickly dropped off, as did the prosperity of the Tihama region in general.

In the beginning of the 1800s, the Tihama was encroached again, this time from the north. The new Wahhabi power in Saudi Arabia had gained control of the Tihama when the local Sharif abu Mizmar swore allegiance to the northern power. Regretting his decision, abu Mizmar withdrew his support, and as a result a

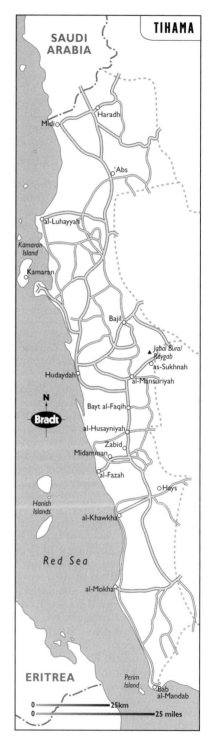

large Wahhabi force marched southward into Yemen and devastated much of the northern Tihama.

The Wahhabis were repelled with the help of the Egyptians, who remained in the country for another two decades until the Ottomans began their second occupation. In the years leading up to World War I, the Italo-Turkish War broke out, and as a result the Italians bombed several locations in the Tihama. With the outbreak of the war, it was the British, who had secured the colony of Aden less than a century earlier, who took to bombing Ottoman sites in the Tihama.

In addition to the many enemies the Ottomans faced in Yemen (the Italians from the air, the British from the south, and Imam Yahya from the east), they soon had to deal with a large revolt within the Tihama itself as Muhammad al-Idrisi began his uprising. It was not hard for al-Idrisi to attract a large following – his great-grandfather had been regarded as a local saint and his family renowned as fair and neutral arbitrators. When the tribes of the area complained to al-Idrisi that the Ottomans were levying unfair taxes upon them, al-Idrisi declared that the Ottoman governor was ousted. Of course, it really was not as easy as that, but al-Idrisi's statement emboldened the tribes to begin a rebellion that would last in some form or another until the Ottomans left the country a decade later.

During the early 1900s the Ottomans, Imam Yahya and al-Idrisi all vied for power in the Tihama. In 1911, Imam Yahya and the Ottomans entered into the Treaty of Da'in, which gave the highlands to the imamate and the Tihama to the occupying forces. In response, al-Idrisi entered into an alliance with the British in Aden three years later. During the course of World War I, the British forces supplied al-Idrisi with funding, training and protection.

Because Imam Yahya never agreed to help the British fight against the Ottomans, the British naturally bequeathed control of the Tihama to al-Idrisi. After taking control of most of the region, al-Idrisi died in 1923. With funding from the Italians, Imam Yahya finally was able to occupy Hudaydah and much of the northern Tihama, although the British maintained control of Kamaran Island.

The Sunni Tihama tribes, however, were not willing to submit to the rule of the Zaydi Imamate. The Zaraniq tribe in particular led a fierce revolt against the imamate which took nearly two years to put down. In 1925, the sheikh of the Zaraniq tribe sent a telegraph to the League of Nations, requesting that the international body recognise an independent Zaraniq state. Imam Yahya dealt harshly with the rebellion, imprisoning nearly 1,000 of the tribesmen in the infamous Nafi' Prison in Hajjah. Over 800 of the prisoners died there.

AL-LUHAYYAH

HISTORY It's hard to believe that the small town of al-Luhayyah was once one of Yemen's biggest ports. The town was founded at the dawn of the 15th century by the local mystic 'Ali az-Zayla'i. The interest in the local saint (who is buried in the town's mosque) quickly attracted new settlers, and within a century the unassuming village had turned into a bustling town.

From the 16th–18th centuries, al-Luhayyah was an economically successful port town, competing with the town of Mokha to the south in exporting coffee. Additionally, pearl diving blossomed in the city once al-Luhayyah acquired a regional reputation for the beauty of its pearls. For several centuries, it vied with its neighbour Massawa across the sea in modern Eritrea in production and quality. Both cities claimed the title 'Pearl of the Red Sea'.

In 1762, Carsten Niebuhr and five other scientists arrived at the port of al-Luhayyah, having been commissioned by the King of Denmark to embark on a scientific expedition of Yemen in search of information on biblical history. At the time, al-Luhayyah was still enjoying its status as a busy port city, and Niebuhr and his companions were welcomed to the city. Niebuhr described the residents of the port city as 'curious, intelligent and polished in their manners'. He may have used the word 'curious' specifically to describe the emir of the town, who took great delight in playing with Niebuhr's microscope.

In the 19th century al-Luhayyah lost the stature it had once held. The rise of al-Hudaydah as a major port, as well as a political and economic centre of the region contributed heavily to al-Luhayyah's downfall. Other factors contributed as well: first, in 1809 shortly after much of the Tihama had been subjugated to the Saudi Wahhabis, a local ruler of northern Tihama tried to reassert control of the area. In response, the Wahhabi forces marched southward and practically burned the city of al-Luhayyah to the ground. Later, in 1911, the city faced another attack as Italian forces bombarded the city at the outset of the Italo-Turkish war. Within a century the bustling town had turned into an unassuming village.

GETTING THERE Due to its northern location and vicinity to Sa'ada, tourists are not allowed to travel to al-Luhayyah except by hiring a private car through a local travel agency.

WHERE TO STAY There are no hotels in al-Luhayyah, so if you are planning on spending the night here, you either need to camp nearby or pull up a mattress on the floor of the police station. There is a decent camping spot *sans* mosquitoes on the northern side of town – ask the police chief to show you where it is.

WHAT TO SEE Today al-Luhayyah is a small fishing village, and little remains of the Old City's port trade or pearl-diving trade. Local divers now look for sea cucumbers, which are shipped off to east Asia. Nevertheless, if you arrive in July (the month of the pearling season) and offer the right financial incentive, you may be able to get one of the fishermen to dive for you.

There is a small souk within the city – kept surprisingly clean by a daily night sweeping. Within the large and multi-domed **Great Mosque** is the tomb of 'Ali al-Zayla'i, the 15th-century mystic who founded the city. The mosque itself, however, only dates back to the 19th-century Turkish occupation. Other evidence of the Ottoman occupation (such as several fortifications) exists just outside the town on the hill of **Jabal al-Milh** ('the Mountain of Salt').

More impressive is the large **mangrove forest** that blossoms up around the region and forms a maze of navigable water channels through the marshes that lead to the sea. Past the mangroves and into the open water, there are several serene and uninhabited **islands** that present good snorkelling and lazy idling opportunities. For anywhere from 5,000–10,000YR, it is possible to hire a boat to go through the mangroves and out to the islands.

If you are planning on doing anything more than a brief stopover in the town (ie: heading out to the islands or camping in the area), it is a good idea to stop first at the local police station to let the local officers know you are in town and what you are planning on doing there. This will save you a lot of grief later.

There is not much to see to the north of al-Luhayyah unless you have a visa for Saudi Arabia. There is a border crossing outside the town of **Haradh**. For information on crossing into Saudi Arabia, see *Chapter 2*, page 45.

KAMARAN ISLAND

HISTORY Popular legend holds that Kamaran Island got its name because island's villagers were able to view the moon's reflection twice in the sea. It's hard to have a lot of faith in the story, given that Kamaran only sounds like the Arabic word for 'two moons' (*qamaran*) and that the moon does not seem to reflect twice in the surrounding waters. Nevertheless, the legend abounds, and Kamaran has acquired the nickname 'the island of the two moons'.

Another legend proposes a different origin: a young Yemeni princess named Kamaran recovered on the island from a life-threatening sickness. In gratitude for the island's role in saving his daughter, the king named it after her. The legend has some merit when you consider that 'Kamaran' is a Kurdish name and that previous occupying forces, such as the Ayyubids and the Rasulids, were of Kurdish origin. The gaping hole in the story, of course, is how anyone in the Middle Ages could have recovered anywhere on the 100 square miles of barren island.

The ruins of an old Persian fortress and tomb dating back to the Persian occupation of the 7th century are the earliest bits of historical evidence we have to shed light on Kamaran's early history. Little about the island is known for the next 1,000 years or so. In the early 16th century, the island was occupied briefly by the Portuguese. By the end of the same century, the island had been taken by the Ottomans.

During the second Ottoman occupation in the 19th century, Kamaran Island enjoyed great prosperity. Health installations were set up, and the island acted as a mandatory quarantine for pilgrims travelling to Mecca. Thousands of pilgrims from Africa and the Indian subcontinent were inspected and treated at the island each year, and the population and development of Kamaran blossomed as a result.

The British forces took control of the island in 1915, using the island as a strategic base and continuing to maintain and even enlarge the quarantine operations. Saudi Arabia decided that the island should not be the sole profiteer in the pilgrimage business. In the early 1950s it constructed its own quarantine camp, demanding that all pilgrims go through the process there. The Kamaran camp closed in 1952; the development that had built up around the camp soon slipped away.

After the British left Yemen in 1967, South Yemen (and shortly thereafter the PDRY) inherited control of the island. During a border dispute with the north in 1972, the PDRY lost the island to the northern YAR. Ownership of the island was a source of constant tension for the two countries until at last Yemen was unified in 1990.

GETTING THERE To get to Kamaran Island, you first need to make your way to the village of as-Salif by turning off the Hudaydah–al-Luhayyah road. Buses and bijous don't frequent the town, so you'll have to have your own transportation. Once in as-Salif, you can hire someone to transport you the 20-minute hop over the sea on a small boat (known locally as a *falūka*) for 7,000YR (roundtrip).

 WHERE TO STAY

Kamaran Island Camp (9 rooms) m 77 711742; e mam@kamaran.net; www.kamaran.net. Located on the northeast side of the island, the camp provides basic Tihama-style straw huts completely isolated from the rest of the island's villages. The hotel offers a number of tours of the island, including the northern mangrove forests (US$45), fishing trips (US$45), donkey treks (US$20) & more ambitious tours to the other islands of the region (US$175). Renting a boat for diving excursions costs between US$75 & US$150 for 3hrs. $$$pp. B&B.

If you want to stay in Kamaran and either do not want to spend the cash on the island hut or just want to be closer to the village, you can get a mattress on the floor at the **Buffeeya**, a small restaurant and store located at the base of the old Turkish fort.

8

WHERE TO EAT The only places to sit down and have a meal on the island are at the **Island Camp** on the northeast side of the island and the small **Buffeeya** in Kamaran village. The restaurant at the former can serve an array of Yemeni dishes (**$$$$**). The Buffeeya, primarily a small supply and tea store, serves up fish and rice for visitors. It may take a while to get your food here – after an order the store owner needs to run back to his house and have his wife cook the food. (**$$**).

WHAT TO SEE Kamaran and the surrounding islands offer excellent **diving opportunities**. The prices offered by Island Camp for equipment and boat rental might be a bit steeper than the sites at Hudaydah or Socotra, but the diving areas around Kamaran are some of the best in the world. The islands make up the tail end of the Farasan Bank, an 800km-long shoal that stretches up into the waters of Saudi Arabia that Jacques Cousteau raved about in his book *The Living Sea*. Noting that the Bank was one of the most interesting diving sites he had explored in the Red Sea, Cousteau noted that learning about the area's 'reef structures and marine biological richness would take a lifetime'. Outside Kamaran, the diving sites of note include the islands of Uqban, Zubayr, and Six Foot Rock.

A large yacht named the ***Katharina Maha*** is normally anchored in the bay of Kamaran village, looking oddly out of place in Yemen. The yacht normally can be booked for sailing and diving trips in the area, although it was out of commission for minor repairs when I was last there. Send an email (*info@ftiyemen.com*) for updates. The name of the Yacht is steeped in gossip.

Kamaran village does not have too much to see in the way of tourist sites – the old **Ottoman fort** is unimpressive. To the north of the island there are **mangrove forests** and a variety of wildlife; boats can be rented from the village or the tourist Island Camp.

HUDAYDAH

HISTORY The first mention of the city of al-Hudaydah appears in documents dating back to 1454 that concern the rise to power of the Tahirid dynasty, but from then until some time afterwards, the port city remained relatively unimportant. Even the traveller Carsten Niebuhr, as late as his expedition in 1763, noted that the three major ports of the Tihama were Aden, al-Mokha and al-Luhayyah. Al-Hudaydah wasn't even on the radar.

The town was raided by the Mamluk forces in 1516, and again during Wahhabi incursion in 1810. The town began to develop in the 1800s – the Ottomans attempted to build up the port to rival the British-controlled Aden to the south. During the Italo-Turkish War, the Italians bombed al-Hudaydah. A British bombardment followed during World War I.

During the war, the British worked closely with Muhammad 'Ali al-Idrisi, the crafty head of the Idrisi clan in Asir. After the Ottomans were defeated and withdrew, the British favoured al-Idrisi over the Zaydi Imam Yahya in northern Yemen, and bestowed upon the former full control of Hudaydah and much of the Tihama.

The independent Idrisid state did not last very long. Al-Idrisi died four years after he had occupied Hudaydah. The rivalry and confusion within the Idrisid state after his death opened the door for Imam Yahya to take Hudaydah.

Both northern Yemen and Saudi Arabia moved to fill the void created by the collapse of the short-lived Asir state. As the two states expanded, conflict became inevitable, and in 1934 war was declared between the two powers. The Saudis won the war decisively, and they had managed to capture Hudaydah in the conflict. Only by signing the Treaty of Taif in the same year, and by giving up their claim to the traditionally recognised Yemeni areas of Asir and Najran, was Imam Yahya able to reacquire Hudaydah.

Around the time of the Yemeni revolution, al-Hudaydah began to gain in commercial importance. Although the port did not have any deep-water capabilities, an extensive project was undertaken by the Soviet Union in the early 1960s, and a new deep-water port was opened outside the city.

Today Hudaydah is the biggest and most important port in Yemen after Aden, and the largest city in the Tihama. Its major economic value continues to lie solely on account of its location along the Red Sea, and as a port it acts as a major zone for imports to the country. Driving down the road from Sana'a to Hudaydah, you will frequently see carrier trucks full of Toyota Landcruisers fresh off the boat making their way to the capital to be sold.

GETTING THERE Buses travel from Hudaydah to Sana'a (1,050YR), Aden (1,300YR), Ta'iz (950YR), Zabid (400YR), and Bayt al-Faqih (200YR). Shared taxis cover the same destinations for roughly the same price.

⌂ WHERE TO STAY

⌂ **Hudaydah Land Resort** (34 rooms) Off Sana'a St, after the turn for the airport; ☎ 03 230512; f 03 230513. In terms of places to stay, the Hudaydah Land Resort is the best thing happening in Hudaydah. In addition to a bedroom, *majlis* & clean Western-style bathroom, each chalet contains its own decently sized outdoor swimming pool enclosed by a wall to ensure privacy. Common areas on the grounds include another swimming pool, restaurant, grocery store, & billiards room. Owner Ali al-Marree is undertaking a complete facelift of the Hudaydah resort. He has already finished the resort & adjoining Hudaydah Land Amusement Park; next on the agenda is a Dubai-like Palm Resort, a large sports centre & a zoo. $$$$; *with private swimming pool* $$$$$

⌂ **Ambassador Hotel** (59 rooms) Sana'a St; ☎ 03 230850; f 03 230808; e ambassadorhotel@y.net.ye. Although the rooms & Western bathrooms are clean, many rooms are pervaded by an unpleasant smell, & some tourists have complained about their stays. $$$; *suites* $$$$

⌂ **Shami Plaza Hotel** (16 rooms) Corniche St; ☎ 03 207467; f 03 207462. Clean rooms on the beach with Western bathrooms. Prices range according to the season. $$$; *suites* $$$$

⌂ **Taj Awsan Hotel** (64 rooms) Sana'a St; ☎ 03 235270; f 03 235277; e tajawsan_hotel@yahoo.com. Nice rooms with clean Western bathrooms. The Bilqis Restaurant & Bar on the top floor has a wide selection of food & drinks. B/fast is included & is served in the lower Arwa Restaurant. Internet available to those with laptops. $$$; *suites* $$$$

⌂ **Al-Kokha Plaza Sweets** (15 rooms) Corniche St; ☎ 03 208262; f 03 208304. The dbl rooms on the lower level are some of the best value in Hudaydah. The 'sweets' are quite spacious, & can easily accommodate 3–4 people. $$; *suites* $$$$

⌂ **Al-Fakhama Hotel** (77 rooms) Corniche St; ☎ 03 213009; f 03 213008. Rooms are decent; get one overlooking the sea. Visa/Mastercard accepted. Prices range slightly between low season & high season. $$$

⌂ **Al-Ikwa Hotel** (38 rooms) Sana'a St; ☎ 03 201148; f 03 201147. Not particularly pleasant, but very gentle on the wallet. $

⌂ **Al-Burg Hotel** (29 rooms) Sana'a St; ☎ 03 201114; f 03 201113. The hotel was undergoing renovations while I was in town, but regardless, the rooms seemed cramped & not particularly clean. $$

✗ WHERE TO EAT

✗ **Bilqis Restaurant & Bar** Sana'a St; ☎ 03 235270; ⏰ 11.30–14.00, 17.30–20.00. Located in the Taj Awsan Hotel, the Bilqis offers a large selection of food & alcohol available from an English menu. $$$

✗ **Al-Sindbad** ⏰ 11.30–14.00, 17.30–20.00. Located directly across from the People's Garden, the al-Sindbad Restaurant is one of the most popular local venues in Hudaydah. The restaurant serves a huge variety of dishes, & there is a large menu printed on the wall. Try the 'Al-Sindbad Special Dish'. $$

✗ **Big Bite Pizza** Corniche St; ☎ 03 207467; ⏰ 11.30–14.00, 17.30–20.00. The restaurant adjoins the Shami Plaza Hotel & serves up tasty seafood & Indian dishes but oddly no pizza. $$

OTHER PRACTICALITIES There are **ATMs** located at the Tadhamon International Islamic Bank (Mina'a St) and the Saba Islamic Bank (Sana'a St).

WHAT TO SEE Hudaydah definitely has a feel of its own. In speaking about the city with two separate travellers on two separate occasions, they both stated that the only thing they could offer to compare the city to was the Mos Eisley Cantina from *Star Wars*. The comparison had more to do with the colour and oddities of the city than with Obi Won's warning to Luke that he would 'never find a more wretched hive of scum and villainy'.

The most interesting site in Hudaydah without a doubt is the local **Fish Market** (⊕ *06.00–09.00 daily*). Located by the docks, you can delve into haggling for your breakfast or simply watch the fishermen bring their large catches to the shore, unload them, and sell them on the spot to willing customers. The fishermen bring in a vast variety from which to choose.

For a surreal experience, stop by the **Hudaydah Land Amusement Park** (⊕ *09.00–23.00 Sat–Thu, 12.30–23.00 Fri; entrance fee: 30YR; rides 50–100YR*). The park offers a variety of rides, games, a swimming pool and a restaurant. While there are regularly several hundred visitors on Thursdays and Fridays, try to stop by if you are in the area during Eid al-Fitr, when the amusement park fills up with over 2,000 Muslims looking for family entertainment and gaiety after the month-long fast of Ramadan.

OUTSIDE HUDAYDAH

JABAL BURA The region around Jabal Bura (⊕ *09.00–dusk; entrance fee: 500YRpp – cars 200YR extra*) is lush with both plant and animal life. Among the animals of the region are baboons, turtles, rock hyraxes and a large assortment of birds and butterflies. (There have been recent reports that a large number of baboons died after the installation of new power lines.) Along with the areas of 'Utmah, Hof, and Socotra, Jabal Bura is one of the Environmentally Protected Areas of Yemen, but Jabal Bura is the only one among the four that has an actual 'nature park' feeling to it.

There are several signs with pictures of animals (such as baboons, rock hyraxes, turtles, and cobras) pointing in various directions. The signs seem to have no relationship whatsoever to where any of these animals can be found. One of the park wardens said that the signs were put up to keep the local Yemenis from littering. Whether because of ingenious sign placement or otherwise, there is little rubbish in the area to spoil the forest views. Previously, tourists were permitted to camp in the area, but it was no longer allowed when I was there. Check with the gatekeeper if you are curious whether the policy has reverted.

Three walking paths are marked with signs in Arabic (معبار), and lead to various villages in the area, ranging in length from three to seven hours. At the end of the road, a path leads up to the village of **Raygab** (1,870 m), the head of the district, perched atop one of the mountains. The walk up will take about ten hours. A much more leisurely stroll can be had by walking from Raygab down to the protected area, which will take about six-and-a-half hours. From Raygab, there is another easy walk to **Wadi Rayjaf** that takes about five hours.

AS-SUKHNAH Located near the base of Jabal Bura, the town of as-Sukhnah is known for its hot spas and vigorous massages. The town served as Imam Ahmed's winter retreat, and the palace and spa he had built there remains. Yemenis still turn up to the town to bathe in the waters in an attempt to cure a variety of ailments.

There are two hammams in town: one in the basement of Imam Ahmed's old palace, and another for the mere common man. Unless you have a particular desire to partake of the old royal hammam, the latter one is actually a bit better. Both hammams contain three separate vats of increasingly hot water.

While there is a number of other important spa towns in Yemen (such as Hammam Damt and Hammam 'Ali) as-Sukhnah is the only one that is also famous for its masseuses. Each trip to the hammams here includes an invigorating massage (including a very painful technique in which the masseuse pulls on some nerves in your armpit). The cost of baths and massage is 1,000YRpp.

Halfway between as-Sukhnah and either Hudaydah or Bayt al-Faqih is the medium-sized town of **Mansuriyyah**. There are a lot of supply stores and local restaurants here, and a weekly market is held on Wednesday.

ZABID

HISTORY The fiercely independent tribes of the Tihama have had a historical tendency toward rebellion against foreign control. Shortly after Muhammad's death, the 'Akk tribes revolted against Medinan control to avoid the Islamic taxes that continued to be levied. Revolts broke out against both the Umayyads and the Abbasids; as late as the 1920s, the Zaraniq tribe (descendants of the 'Akk tribes) led an important uprising against Imam Yahya.

In each of these instances, the rebellions were crushed – but it was in quelling one of these uprisings that the city of Zabid was founded. In the early 9th century the 'Akk and Asha'ir tribes led a Tihama-wide revolt against the Baghdad-based Abbasid Caliphate. The Abbasids had been trying to exert control of the Tihama region for over 70 years. On the advice of his vizier, Caliph al-Ma'mun sent Muhammad bin Ziyad to the region to extinguish the rebellion and to establish a local capital to ensure another did not arise.

Ziyad began his task in 819 and made significant progress toward bullying the tribes into submission. The next year, he established his military capital at the village of al-Husayb, which lay on the important pilgrimage route from Aden to Mecca. Serving as an ideal spot both strategically and economically, the village expanded until the small town became the large city of Zabid. (The new city took its name from the neighbouring wadi.)

Perhaps feeling a little homesick, or else in order to impress the surrounding tribes, Ziyad had the new city designed with a circular layout similar to the Abbasid capital of Baghdad. Accordingly, Zabid quickly acquired the nickname 'the Baghdad of Yemen' – not a particularly pleasant appellation today. Over time, however, Zabid had as many as four defensive walls built around it. The round city, encircled by a number of concentric rings, began to look more like a picture of Saturn than Baghdad. Of course, this might very well have been the idea; the Yemenis have always had a soft spot for astrology.

When Ziyad first arrived in the city the al-Asha'ir Mosque was already standing, but he soon ordered the construction of the Great Mosque and several others, which would help establish Zabid's reputation as a centre of Islam. The rule of Ziyad's dynasty – the Ziyadids – lasted until 1018. Throughout that time Zabid continued to grow in stature as an economic and religious centre of the country.

After the Ziyadid dynasty fell, control of Zabid passed on to the brothers Najah and Nafis, two Abyssinians who had been slaves of the Ziyadids. Shortly after their rise to power, Najah dispatched with Nafis and assumed sole control of Zabid and much of the Tihama, founding the Najahid dynasty that would play an important role in the city until 1158.

Two decades after Najah came to power, 'Ali al-Sulayhi quickly rose to power in the Haraz Mountains and began conquering much of Yemen. As a purported sign of friendship and goodwill, al-Sulayhi sent Najah a beautiful slave girl who had been instructed to poison the ruler in Zabid. Al-Sulayhi's ruse worked – Najah readily accepted the girl, and he died shortly thereafter.

Of course al-Sulayhi's foul play permanently soured relations between the Najahids and the Sulayhids, and the next 100 years or so saw a series of murders and several shifts of the control of Zabid. Najah's son Sa'id 'the squinty' avenged his father by murdering al-Sulayhi and absconding with his beautiful wife Asma back to Zabid. Asma was eventually rescued (although not before becoming pregnant with Sa'id's child). Sa'id was eventually killed when he was invited to a meeting to discuss how to overthrow Queen Arwa al-Sulayhi. The meeting had been set up as a ruse by Arwa herself.

The last Najahid ruler was murdered in Zabid by the ruthless 'Ali bin Mahdi, founder of the equally ruthless Mahdid dynasty. Luckily for the people of Zabid, the Mahdid reign did not last for long. The dynasty was overrun by the Kurdish Ayyubids of the famous Saladin in 1173, less than two decades after taking power.

During the two centuries of Rasulid rule, Zabid gained further in stature and reputation. The city was used as a winter home for the Rasulid rulers, who continued to build mosques and schools in the scholarly city. A late 14th-century survey of the city revealed over 230 mosques and schools.

By the middle of the 15th century the Rasulid dynasty had ended and Zabid began its gradual decline toward decay. During the Ottoman occupation the Turks used the city as a military base, and the frequent attacks on the city by the surrounding tribes took its toll. Additionally, Zabid began to lose its financial viability. As the coffee trade blossomed, so did the economic importance of those areas where the beans could be grown, gathered, or shipped. Zabid was not any of these.

In 1993, Zabid became one of three Yemeni cities (along with Sana'a and Shibam Hadhramawt) proclaimed by UNESCO as a World Heritage Site. In 2000, it was the only city in Yemen to be given 'World Heritage Site in Danger' status.

GETTING THERE Zabid can be reached by bus from Ta'iz (600YR), Aden (1,100YR) and Hudaydah (400YR). Destinations *en route* to any of these places are available at a lower cost.

🏠 WHERE TO STAY

🏠 **Istrahah Zabid Hotel** (4 rooms) 📞 03 341270. Located behind the Zabid citadel, the quaint hotel offers a number of cots in hostel-style rooms. There are three shared bathrooms, and a large sitting area. $$

WHAT TO SEE Not much remains of Zabid's glorious past. While the 14th-century city contained over 230 mosques and schools, modern Zabid now numbers 29 mosques and 53 schools. Ruins of the old wall remain where once there were four concentric circles of protection. The souks in the centre of the town are not of much interest.

There are four gates to the city, each of which has retained its name since at least the age of the Rasulids. The eastern gate is known as Bab Shubariq, the northern as Bab Shiham, and the southern as Bab Ghurtub – each of these names refer to a different area of the country to which each gate points. The western gate, known today as Bab an-Nakhil ('the Gate of Dates') was previously known as Bab Ghulayfiga, which referred to a region of the Tihama along the sea. During the reign of the Rasulids, the name of the gate was changed, probably in reference to the wildly popular Subut an-Nakhil ('the Sabbaths of the Dates'), a decadent date-harvesting festival that included activities such as co-ed group bathing.

Of the mosques that remain in Zabid, three are worthy of particular note. The oldest mosque in the city, the **al-Asha'ir Mosque**, was built during Muhammad's lifetime in AD629 by Abu Musa al-Asha'iri after he led a tribal delegation to Mecca to profess allegiance to Islam. Since its construction the mosque has undergone several major restorations: once by al-Hussein bin Salama in 1016 and once by al-Mansur 'Abd al-Wahhab of the Tahirid dynasty in 1486. The **Great Mosque** was built shortly after the founding of Zabid proper in 820.

The **Iksander Mosque** dates back to the 13th-century reign of the Ayyubids, although the minaret dates to the later Ottoman occupation. The best thing about the Iksander Mosque is that it is generally open to tourists (dress appropriately). This mosque and the al-'Ashrafiyah Mosque in Ta'iz are your best opportunities to enter and examine a beautiful medieval mosque in Yemen. Within the Iksander Mosque there are some restoration efforts underway, but it is still possible to see the beautiful relief work and the intricate calligraphy that spells out the 99 names of God listed in the Koran. A huge dome rises from the centre. The Iksander Mosque is within the larger **Zabid Citadel**, which also includes the **Nasr Palace**, an Ottoman building dating from the early 1800s.

There is an ornately decorated house in the town once used by the Italian director **Pier Paolo Pasolini** in his film *Il fiore delle Mille e una Notte* ('The Flower of the 1001 Arabian Nights'). Pasolini filmed scenes in the movie in both Zabid and Sana'a, and he fell in love with the country. He referred to Yemen as the most beautiful country in the world, and his pleas to UNESCO were instrumental in getting Zabid recognised as a World Heritage Site. The main room of the building is a lovely little *diwan* that is perfect for taking a short, relaxing break. Entrance is free, but the owner always appreciates a generous tip.

BAYT AL-FAQIH

History The town of Bayt al-Faqih is located 40km to the north of Zabid. It was founded in the 13th century by the travelling scholar Ahmed bin Musa al-'Ujayl, who is buried in the town. 'Ujayl, venerated as an important saint in the area, seems to have been more focused on the sciences than mysticism – there are far fewer miracles attributed to him than al-'Aydarus of Aden or al-Suwayni of Tarim. After his death, the city took on its current name, meaning 'House of the Scholar'.

Bayt al-Faqih quickly expanded as a major commercial centre as the demand for coffee grew from the 16th century onward. Coffee beans were gathered in various regions of the Yemeni highlands and shipped onward to Bayt al-Faqih, where a large market sprung up to deal with the trade. When Carsten Niebuhr's expedition arrived in the city in 1763, he noted that merchants had come from Europe, Persia and India.

Getting there & away Shared taxis run to Zabid (50YR, ½hr) and Hudaydah (200YR, 3hrs).

What to see The primary attraction of Bayt al-Faqih remains the **weekly market** that began to accommodate the coffee trade. The market, which takes place on Friday mornings, is one of the largest in the country, and people come out in droves for the shopping. Coffee is no longer the main commodity – today, the merchants' wares include fruit and vegetables, live animals, clothing, handicrafts, and a variety of odds and ends.

The **Zabid Fortress** was used as a garrison to control the region during the time of Imam Yahya. While there are plans to repair the building, they are not likely to be implemented any time soon. Even so, the castle is not in that bad a condition. The mosque inside the fortress was built in 1930, and there is some relief work on the walls near the religious structure. The guard tower is currently inhabited by bats. There is no fee to enter the castle, but you should tip the doorman 200–300YR.

Zabid has long been known for the quality of its textiles, and although the weavers are not as prominent as they once were, there is a small **handicraft workshop** in the backstreets of the town where a couple of men maintain the tradition. The workshop contains two large looms that are used to create the *mawwaz*, the wrap-around skirts worn by many Yemeni men. In addition to being able to purchase the *mawwaz* made at the site (4,000–10,000YR), you'll be able to watch the men work the loom. To find the place, ask around for the 'al-maHaylika' (المحيلكه).

AL-HUSAYNIYAH The small town of al-Husayniyah is centred between the cities of Zabid and Bayt al-Faqih – about 20km from each. Although the town has a few small restaurants and stores to stock up on basic supplies, there is not much reason to stop here unless you want to see the famed camel jumpers.

History Al-Husayniyah was built on the site of an older village named Fashal. In the mid 14th century, the village was burned to the ground as a result of rivalries between members of the Rasulid dynasty. About 100 years after its destruction, the town was rebuilt by and took its name from Husayn bin Salman al-Ahdal.

Getting there & away It is possible to take a shared taxi from either Zabid or Bayt al-Faqih (50YR, ½hr), although practically speaking, it is better to come by private vehicle. (This way, for instance, if you are coming from Zabid, you can stop in the town and ask about the camel jumping. If it will take a while to organize, or is not

Life isn't a bowl of cherries for the camel-jumping elite. They may win the esteem of their fellow townsmen and even President Ali Abdullah Saleh himself, but all that praise can come at a steep price. Those who receive praise must also take steps to guard against the Evil Eye.

Yemenis, like people of many other cultures, put a lot of stock in the notion of the Evil Eye – that one's fortunes can be turned to disaster by the envious stares of others. Thus, when admiration is expressed (and in particular of women), Yemenis will often add the phrase *ma sha` Allah* ('what God wishes') to prevent the Evil Eye from doing any harm.

Salam 'Ali was one of the best camel jumpers al-Husayniyah had ever seen, his mystical jumping abilities allowing him on occasion to leap over seven camels. It is common knowledge in al-Husayniyah that Salam 'Ali had an accident that has prevented his participation in the sport because everyone was jealous of his jumping abilities. We are hoping that the great jumper can recover at some point and continue to follow his passion.

possible to see at the moment, you can continue on to Bayt al-Faqih, and return later as needed.)

What to see There is not much to see in al-Husayniyah in terms of sites, but the town has a great athletic tradition that has to be seen to be fully appreciated. On an irregular basis, the town hosts the **Husayniyah Sports Festival**, and the city's racetrack stadium fills up with tens of thousands to watch the horse- and camel-racing events. The six-day festival draws a pool of over 500 athletes, mainly from the Tihama, lowlands, and desert regions of the country.

In addition to the races, the festival also holds **camel-jumping competitions**, where men run headlong at a row of camels before springing off a half-metre dirt mound in an attempt to leap over the animals. The goal of the contest is to jump over as many camels as possible in a single leap. Camel jumpers who can clear as many as six camels usually take the prize.

This festival is held on an irregular basis. You may be able to find out if one will be occurring during your visit by contacting the Ministry of Youth and Sports in Sana'a (↘ *01 426810*). Even if there is no festival planned, it is possible to arrange a private viewing of the athletes doing what they do best if you are or have with you an Arabic speaker. There is no official procedure for arranging an exhibition – basically if you get the word out in town that you are interested, someone will find some camel jumpers for you (although it may take a couple of hours to arrange). Just do a little asking around. You'll probably pay around 10,000YR for the privilege.

MIDAMMAN The small village of Midamman is located 21km from Zabid along the road to al-Fazah, a stretch of road covered with dense date palm trees. The village of Midamman is not noteworthy except for its connection to '**Yemen Henge**', a series of Bronze-Age megaliths long known to the inhabitants of the region, and only recently found by Western archaeologists. The megaliths are a little hard to find – they stand about 5km outside Midamman, reached by dirt roads heading toward the north.

AL-KHAWKHA

Most tourists who come to al-Khawkha never actually see the village. The tourism industry here revolves around several hotels and palm tree-lined beaches that offer

It is possible to travel to African destinations from the port of al-Mokha by boat depending on when you are there. When I was there, however, the only destination to which one could travel was Djibouti. In order to get first-hand information for this guide, and because travelling by boat across the Red Sea sounded like a lovely and romantic idea, I decided to make the journey.

The first order of business is to get a visa for your country of destination. If you do not do this before coming to Yemen, you can take care of it in Sana'a. The next step is to visit the al-Mokha Port Authority. Note that no English will be spoken, so Arabic really is a must – you have to ensure not only that you elucidate what you want to do, but also that you are explaining it to the right person. You will buy your ticket there usually from the captain of the boat on the day that you want to travel. (If he is not at the port, you will be given directions to his house.) Boats typically set sail late in the evening, so if you begin the process in the morning or early afternoon (before lunchtime) you should be fine. Once you have your ticket, you will surrender your passport to the officer at the port. It will be given to the captain of your boat, and you won't see it again until you reach your destination.

The boat was supposed to set sail at 21.00, but we were not permitted to board until nearly midnight. The nearly three hours of sitting at the port, passing the time by watching the several cockroaches scurry around on the questionably seaworthy vessel that I would soon be boarding, did much to dispel any romantic notions that I previously had. Luckily once we departed, the cockroaches mysteriously all disappeared, popping up only briefly and infrequently throughout the voyage.

The passengers were equally split between men and women – the men were mostly Yemeni and the women mostly Djiboutian. Each group of about 20 or so members was herded onto a small section of wooden planks about 7m^2 to sleep.

The trip was supposed to take about 14 hours. Overnight we sailed south down the coast of Yemen toward Bab al-Mandab, where we would make the crossing. However, because the winds had grown in ferocity, the captain decided to sit out the weather by throwing down anchor about 1km from the southern tip of Yemen. Asked how long before the boat would resume the journey, the captain said, 'Whenever the winds calm. Maybe three hours; maybe three days.' Protests to push onward fell on deaf ears; the message was clear: those for whom time is a concern do not travel by boat. After 20 hours of sitting on a stationary boat at sea, we set off again. The captain was right – the winds were indeed fierce. The boat was frequently tossed about during the crossing, and we arrived in Djibouti about 36 hours after we had left Mokha. (Basic meals were provided for free on the boat.)

swimming and snorkelling opportunities, all of which are about 1km or so out from the village proper. Even many of the restaurants lie outside the town boundary. The small fishing village, however, does have a charm of its own, especially on the main dirt road where the tiny market unfolds.

The area is the launching point to visit the islands of **Hanish** and **Zuqar**, which offer some of the best snorkelling opportunities in the Red Sea. Unfortunately, visitation permits are not granted to foreigners due to the military presence on the latter. In the mid 1990s, Yemen and Eritrea had a brief scuffle over the ownership of the islands, during which nearly 200 Yemenis were captured and taken prisoner by the Eritrean forces. The prisoners were released soon afterwards, and the two countries presented their claims to the Permanent Court of Arbitration. In 1998, the court awarded full ownership of the islands to Yemen.

WHERE TO STAY

Al-Khokha Tourist Village (30 rooms) ✆ 03 362779; f 03 362780. The rooms are a little cramped, but the hotel does have its own beach. Upgrade to the suites if you need a bit more room. All rooms come with Western bathrooms. $$.

La Moka Marina Village (20 rooms) ✆ 03 362770; f 03 362771. The clean rooms that appear in the 10 different bungalows at the 'village' are the best going in al-Khawkha. While you'll have to walk about 500m to find the beach, you can idle comfortably in the shade of the hotel grounds when you return. $$. There is a large *diwan* to complete your qat-chewing experience, & a nicely equipped restaurant (*b/fast* $; *lunch/dinner* $$$).

Sindbad Hotel (12 rooms) ✆ 03 363872. Rooms here resemble small bungalows with straw ceilings, & the grounds are very peaceful. The rooms do not have AC or private bathrooms, & the nearby sea is filled with fishing boats. $. FB.

✗ WHERE TO EAT There are several small restaurants in al-Khawkha. The cleanest and best is **Mat'am Nana** (⏱ *11.30–14.00, 17.30–20.00*), which serves grilled fish. *Mains* $$

WHAT TO SEE While you may not be able to make it to Hanish Island, that's not to say that there are no snorkelling opportunities for you to enjoy here. By enquiring at any of the hotels listed above, you should be able to rent snorkelling equipment (1,000YR) or hire a boat to take you out to explore the corals (4,000YR). Otherwise, travellers come here simply to relax at the hotel beaches before continuing onward to other locations.

AL-MOKHA *Telephone code 04*

HISTORY The port city of al-Mokha is famous for being the place through which most of Yemen's coffee passed, bound for the destinations of Europe, Turkey and India to satisfy the world's growing hunger for the drink. The port was so synonymous with the bean that it lent its name to 'mocha' coffee.

The first large order of coffee beans purchased at al-Mokha for European consumption was by a group of Dutch traders in 1638. In the century that followed, al-Mokha became the main hub for the coffee trade, frequented by Dutch, Portuguese and French traders among others.

The importance of the port city dwindled after Yemen lost its relative monopoly on the coffee trade. In the late 17th century, the Dutch had managed to grow coffee on the island of Java, and Yemen's days as the sole provider of the bean ended. Mocha remained competitive in the coffee-shipping business for several more decades, until the Yemeni farms were not able to keep up with the new production at the colonies.

WHERE TO STAY

Funduq ar-Rasheed Siyyahi (19 rooms) ✆ 04 362357. If you want to spend the night in al-Mokha, the town's sole hotel has adequate rooms with Yemeni bathrooms. The AC units in the room appear to date back to World War II, but work sufficiently well to protect you from the Tihama heat. $$

WHAT TO SEE There's not much going on in al-Mokha worth checking out these days. In fact, unless you are planning on taking a boat to Djibouti or need a place to base yourself while exploring the southern Tihama, there is not much reason to come to the town. If you do find yourself in the area, the white domes and minaret of the 15th-century **ash-Shadhili Mosque** may be of interest.

8

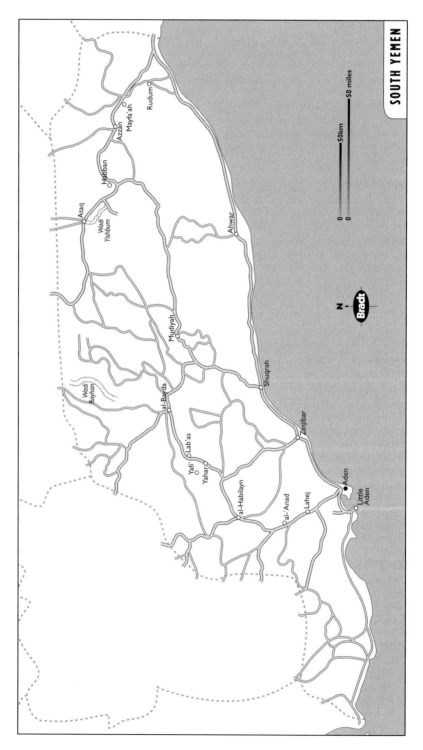

SOUTH YEMEN

0 50km
0 50 miles

N

Bradt

Rudum

Mayfa'ah
Azzan
Habban
Ataq
Wadi Yishbum
Ahwar
Mudiyah
Wadi Bayhan
al-Bayda
Shuqrah
Lab'as
Yafi'
Yahar
Zinjibar
al-Habilayn
al-'Anad
Lahej
Aden
Little Aden

9

South Yemen

Telephone code 02

ADEN

HISTORY Like many places in Yemen, Aden claims a connection to early biblical and Koranic stories. While Sana'a may claim it was founded by Noah's son Shem, local legends give Aden a more ancient claim – not only as the departure point for Noah's Ark, but also as the city founded by Cain and Abel. The tomb of Abel (who according to the Koran was buried by Cain after being instructed how to do so by a raven) is reputed to be located on Jabal Hadid.

Aden served as the main port of the Awsan Kingdom between the 9th and 7th centuries BC. In 685BC, the port was captured by the great Sabaean King Karib'il Watar, who through his campaigns brought the Kingdom of Awsan to an end. In the mid 1st century AD the *Periplus of the Erythraean Sea* notes that Aden is called 'Eudaemon Arabia' ('Happy Arabia'). The epithet would stick and apply to the entire country, particularly under its Latin version 'Arabia Felix'. Despite its description that the port was strategically located and that it had previously served a large number of ships crossing through the region, the *Periplus* noted that the port had previously been largely destroyed by the Himyarites.

Descriptions of Aden appear throughout the Islamic era of Yemen. Although the original three centres of Islamic governance had been Sana'a, Hadhramawt, and al-Janad, the Abbasid rulers of Baghdad began to move their focus from the last city to that of Aden in the mid 8th century. Several centuries later, the historians reported that Queen Arwa received the yearly revenue of Aden as part of her marriage dowry.

In the early 1500s Ludovico di Varthema, the Italian explorer who was the first non-Muslim to enter Mecca, wrote that: 'Aden was the strongest city that was ever seen on level ground.' At the time of his visit, Aden was controlled by the Tahirid dynasty. He writes in the account of his travels that ships from India, Ethiopia, and Persia, as well as all vessels headed for Mecca, docked at the port under the imposing watch of Sirwah Fortress and paid dues to the Tahirid Sultan. He also

IF ONLY THERE HAD BEEN A QAT-CHEWING COMPETITION

In 1962, Aden competed in the Commonwealth Games held at Perth, Australia, games remembered for 'heat, dust and glory'. The Aden team, comprising a mere two individuals, competed in seven different racing events. Aden reappeared at the 1966 games in Kingston, Jamaica as the Federation of South Arabia and added men's featherweight wrestling to the events in which they participated. The colony did not take any medals in either of the games. Perhaps the best athletes were back in Yemen, preparing for the revolution during the earlier games and fighting in the Radfan Mountains during the later ones.

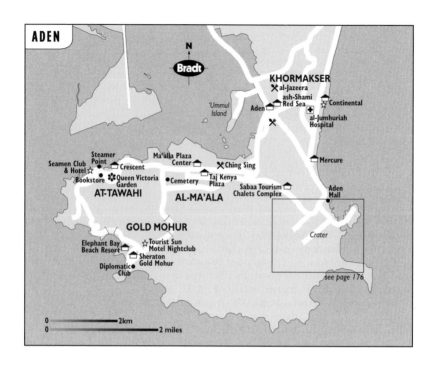

ADEN

N

Bradt

KHORMAKSER

✕ al-Jazeera
ash-Shami
Red Sea
Aden
☆ Continental
✚ al-Jumhuriah
Hospital
✕

🏠 Mercure

Steamer
Point
🏠 Ma'alla Plaza
Center
Seamen Club
& Hotel ☆ 🏠 Crescent
✕ Ching Sing
🏠 Bookstore ✿ Queen Victoria
Garden
● Cemetery
Taj Kenya
Plaza
AT-TAWAHI
AL-MA'ALA
Sabaa Tourism
Chalets Complex 🏠
Aden
Mall

GOLD MOHUR

Crater

Elephant Bay
Beach Resort 🏠 ☆ Tourist Sun
Motel Nightclub
🏠 Sheraton
Gold Mohur
Diplomatic ●
Club

see page 176

0 ――――― 2km
0 ――――― 2 miles

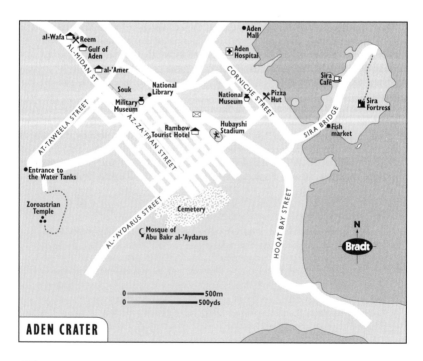

al-Wafa 🏠 ✕ Reem
🏠 Gulf of
Aden
● Aden
Mall
AL-MIDAN ST
✚ Aden
Hospital
🏠 al-'Amer
Souk
National
Library
CORNICHE STREET
Sira
Café
AT-TAWEELA STREET
Military
Museum
National
Museum
✕ Pizza
Hut
Sira
Fortress
AZ-ZA'FRAN STREET
✉
Rambow
Tourist Hotel
✳
Hubayshi
Stadium
SIRA BRIDGE
● Fish
market
● Entrance to
the Water Tanks
Zoroastrian
Temple
AL-'AYDARUS STREET
Cemetery
HOQAT BAY STREET
Mosque of
Abu Bakr al-'Aydarus
N

Bradt

0 ――――― 500m
0 ――――― 500yds

ADEN CRATER

notes that the city housed up to 6,000 families. Ludovico suffered harsh treatment at the hands of the sultan's underlings – he was chained and imprisoned for 65 days as a suspected Christian spy – but it did not seem to dampen his opinion of the city, which he found 'extremely beautiful'.

On 19 January 1839, Captain Stafford Bettesworth Haines captured Aden, and the city was annexed to British India. The British had been looking for an ideal spot to serve as a coaling station for the ships travelling to and from India. In the previous years, British settlements appeared on Socotra and Perim Island, but were abandoned once the port at Aden had been seized. The capture of Aden marked the first expansion of the British Empire under the reign of Queen Victoria.

Aden had changed significantly since its early 16th-century heyday. The port had lost its significance as Vasco da Gama's route to India around the Cape of Good Hope was utilised more and more often on the one hand, and as the coffee boom developed the Red Sea ports of al-Mokha and al-Luhayyah on the other. Compared with the 6,000 families present during Ludovico di Varthema's visit, the city only boasted an entire population of 600 people when Captain Haines took over.

During the early years of the British Occupation the city of Aden began to grow in size, particularly once the Suez Canal opened in 1869. In the 128 years of British rule, the city's population grew from 600 to over 250,000 and trade revenues exploded from £30,000 to £154 million. By the 1950s Aden was the fourth-largest tax-free port in the world, and it saw over 6,300 ships annually.

The British colony of Aden served as a crossroads for many of the 19th-century explorers – Burton, Speke, Baker and Stanley all passed through the port town. The poet Arthur Rimbaud lived in Aden as well, although he had long given up poetry by that point. The city hosted royal visitors too. In 1872, the future King Edward VII stopped in at Aden on his way to India; Queen Elizabeth II made a more prolonged visit in 1954.

The British used Aden as their base for exerting control over much of south Arabia. Starting in the 1880s, the British began signing treaties of friendship and protection with the various sultanates of southern Yemen that made them officially part of the Aden Protectorates. Eventually these protectorates would be organised and separated into the Eastern and Western Aden Protectorates.

Britain's growing presence in Arabia soon put it at odds with the Ottoman presence in the north. The first major clash between the two colonial powers occurred in 1873 as the spheres of Aden and Sana'a began to overlap. Over the next 30 years conflicts would continue to spark – at times with great severity. At last the two powers agreed to a line separating their respective areas of control. The Anglo-

THE CUNNING USE OF FLAGS

While Aden has hosted such greats as Rimbaud, Richard Burton and Queen Elizabeth II, it also was the birthplace of British actor Eddie Izzard, who launched his career as a transvestite stand-up comedian. On his website, Izzard notes that his father worked for BP and: 'ended up taking this post in Aden, which is a bit like saying, "I'm going to the moon." It's still miles away, but this was in the fifties.' Izzard's mother, who was working in Aden as a nurse, met and married his father while in Yemen.

In an interview with Eirik Knutzen, Izzard stated that his Yemeni birth was an initial obstacle to entering the United States: 'They were focused on my birth (in Yemen), and it didn't ease up until I got off a plane wearing a dress and makeup. Bizarrely, it made things easier for me. They seemed to think, "Oh, he's a transvestite ... he doesn't look like al-Qaeda... what the hell, let him in."'

Ottoman Line was agreed to in 1905 and stretched from the Bab al-Mandab in the southwest to the town of Harib in the northeast. Even after the revolutions of North and South Yemen in the 1960s, the line would serve as the basic border between the Yemen Arab Republic and the People's Democratic Republic of Yemen until unification in 1990.

In 1937, Aden was removed from the jurisdiction of British India and became a crown colony in its own right. Beginning around the same time, and as a result of the adoption of the 'Forward Policy' – the movement favouring greater intervention in the governance and development of the British protectorates – the British in Aden began signing more intrusive 'advisory treaties' with the Aden Protectorates. A series of limited constitutional reforms were propagated throughout the protectorates until the 1950s.

In 1959, the Western Aden Protectorates formed the Federation of Arab Emirates of the South. Despite a local outcry, Aden joined the Federation in 1963. The larger body became the Federation of South Arabia, but it would not last long. That same year, an intense rebellion in the Radfan Mountains against the British was led by the National Liberation Front (NLF). For several years Aden became an intense war zone as the NLF and the Front for the Liberation of Occupied South Yemen (FLOSY) carried out guerrilla attacks against the British, the colonial power responding with a particularly brutal counter-insurgency. Aden was a battlefield, and the area of Crater saw bomb and grenade explosions on a daily basis.

With the decision to withdraw from all military bases 'East of Suez', the British issued a defence policy paper declaring that all military forces would leave Aden by the end of 1968. Following the announcement, fighting increased as the Marxist-leaning NLF and the Egyptian-backed FLOSY vied for power. Because of the situation in the city, the British were forced to expedite the removal process, and the last British soldiers flew out of the country on 30 November 1967 – the date now celebrated as Independence Day.

As the British left, the NLF assumed power in the newly formed People's Republic of South Yemen. In 1969, the leftist contingent of the NLF acquired control of the party, instituting drastic socialist reforms labelled as the 'Corrective Move' – a policy which would lead to the formation in 1970 of the People's Democratic Republic of Yemen, the only Marxist state to have ever existed in the Middle East.

Rivalry within the Yemeni Socialist Party led to another brutal war in Aden in January 1986. Head of State Ali Nasir Muhammad al-Hasani and the recently returned-from-exile ex-leader Abd al-Fatah Ismail both rallied their forces to see who could assassinate the other first. Al-Hasani won that game, but eventually he was forced to flee from the country as well. The 'January events' led to a ten-day civil war that resulted in 13,000 civilian casualties and the emigration of over 60,000 South Yemenis to the north.

Following the collapse of the Soviet Union, the People's Republic of South Yemen lost its sole benefactor, and the long-contemplated union with the Yemen Arab Republic was formalised on 22 May 1990. Aden was declared the 'economic capital' of the Republic of Yemen, but it is not exactly clear what this meant. After unification Aden was largely neglected until the civil war of 1994. For the third time in 40 years, Aden became the scene of large-scale fighting. Aden has been built up again over the last decade and a half, and the promise of the Aden Free Zone has led to speculation that further development will soon follow.

Unfortunately, Aden is probably best known in the world today as the location where the *USS Cole* was bombed in 2000, an al-Qaeda attack viewed as an important precursor to the attacks of 11 September 2001.

GETTING THERE

By bus The Al-Esayi bus company offers trips to the following locations: Sana'a (1,350YR, 7hrs), Ta'iz (600YR, 2½hrs), Mukalla (1,700YR, 7½hrs), Hudaydah (1,800YR, 7hrs), Seiyun (2,800YR, 11hrs), Dhamar (1,100YR, 5hrs), Yarim (1,000YR, 4½hrs), Zabid (1,050YR, 5hrs).

Simlarly, the slightly pricier Yemitco travels to the following: Sana'a (1,400YR), Ta'iz (600YR, 2½hrs), Mukalla (2,000YR, 7½hrs), Hudaydah (1,300YR, 7hrs), Dhamar (1,100YR, 5hrs).

By shared taxi Bijou shared taxis gather and head to the following destinations once full of passengers: Sana'a (1,400YR, 6hrs), Ta'iz (650YR, 2hrs), Mukalla (1,800YR, 6½hrs), Hudaydah (1,400YR, 6½hrs), Ibb (850YR, 3hrs).

By air Air Yemenia operates flights to Sana'a (daily), al-Ghayda (Monday), Mukalla (Monday and Saturday), Socotra (Monday) and Seiyun (Tuesday and Wednesday).

WHERE TO STAY
Exclusive $$$$$

🏠 **Aden Hotel** (186 rooms) Khormakser; ☎ 02 232911; f 02 235655; e admin@goldentulipadenhotel.com; www.goldentulipadenhotel.com. Aden Hotel is well situated at the Khormakser roundabout, convenient to that area of town as well as Ma'alla & Crater. The hotel used to be run by Moevenpick, & most people still refer to it by that name. Wireless internet is available in the lobby; the suites have high-speed connections. Other amenities include the private pool (entrance fee for non-guests: 800YR/adult; 450YR/child), the **Tawila Bar**, **Abu Nuwas Nightclub**, & 2 restaurants.

🏠 **Mercure Hotel** (76 rooms) Khormakser; ☎ 02 238666; f 02 238660; e mercureaden@ accoryemen.com; www.accoryemen.com/mercureaden. Most rooms have an apt-style layout which are quite nice but a little pricey. Like the apts, all rooms have balconies & an ocean-side view. The hotel also has a

swimming pool & restaurant. Note that on the Accor international website (www.accorhotels.com) the prices are significantly cheaper.

🏠 **Sheraton Gold Mohur** (130 rooms) Off Gold Mohur Rd; ☎ 02 204010; f 02 205158; e reservations.aden.yemen@sheraton.com; www.sheraton.com/goldmohur. Located right on the beach near Elephant's Bay, the Sheraton Hotel is best available in Aden. There is a private beach & pool (entrance fee: 1,500YR for non-guests), a sauna & health club (1,000YR), as well as several great restaurants. There are plans to install wireless internet in the lobby; in the meantime, guests can use the small business centre (20YR/min). Accepts credit cards. Prices vary according to season (low/high), although you can always get the low season rate by booking through the website. Boat rentals: 5,000YR/hr.

Upmarket $$$$

🏠 **Crescent Hotel** (65 rooms) 'Ali Mohsan St; ☎ 02 203471; f 02 204597. Queen Elizabeth II visited Aden in 1954, & when she did, she stayed at this hotel built by the British. She is supposed to have brought a piano & various other equipment with her, which the staff & management of the hotel seem to have misplaced (no-one could figure out where it was; although some were quite sure they had it lying around somewhere). While the hotel might not be clean enough for Her Majesty these days, the old colonial-style building has a distinct character to it. If you decide to stay here, you might as well stay in the Queen's room (Room 121 – US$40).

🏠 **Elephant Bay Beach Resort** (31 rooms) Off Gold Mohur Rd; ☎ 02 201590; f 02 201082; e abbraden@y.net.ye;

www.elephantbaybeachresort.com. A very quiet resort with pleasant rooms & private beach (entrance fee for non-guests: 600YR). If you are looking for something relaxing & low key, this is a good hotel. As an added bonus, the **Casablanca** is about as close to a dive bar as you can come in Yemen, complete with dartboard & billiards table. Wireless internet in the lobby. Accepts MasterCard. Jet-ski rental: 15,000YR/hr; boat rental: 5,000YR/90min.

🏠 **Ma'alla Plaza Center** (46 rooms) Ma'alla Main St (next to the FedEx/DHL buildings, & under the sign for the Oasis Restaurant); ☎ 02 245610; f 02 245643. A nice apt-style complex that caters mostly to northern Yemenis staying in Aden for longer periods of time. The 'super deluxe' rooms are quite spacious, coming with 2 bedrooms, 2 bathrooms, & a living room. The 'deluxe' rooms have no AC. The receptionist & manager speak English, & the Oasis Restaurant (meals: 500–2,000YR) is housed in the basement.

🏠 **Sabaa Tourism Chalets Complex** (56 rooms) Queen Arwa Rd; ☎ 02 248797; ƒ 02 248796. Very

nice apt-style/suite rooms in lovely chalets, set up with multiple bedrooms & kitchen. Many of the rooms have great views of the Ma'alla area of town. These are a great bargain for the price. *Royal rooms:* $$$$.

Mid-range $$$

🏠 **Al-'Arusa Tourism Complex** (45 rooms) ☎ 02 205561; ƒ 02 204956. Most rooms are quite small, but they are clean, come with a patio & Western bathroom, & are nicely situated near the beach. Staying at the hotel also grants you access to the pool, basketball courts, & private beach. *Suites* $$$$.

🏠 **Taj Kenya Plaza** (57 rooms) Ma'alla Main St; ☎ 02 247000; ƒ 02 247011. Spacious rooms overlooking the section of Main St where children gather to play billiards. No English-speaking staff. *Apt-style rooms:* $$$$

Budget $$

🏠 **Al-'Amer Hotel** (24 rooms) Midan St; ☎ 02 250000; ƒ 02 256304; e alamer_group@y.net.ye. The best hotel in the budget range. Working AC, Western bathrooms, & a small Yemeni restaurant located next door. Plus you are located in central Crater.

🏠 **Ash-Shami Red Sea Hotel** (43 rooms) Khormakser, next to the Aden Hotel; ☎ 02 236866; ƒ 02 236869. A small establishment, but clean with AC & Western bathrooms. There is a small restaurant attached as well as a 24hr coffee shop.

🏠 **Rambow Tourist Hotel** (20 rooms) Queen Arwa St. After it was discovered that the poet Rimbaud had lived in this house during his tortuous stay in Aden, the French government quickly converted it into the French Cultural Centre. Eventually, the cultural centre disappeared and the building changed to house the hotel and adjoining bank. It's not exactly a season in hell, but it's not the cleanest establishment either.

Cheap $

🏠 **Al-Wafa Hotel** (20 rooms) Ghandi St (Crater); ☎ 02 256340. Cheap rooms in Crater. Not bad if you don't mind a bit of insect company.

🏠 **Gulf of Aden Hotel** (25 rooms) Ghandi St (Crater); ☎ 02 253900. Relatively cheap but not particularly clean. Some rooms have Western bathrooms. Mind the cockroaches.

✖ **WHERE TO EAT** In addition to the restaurants listed below, there are a number of fast-food restaurants located in the food court of the Aden Mall.

✖ **Reem Restaurant** Ghandi St (Crater); ⏰ 07.00–14.00, 17.30–22.00. One of the most popular restaurants in Aden, particularly among locals. Reem dishes out standard Yemeni fare. $$

✖ **Al-Jazeera** Khormakser; ⏰ 11.30–14.00, 17.30–22.00. Popular Yemeni-style seafood restaurant. $$

✖ **Ching Sing** Ma'ala Main St (Ma'ala); ⏰ 18.00–23.00 (closed Fridays). This Chinese restaurant was established in 1963, & is very popular with expats. Good food & ambiance; alcohol available. $$$

✖ **Pizza Hut** Corniche Rd (Crater) ⏰ 11.30–14.00, 17.30–23.00.

Hotel restaurants

✖ **Reedan** Khormakser roundabout (Aden Hotel) ⏰ 06.00–10.30, 12.00–15.30, 19.00–22.30. Buffet-style restaurant serving a variety of foods. *Mains:* $$$$

✖ **La Veranda** Khormakser roundabout (Aden Hotel) ⏰ 06.00–10.30, 12.00–15.30, 19.00–22.30. Serves both Yemeni & Italian cuisine. *Mains:* $$$$

✖ **Silk Route Restaurant** Off Gold Mohur Rd (Elephant Bay Beach Resort); ⏰ 11.30–14.00, 17.30–23.00. Serves Indian & Chinese dishes. *Mains:* $$$$$

✖ **Al-Safina** Off Gold Mohur Rd (Sheraton Gold Mohur Hotel); ⏰ 18.00–23.00. Buffet-style restaurant featuring a different cuisine daily. *Buffet:* $$$$

✕ **Pink Pearl Chinese Restaurant** Off Gold Mohur Rd (Sheraton Gold Mohur Hotel); ⏱ 19.00–23.45. The Sheraton's Chinese cuisine restaurant. More exclusive than Ching Sing in Ma'ala, but without the atmosphere. *Mains:* $$$$

✕ **Fish Market Restaurant** Off Gold Mohur Rd (Sheraton Gold Mohur Hotel); ⏱ 11.00–23.30. Seafood restaurant located on the Sheraton's private beach. The place is usually deserted. *Mains:* $$$$

ENTERTAINMENT AND NIGHTLIFE

Nightclubs Aden is one of the few cities in Yemen that warrant a brief entertainment section. Most of the nightlife in the city centres on a number of nightclubs – hotspots of live music, dancing and alcohol. Some venues are sketchier than others, and many of the women you will meet work for the establishment. Indeed, the attached hotel at the Tourist Sun seems little more than a scene for continuing the evening's festivities in private.

In addition to dancing and drinking, the patrons of the nightclub participate in 'money throwing', where men with large stacks of 100, 200 or 500YR notes demonstrate both their wealth and their appreciation of a dancer or friends by cascading the notes over them. The money-littered floor is quickly swept in between songs by the nightclub staff.

The nightclubs typically stay open daily from 23.00–04.00. Admission ranges from 2,000–4,000YR. A range of Yemeni and Western food can also be served, and a late dinner is often included in the admission price.

☆ **Abu Nuwas** Khormakser (Aden Hotel) Located in the Aden Hotel, the Abu Nuwas nightclub is one of the more respectable nightclub establishments in the city.
☆ **Safari Club** Off Gold Mohur Rd (Sheraton Gold Mohur) Considered to be one of the more prestigious locales, this is perhaps the best place to watch men spend the entire night throwing money in the air at each other or nearby dancing women.

☆ **Seamen Club & Hotel** al-Muhsen St. Although no longer a functioning hotel, the waterfront nightclub continues to thrive.
☆ **Diplomatic Club** Gold Mohur Rd. A much more 'family-style' nightclub, where people often just sit and listen to the music.
☆ **Tourist Sun Motel Nightclub** Off Gold Mohur Rd. Not for the fainthearted.

Other activities The sports facilities at the **al-'Arusa Hotel** (entrance fee: 500YR/family or 200YRpp) are great if you want to pass some time on the basketball courts. There is also a swimming pool and beach, as well as a restaurant.

The Aden Mall now operates **bowling lanes** (500 YR/game), located next to the food court. The large glass windows looking out into the seating area always ensures that there will be a wealth of spectators cheering you on.

SHOPPING For shopping opportunities in Aden, there is the souk in Crater, which hosts a row of cheap clothing stores, and the **Aden Mall**, a new addition to the city that contains more upper-end stores that cater to Aden's wealthier elite.

South Yemen   ADEN

9

OTHER PRACTICALITIES
Hospitals
✚ **Al-Jumhuriah Hospital** Khormakser; ✆ 02 233033
✚ **Ar-Razi Specialised Hospital** Khormakser; ✆ 02 234006
✚ **Aden Hospital** Corniche Rd (Crater); ✆ 02 254812

Banks
$ **CAC Bank** Abdullaziz St; ✆ 02 232132
$ **International Bank of Yemen** Queen Arwa St (Crater); ✆ 02 255795

$ **National Bank of Yemen** Queen Arwa St (Crater); ✆ 02 253484

There are plenty of **ATMs** throughout the city of Aden. You can find the machines at any of the major bank branches or in the **Aden Mall**.

Internet The best place to go for internet access is **Ma'alla Main Street**, which hosts about five internet cafés. There is also an internet café in Crater on Souk at-Taweel Street.

WHAT TO SEE The city of Aden is a combination of several different neighbourhoods – Crater, Ma'alla, Tawahi, Gold Mohur and Khormakser. Each is known for something in particular. **Crater** is the old district of the city and served as the original ancient port; it contains the modern souk as well as many of the city's sights. The neighbourhood's name is taken from its location. It was built in the crater of Aden's extinct volcano.

Ma'alla is the area that was built up during the British occupation. The two long rows of rather depressing, Soviet-looking buildings that line both sides of Ma'alla Main Street were constructed by the British and used as residences. The area now functions as the modern port and overlooks the new Aden Free Zone. The region of **Tawahi** was used as the port during the British occupation.

The city's modern growth has taken place mainly in the area of **Khormakser**, and as such, there is not much to see in the area. The neighbourhood contains the city's major hospitals and universities, as well as the diplomatic region. The highly secluded region of **Gold Mohur** contains the majority of Aden's resorts, private beaches, and nightclubs. Outside the city limits are several important suburbs, such as **Sheikh 'Uthman**, the gathering place for shared taxis and buses, **al-Mansura**, and **Madinat ash-Sha'b**.

Aden Water Tanks (⊕ *7.30–12.00, 14.00–17.30; entrance fee: 100YR*) The Aden Water Tanks (or 'Cisterns of Taweela') are located on the western edge of Crater, at the end of ravines coming down from the nearby peak. The 13 interlinked chambers, of which there were originally 52, were designed to capture and store the water rushing down the mountain side after a large rain in order to provide clean water to the city and help with flood prevention. The tanks have been said to hold anywhere from 15 to 100 million litres of water, although the former is probably closer to the truth. Even still, a storage device for 15 million litres of water is quite an impressive feat for ancient archaeology.

Just how ancient the tanks exactly are, however, is up for debate. The cisterns have been claimed to date back to the 1st century AD, to the reign of the Himyarites, but they may well have been built later by some of Yemen's earlier Islamic dynasties. At least one author claimed that the tanks may have been built as late as the 11th century AD by the Zuray'ids, a Fatimid dynasty whose centre of power was in Aden. The Zuray'id theory on first glance seems plausible – the revenue of the city of Aden during the reign of the Zuray'ids was handed over to Queen Arwa, whose name means '*thirst quencher*' and who is said to have spent an entire year's budget on public works such as aqueducts. The water tanks are noted by earlier historians and geographers, however, including a mention by al-Hamdani in the 10th century AD. Therefore, the tanks must have been built at an earlier date, but as a plaque dating from 1899 at the entrance of the tank verily notes: 'nothing is accurately known' about the original construction of the tanks.

At some point during the history of the city, the large cisterns fell into disuse, and year after year, rainfall continued to fill the tanks with debris it collected while coursing down the mountain. Eventually the tanks became completely immersed in 'rubbish and debris'. The front plaque notes that this was the state the tanks were in when they were rediscovered in 1854 by Sir R Lambert Playfair, who was at that time the Assistant Resident at Aden, and who later went on to serve as the British Consul General for the Territory of Algeria, among other foreign postings.

Today the tanks no longer serve their original purpose, although they are said still to be used to irrigate the local gardens. The tanks act mainly as the setting for this park and gardens area. A building labelled 'Aden Museum' is also located on the park grounds, but it has been closed for some time and there seem to be no plans to reopen. Perhaps the curator had been worried about the odd local belief associated with the tanks – that three deaths by drowning will occur every time the cisterns fill to the brim.

Beaches One of the draws of Aden, especially for foreigners living in Yemen, is the chance to relax at the city's beaches. Within the city itself, you need to head to the **Gold Mohur** district. **Lover's Bay Beach** is regarded as the best public beach. At the time of writing there was no entrance fee, although there was a resort currently being constructed. It appears, however, that those plans ultimately may be abandoned. Two great private beaches can be found at the **Sheraton Gold Mohur** (entrance fee: 1,500YR for non-guests) and the **Elephant Bay Beach Resort** (entrance fee: 600YR for non-guests). The **Blue Beach** outside the city in **Little Aden** is also quite nice.

Museums and libraries
National Library (*al-Mathaf St;* ☎ *02 253507;* ⊕ *08.00–13.30, 15.30–19.00 Sat–Wed;* entrance: free) is located next to the Military Museum. It has a large section of foreign books – including Rimbaud in French – and a section of various English books on Yemen.

Military Museum (*al-Mathaf St;* ☎ *02 253243;* ⊕ *09.00–12.00, 16.00–19.00 Sat–Wed; entrance fee: 500YR*) was closed for renovations while this book was being researched. The museum is said to display a large collection of items regarding the British occupation and subsequent revolution.

National Museum (*al-Aydarus St;* ⊕ *08.00–13.30 Sat–Wed; entrance fee: 500YR*) is housed in the old palace of the Sultan of Lahej. It was plundered during the civil war in 1994, when rogue members of the northern forces decided to pick up some free decorations for their houses back home. Artefacts are mostly from the old kingdom and are accompanied by English descriptions, even if they are not always that helpful.

The second floor houses the **Museum of People's Traditions**, which has some interesting displays but could be improved to better cover southern Yemen. You will be asked to sign the guestbook on both floors.

ARTHUR RIMBAUD

Melanie H P Miller

The 19th-century French poet Arthur Rimbaud is best known as the child prodigy of the Decadence, the literary movement on the cusp between Romanticism and Modernism. Rimbaud's poetry was filled with visionary imagery and resonated with all the power and beauty of untamed, rebellious youth. His playful, witty verse described the heady life of pleasure that surrounded him. Unfortunately for his future readers, the implosion of his tumultuous, high-profile relationship with fellow poet Paul Verlaine, combined with the mediocre reviews of his poetry by the critics of the day prompted Rimbaud to give up writing and leave France entirely.

By age 20, Arthur Rimbaud was living in Aden and working as a merchant. The only writing he did at that time was in the form of letters to his mother and sister. In them, he complained about everything in Aden, from the dryness of the weather to the meagreness of his earnings. For him, Aden was 'a volcanic rock, without a single blade of grass or drop of water'. He described himself as 'aging very quickly in these stupid jobs, and in the company of savages and fools'. Rimbaud was happy to be promoted to a position that took him to Djibouti, Ethiopia, and other parts of north Africa, where European merchants were hoping to capitalise on an Abyssinian power struggle. Rimbaud did not enjoy the promotion for long – he fell ill and was forced to return to Marseilles to have his leg amputated.

Despite his initial disenchantment with life in Yemen, on his deathbed in Marseilles, Rimbaud wanted nothing more than to return to Aden, writing to his sister, 'I hope to go back where I was, where I have friends of ten years' standing… I shall always live there, for in France, except for you, I have neither friends nor acquaintances, nobody… In any case it is essential I go there.' Deep in the throes of his illness, he asked his sister to book passage for him on the next steamship to Aden. He died the next day.

Shortly after his death and the posthumous publishing of his work, poets who had suddenly become great fans tried to trace Rimbaud's path through Aden. Three separate failed attempts to find Rimbaud's house were recorded in 1905, 1936, and 1976. Rimbaud's poetry enjoyed yet another surge in popularity in the 1960s, when his passionate, vivid descriptions of drugs, sex, and depravity struck chords with rock geniuses like Bob Dylan and Jim Morrison.

In 1991, on the advice of Adeni historians, some poets met in Aden to search for traces of Rimbaud's life in Crater. They discovered the coffee warehouse where Rimbaud had worked, overseeing a team of Hindu women who sorted, graded, and packed green Yemeni coffee for sale. With great fanfare, a sign that read 'Rimbaud's House' in French and Arabic was placed on the warehouse. The building was later renamed as 'The Franco-Arab Cultural Center: Rimbaud's House' and colloquially called 'The Poetry House'. As a site for cultural exchange, Rimbaud's House was designated as 'a space for poetry, translation, and creativity'. Very much like the artist, however, the Poetry House gave up its French cultural ambitions early and turned instead to Adeni business ventures. The building now hosts the **Rambow Tourist Hotel** and the **Yemen Bank for Reconstruction & Development**.

Religious structures

Mosque of Abu Bakr al-'Aydarus Al-'Aydarus was a descendant of the Prophet Muhammad through 'Ahmed bin 'Isa the Migrant, who travelled from Iraq to Hadhramawt in the 10th century. 'Ali bin 'Isa was the founder of the Hadhrami Sayyids, centred in Tarim, and his line introduced Sufism to the region in the early

13th century. Al-'Aydarus was born in Tarim in 1447. After completing his religious schooling, he was sent to Aden to build a mosque and undertake efforts to found a Sufi school in the region. His work in doing so garnered him the title of the Patron Saint of Aden, or more simply, the *Adeni*.

Stories of al-'Aydarus's mystical powers abound. In one tale, for example, it is said that the holy man was tired and did not feel like climbing up over the mountain to get to the next village. He took his *miswak* (the small twig of wood used to clean the teeth) and flung it at the mound of earth. When the twig hit the ground, the mountain was crushed, and he proceeded to the village with ease.

Even after his death, al-'Aydarus's powers are believed to have lived on. One particularly famous story is that of a Sikh suffering from belly-ache who, after having visited countless doctors and having tried just as many remedies, was told to visit and recite sections of the Koran over the tomb of the recently deceased al-'Aydarus. Having made his way from India, the man did as he was told. When he fell asleep next to the tomb after the Koran recitation, al-'Aydarus appeared to him in his dream and told him go and get a bath in the nearby waters. He woke up and followed his given instructions faithfully once more. He recovered instantly.

To show his gratitude, he constructed the mosque and dome over al-'Aydarus's tomb, and returned to India with a promise to the locals to provide the doors shortly. After a long delay, al-'Aydarus appeared to him in another dream, telling him to send the wood for the doors as he had promised. The Sikh asked the dream apparition how he could get the wood all the way to Yemen. He was told in the dream to throw it in the water; the sea and providence would take care of the rest. Ever obedient, the Sikh woke up and tossed several fine pieces of timber into the ocean. Making its way across the Indian Ocean, the wood for the doors later washed ashore at Sira', with an inscription denoting their intended use in the mosque.

Regardless of whether the wood actually made a solo trip across the ocean, the old doors of the mosque did date back over 500 years. Unfortunately, it is now impossible to see the inscription on the old doors, as they (along with most of the mosque) were destroyed by North Yemeni Islamic fundamentalists during the 1994 civil war. Striking out at what they called 'Sufi grave worshippers', the soldiers attacked the mosque with guns, grenades and rockets, burning copies of the Koran and uprooting tombs in the courtyard – a sad reminder of the consequences of religious intolerance. The mosque has been rebuilt somewhat, although renovations are still going on.

In addition to his supernatural powers, Aden's patron saint was also the city's poet laureate. During his lifetime he wrote a wealth of Sufi poetry and introduced musical gatherings to the city of Aden. Engseng Ho describes him as having been 'religiously musical'.

Today, the Mosque of Abu Bakr al-'Aydarus is the centre of Sufi learning in Aden. Although the original mosque was built in the late 15th or early 16th century, the mosque was rebuilt in the 19th century. Of course, large rebuilding efforts were also required after the devastation following the 1994 civil war. The musical poetry sessions that al-'Aydarus started continue to this day, and there are special poetry recitations on Mondays. Tourists are allowed to enter, but should proceed with respect and caution – the recent destruction of the mosque has made local adherents cautious of speaking with outsiders.

There is also a large festival that occurs yearly on 14 Shawal, the date of al-'Aydarus's death (15 October 2008, 4 October 2009). After a procession to the mosque, there is a series of sermons and lectures. Needless to say, all the proceedings are in Arabic.

Zoroastrian Tower of Silence ruins The Zoroastrian faith is an ancient one; the prophet Zoroaster is believed to have lived sometime around the 11th century BC. The tower here, however, has no such claims to antiquity. It was built in the 19th century to serve the members of the faith that came to Aden from India during the British occupation.

The tower itself was used as part of the Zoroastrian death rituals. When a member of the faith died, he would be dragged to the tower and left naked in the centre circle to be consumed by vultures. For the believers, cremation was not an option – the body was too unclean to be placed in holy fire. Neither was burial – the uncleanliness of the corpse would contaminate the earth. Air burial thus served a dual purpose: consumption by vultures was believed to have cleansed the impurity of the body while at the same time freeing the soul for release.

The tower is constructed of several small concentric circles. The bodies of men were put in the outermost ring, with those of women and children in the middle and innermost ring, respectively. While the structure still exists in the form, it is unclear how long it will do so. Locals living nearby on the mountain seem to be taking stones from the tower with increasing frequency to construct their own homes.

The ruins of the Zoroastrian Tower of Silence are located about 300m to the southwest of the Aden Water Tanks. To get there, face the entrance to the Water Tank Park, turn left and walk to the end of the wall. Make the first right you see and climb the footpath to the top. For a more perilous road, there is a small rocky path that leads up the mountain from within the Water Tank Park.

Sights of colonial interest The old harbour of the British-occupied port of Aden is **Steamer Point** (⊕ *09.00–12.00 & 15.00–18.00*) in the at-Tawahi neighbourhood. The old port has been refashioned as a tourist destination, with pictures and captions of the old area hung throughout. A small souvenir store sells various trinkets, old stamps and books.

For a small fee (US$30) you can rent a boat that holds up to ten passengers and traverse the area around the Aden Free Zone and Ma'alla pier before returning to the old port. The trip takes about 90 minutes. With a little more money you will get a longer trip and be able to travel to any of the local destinations.

Across from Steamer Point is the **Hogg Clock Tower**, often described nowadays as 'Little Ben'. The clock tower was built to commemorate Brigadier-General A F G Hogg, the political resident and commander-in-chief in Aden from 1885–90.

Other interesting sights include the **British Cemetery**, a collection of old tombs, mostly from the world wars, but some from the early 1900s, and the largely unkept **Queen Victoria Garden**, which boasts a large statue of the monarch.

OUTSIDE ADEN

LITTLE ADEN Although the town has mainly developed around oil refineries, Little Aden also provides a great contrast from its big brother in terms of the peace and quiet you can find on its sparsely populated beaches.

Getting there and away The most exciting way to get to Little Aden, or to return to Aden, is to take a boat across the water. The trip takes about 90 minutes, and it costs 7,000YR to rent the boat.

 Where to stay

Al-Kdeer Suites Rooms (35 rooms) ☎ 02 275822; f 02 275820. Rooms are very clean, & let you enjoy the tranquillity of Little Aden. Sea-view rooms are particularly nice, & all come with Yemeni bathrooms. Truly great value! $

✕ Where to eat Meals are available at the al-Kdeer Suites Rooms hotel.

What to see and do The joy of coming to Little Aden stems from enjoying the beaches here. The lovely **Blue Beach** is touted as one of the best public beaches in the area, although it seems to be seldom used. Next to the beach is the mountain of **Jabal al-Ghadeer**. There are 600 stairs to the top, and also a newly opened chairlift that makes the climb all the easier. There is a deceptive sign for a Marine Museum, but do not be fooled; no such museum exists!

NORTH OF ADEN

LAHEJ Until 1967 the city was the seat of government of the Lahej Sultanate. The one major site in the town is the **Lahej Sultan's Palace**, the former residence of Abdul Kareem bin Fadl bin Ali al-ʿAbduli. At one point the palace had been transformed into a museum, but now it's the home of the radio station of Lahej and Yemen News. Tourists are no longer allowed to enter.

AL-ʿANAD During the civil war of 1994 south Yemeni generals claimed al-ʿAnad had an impenetrable base and a famed military – after all, it was reputed to have been the largest military base built by the Soviet Union in the Middle East. After several key attacks by the north, however, the city fell.

Today the town primarily is known as *the* place in Yemen to buy delectable sweets – and for good reason! Stopping to buy large quantities of the sugar-laden treats is practically a requirement for family members travelling home from Aden. Some of the best offerings are ʿAraysi (500YR/kg), Hareesa (350YR/kg), and my personal favourite, Abu Baggarah (450YR/kg).

EAST OF ADEN

YAFIʾ The road from al-Habilayn to al-Bayda passes through the countryside of Yafiʾ. The area is heavily touted for its spectacular views, but they do not compare to the scenery offered in much of the highlands, and I would not recommend going out of your way to see it. Still, if you are coming to al-Bayda from Aden, the landscape makes for a more exciting drive than if you went up the coast.

The architecture of the buildings is unique to this area of Yemen. Nearly every building in the wadis is constructed using large stones that are reserved for mosques in most other towns. Additionally, the buildings have palatial peaks on all of their corners. I do not know where the architectural influence for the area comes from, but it definitely differs from other styles of the region.

The town of **Yahar** is well known for its coffee production, and you should be able to pick some up during the weekly Tuesday market. Further up the road to al-Bayda, the town of Labʾoos has an old run-down communist monument – an alien reminder of South Yemen's Marxist history.

AL-BAYDA Although al-Bayda is the provincial capital of the region and the largest city for a good distance, there is surprisingly little to see here. Given the extensive security guards who must accompany you during any stay in the city, there is little reason to linger in the town unless you are planning on making the trip up Wadi Bayhan.

Getting there and away At the time of writing, tourists were only allowed to travel in and out of al-Bayda accompanied by what seems like a small army. Accordingly, travel by bus and shared taxi is strictly forbidden. It is essential for you to arrange your travel through a Yemeni tour operator.

Where to stay

🏠 **Al-Riyadh Tourist Hotel** (40 rooms) al-'Am St; ☎ 06 538003; f 06 534310. Standard, clean rooms with Western bathrooms. An **ATM** is located within the hotel premises. $$

🏠 **Al-Khaleej Tourist Hotel** (30 rooms) al-'Am St; ☎ 06 534333. The hotel offers standard, mostly clean rooms with a mixture of Yemeni & Western bathrooms.

$. Rooms with shared bathrooms are 500YR cheaper.

🏠 **Al-Baeda Plaza** (30 rooms) ☎ 06 530406; f 06 538166. Located in front of the ath-Thawra Hospital, the hotel offers rooms with a little less quality. Some of the trpl rooms have Western bathrooms. $

🏠 Where to eat

The three local restaurants in town all serve basic meals. There is also a small restaurant serving basic meat and rice dishes on al-'Am St.

WADI BAYHAN Recent excavations of Wadi Bayhan – the valley that runs from al-Bayda northeast toward Bayhan – has revealed that the area was the site of a large battle between the ancient kingdoms of the Sabaeans and the Himyarites. In more modern times, the valley was used strategically in the conflict between the British and the Turks, and later by the republican and royalist armies during the 1962 revolution.

With the days of these conflicts now long over, you can traverse the rough terrain of Wadi Bayhan with an excellent drive that will take about five hours. The road is unpaved for nearly the entire trip, but the opportunities to see amazing views of nature and wildlife are terrific. There is a large variety of birds, and clans of Hamadryas baboons often make appearances. The entire trip would make a wonderful extended hiking expedition, but security concerns make it unlikely that you would be able to get permission for such an outing.

BAYHAN The actual city of Bayhan is simply called 'Souk' ('Market') by the locals, who use the word 'Bayhan' to refer to the larger area encompassing the town. There is a couple of restaurants and supply stores in town, and it could be a good place to stop and refresh before or after venturing to nearby **Timna'**. There used to be a museum in the city dedicated to artefacts found at the ancient site, but it has since closed.

TIMNA' The site of Timna', the ancient capital of the Qataban Kingdom, is located directly outside the city of Bayhan. There is a couple of sites of ruins, both of which are completely fenced off, so close examination is unfortunately not possible.

There are plans to build a new museum at the site to store the artefacts from Timna' that used to grace the old Bayhan museum. As with many local Yemeni museums, the initial capital usually comes from foreign help, and it is unclear when the museum is expected to be finished.

One of the more interesting pieces that was unearthed here was a large obelisk upon which were carved Qatabani laws – Yemen's ancient equivalent to Hammurabi's Code.

ATAQ

With the glory of the city of Shabwa now long gone, Ataq is the capital of the Shabwa governorate. Given the combination of the area's heightened security concerns along with the fact that there is relatively little to see, there should not be much reason to schedule a trip to the city on an itinerary of any brevity whatsoever. However, if you do find yourself in the Ataq, the local museum is quite nice and should whet your appetite.

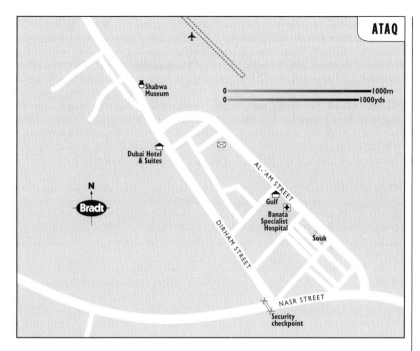

ATAQ

WHERE TO STAY

🏠 **Dubai Hotel & Suites** (40 rooms) Dirham St; ☎ 05 201041; f 05 203825. While it may not be able to compete with Dubai's 7-star resorts, the hotel offers clean & adequately spacious rooms that are equipped with Western bathrooms. A small restaurant on the first floor serves typical Yemeni dishes (200–800YR). $$

🏠 **Gulf Hotel** (36 Rooms) al-'Am St; ☎ 202142; f 202145. While the rooms are a little bit less clean than those offered by its counterpart, they are not too bad. Additionally, the rooms come with a desk, a balcony, & Western bathrooms. $

✕ WHERE TO EAT
Ataq is not known for its culinary wonders, but there are a few small restaurants on Nasr Street.

WHAT TO SEE
Shabwa Museum (Dirham St ⊕ 08.00–12.30, Sat–Wed) The museum has a surprisingly good collection of pieces given its location in the middle of Ataq. In particular, it has a nice set of alabaster funerary *stelas* (stone slabs). Also on display are artefacts from the excavation of Shabwa, Timna' and Qana, as well as various bits from the Stone Age.

AROUND ATAQ

WADI YISHBUM If you're passing through Ataq, you may want to take a slight detour through Wadi Yishbum. Unlike most of the wadis you will pass through in Yemen, Yishbum is much narrower, and the cliff faces shoot up to impressive heights at right angles. You'll pass a number of little villages perched up against the cliffs. The drive will only take you about 30 minutes from when you leave the main road to when you return, and it can make for some nice photo opportunities.

South Yemen **AROUND ATAQ**

9

189

AZZAN The village is known (although not by Yemenis) as being the supposed starting point of one of the three wise men who visited Jesus in Bethlehem. No-one in the village, however, has any knowledge about either the biblical story or the excavation that took place later. As one of the locals told me, 'You can't ask us about anything that happened over 200 years ago.'

OUTSIDE AZZAN Several kilometres outside the village of Azzan lie the ruins of **Nagib al-Hajar Castle**. The ruins date back to the caravan kingdoms, and the style of the fortification is similar to the one you can see at Baraqish near Marib.

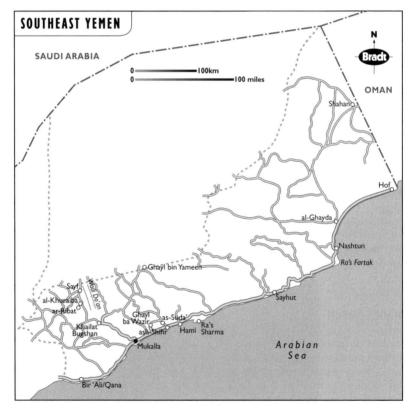

10

Southeast Yemen

Telephone code 05

MUKALLA

HISTORY In light of Yemen's long history, Mukalla has not held its place as one of the country's major ports for very long. By the time the nearby ancient port of Qana had lost its prestige, the city had probably not even achieved the status of a small fishing village.

The earliest settlement here probably sprang up sometime around the 12th century AD, but it was not until the Qu'aiti Sultan Ahmed al-Kasadi established his seat of power in the town in 1625 that the city took on any real importance. By the 18th century, however, Mukalla had been transformed into a bustling port city.

Over the next century and a half, the city became another stage bearing witness to the power struggle between the Qu'aiti and Kathiri sultanates. With some support from the British in Aden, the Qu'aitis gained control of Mukalla in the late 19th century, and they controlled the port until the 1967 revolution. Since the revolution Mukalla has continued to play its role as a major port city.

Mukalla came to be known for its glistening white-washed building that rose up out of the lapping of the wave. The scene impressed the early 20th century British traveller Freya Stark so much that she remarked that "if ever [she] were to have a honeymoon, it would be pleasant to spend it on the curving beaches of Mukalla, where the rolling of the world is scarcely felt." Although the city had lost much of its charm over the years, a recent beautification project has restored much of the old lustre. Even still, it is hard to imagine the city blossoming into a honeymoon resort any time soon.

GETTING THERE AND AWAY

By bus Al-Esayi buses travel to Sana'a (1,900YR, 10hrs) and Aden (1,700YR, 7hrs). Yemitco buses travel to the same destinations (2,000YR each) and to al-Ghayda (1,500YR, 5½hrs).

By shared taxi Shared taxis depart for Aden (1,800YR, 7hrs). All other destinations must be negotiated on a private taxi rate, although many destinations, such as those surrounding Ataq, will only be reachable by arrangements with a private tourism company.

WHERE TO STAY

☐ **Holiday Inn Mukalla** (112 rooms) Khalf St; 📞 05 306160; f 05 306150; e himuk_fc@y.net.ye; www.ichotelsgroup.com. For security, the hotel is the best in Mukalla. Every vehicle entering the car park is stopped & searched. The rooms are excellent, & all face the sea. The hotel also offers tennis courts (3,000YR/hr for non-guests), a private beach (entrance fee: 500YR for non-guests), & wireless internet in the hotel lobby & restaurant. Significant discount usually given on request. Alternatively, booking rooms through the website can reduce the price by up to 40%. $$$$$.

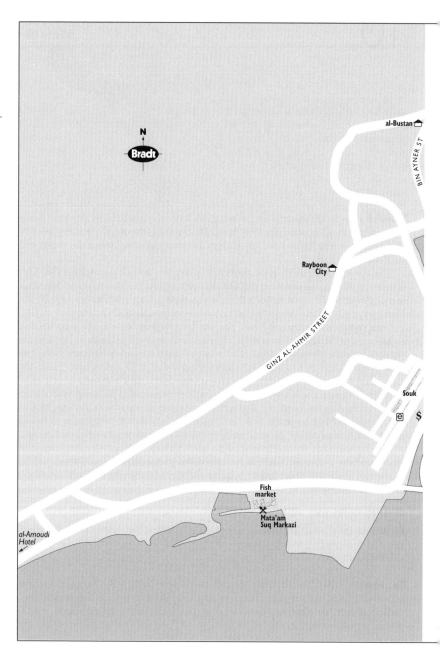

🏠 **Al-Amoudi Hotel** (80 rooms) Ibn Seen St;
📞 05 360360; f 05 361744;
e al-amoudihotel@hotmail.com. The prices are a little steep, & the hotel is located about 15km from the city centre, but it may be perfect if your main concern is staying in a quiet area. In addition to

the internet café & swimming pool, the hotel has a **restaurant** that offers a large buffet for 2,500YRpp.
💲💲💲💲.

🏠 **Al-Bustan Hotel** (64 rooms) Bin 'Amer St; 📞 05 318771; f 05 318770. Perhaps the best deal of the high-end hotels. The waterway is planned to extend

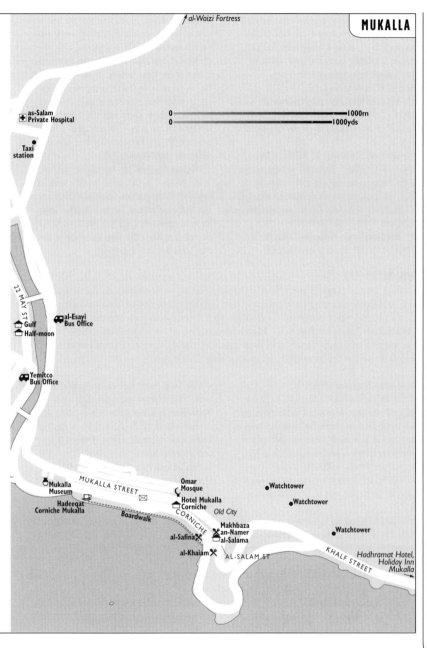

al-Waizi Fortress

0 ——————————————————— 1000m
0 ——————————————————— 1000yds

as-Salam
Private Hospital

Taxi
station

22 MAY ST

al-Esayi
Bus Office

Gulf
Half-moon

Yemitco
Bus Office

Mukalla
Museum

MUKALLA STREET

Omar
Mosque

Watchtower

Hadeeqat
Corniche Mukalla

Hotel Mukalla
Corniche

CORNICHE

Old City

Watchtower

Boardwalk

Makhbaza
an-Namer
al-Salama

Watchtower

al-Safina

al-Khaiam

AL-SALAM ST

KHALF STREET

Hadhramat Hotel,
Holiday Inn
Mukalla

all the way to the back of the hotel, which should make it even better. The apt-style rooms are fantastic. Furthermore, the scrumptious fare of the **al-Bustan Sweets Shop** is right next door. $$$$.
Hadhramaut Hotel (64 rooms) Khalf St; ✆ 05 302060; f 05 303134; e hadmot.htl@y.net.ye;

www.hadmothtl.com.ye. In the past, this hotel was the only available upmarket option in Mukalla. Today, it is beaten in service & design by the Holiday Inn & in value by the al-Bustan. The Hadhramaut, however, does retain some of its charm. Ask to stay in the chalets, which are quaint &

located in the middle of a garden area. The hotel is good to stay at particularly if you want to take advantage of the **diving & fishing centre** located therein. Additionally, prices are nearly halved for non-nationals with residency visas. Accepts MasterCard/Visa/American Express. $$$$.

🏠 **Al-Salama Hotel** (25 rooms) al-Salam St; ✆ 05 305211; f 05 303373. If you are looking for a cheap hotel in the centre of the Old City, this place is great. $$.

🏠 **Gulf Hotel** (20 rooms) 22 May St; ✆ 05 304147; f 05 303427. Rooms are pleasant enough, & the strong, permeating odour of perfume in the lobby will guarantee you smell your best when you hit the streets of Mukalla. Rooms come with Western bathrooms. $$.

🏠 **Half-Moon Hotel** (25 rooms) 22 May St; ✆ 05 302767; f 05 302778; e halfmoonhotel@

yemen.net.ye. If you prefer to be near the new parts of town to the old, you can't go wrong with the Half-Moon, a favourite with tourists. $$.

🏠 **Hotel Mukalla Corniche** (46 Rooms) Corniche St, in front of the 'Omar Mosque; ✆ 319441; f 319445. The live falcon in the hallway might seem a little odd to comprehend, regardless of how many times you come across it during your stay. Rooms are very good for the price – decently clean & most come with Western bathrooms. The best value of the inexpensive establishments. $$.

🏠 **Rayboon City Hotel** (51 Rooms) Ghar al-Ahmar St; ✆ 05 303606; f 05 304211; e info@rc-hotels.com; www.rc-hotels.com. Rayboon City Hotel is a little more than double the price of the Hotel Mukalla Corniche. The extra money you spend gets you access to the car park & a 24hr coffee shop, but in general the place seems a little run down. $$

✗ **WHERE TO EAT** There is a number of good local eateries in Mukalla. Most are located on the edge of the Old City where Corniche Street bends out toward the sea, and there is a small eatery at the fish market on the other side of town where you can have your purchase cooked for you. Otherwise, most of the major hotels (**Holiday Inn**, **al-Bustan**, **Hadhramaut**, and **al-Amoudi**) have decent restaurants offering Yemeni and Western dishes, and there is a **Pizza Hut** on Khalf Street between the Hadhramaut and Holiday Inn hotels.

✗ **Al-Safina Restaurant** Corniche St; ⊕ 06.00–10.30, 12.00–15.30, 18.00–22.30. You can't miss the large boat-shaped restaurant at the end of the Corniche stretch. The restaurant caters to both tourists & locals, & it can turn out some nice curries & Lebanese appetisers in addition to its seafood fare (lobster: 4,000YR/kg; shrimp: 4,000YR/kg; fish: 2,000YR/kg). The rooftop patio is great for an evening view of the sea & Old City. $$$

✗ **Al-Khaiam Restaurant** Across from al-Salama Hotel; ⊕ 06.00–10.30, 12.00–15.30, 18.00–22.30. Perhaps the most popular local restaurant in town

– & for good reason. The seafood is almost as good as the harried Yemeni atmosphere. $$

✗ **Makhbaza an-Namer** Across from al-Salama Hotel; ⊕ 06.00–10.30, 12.00–15.30, 18.00–22.30. Good local seafood restaurant, serving up dishes of fish sized according to your requirements. $$

✗ **Mata'am Souk Markazi** ⊕ 06.00–10.30, 12.00–15.30, 18.00–22.30. Located in the centre of the fish market, surrounded by rows & rows of fresh-fish vendors. Buy your catch (shark, lobster, shrimp or fish) & have the restaurant cook it up for an extra 200YR while you relax at a table near the water – a great experience! $$

OTHER PRACTICALITIES **As-Salam Private Hospital**, the best in town, is located across the street from the al-Bustan Hotel.

The **International Bank of Yemen**, the **National Bank of Yemen**, and the **Commercial Agricultural Bank of Yemen** are all located in Hay al-Umal, near the inlet.

WHAT TO SEE One of the oft-photographed sights of Mukalla is the seemingly abandoned **al-Waizi Fortress**, a miniature palace-style building that originally stood to guard the main entrance of the town. Today, entrance into the fortress is not possible, but you can walk around the outer grounds of the building. Closer to the centre of the city is the impressive **Mukalla Museum** (⊕ *09.00–12.00, Sat–Wed; entrance fee 500YR*), a large, former palace dedicated to items from the time of the Qu'aiti Sultanate. Walking through the halls of the museum offer you a glimpse of a very different past (at least for a small portion of society) that seems quite out of place now in modern Mukalla.

OUTSIDE MUKALLA

NORTH OF MUKALLA

Wadi Do'an The valley of Wadi Do'an leads from Mukalla up to the towns of Wadi Hadhramawt, and it provides one of the more interesting journeys in the Yemen. The first checkpoint outside Mukalla lies at the base of a mountain leading to the **Abd al-Gharib Pass**. As you wait to pass through the control, you may want to take the opportunity to buy some fresh coconuts (50YR/coconut) from the children who often set their stands up there.

With coconuts in hand, the road quickly rises 600m, bringing you to the Abd al-Gharib Pass. Continuing another 10km northward into Wadi Do'an, you enter the area known as **Khaila**. The entire area has been under the continuous patronage of **Sheikh Abdullah Ahmed Bugshan**, who had the roads constructed, provided electricity to the region, and built a number of the schools and homes that dot the valley. His help and support have been so great that most people in Yemen now refer to the area as **Khailat Bugshan**. Currently, he is planning the construction of a 'Tourist City' atop one of the mountains. Details are scarce, but the site will probably be completed around the year 2010.

🏠 *Where to stay*

🏠 **Khailah Palace Tourist Hotel** (37 rooms) ☎ 05 515030; f 05 515034. If you are driving up Wadi Do'an, a stop (if not a night's stay) at the Khailah Palace Hotel in the area of Khailat Bugshan should be mandatory. The hotel looks as though it was made to advertise the variety of colours you can get by purchasing a box of Crayola crayons; the ornate design is a testament to Yemeni eccentricity & is another product of the rebuilding of Sheikh Bugshan. Even if you are not staying at the hotel, the staff are very friendly, & will let you tour the place & see some of the rooms. The interior design of the rooms has a colonial feel, decorated with pillars & crown reliefs. The hotel is a good base for setting out to explore the wadi. If you are staying here, try to get one of the corner rooms. $$$$

Al-Khuraiba Al-Khuraiba is the district centre of the region, and serves a number of important functions for the area. Beyond its governmental duties, the village is also an important seat of learning. The mountain Bedouin of the region bring their children to the schools here to study. The town is also the educational centre of the region for members of the Sufi sect. The hospital of al-Khuraiba serves the entire area, and is well known for offering its services for free to the poor.

 Where to stay

🏠 **Al-Khouraebah Tourist Hotel** (9 rooms) ☏ 05 495040. This quaint guesthouse offers small, clean rooms with balconies & Yemeni bathrooms. A small restaurant on the first floor serves typical Yemeni dishes. $$

🏠 **Funduq an-Nasr** (3 rooms) ☏ 05 495090. There are no mattresses, sheets or pillows; the guesthouse offers a hard floor to sleep on & the amenities provided by a shared bathroom. $

Shopping There is a small **antique shop** in town, offering old wooden carved reliefs and other local handicrafts, that is open infrequently. If you would like to peruse the wares, ask Salem at the **al-Khouraebah Tourist Hotel** to track down the owner, who will gladly open it for you.

What to see and do On the west side of town, a path leads up the cliffside to the apex of the adjacent mountain, where you will be rewarded with frankincense trees and picturesque views of the countryside. The walk up the path is pleasant, requiring no hard climbing, and takes about 60–90 minutes to reach the top.

Ar-Ribat This is the next village to al-Khuraiba, and it has a weekly Friday market. Its claim to fame comes from being the **hometown of Osama bin Laden's father**, Muhammad bin Laden. Whenever newspapers portray Yemen in a negative light, the articles often state that the country is 'the ancestral home of Osama bin Laden'. (The exact phrase has been used by BBC, CNN, the *Guardian Unlimited*, *The New York Times*, *Forbes* magazine, and al-Jazeera, to name a few.) This is the village that they are referring to.

The house in which Papa bin Laden grew up still stands in the village, and the bin Laden family rents it out. Currently, the building is used as a school and education office. While many of Osama bin Laden's 24 brothers have paid a visit to the village, the terrorist mastermind himself is not believed to have dropped by. Muhammad bin Laden left the village as a poor emigrant prior to World War II. He moved to Saudi Arabia where he would later earn his vast fortunes.

Sayf The administrative centre of Wadi Do'an is known for the painting style of its houses – a much more moderate version of what you can see to the south at the Khaila Palace Tourist Hotel. The houses utilise well-placed touches of colour and design to make the otherwise normal architecture more interesting.

Where to stay

ar-Rayboon Tourist Hotel (4 rooms) 05 513590. The rooms at the small guesthouse include mattresses on the floor. There are 3 shared Yemeni bathrooms for the 4 rooms, so it's unlikely there will be much of a queue. If you are interested, you can also request to sleep on the roof. The manager sells local honey as well, although you'll have to bargain him down to get a decent price. *Rooms 2,000YRpp. B/fast & dinner inc in the hotel restaurant.*

WEST OF MUKALLA

Bir 'Ali/Qana Bir 'Ali is a small town on the southern coast of Yemen that has become a frequent stopover point for tourists who wish to dip in at its nearby pristine beaches, complete with nearby schools of dolphins and the ruins of an ancient port known since biblical times.

Qana was the ancient port of the Hadhramawt Kingdom, which ruled from the desert city of Shabwa between the years of 1000BC and AD350. The kingdom thrived by capitalizing on the incense trade, and Qana was an important part of that equation. It was at this ancient port where the ancient rulers received the large quantities of frankincense and myrrh that were then sent on the long caravan journey across mainland Yemen, through the city of Shabwa and onward toward Marib and the rest of the incense-demanding world.

Getting there At the time of writing, Bir 'Ali was not accessible by public transportation. Because of its location in the sometimes volatile Shabwa Governorate, travellers are required to travel to the area by hiring a private car and driver through a local tour operator.

Where to stay

Qana Tourist Complex (12 rooms) 05 211169; e qana-birali-yemen@yahoo.com. This camping site sprang up to capitalise on the increasing number of tourists who make their way to enjoy the beach adjacent to the old site of Qana & the island of Hillayaniah. The private beach is only enhanced by the bungalows, adequate restaurant (b/fast: 400YR; lunch/dinner: 800YR) & restroom facilities. Even if you're not staying here, it's a good place to while away the afternoon hours. *Bungalow: 2,000YRpp; inside room (holds up to 4 people): 6,000YR.*

What to see Looking at the Husn Ghuraf mountain to the west from the Qana Tourist Complex, there is a steep sand path visible. It makes for a very difficult climb to the top, but brings you right to the old temple.

A much easier walk up the mountain can be had by finding the old road on the northern side of the mountain (opposite the sea). Walk around to the northern side until you see the ancient wall begin on your right and several excavated ruins on your left.

The path eventually levels off for a small stretch right before the entrance to the old fort. About halfway into the level area, you can see the old inscription first 'discovered' by several gentlemen from the East India Company. There are four large water tanks and various buildings, as well as a temple on the high part of the western side.

Between the beach at the Qana Tourist Complex and the island of **Hillayaniah**, dolphins are frequently swimming about. You can rent a boat for around 4,000YR to motor out and join them, and then hit a few of the other islands nearby. The beaches of the islands are completely isolated, and there are great snorkelling opportunities.

Ghayl ba Wazir The area of Ghayl ba Wazir is known for its natural water springs, tobacco and henna. The best spring in terms of swimming is called Homat Sa'ad. Watch out for the little fish that like to nibble on your legs.

As-Suda' The small town of as-Suda' ('the headache') contains an old fort named **al-Awaalag** that dates from the time of al-Qu'aiti Sultanate. As recently as 50 years ago the building was standing tall, but each year takes its toll. The fort is now mostly ruinous.

Ash-Shihr Ash-Shihr was one of the three major cities of the al-Qu'aiti Sultanate (along with Mukalla and Shibam). Today, the city is starting to grow into a decent-sized place, and within ten years will probably be one of the major economic centres of Yemen. Two large gates with cannons meet you at the edge of the city's old boundary, although the urban growth has now bubbled on significantly past there.

The government is currently in the process of building a new port here. The long beachfront along the city contains many small fishing boats going back and forth with their catches.

Getting there & away Ash-Shihr lies on the road between Mukalla and al-Ghayda. There are a few shared taxis that travel between the growing city and Mukalla (300YR).

🏠 **Where to stay**

🏠 **City Center Tourist Hotel** (22 rooms) al-'Am St (in the Khour area of town); ☏ 05 334621; f 05 334623. If you need a place to stay in ash-Shihr, City Center is about as good as it comes, at least for now. Rooms are decent with Western bathrooms. There is a 200YR discount on rooms with shared bathrooms. $

✗ **Where to eat**

✗ The **Fish market** (⏱ 06.00–12.00) is the gathering point for the local fishermen, although most of the prime catches are trucked off to Saudi Arabia or Oman or shipped by boat to countries of the European Union. Local restaurants in the area specialise in cooking up a tasty sauce made from fresh squid. You can buy yours here and take it to any of the local eateries around. Tuna: 700YR/fish; squid: 530YR/kg.

AL-GHAYDA

Al-Ghayda is the capital of the al-Mahra governorate. Al-Ghayda is situated on a curve of the Yemeni coastline that continues northeast toward Oman and south toward Ra's Fartak. The typically unoccupied beaches lie east of the city, and the domestic airport is situated to the south.

The city is pleasant enough, and you may find the need to stop in here if you are travelling to Hof or Oman. The city would also make a good base for studying or doing fieldwork on Mahri, the most widely spoken language of the unwritten Modern South Arabian languages.

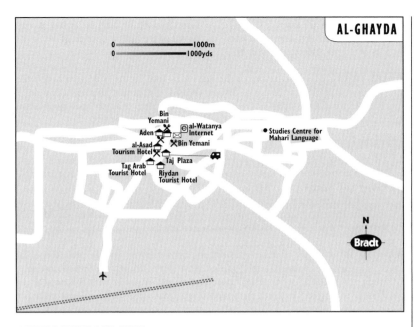

GETTING THERE AND AWAY

By air Air Yemenia flies between al-Ghayda and Sana'a (Sunday, 2hrs).

By bus The al-Esayi office is located in the building adjacent to the Taj Plaza Hotel, and buses gather at the same point. Buses run to Mukalla (1,200YR, 5½hrs), Aden (2,000YR 13hrs), and Sana'a (2,000YR, 14hrs).

By shared taxi Bijous gather in the car park lot to the east of the Taj Plaza Hotel. Daily trips are made to Seiyun (1,000YR, 3½hrs) and Mukalla (1,500YR, 5hrs). There are also shared taxis going to the local, small fishing villages of Haifif (50YR) and Thabut (150YR), described as 'a town with a grocery store'.

WHERE TO STAY

Tag Arab Tourist Hotel (33 rooms) ☎ 05 610625. As with the Taj Plaza, the suites are the place to stay, although the standard rooms are also decent. Rooms come with Western toilets & balconies. $$

Taj Plaza Hotel (105 rooms) ☎ 05 611222; f 05 610601. The best hotel in al-Ghayda, & not that expensive. Rooms are OK, but the only slightly more expensive suites are much better. Bring some fresh catches from the fish market to the veranda restaurant (the only restaurant in town to boast an English menu) to have them cook up a tasty curry. $$

Aden Hotel (41 rooms) ☎ 05 610822. The linoleum floors may remind you of a school cafeteria. Rooms are relatively clean. All rooms utilise shared Yemeni bathrooms that do not have hot water. $

Al-Asad Tourism Hotel (40 rooms) ☎ 05 611061; f 05 611068. There is no sign outside the hotel, so you may have to ask around for it. Rooms come with seatless Western bathrooms & hot water. The keys also have an interesting animal theme. There is a 500YR discount on rooms with no AC. $

Al-Taher Tourist Hotel (28 rooms) ☎ 05 612667; f 05 612668. The hotel is about a 10–15min walk from the town centre. The rooms are clean & come with Western bathrooms & hot water. Rooms vary in quality – get one with carpeting & a couch for no extra cost. $

Bin Yemani Hotel (64 rooms) ☎ 05 612371; f 05 612372. Rooms are spacious but not particularly clean. The hotel is located on the main shopping street, & has an attached restaurant. Yemeni bathrooms with no hot water. $

🏠 **Riydan Tourist Hotel** (20 rooms) ☎ 05 611672; 🖷 05 611633. The hotel offers decent, clean rooms for a low price. Yemeni bathrooms are clean, but without hot water. The hotel's AC is turned on when the management thinks it is hot enough. ⑤

✖ **WHERE TO EAT** The restaurants in the Taj Plaza and Tag Arab Tourist hotels are pretty good, and offer a variety of dishes. Outside the hotels, there is a couple of local restaurants. One open-air restaurant in the centre of town also has billiard tables, so you can pot a few balls if your fish is too long in coming.

OTHER PRACTICALITIES If you need to check your email, the **Al-Watanya Internet** (⊕ 08.30–12.00, 14.00–23.00; 3YR/min) is located on the same road as the Taj Plaza Hotel. On the same road, in the opposite direction is the small and questionable **Al-Ghayda Clinic** (☎ 612543)

If you have any interest in spending more time in the area and trying to pick up some of the local language while you are here, try the **Studies Center for Mahari Language** (☎ 612322; m 711 914200), located on the southern side of the city.

WHAT TO SEE AND DO The street that runs from the city square toward the Taj Plaza and Tag Arab Tourist hotels is filled with stores. Mostly clothes are for sale, although you will find some other household items for sale as well. There is also a small store selling local sweets. Although it is a small city, it's the biggest place for some distance – Mukalla is over 500km away – and so you will see quite a few people walking the road to look for good deals in the biggest market around.

The fish and qat markets lie to the east of Market Street. Al-Ghayda is, after all, simply a glorified fishing village, and so if you are planning on staying here you should purchase some of the very cheap fish, shrimp and lobster and have your hotel cook up a dish for you.

OUTSIDE AL-GHAYDA

HOF The small village of Hof sits near the border with Oman. The region is one of Yemen's four environmentally protected regions, and even orchids are said to grow in parts of the mountains during the rainy season. Outside the brief rainfalls, however, the village and surrounding country side are not as visibly appealing. There is a small restaurant in the village that seems to serve nothing but seafood.

11

Hadhramawt

Telephone code 05

HISTORY

EARLY HISTORY There are several different theories as to the origin of the name 'Hadhramawt'. The oft-visited tomb of the Prophet Hud lies within the wadi, and the similarity between his name and the beginning of Hadhramawt has led some to speculate that the region's name is derived from its prophet. Another line of thought holds that the word 'Hadhramawt' – which literally means 'death comes' – originates from the last words that the Prophet Hud spoke. On the other side of the spectrum there are tales of a tribal chief named 'Amr, who fought so fiercely in battles that it was said that 'death comes' with him.

In any event, both the name and the civilization of Hadhramawt extend well into antiquity. Hadhramawt is referred to in the 10th chapter of Genesis as Hazarmaveth, one of the 13 listed sons of Joktan, correlating to the great Yemeni forefather Qahtan. The area has been inhabited since the Stone Age, and the ancient capital of the region, Shabwa, likely began as a settlement in the 2nd millennium BC. Sometime around the beginning of the 1st millennium BC, the tribes of the region formed the Hadhramawt Kingdom, a power which would exist for nearly 1,300 years.

DURING THE EARLY AGE OF ISLAM

Delegation After the death of the Prophet Muhammad, many regions that were once loyal to Islam began to fall from the fold. This led to a series of battles across the Arabian Peninsula known as the Wars of Apostasy.

In Hadhramawt, trouble was brewing as well, but it was not quite as simple as merely a revolt against paying Islamic taxes, as was the case in other areas of the peninsula. Disagreements between the local tribes in the area had spiralled out of control into all-out war. Local historians say that members of the Banu Mu'awiya tribe had become involved in a dispute with Ziyad bin Labid, the Medinan-appointed governor, and with the Hadrami tribes of the region, concerning the methods of collection and distribution for the Islamic alms taxes and concerning a scandal regarding Ziyad's refusal to return a Banu Mu'awiya she-camel.

With the support of the local Hadrami tribes, Ziyad had initial success against the Banu Mu'awiya, killing many of the tribe's leaders in a surprise night attack. But the attack did not succeed in putting down the revolt. Rising to defend the honour of his fallen leaders, Abu Muhammad al-Ash'ath bin Qays led his forces to mount a counter-attack. Known for his strategic planning and unfamiliarity with a hairbrush (his nom de guerre, 'al-Ash'ath', means 'the one with crazy hair'), al-Ash'ath defeated Ziyad's army near Tarim.

When al-Ash'ath learned that the Medinan General al-Muhajir was marching toward Hadhramawt with a large Muslim army, he and his troops walled up in the fort of Nudjayr and waited for the army to approach. Al-Muhajir besieged the fort with great success.

HADHRAMAWT

SAUDI ARABIA

N

100km
100 miles

Rimah
Thamud

Qabr
an-Nabi Hud
Tarim   Ayanat   Bir Barhut
Seiyun   Husn
Shibam   al-'Urr
al-Ghurat
Huraydah
Mashhad   Ghayl bin Yameen

Arabian
Sea

Sensing that his defeat was nigh, al-Ash'ath secretly agreed with al-Muhajir that he would open the doors to the fort in return for the safe passage of nine to-be-named family members. With the gates to the stronghold opened, the Muslim army entered and dispatched over 1,000 members of the rebel army. Al-Ash'ath almost met with an untimely end as well, as he clumsily had forgotten to write his own name down on the list of nine to receive amnesty. In the end, the general decided to spare his life and sent him to Medina as a prisoner.

Ibadiyyas in Hadhramawt Around the year AD685, a group of individuals settled in Hadhramawt from the Kharajite branch of Islam, the sect that formed to oppose 'Ali and Mu'awiya after the arbitration at Siffin, in an attempt to flee the harsh persecution they were facing back in their native Iraq. This early introduction to the Kharajite ideas most likely made it easier for the Ibadhis, a moderate branch of that group, to attain power in the region.

In AD746, 'Abdullah ibn Yahya, known commonly as Talib al-Haqq ('the Student of Truth'), travelled to Mecca from Hadhramawt during the pilgrimage and met with the Basra-native Abu Hamza al-Mukhtar bin 'Awf al-Azdi. The Umayyad dynasty was in its final throes of reigning over the territories of Yemen, and Talib al-Haqq and Abu Hamza agreed to travel together back to Hadhramawt in an attempt to spread the Ibadhi faith and to overthrow Umayyad rule there.

Perhaps because of the early Kharajite influence, the two were very successful initially. Talib al-Haqq and Abu Hamza raised a small army of several thousand soldiers and easily defeated the Umayyad governor stationed there. With all of the

Hadhramawt under their sway the pair set out with their army and took over Sana'a as well.

The Umayyad Caliph was busy expanding the Muslim Empire, and the insurrection in Yemen did not concern him much. The Sana'ani population was growing tired of Umayyad rule. The Ibadhis were able to defeat the governor there without much effort. With Sana'a under his control Talib al-Haqq managed to raise a large army, and he sent Abu Hamza north, occupying Mecca and Medina and challenging the Umayyad rule there.

Marwan bin Muhammad, the last caliph of the Umayyad dynasty acted quickly once the Ibadhi rebellion broke into the Hijaz region and threatened his rule in Syria. He dispatched an army of over 4,000 soldiers that met and defeated Abu Hamza and his forces in Mecca. Following that victory, the Syrians marched south to Sana'a where they had a decisive victory over Talib al-Haqq. The remaining members of the Ibadhi army fled to Shibam to join up with the Ibadhi-appointed governor there.

The caliph's army attempted to end the Ibadhi threat once and for all, and set out from Sana'a to meet them in Hadhramawt. In a swift night attack, the Umayyad army routed the Ibadhis and secured the city of Shibam. Troubles back in Syria, however, required the Umayyad army to broker a quick peace with the few remaining Ibadhis before heading back home. Members of the faith continued to live in the region, having moved from Shibam to the city of Do'an. They paid taxes to the head Ibadhis in Oman, until the Sulayhids seriously crippled the group's numbers in the 11th century. By the end of the 12th century, they were expelled from their mosque in Shibam.

Their reputation for inhabiting the area lived on for some time, however. Writing in the 14th century Ibn Khaldun wrote that the inhabitants of

IBADHIS

Following the death of Muhammad, the Islamic world expanded rapidly. The first caliph Abu Bakr brought the entire Arabian Peninsula into the Islamic fold, while the next two caliphs, 'Omar and 'Uthman, expanded the empire to include land as far away as Libya, Turkey, and Pakistan.

With the assassination of 'Uthman the Muslim world faced its first civil war. Both 'Ali and Mu'awiya claimed the right to be the next caliph, and the forces of the two men ultimately met on the battlefield at Siffin. Mu'awiya tricked 'Ali into arbitration before the latter could finish a military victory.

The arbitration upset a lot of people. In particular a group of 'Ali's supporters broke away from him, arguing that he had no right to use the high position of caliph as a bargaining chip. The group became known as the Kharajites. They bitterly opposed both 'Ali and Mu'awiya, arguing that the caliphate should pass to the most qualified individual and not necessarily to someone of Muhammad's family (as the Shi'ite hold) or to Muhammad's tribe (as the Sunni hold).

Back in Iraq, the Kharajites faced large persecution and became quite extremist. Abdullah ibn Ibadhi broke away from the more radical groups and founded the moderate Ibadhi sect. Unlike their fellow Kharajites in Iraq, the Ibadhis rejected assassination and did not view non-Kharajite Muslims as infidels. Furthermore, the Ibadhis do not view the existence of the imam as necessary – if no-one alive is fit for the job, they will wait until someone comes around.

The Ibadhi population in Yemen has dwindled significantly, but it has a large presence in neighbouring Oman.

Hadhramawt 'abhor 'Ali for having consented to submit his rights to human judgement' – a reference to the Ibadhi faith. In any event, while the sect no longer survives in Hadhramawt today, the faith continues to exist to the east in Oman.

The Hadhrami Sayyids In AD932, a man by the name of Ahmed bin 'Isa (appropriately known as 'the Migrant') migrated from Basra, Iraq to Wadi Hadhramawt. He settled in the area and became the ancestor of all the Hadhrami Sayyids – the descendants of the Prophet Muhammad in the region. (Ahmed himself was nine generations removed from Muhammad.) His descendants moved eastward along Wadi Hadhramawt, settling in various areas along the way.

Nearly 200 years later 'Ali bin Alawi the Endower, the great-great-great-grandson of the Migrant settled in Tarim, which became a permanent base for the Sayyids. More importantly, the Sayyids finally became viewed as a permanent fixture of Hadhramawt rather than as a band of migrants. They supported the area economically and easily befriended and assimilated into the native Hadhrami society.

In the 13th century, the Hadhrami Sayyids turned to Sufism. Muhammad bin 'Ali, who was the grandson of 'Ali the Endower and who is known as 'the Great Teacher', met with a Sufi theologian who had been sent by the great north African Sufi saint Abu Madyan Shu'ayb. Together, they helped spread the faith.

SHIBAM

HISTORY Around the 3rd century AD the ancient Hadhramawt capital of Shabwa was destroyed, and Shibam became the new capital of the region. The city had existed for several centuries before its promotion, and it had been besieged in previous years before the Himyarite Kingdom finally proved superior to that of Hadhramawt.

Like many other cities in Yemen, there is no dearth of theories regarding the origin of its name. According to al-Hamdani the town's name was changed to Shibam from the similar-sounding Shibat. The origins of both names may lie in their similarity with that of Shabwa. 'Shibam', however, is quite a common town appellation in Yemen – there are actually four different places named Shibam in different parts of the country. (This Shibam is known as Shibam Hadhramawt when the need for differentiation arises.)

If, as another theory states, all the four separate towns were named after a great king or tribal leader, little to no record remains of him. Popular legend strings together a number of important words to put the leader's full name Shibam bin Hadhramawt bin Saba' al-Asghar. The most well-known (and historically verified) king of the city, however, was Qaisabah ibn Kalthum al-Kindi, who played a decisive role in the Muslim conquest of Egypt.

Little remains of the city as it would have existed following the exodus from Shabwa. In fact, the city has gone through several iterations since that time. In the early 10th century, the city's buildings and mosques were destroyed during an attack from the Kindah tribes. Shibam also had to be rebuilt after disastrous floods in 1298 and in 1532.

Despite its frequent destructions, Shibam had served as the capital of Wadi Hadhramawt up until the 16th century. During the lifetime of Muhammad, and shortly after his death, the Medinan-appointed Governor Ziyad bin Labid used the city as his base of operations, as did the Ibadhi revolutionaries Talib al-Haqq and Abu Hamza a century later in their struggle against the Umayyads. The city was used again as the focal point of the Ibadhi faith in the 11th and 12th centuries, until they were driven out of the city in 1194. In 1219, Shibam was conquered by the

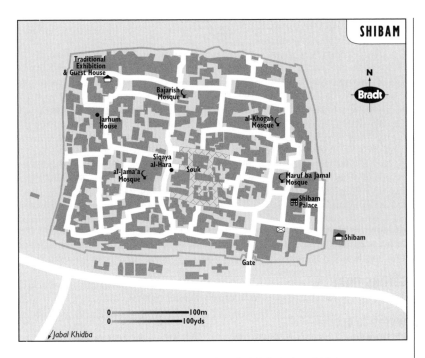

forces of Ibn Mahdi, who were connected with Saladin's Ayyubid dynasty.

While neighbouring Tarim continued to blossom as the scholastic capital of the region, Shibam maintained its hold as the political and commercial capital for another 300 years. It was not until 1520, a short 25 years after the Kathiri tribesmen had conquered Shibam, that the Kathiri leader moved the capital of his new sultanate from Shibam to Tarim. The Kathiris continued to maintain and govern the city, and after the devastating flood in 1528, the Kathiris helped construct the series of small dams and canals outside the city that has helped prevent a recurrence of this disaster.

The Kathiri Sultanate eventually lost total control of Shibam to the rising power of the Qu'aitis. Early in the 19th century, the Kathiri owner of Shibam sold half of his city to the Qu'aitis in order to fund his infighting with another prominent Kathiri ruler. When the Kathiri Sultan later wanted to buy back the half he had sold, the expansive-looking Qu'aitis were not willing to sell.

The Kathiris decided to win back the city by other means. While most of the Qu'aitis were attending a festival in the nearby town of al-Qatn, the Kathiris massacred the small number of Qu'aitis who had been left behind and took command of the entire city. The Qu'aitis responded by attacking Seiyun and by laying a lengthy siege to Shibam, during which time its inhabitants resorted to eating leather in order to survive.

The Qu'aitis and the Kathiris agreed to split the city again after arbitration, but both sides quickly set to work assassinating the other during deadly dining soirees – the *amuse-bouche* often exploded and was then followed by a knife in the back. The Qu'aitis proved masters at the 'why don't you come over for dinner?' ploy, and the Kathiris fled the city. The Qu'aitis maintained their rule of the city until the fall of their sultanate in 1967.

Inhabitants of Shibam talk about the city's 'three fives' – the current city is approximately 500 years old, there are about 500 buildings, and the population of the town is about 5,000. Other estimates put the population at 7,000–8,000, but either way, unlike other towns and cities across Yemen, Shibam has not changed much in terms of its shape, size or population over the last several hundred years.

GETTING THERE The easiest way to get to Shibam other than by a private vehicle is to take one of the shared taxis from nearby Seiyun (600YR, 1/2hr).

WHERE TO STAY

Shibam Hotel (7 rooms) ☎ 05 420425; f 05 420424; e alhawtahtl@y.net.ye. Being the only hotel in Shibam, the prices are a little higher than one might expect for the rooms provided. Nevertheless, the rooms are clean & have Western toilets. While located within the walled city itself, it is right outside the gate, on the southeast corner. Many rooms have private balconies where you can gaze up at the tall buildings before you. $$$

WHERE TO EAT

There are no restaurants within Shibam. The small, outdoor **Café al-Saffra** inside the city gate serves tea, *shisha*, and sandwiches. During the evening hours, many of the townsmen gather in this square to play dominoes and smoke *shisha*. The rules of the square are simple: you can sit and play dominoes as long as you like for no charge, but you must buy tea (10YR). For greater food variety, you can buy snacks at local stores.

OTHER PRACTICALITIES There is a **post office** located within the main square, to the right after walking through the city gate. There are no banks or ATMs, but you can exchange money at local exchange outlets.

WHAT TO SEE Most tourists come to Shibam to see the city itself. In the early 1930s, Freya Stark and Hans Helfritz made separate journeys to Shibam, the former coining the town the 'Manhattan of the Desert' and the latter the 'Chicago of the Desert'. The city is a marvel of mud-brick skyscrapers, densely packed together on a small mound, and which extend upward some five to eight storeys. Since 1982, the city has been recognised as a World Heritage Site by UNESCO.

The architectural style and design of the city on the whole is unlike anything else in Yemen. The most popular theory to account for this is that residents fleeing from the destroyed city of Shabwa rebuilt Shibam, their new home, based on the design and structure of Shaqir, the great palace of Shabwa. The theory makes sense – the inhabitants would no doubt long for a piece of their old home with them. In the same vein, many of the tower houses of Sana'a are believed to be modelled after the long-gone Ghumdan Palace.

The image of these monolithic buildings jutting heavenward in the isolation of the surrounding countryside is truly spectacular, and viewing the panoramic image at sunset, when the sky and buildings become playful with colours, makes your camera finger itch to take a snapshot like little else can. The best place to relieve that itch is on the mountain of **Jabal Khidba**, where you can get a bird's-eye view of the city by climbing only a short distance up the path. Nearly every visitor to the city comes to the area for the obligatory photograph of Shibam – and with the way the sun hits the city at day's end, it's likely you'll want one too. There is an old fortification about 10–15 minutes' walk from the base, where most people stop before snapping a quick photograph and returning.

You will be further rewarded if you make your way to the top of the mountain with a better perspective of Shibam and great views of the surrounding countryside as well. If you plan on hiking to the top, you should leave about an hour and a half before sunset (when the sun will be right where you want it), giving you an hour to make the climb and enjoy the view before embarking on the half-hour descent.

From the old fortification or from the top of the mountain, you will be able to see the entire city, including the town gate, the walled fortification that surrounds Shibam, and the large **Maruf ba Jamal Mosque** to the left of the town. There is another mosque of the same name within the city walls. Both were founded by the 16th-century scholar who lent them his name.

Just inside the main gate, and to the east of the square, is the old **Shibam Palace**. The palace was built in the 13th century by the followers of Ibn Mahdi. During the

FREYA STARK

Allison Otto

Dame Freya Stark (1893–1993) was one of the first Western women and one of the first Europeans to visit Hadhramawt and to travel through the remote regions of Yemen. Her first journey was an attempt to travel the Incense Road from Aden to Shabwa and to explore the ancient trade routes whose cities are only just being excavated now, after her death. An attack of fever prevented her from reaching her destination, but her historic journey across southern Yemen is chronicled in her book *The Southern Gates of Arabia*. She returned to Yemen several times over the next 60 years, as a traveller, as a diplomatic employee and propagandist during World War II, and as a guest of the British embassy.

A review of a relatively recent biography of Stark describes her as existing in 'the borderland between literature, politics and exploration'; her travels both helped to open the Middle East to Westerners and brought the cultures and the people of Yemen to the West through her writings and photographs. A second book, *A Winter in Arabia*, chronicled another expedition through the Yemeni desert in the company of a Bedouin caravan. Stark was knighted a Dame Commander of the Order of the British Empire (DBE) by Queen Elizabeth II in 1972.

One of Stark's most evocative descriptions of the other-wordly region she came to love is found in the introduction to *The Southern Gates of Arabia*, when she envisions the sight first observed by an anonymous Greek sea captain who described the Yemeni coast 2,000 years ago for his fellow sailors: Here are the high-shouldered mountains of Yemen, dark with abysses and overhanging summits, beyond a yellow foreground of sand a two days journey... Their colour, seen from the sea, is not that of the temperate mountains of earth, but is smouldering and dusky, as if the black volcanic points were coated with desert sand, and the red sandstones subdued by ashes of volcanoes – like embers of coal dying in a crust of cinders.

| |

reign of the Kathiris, the palace ceased to be the governmental seat and became the house of the sultan's extended family. A little further to the north is the **al-Khogah Mosque**, reputed to be 1,000 years old. The mosque was used as the centre of the Ibadhi faith until its adherents were finally expelled in the 12th century.

Walking through the streets of Shibam, you can view the large houses in more intimate detail. From this perspective, one of the most interesting things about the buildings is their elaborately carved wooden doors, doorframes, and locks. Some of the doorframes, in particular, are quite old – the one from Bayt Abdullah bin Fakik is said to date back to 1609, and that of Bayt 'Ali ibn Hayasa to 1717.

As you walk through the streets, you will notice ropes overhead extending from the upper-floor windows of many houses to the elevated windows of their neighbours, giving the appearance of a half-finished spider web. The ropes are used to transport items between the houses. After all, taking a batch of leftovers from the top floor of one eight-storey building to the top floor of another would involve a lot of work otherwise.

In addition to the inter-house rope transportation system, the inhabitants of Shibam have developed another novelty to make life in the skyscrapers easier. The locals claim that every building's single entrance door produces a pitch and tone combination unique to that particular house. This allows the inhabitants to know whether the guests on the street are knocking at their house or at one of the neighbours' without budging from the upper levels. Ask for a demonstration and see if you can discern the differences.

One of the (if not *the*) oldest house standing in Shibam is the **Jarhum House**, known locally as *Bayt Jarhum* (⊕ *09.00–13.00, 16.30–17.30 Sat–Thu; entrance: free*), which is said to date back to before the last great flood that wreaked havoc on the town in 1528. The house was purchased by UNESCO, and now contains pictures of Wadi Hadhramawt with accompanying English placards. There are plans to extend the material on display and transform it into a true museum.

Near the Jarhum House is the **Traditional Exhibition & Guest House**, known locally as *al-Bayt at-Tagleedi* (⊕ *08.30–13.30, 15.30–16.30 Sat–Thu; entrance: 300YR*). The traditional house is an excellent museum, as it not only offers information on the culture, architecture and lifestyles of the city, but it also affords you the opportunity to explore the inside of a well-kept Shibam house. Tea is served on the top floor after you have exhausted the museum's offerings.

In the centre of the town is the **souk**, although you can find tourist shops selling all types of Hadhramawt souvenirs on virtually every street corner. On the northern side of the souk, there used to be a tree trunk displayed that was used to support the large measuring scales. For some reason, it appears to be covered up now. On the western side of the souk is the **al-Jama'a Mosque** ('The Friday Mosque'). Originally built in AD762, it is the oldest building in Shibam. Repairs were undertaken by the famous Caliph Harun ar-Rashid (of *1001 Arabian Nights* fame) – the red-baked bricks are evidence of his ordered repairs that occurred sometime in the late 8th or early 9th century. The minaret dates back to the 16th century.

Outside the doors of the Jama'a Mosque, in the al-Jama'a Courtyard, sits the equally old well **Siqaya al-Hiara** ('The Well of Confusion'). In days past the well was an important gathering place for the poor, who would sit at its steps and receive alms from passers-by. The well derived its name from also being a gathering place for the town inhabitants who were in need of advice. Some villagers would gather, listen to the individual's problems, and offer advice. The practice no longer takes place, and the well is but a vestigial remainder of a recent custom.

With the rise of its larger sister Seiyun 35km to the west, Tarim is not as prominent in the Hadhramawt region as it once was. In the past, it served as the seat of the kings of the region as well as an important centre of scholarship and the Muslim faith. Today, Tarim maintains its reputation as a place of learning: there are plenty of mosque universities and the al-Ahqaf Library has the largest collection of manuscripts in Yemen outside the House of Manuscripts in Sana'a.

HISTORY Tarim's origins lie in antiquity. It is mentioned in the ancient inscriptions of the old kingdoms, and its history extends to at least the 5th century BC. The 10th-century historian al-Hamdani describes the city as one of the royal strongholds of the region, after the city had served as the seat of power for many kings of the Kindah Kingdom, an offshoot and vassal of the Himyarite Kingdom. Accordingly, tradition holds that the name of the city is taken from one of these kings – Tarim bin as-Sakun bin Kindah. A competing theory claims that the name originates from a more distant ancestor, Tarim bin Hadhramawt al-Asghar, believed to have been the first to settle in the region.

Tarim established itself as a city devoted to Islam early in the course of the religion's history. Yemenis from the city played an important part in aiding Muhammad in the Medinan war against the Meccans, and the 'blessed grave' is said to hold the graves of 40 soldiers killed in the famous Battle of Badr, the first battle between the two cities that was won by Muhammad and the Medinans.

Following Muhammad's death, Tarim is reputed as being the only city in northern Hadhramawt that remained completely faithful to the Meccan authority during the Wars of Apostasy. The first caliph, Abu Bakr, sent 70 of the Companions to Tarim to serve under Ziyad bin Labid, the governor of the region who had been appointed originally by Muhammad. Early in the 12th century 'Ali bin Alawi 'the Endower', the fifth descendant of Ahmed bin 'Isa 'the Migrant', settled in Tarim. Since then, the city has been the centre for the prominent Ba Alawi family, many of whom are buried also in the cemetery of Zanbal. During the life of 'Ali bin Alawi's grandson, Muhammad bin 'Ali – 'the Great Teacher', the Ba Alawi's added the mystical nature of Sufism to their way of life. For the last 800 years, Tarim has been an important centre for the religion.

GETTING THERE Shared taxis run regularly to and from Seiyun (600YR, 1hr).

 WHERE TO STAY

Bahani Apartments (8 rooms) \ 05 413333; f 05 414955. A little difficult to find – off a side street & with a sign in Arabic only – but well worth it. The apt-style hotel rooms offer the best stay in Tarim, with spacious bedrooms and kitchens. Rooms have a mixture of Yemeni & Western bathrooms. Apts $$

Brothers Pension Tourist (7 rooms) Located in the Main Square. The hotel is mainly a location where local Yemenis stay while passing through the town. Brothers Pension defines the meaning of bare necessities, but you may be able to request some sheets. Shared Yemeni bathrooms. $

Kenya Hotel Tarim (11 rooms) \ 05 417550; f 05 415720; e kenya_hotel@yemen.net.ye. Basic, clean rooms with Western bathrooms. Rooms without AC have a 500YR discount. $

X WHERE TO EAT There are several local restaurants in the main town square and in the area of the town's souk.

WHAT TO SEE The city of Tarim is renowned as a centre for scholarship, and there is no better place to see why than in the **al-Ahqaf Library** (⊕ *08.00–16.00*

Sat–Wed). The library is located in the al-Jam'a Mosque. The mosque itself is located in the main town square, and the main entrance is on the side of the building that faces the square. The entrance to the library, however, is up the ramp on the opposite side of the building. The library takes its name from the title of one of the chapters of the Koran, which is thought to refer to the nearby environs of Hadhramawt where the Prophet Hud preached to the people of 'Ad.

The library was established in 1972 and serves as a testament to the important role Tarim played in the sphere of Islamic learning in ages past – the majority of the 6,000 manuscripts, most of which dating back to the 16th and 17th centuries – with some as old as the 11th century – were written by Hadhrami authors. While Tarim's significance in the academic world has slipped since its glory days, the library itself is still very impressive. The library serves today as one of the major centres for Islamic study, and it receives over 5,000 visitors each year.

The manuscripts of the library cover a wide range of Islamic subjects, including Sufism, the Hadith, jurisprudence, medicine, history, and literature. All of the old manuscripts, of course, are in Arabic, but there is a small collection of English books on Arabic manuscripts in one of the shelves of the showroom.

The showroom of the library displays and explains some of the more interesting illuminated works. One of the best pieces of the library is a map of the world drawn by Mudhafar ibn al-Wardi over 500 years ago. The book containing the map is on display, but it is turned to another illumination showing the relationship of the Qa'aba in Mecca to other Muslim regions. Glossy reproductions of the illuminations are available for purchase from the librarian in the showroom for 500YR.

Although non-Muslims typically are not allowed to enter the al-Jam'a Mosque, fortunately you may enter the al-Ahqaf Library and explore the showroom and reading rooms. A guard at the bottom of the staircase will take your name and nationality, and you will be asked to remove your shoes before entering the library. The librarian speaks English, and he will be happy to answer any questions you may have or to show you around.

While the city of Tarim is known primarily as a place of scholarship, it is also a prominent burial ground. The city's **three cemeteries** – Zanbal, Furayt, and Akdar – are believed to hold over 10,000 holy men. Of the three, Zanbal is the most prestigious, and burial there is generally reserved for members of *Ahl al-Bayt*, the descendants of the Prophet Muhammad. Forty warriors from Tarim who fought with Muhammad at the Battle of Badr are buried in the cemetery of Zanbal, as well as the 70 companions of Muhammad who were sent to Tarim by Abu Bakr to help put down a religious insurrection in the region. The cemeteries hold a number of other individuals of note, including two martyrs who had rebelled against Ayyubid authority in the 12th century, the supernaturally gifted farmer and poet Sa'd al-Suwayni of the 15th century, and many of the important Ba Alawi sheikhs.

The abundance of saints buried in Tarim has ensured that the city has always maintained some degree of importance. Partly because of its holy inhabitants, the city is known as 'al-Ghanaa' – the melodious voice; the lush garden. According to one Hadith, the ground below the city holds one of the hidden gardens of paradise. Of course, it's unlikely that everyone buried in the city lived a life of saintly virtue. Given the locally held belief that both the saints and sinners buried in Tarim will be chauffeured into heaven by Abu Bakr, the burial locale probably holds a certain allure for the more non-saintly, whose actions otherwise may have left them unsure of their other-worldly fates.

Generally, the city is more renowned for its **number of mosques** than its number of saints or the vouchsafing properties of the cemeteries. An early 18th-century poet wrote that Tarim contained 360 mosques, the number of which allowed its citizens to visit a different mosque each day of the lunar year. Of course, no-one would deny a poet his God-given license for liberal exaggeration – and the poet in question apparently wasn't afraid to use it. A recent count of the town turned up approximately 185 places of worship. To be fair to the poet, neighbouring mosques have since combined, and his survey may have included all of Tarim's surrounding villages. In any event, the story that the city has a mosque for each day of the year has persisted to the present day.

Tarim's most prominent mosque is the **al-Mihdar Mosque**. The oft-photographed, looming 54m (175ft) mud-brick minaret of the al-Mihdar Mosque is one of the great prides of Tarim. The mosque takes its name from a 15th-century saint who also lent his name to the large rock by the holy river at Qabr an-Nabi Hud. The mosque itself, however, only dates back to the early 1900s. Outside the mosque, you will notice some poles that have been erected in the centre of the road. In the past, as large trucks drove past the mosque, the motorised behemoths would cause the large minaret to wobble. Understandably concerned, the locals put up roadblocks that would prohibit these large vehicles from passing through. Non-Muslims are typically not permitted to enter the mosque.

One of the reasons for the large number of mosques in the city is the historical tendency of the town's citizens to emigrate to other lands or to travel by sea to make their fortunes. For many who are successful in their endeavours abroad, they demonstrate their thanks to God by constructing a mosque in the town upon their return.

In addition to mosques, many wealthy families have also constructed mud-brick palaces after their return to Tarim. The city currently has 25 such buildings, many of which were constructed in the 1940s and 1950s as a means to boost the local economy, which had suffered during World War II. The wealthy families took care to use mostly local materials and employ the citizens of Tarim in the construction of the buildings. The most commonly known of these is the **Qisr al-Kaf** (⊕ *08.00–13.30 Sat–Thu; entrance fee: 150YR*), which was converted into a museum in 1997, in part to pay for the upkeep of the structure. Like most of the palaces in Tarim, Qisr al-Kaf is a wonderful cocktail of Hadhrami, southeast Asian and colonial architecture.

There is a small **souk** in the centre of town near where the shared taxis gather. The three most common items for sale – teacups, dried fish, and gold jewellery – will help ensure that you are not left wanting if you are hit with the sudden desire to take tea and a small snack fashionably.

SEIYUN

HISTORY Seiyun is not an ancient town. Perhaps the earliest-known date in which the city is mentioned occurred late in the 15th century, when a band of Kathiri tribesmen some 10,000 members strong left their home region north of Sana'a in 1494. Spying a golden opportunity in Hadhramawt, the tribesmen invaded Seiyun and the surrounding area. Under the leadership of Badr abu Tuwairiq, the Kathiris successfully conquered the area and set up a capital in Tarim. Shortly thereafter, however, the capital was moved to Seiyun, where the Kathiri sultans governed until 1967.

To establish order in the Hadhramawt, the Kathiris employed mercenary tribal fighters to do their dirty work for them. Most frequently, the Kathiris brought in tribesmen from the renowned *have gun, will travel* tribe of Yafi' from the highlands of central Yemen.

Eventually, the increasing number of Yafi' tribesmen that settled in the area began to vie for power with the Kathiris. The Yafi' tribesmen formed the Qu'aiti Sultanate, which ruled the southern half of the Hadhramawt and which would

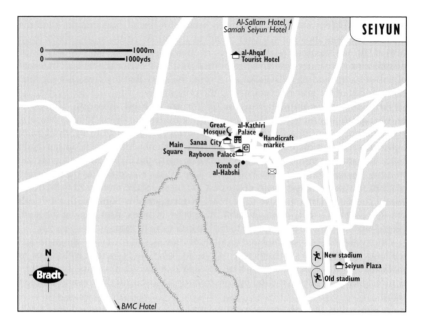

rival the Kathiri Sultanate in Seiyun. In the late 19th century, the two rivals fought each other in a bitter war until the British stepped in and imposed peace.

By the end of the 19th century, the Kathiri state became part of the Aden Protectorate, a conglomeration of tribal groupings and kingdoms in what would become South Yemen outside the British colony at Aden. The British powers at Aden favoured the Qu'aitis considerably, and for much of the 20th century the Kathiri Sultanate was relegated to nominal control of the northeast section of Wadi Hadhramawt.

In 1939, the Kathiri Sultanate became a member of the Eastern Aden Protectorate, along with the Qu'aiti and al-Mahra sultanates. In the early 1960s, the colony of Aden and the surrounding states formed the Federation of South Arabia. The Kathiri sultanate did not join, becoming instead part of the Protectorate of South Arabia along with Qu'aiti and al-Mahra. The protectorate dissolved immediately on the 1967 revolution, and the Kathiri state disappeared soon after that.

Today, Seiyun is the unofficial capital of the region. Although the nearby city of Tarim has the lasting reputation as the centre of scholarship, Seiyun has taken over as a more important city for Islamic studies. In terms of visiting the various sites of Wadi Hadhramawt, Seiyun's central location between Shibam and Tarim, as well as its number of hotels, make it an excellent choice to use as a base.

GETTING THERE Yemitco on al-Jaza'ir Street has a daily service to Sana'a (1,500YR) that takes seven hours. Although buses depart at 05.00 and 13.30, only the latter bus is open for foreigners. The earlier bus continues from Sana'a on to Saudi Arabia, and foreigners are prohibited because the extra time needed to acquire security at the checkpoints would cause undue delay for the other passengers continuing northward.

Yemenia Airways operates a number of domestic flights to the following destinations from the airport: Sana'a (Monday, Wednesday, Thursday, and Saturday; flight duration one hour) and Aden (Tuesday and Wednesday; flight duration one hour).

WHERE TO STAY

Samah Seiyun Hotel (38 rooms) Maryamh St; 05 402777; f 05 403623; e samahhotel@ hotmail.com; www.bazaratravel.com/samah.html. Nice, clean rooms. Several of the dbl rooms include an extra Yemeni-style sitting room that is quite nice, but the ambience suffers slightly from the noise associated with being on one of the main thoroughfares into the city. Inner courtyard houses a large swimming pool, & the hotel restaurant offers a lunch/dinner buffet for 2,000YR. $$$, inc b/fast.

Seiyun Plaza Hotel (68 rooms) President's St (across the road from the football stadium & the presidential palace); 400791; f 401294; e seiyun-plaza@y.net.ye. An excellent hotel with spacious, clean rooms, large swimming pool, & English-speaking staff. On the roof of the hotel there is a domed observation room that affords lovely views of the city. Upon request, the hotel can bring in a local group to provide an entertaining show of folkloric dance for only 2,000YR (all the money goes directly to the performers). The hotel restaurant has buffets for b/fast ($$) & dinner ($$$), with lunch options ranging from entrees to a large Yemeni spread ($$$). Accepts credit cards. $$$

Al-Ahgaf Tourist Hotel (80 rooms) Airport St; 408668; f 408669. Lovely, peaceful rooms with balconies – half of which overlook the swimming pool. While not located in the town centre, it is not too far away, & the hotel makes for one of the best-value places to stay in Seiyun. The hotel restaurant also serves local dishes for lunch ($$$) & dinner ($$). $$, inc b/fast.

BMC Hotel (82 rooms) 05 428040; f 05 428042. Located in the village of al-Ghurfa on the other side of the al-Ahagaf mountain, BMC is about a 12km drive from the city centre. Nevertheless, groups of tourists always seem to enjoy their stay here. Rooms are pleasant, with Western bathrooms. The swimming pool is large, but although the water is changed every other day, the slimy floor could use a good scrubbing. $$

Sanaa City Hotel (20 rooms) Main Sq, opposite al-Kathiri Palace; 05 407082. Decent & spacious rooms (albeit sparsely furnished) located in the heart of Seiyun. A good choice. Western bathrooms. $$

Al-Sallam Hotel (45 rooms) Maryamh St; 05 403208; f 05 403181. Al-Sallam was the first & only hotel in Seiyun for some time. During the early 1970s, the communist government expropriated the building from a local family & turned it into a grand hotel. Even after reunification, the hotel was one of the nicest in Yemen. It is currently operated by the Yemeni government, although plans are underway to return the property to the original family line (who will no doubt continue to run it as a hotel). Rooms are fair, with Western bathrooms, & are decorated in an interesting mix of styles. $

Al-Tawela Palace Hotel (15 rooms) Main Sq; 405264. Rooms are cheap, but it's in no way the most pristine establishment in Seiyun. Yemeni toilets. $

Rayboon Palace Hotel (9 rooms) Main Sq; 05 405393; f 402686. Rooms are decent & somewhat clean. Bathrooms are Western, but you may need to request one with a toilet seat. Rooms without AC are slightly cheaper. $

WHERE TO EAT Outside the hotels, the restaurants in Seiyun are mostly concentrated in the environs of the central town square, including the more prominently displayed **Mat'am ash-Shaab** ('the People's Restaurant') and the **Park Café**.

OTHER PRACTICALITIES There is an **internet café** located next to the al-Kathiri Palace, across from the Garden Restaurant (2YR/min).

There is a number of hospitals in Seiyun. The two most highly recommended are the private **Al-Wadi Medical Hospital** and the government-run **General Hospital**.

There are several banks in Seiyun with ATMs, including the **National Bank of Yemen**, the **Commercial & Agricultural (CAC) Bank**, and the **International Bank of Yemen**. Currency can also be exchanged easily in the area around the town square.

WHAT TO SEE

Al-Kathiri Palace (⏰ 08.00–12.30 Sat–Wed; entrance fee: 500YR) The al-Kathiri Palace stands prominently in the centre of Seiyun, watching over the city as a constant guardian. The palace was built in the mid 19th century by the Kathiri Sultan Ghalib bin Mohsen and saw several renovations thereafter. After South Yemen won its independence in 1967, the palace was taken away from the sultan in typical Marxist fashion and transformed into the headquarters for the local police. In 1984, the palace was converted into the Seiyun Museum.

In general the museum does a great job with presentation. There are many detailed description cards in English, and the palace's four floors are filled with a wide array of artefacts. The first-floor display is dedicated to Ancient Yemen and contains a large number of inscriptions from the nearby site of Rayboon. Unlike other museums in Yemen, the museum also contains several artistic renderings of what Rayboon looked like in the past. The drawings, the pieces in the museum, and the actual site nearby make it possible for you to get a good feel for the ancient city.

The second floor contains two rooms featuring photography by Freya Stark while she was in the region and one slightly out-of-place display on the city of Mecca. Additional photographs taken by Daniel van der Meulen adorn the walls of the third floor. The top floor of the museum has three displays, all very interesting: the Kathiri Sultanate in Hadhramawt, traditional Arab medicine, and handicrafts and customs.

Tomb of al-Habshi Near the town square lies the tomb and mosque of Habib 'Ali al-Habshi, an important preacher and scholar of the late 19th and early 20th centuries who obtained a cult-like following during his tenure at Seiyun. Al-Habshi was born in a small town just outside Tarim in 1843. He began teaching in Seiyun after studying for two years in Mecca, and his charismatic and passionate delivery won him a large following.

Shortly after al-Habshi's death in 1915, his followers established an annual pilgrimage to his tomb and mosque. Over the last 100 years, al-Habshi's prominence has not diminished – his tomb and the monuments around it maintain an important status in Seiyun, and the annual pilgrimage continues. During the days of 18–20 in the Islamic month of Rabi' ath-Thani, pilgrims gather to read the Koran, the Hadith and poetry, to beat their drums, and to weep in worship – just as the Muslim adherents had done while al-Habshi was preaching. Additionally, a smaller crowd gathers during the Islamic month of Sha'ban after the pilgrimage to the tomb at Qabr an-Nabi Hud. Signs reading 'Entrance for Muslims only' are displayed prominently.

Handicraft Market (☉ *08.00–12.00 Sat–Thu*) If you are in the market for some authentic Hadrami souvenirs, this market near the central square offers items such as straw hats and bowls, and caters mainly to locals. You won't find any of the old-style wood carvings here, but if you look around the area of the al-Kathiri Palace, you'll find a couple of antique stores that sell old and expensive wooden doors or pillars (ornately carved doors can be as much as US$1,000).

If sporting events are more your style, there is a **football stadium** in the southern part of town. During the regular season, the local teams take on challengers on Thursdays and Fridays at 16.00.

OUTSIDE SEIYUN

QABR AN-NABI HUD The town of Qabr an-Nabi Hud ('the tomb of the Prophet Hud') is empty for the majority of the year; the many buildings that surround the prophet's tomb uninhabited outside the month of the yearly *ziyyara* (see below). The town is located 94km east of Seiyun.

History The Prophet Hud is known in the Koran as the first of the five Arab prophets – the other four being Saleh, Abraham (who was not actually Arab), Shu'ayb, and Muhammad. According to tradition, Hud was the great-great-grandson of Noah, and he is often identified with Eber of the Old Testament (Genesis 10:24–25). In addition to the genealogies matching up, the roots of the name are also very similar. The English word 'Hebrew' is derived from the name 'Eber', just as the Arabic word for 'Hebrew', *yahudi* (يهودي), is derived from the name 'Hud'.

Tradition holds that Hud was the father of Qahtan, the ancestor of the south Arabian tribes and the father of all Yemenis. According to the Book of Genesis, not only did Eber's progeny include Joktan (Qahtan), Eber also fathered Peleg, from whom Abraham descended. Thus, Hud is considered to be the first common ancestor of all the Jewish and Arab peoples. Considering that his offspring would found the entire Judeo-Christian-Islamic line of religions, it is no wonder that his tomb continues to attract a large gathering every year (even if not exactly for that reason).

The Koran has a lot to say about the Prophet Hud, discussing and making reference to his prophethood no less than 17 times. The mighty nation of the people of 'Ad were said to have ruled directly after Noah's flood in the land of al-Ahqaf, a term which may mean 'sand dunes' but that has been connected with the Hadhramawt region.

As mighty nations are prone to do in these stories, the people slipped into feelings of pride and general haughtiness; the Koran relates that they built a tower on every hilltop, just to amuse themselves. Much like the Israelites after the parting of the Red Sea, the people turned to idolatry. God sent them Hud, an 'Adi himself, to bring them back unto the folds of monotheism. It did not work.

As would later be the case with both Jesus and Muhammad, Hud discovered that a prophet is without honour in his home town. Flinging fighting words at Hud such as *imbecile* and *liar*, the people of 'Ad rejected his message.

The rejection of God's message by the people of 'Ad occurred not long after the flood. Though He was angry, God no doubt remembered the promise He had made in Genesis 8:21 to never again smite the human race as He had done, ie: to smite them by flood. Cleverly, God sent a drought.

The people of 'Ad were not deterred from their apostasy by a lack of water and so God resorted to stronger measures. The Koran relates that the people of 'Ad ultimately were destroyed by a roaring and violent storm wind that swept across the al-Ahqaf region for eight days and seven nights non-stop: the people of 'Ad were no more.

When it came time for Hud to die, he is said to have gone to the large stone where his tomb now sits. With God opening the rock before him, Hud entered the stone, and God closed the rock behind him. One version of the story says that God opened the rock to protect Hud, who was being pursued by his enemies – perhaps some 'Adi rebels who had survived the storm or some of Hud's followers gone bad. In any event, the rock still has a large fissure, the result of not having closed completely.

The Ziyyara Every year for four days during the Islamic month of Sha'ban, pilgrims flock to the town of Qabr an-Nabi Hud to partake in a festival that dates back to ancient times. To understand the nature of the pilgrimage and festival, it is necessary to understand how seasonal markets in the ancient Arabian Peninsula worked.

Throughout the Arabian Peninsula in pre-Islamic times, there were several gathering areas that held seasonal markets once or twice a year. To a greater or lesser degree, the market areas were located often on holy ground, and the time of the market coincided with the time of pilgrimage to these sites, thus doubling the attendance. The pilgrimage to the Kaaba in Mecca, for example, which now forms one of the five pillars of Islam, originated out of a seasonal market connected to a pagan pilgrimage to the Kaaba.

During these markets, the various tribes of the region would gather together and put aside their differences. The markets were considered sanctuaries, similar to the way that Sana'a is viewed today. As these markets were held only once or twice a year, the tribesmen would buy enough supplies to see them through to the next market.

The markets were more than merely a place for tradesmen, however. The large gathering of various people in relative safety provided a good forum for artists as well, giving local poets a chance to show off their skills.

The market at the site of Qabr an-Nabi Hud was known as Souk ash-Shihr, and it specialised in the sale of leather, frankincense, and myrrh. Sheikh 'Abd al-Qadir notes that buying and selling was accomplished by means of games of chance, such as by throwing stones.

Because most of these markets were connected to the worship of idols, they were stamped out with the onset of Islam – the two major exceptions being the pilgrimages to Mecca and Qabr an-Nabi Hud. The former was officially brought into the scope of Islam by Muhammad, while the latter was able to maintain its existence because Muhammad himself mentioned that Hud was a prophet of God in the Koran.

Increasing wars between some of the tribal factions in the Hadhramawt after the coming of Islam decreased the ability of the region to host a large seasonal market, but the market gradually reclaimed its original importance. During the 15th century, al-'Aydarus helped to transform the market and pilgrimage into the religious experience it resembles today by turning the affair into a Sufi pilgrimage.

Once the Sufis adopted the *ziyyara*, the pilgrimage lost much of its commercial aspect. Today, for instance, there is hardly any trading that occurs. The number of religious pilgrims who fill up the tiny town, however, is staggering. The *Yemen Times* reported that over 160,000 pilgrims made the trek to the tomb in the four-day period surrounding the *ziyyara* in 2000.

While you won't be able to stop in and pick up leather and myrrh, the *ziyyara* offers something much more important. With its remnants of ancient customs, the site offers a glimpse into the workings of the ancient Arab world. In 2008, the *ziyyara* will run from 10–13 August; in 2009, from 30 July–2 August; and in 2010, from 19–22 July. The *ziyyara* is only open to Muslim men.

Getting there The only way to reach Qabr an-Nabi Hud is by private vehicle. At the time of writing, the asphalt road connecting the town to the main thoroughfare had not yet been completed, and some slight off-road driving was required.

What to see Entering the town, you will first cross the small river where supplicants first perform their ablution and drink from the hands of their religious leader during the pilgrimage. Near the river, you will find the first of three important rocks. The riverside stone is called the **Rock of 'Umar al-Mihdar**, a 15th-century saint from the time when the *ziyyara* took on a Sufi nature. The main mosque in Tarim also takes his name.

Inside the town's gates, the first landmark of note is **Bir Tesloom** ('the Well of Greeting'). Although no longer a functioning well, the old fount is thought to be a meeting place of the righteous. During the *ziyyara*, the pilgrims stand in front of the well, saying *sallam 'alaykum* to the prophets mentioned in the Koran (from Muhammad to Adam) and then to the number of angels who grace the watering hole as well.

Outside the *ziyyara*, women are allowed to enter the grounds of the town and may even enter the dome which houses the **tomb of the Prophet Hud**. As you walk through the town, however, you may notice an old sign that reads 'Muslims Only' that has been uprooted and leans against one of the buildings, pointing to nowhere in particular. I was told that the sign had originally been erected after several female tourists attempted to visit during the *ziyyara*.

Whether non-Muslims are allowed to enter the holy site today is ambiguous. The tomb of the Prophet Hud is a deeply religious place for the Sufi sect that gathers here, and your presence might be welcome or frowned upon, depending on who is visiting the tomb on any given day.

Regardless, you should respect the wishes of the locals. On the one hand, the Sufis in Yemen are wary of people outside their way of faith, especially when it comes to the veneration of the tombs of holy men – the destruction of the temple of al-'Aydarus in Aden and other Sufi sites by Islamic fundamentalists in 1994 weighs heavily on the memory. Outsiders in general, and foreigners in particular, may be viewed as a threat – a means by which knowledge is disseminated and which may bring back the wrath of the fundamentalists. On the other hand, while some members of the faith may be very welcoming to those who visit the site and want to learn more about it, others believe that the presence of non-Muslims demeans the religiousness of the tomb. Just be aware that you may or may not be able to proceed.

Beginning up the stairs to the tomb, a large rock juts out of the ground – the second of the three important stones in the town. The rock is believed by many to be **Hud's she-camel**, which God turned to stone after Hud entered his tomb. Another interpretation of the she-camel tale is that the word for 'rock' and 'she-camel' in Arabic are the same: *naqah* (ناقة). However, given that the Arabic legends hold that Hud's son, Qahtan, was the first speaker of Arabic, perhaps he gave the same word to 'she-camel' and 'rock' after witnessing the transformation of one into the other.

Next to the Rock of the She-Camel, there is a whitewashed stone building dating from the 1980s where pilgrims sit to ask for further supplications after visiting the tomb above. Outside the building, on the second platform before the staircase splits in different directions, there is an out-of-place stone with a large depression in it. The mark is said to have been left by Hud's camel – the last footprint she left before sitting down and turning to stone.

At the top of the stairs lies the **Tomb of the Prophet Hud**, partially enclosed within a small domed building. Originally a large pile of rocks, the tomb was first renovated in the late 15th century and a small dome structure erected. The current white dome dates back to the late 17th century. If you are entering the tomb, you should take your shoes off once you reach the top platform of the dome.

Inside the dome, the tomb starts at the fissured rock and continues for roughly 28m (92ft). The Koran states, after all, that both Hud and his 'Adi kin were giants. The fissure in the rock has been smoothed over, the result of millennia of pilgrims' hands passing over it in reverence. This rock is the third and most important of the stones in the town. It was this rock that God is believed to have opened to permit Hud to enter, closing it all but for the fissure after Hud had laid down to die. Outside the dome, there are several tombs that date back about 200 years.

BIR BARHUT Bir Barhut, or the 'well of Barhut', was known in pre-Islamic traditions as the worst well on earth. Early authors described it as a volcanic pit and noted that the well threw forth red-hot coals as large as mountains, supposedly crying out into the night with a voice like thunder that shook the countryside for miles while doing so.

As if that were not enough, the well was also accompanied by a putrid smell of sulphur and was the haunting ground for the souls of infidels and hypocrites. Tales abounded that one could hear the screams and cries of these dark souls being tortured within the depths of Barhut's gloomy waters. Another story followed that whenever a particularly odious stench issued forth from Bir Barhut, it would be followed quickly by news that one of the most prominent unbelievers had died. Al-Hamdani noted that it was common to use the name of Bir Barhut in cursing others – an ancient variant on 'go to hell'.

Bir Barhut is actually a cave, and no trace of a well remains. Explorers who have visited it in the last century or two have found no evidence of volcanic activity either. The cave walls have objects which resemble seashells peeking out, and are covered in many places by a white substance that looks like salt. In the account of his travels to the region, van der Meulen notes that the 'curious but innocuous smell' was caused by bats or by rock weathering, not by 'sulphurous vapours'. As I walked through the cave, I did not notice any discernible odour. Thus, the infamous and feared Bir Barhut is neither foul smelling, volcanic, nor water-producing. The cave is rather hot, and in some passages the temperature rises significantly. Additionally, you can take some small comfort as I did, that if you are not a Muslim, at least there will be souls of infidels therein whenever you visit.

How exactly the innocuous cave of Barhut became known as a foul-smelling sulphur pit that housed the ghosts of unbelievers is something of a mystery. Most likely, Bir Barhut got its reputation by its association and proximity to the tomb of the Prophet Hud. After Hud's warnings to the people of 'Ad were received in vain, God is said to have wrought destruction upon them, wiping the Hadhramawt slate clean. The Koran states that the people of 'Ad: 'were destroyed by a fierce roaring wind, which He imposed on them for seven long nights and eight long days so that thou mightest have seen men lying overthrown, as they were hollow trunks of palm-trees.' Additionally, at least one geographer claimed that the area to which Hud was sent, known as al-Ahqaf, was a mountain and a cave. Thus, a legend of an entire people of unbelievers dying in one place could give rise to a folk legend that the local cave housed all their souls. Furthermore, the darkness and despair of Bir Barhut act as the perfect foil to the Bir Tesloom (the 'Well of Greeting'), thought to be the watering hole (literally and figuratively) of all the pious souls, angels, and prophets, and which sits just off the tomb of the Prophet Hud.

Getting there To get to Bir Barhut, continue past Qabr an-Nabi Hud down the valley road of Wadi Sana. From the last gate leading to the town of Qabr an-Nabi Hud, it is 9.8km until the entrance to the cave. On your right-hand side, you can see a small zig-zagging path that goes up about two-thirds of the mountainside and ends at the large cave entrance. Despite (or perhaps due to) the dubious folkloric claims, the cave is actually quite lovely; passageways open up to large chambers, and much of the cave can be traversed without need of climbing within. Make sure you bring good light sources, additional batteries, and a compass if you decide to do any serious exploration.

If you had your heart set on exploring a cave inhabited by evil spirits and dark odours, I recommend the cave near ar-Riyyadi in al-Mahweet. The inner sanctuaries of the cave are said to be inhabited by jinn, and the stench of bat guano has built up to such a level that your every breath will make you feel as though you are incurring God's wrath.

AL-HAWTA As Hadrami families received their remittances from abroad, they were able to branch out and found new dwelling areas. New buildings were not complete without a vast array of date palms, and so the trees were planted to comprise a large garden, known as a *hawta*. The town of al-Hawta derives its name from these gardens, and was likely founded on remittance money a couple of centuries ago. The main palace has been converted into a tourist hotel, and it is *the* place to stay in Wadi Hadhramawt.

Getting there Staying at the al-Hawta Palace Hotel will virtually require that you have private means of transportation – such as through a travel agency. While al-Hawta can be reached easily enough by taking a shared taxi between Seiyun and Shibam, trying to leave the small town by public transportation will prove more difficult.

Where to stay

 Al-Hawta Palace Hotel (58 rooms) ✆ 05 425010; f 05 425013; e alhawta@ universal.yemen.com. Located only 16km from Seiyun, this hotel is the best place from which to explore the entire region (if you don't mind the small drive & can afford the price). The old building of the hotel retains its old Hadhrami style, even in the gorgeous rooms, & is a much better place to stay than the newer, modern-style building. Ask for a room with a balcony. The grassy grounds are very peaceful as well; they include a swimming pool, antique shop (🕐 17.30–22.00, 7 days/week), & a large restaurant ($$$$). Alex, the manager of the hotel, speaks English very well & is happy to assist with any questions you may have. Internet access is available (20YR/min). Accepts credit cards. $$$$$

TOMB OF AHMED BIN 'ISA On the road from Seiyun to Tarim is the Tomb of Ahmed bin 'Isa Ahmed bin 'Isa is known by the appellation 'the Migrant', having moved to Hadhramawt from Basra, Iraq around AD932. The Migrant was the founder of the Hadhrami Sayyids – the descendants of the Prophet Muhammad. In Hadhramawt, the Sayyid families of the area trace their ancestry back to Muhammad through Ahmed bin 'Isa. All the important graves you will see in the area are his descendants. Not a bad lineage!

MASHHAD The little town of Mashhad contains yet another tomb of religious importance. Within the small dome is the grave of **'Ali bin Hassan al-'Attas**, the grandson of Ahmed bin 'Isa. According to legend, by the time 'Ali al-'Attas arrived in Mashhad, the area had become a hotbed for thieves and murderers. Undeterred, 'Ali al-'Attas settled in the region and began the process of cleaning up the riff-raff. In addition to building a mosque, he is said to have rediscovered an ancient, dry well that issued forth with water upon his approach. His mosque-building and water-producing skills were not without effect; the town is said to have become safe again by the time of his death.

Perhaps the well that al-'Attas discovered had previously been used by the residents of the ancient site of Rayboon, which lies across the street on a nearby mound. Although the temple was excavated several decades ago, it has largely been covered again by the shifting sands. You can still see a small portion of the temple floor and wall.

GHAYL BIN YAMEEN At the small village of **Ghayl bin Yameen** there is an old mud-brick fort known as **Qarn adh-Dhabi** ('the Deer's Antler'). Like many of the old fortifications in the country, the Antler is in a state of disrepair. The main problem, however, is getting there. The trip requires a long drive on an unpaved road. Much of the trek is over land being explored by the **Canadian Nexen** oil company, and there are many security checkpoints scattered throughout to ensure their safety.

RIMAH Rimah is the first major stop coming from the Shahan border crossing at Oman. Importing cars from Oman and Dubai into Yemen is a lucrative business, and Rimah, directly over the border, is one of the main places where these vehicles are sold. Yemenis used to flock to the town in large numbers to buy a vehicle for a significantly cheaper price than they could in other parts of the country. While the sales still continue to some degree, the prices have more or less evened out.

Where to stay

⌂ **Green Mountain Hotel** (37 rooms) ☎ 05 482204. The 'Green Mountain' is actually a small hill graced by some patches of grass, but I suppose that is impressive enough in the middle of the desert. The hotel serves mainly as a stop for those travelling between the Yemen and Oman or calling into the town to buy a new imported car.$$

12

Socotra

Telephone code 05

Socotra is an earthly paradise, with a vast variety of plants and wildlife. Endemics pop up at every turn, and odd shaped trees twist and turn out of the ground, looking like they might be more at home in a Dr Seuss book. The island is rich in history and mythology, believed to have been visited by the apostle Thomas, the fiery Phoenix, and numerous pirates. There are abundant opportunities for birdwatching, hiking, snorkelling, caving or just relaxing on the beach. Enjoy, but remember: conservation is key.

NATURAL HISTORY with Dominic Ashby, Kate Reimer and David Scoville

The Socotran Archipelago is one of Yemen's greatest treasures of biodiversity. Located about 400km south of the mainland in the Indian Ocean, these arid islands play host to a stunning array of plant and animal life. An estimated 30% of the island chain's plant life is endemic, as are many of the birds found there. Socotra is an ecotourist's dream – not all of the region's animal species have been identified, and the waters surrounding the archipelago are relatively unexplored.

GEOLOGY The Socotran Archipelago is of continental origin, formed as part of the same process of continental drift that shaped the Arabian Peninsula. The archipelago comprises four islands: the main island of Socotra and three smaller islands, known as the 'brothers' – 'Abd al-Kuri, Samhah, and Darsah. The main island of Socotra, covering an area of 3,626km², consists of coastal plains, inland limestone plateaux, and the Haghier Mountains in the northwest, which reach a height of 1,525m. The climate is arid, with seasonal monsoons occurring from March to May.

FLORA The plant life on Socotra is surprisingly diverse. There are over 900 known plant species on the island, a full 30% of which are endemic. Perhaps the most noteworthy of these is the dragon's blood tree (*Dracaena cinnabari*). The tree is so named for the bright red colour of its resin. The resin was a major export from the island and a part of the spice trade of the region. It was used as a varnish and dye, as an incense, and body oil. 'Dragon's blood' was also in demand for numerous medicinal purposes, including as a coagulant, a fever reducer, and to treat ulcers, diarrhoea, dysentery, and skin conditions. It is still used today on the island for its medicinal purposes. Elsewhere, it is still used for varnishes, oils, and incense. The dragon's blood tree, which is identifiable by its unique umbrella shape, is found primarily in the mountain highlands of the island; these unique trees stand between 3m and 10m in height. Also dwelling in the highlands are numerous shrubs, most prominently *Rhus thyrsiflora*, *Cephalocroton soqotrans*, and *Allophylus rhoidiphyllus*. Socotran aloes (*Aloe perryl*) also occur in the higher altitudes.

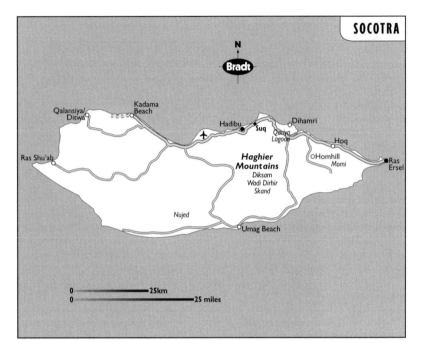

At the foothills of the mountains of Socotra there is a rich shrub land. One of the most distinct plants in this area is the Socotran desert rose (*Adenium obesum ssp sokotranum*). This unique plant is also known as the 'bottle tree' for its thick bottle-shaped trunk. Other succulents in the area include the cucumber tree (*Dendrosicyos socotrana*) as well as both frankincense and myrrh. *Jatropha unicostata*, which occurs on the lower slopes of the mountains, is prized for its medicinal uses. Its sap is used as an antiseptic, an emetic, and to treat wounds and skin irritation.

On the plains and lowlands of the island the shrub *Croton socotranus* is the predominant flora. Also prevalent is the tree-euphorbia (*Euphorbia arbuscula*), which rises above the shorter shrubs.

Other plants of note are the Socotran begonia (*Begonia Socotrana*) and the *Punica protopunica*, a relative of the pomegranate, and the Persian violet (*Exacum affine*).

FAUNA

Birds Birdlife on Socotra is as rich as on mainland Yemen. Over 140 species can be found on the island with at least six known endemics. These are the Socotra sparrow (*Passer insularis*), Socotra sunbird (*Nectarine balfouri*), Socotra warbler (*Incana incana*), the black Socotra starling with its yellow underwing (*Onychognathus frater*), Socotra cisticola (*Cisticola haesitata*), and Socotra bunting (*Emberiza socotrana*) with its distinct black-and-white head stripes. Local raptors include the Lanner falcon (*Falco biarmicus*), Socotra buzzard (*Buteo buteo subspecies*), and the African scops owl (*Otus senegalensis*). Ever present is the Egyptian vulture (*Neophron percnopterus*).

The island is an important breeding ground for many visiting birds. Among them is the masked booby (*Sula dactylatra*). This seabird is the largest booby with wingspans of up to 152cm. They can be distinguished by their black wingtips and characteristic mask. The brown booby (*Sula leucogaster*) also comes to Socotra for nesting. In contrast to the masked booby, the brown booby has rich brown plumage with a white underside. Other regulars on Socotra's shores include the bridled tern (*Sterna anaethetus*), Persian shearwater (*Puffinus persicus*), and red-billed tropicbird (*Phaeton aethereus*). Visitors are quite likely to catch sight of the Socotra cormorant (*Phalacrocorz nigrogularis*); these large birds are almost all black with slight white markings on the wings and eyes, and can achieve wingspans of up to 300cm. They often congregate in flocks ranging into the thousands or even tens of thousands. Great numbers of Jouanin's petrels (*Bulweria fallax*), which only come to land in order to breed, can also be found on Socotra.

Mammals Interestingly enough, for all its biodiversity, Socotra is almost devoid of mammals. There are several species of bats, and rats and mice have been introduced by humans. Predators include the small Indian civet (*Viverricula indica*), and a breed of feral cat. Common domestic mammals on the island include cattle, goats, sheep, and camels.

Reptiles, turtles, and arthropods Reptile life on Socotra is extremely endemic. Of the 22 known species of reptile, 19 are unique to the islands. These include some 16 species of gecko, and a single species of chameleon (*Chamaeleo monachus*). Of the snakes on the islands, most are small and unobtrusive, such as the several species of blind snakes. These tiny snakes often dwell in termite nests. There are no known land turtles on the island, but green turtles (*Chelonia mydas*) are thought to nest on the coast. There are at least two types of freshwater crab: *Potamon socotrensis*, and *Socotra pseudocardisoma*, as well as a large land crab (*Cardisoma carnifex*). The last can be found near mangroves and palms where they dig their burrows. Socotra has its share of arachnids, including several species of scorpion. Much of its insect life remains unclassified. One recurring characteristic among the known species is reduced wing size, a common trait among island species, developed in order to keep the insects from being blown away from land by heavy winds.

HISTORY

According to the legend of the island, Aristotle advised Alexander the Great to send a colony of Greeks from the philosopher's home town to Socotra in the 4th century BC. The goal of the expedition was to take advantage of the abundance of aloe and other plants that grew freely on the island. After all, the Indians who occupied the island before the Greeks had named it *Dvipa Sukhadara* – Sanskrit for 'the Island of Bliss'. When the Greeks landed on Socotra, they unseated the Indian colony and started their own reign of the island. The island's newest inhabitants adapted the old Sanskrit name to the Greek language as 'Dioscorida'. From this Sanskrit appellation as well, the island's modern name 'Socotra' was derived.

There are several other theories accounting for the origin of Socotra's name. One commonly put forward hypothesis is that the name reflected the business of the island – in addition to frankincense the island was known for exporting the sap of the dragon's blood tree. According to the Arabian geographer Yaqut al-Hamawi, this tree was known locally as *al-Qatir*; thus, Souk al-Qatir ('the Dragon's Blood Tree Market') is feasible. Likewise, the *Periplus of the Erythraean Sea* noted that the islanders collected the substance by gathering the drops that fell from the trees – Souk al-Qutra ('the Market of the Drop') is also possible.

The Greeks formed a colony on Socotra, and they may have influenced the indigenous and Indian populations on the island with their history of democracy. By the 1st century BC, Socotra had developed a reputation as a shining utopia. At

12

that time, Diodorus of Sicily described Socotra as a thriving democracy and religious society whose warlike people elected its presidents annually and rode about the island on chariots. Perhaps this is what Aristotle had in mind when picking out the families to form a colony on the island. In Books VII and VIII of his *Politics*, Aristotle discusses the conditions of 'the ideal or perfect state'. In Aristotle's perfect state, in which he allows himself 'to presuppose many purely imaginary conditions', he envisions a type of electorate – with a population not too large, land connected to the sea, and populated by a class of warriors. Perhaps the island of Socotra provided the perfect arena for experimentation in democracy.

In any event Diodorus provides an interesting description of the island that is a bit absurd at times. His account must be treated cautiously – he had never visited the island and he was copying largely from a previous geographer who had not visited it either. That being said, he describes Socotra (using its Egyptian name of 'Panchaea') as an island on which is built a massive temple dedicated to Saturn containing large statues of the gods, and he notes that Abd al-Kuri was a holy island in which the inhabitants refused to bury their dead. More common to today's understanding of the island, he notes that Socotra is rich in frankincense and myrrh, filled with an abundance and great variety of wildlife – although his account includes a large number of elephants.

Elephants were not the only unlikely creature claimed to make their home on Socotra. The *Periplus of the Erythraean Sea* notes the presence of crocodiles, large lizards and a white tortoise. More fancifully, the stories of Sindbad note the presence of the roc, a large mythological bird often described as being large enough to carry off an elephant. (Perhaps that's where all of Diodorus's animals went.) For the Phoenicians, Socotra was home to the legendary phoenix. Every 500 years, the sacred bird would burn upon a funeral pyre of incense and dragon's blood tree twigs. A young worm would arise from the ashes that would eventually become the new phoenix; he would gather the ashes of his father and carry them to Heliopolis in Egypt before returning to the island.

In the mid 1st century AD, the Apostle Thomas was shipwrecked on Socotra while *en route* to India. Building the island's first church from the wreckage, he converted the island's inhabitants to Christianity. The legacy of the apostle and of those who followed shortly thereafter him would be a long one – for the next 1,500 years writers would note the strong presence of Christianity on the island. By the 4th century the Church on Socotra had grown so strongly that it was able to send missionaries to mainland Yemen. Emperor Constantine II is said to have sent Bishop Theophilus Indus to the Himyarite capital of Dhafar, where the bishop founded a church and helped to propagate Christianity as the official state religion for a brief period of time.

One such account that referenced the continued Christian presence on the island was that of Cosmas Indicopleustes, who set out in the mid 6th century on a journey to prove that the world was indeed flat. During his voyages to refute the pre-Christian geographers, Cosmas sailed past the island of Socotra. In his account he noted that the island's Christians were under the authority of the Assyrian Church of the East; Cosmas's claim was confirmed by Marco Polo in his own account of the island some 700 years later.

The Assyrian Church of the East, often referred to as the Nestorian Church, split from the Roman Catholic Church in the 5th century when Nestorius, then Bishop of Constantinople, refused to address Mary as the 'Mother of God'. According to the Church's theology, Jesus's divinity and humanity were two separate entities within the unified Christ, and that God had nothing to do with the latter, and Mary nothing to do with the former. Accordingly, Nestorius would only grant Mary the title 'Mother of Christ'. The Assyrian Church is reputed to have been founded by the Apostle Thomas – which either helps to confirm his presence on the island or explain how the myth of his visit began.

In addition to Christians Socotra became famous as a haven for pirates between the 10th and 15th centuries. There is evidence to suggest that the island may have had a female ruler in the early 15th century. Female rulers are surprisingly prevalent in Yemen's history – the Queen of Sheba had ruled the Sabaean Kingdom, and Queen Arwa ruled much of Yemen in the 11th century – so the idea that Socotra also had a female ruler is plausible.

In 1507, Socotra was occupied briefly by the Portuguese. In a bloody attack, the Portuguese were able to overcome a fortress occupied by Mahri forces near the town of Souk. Four years later, the Mahri sultans sent forces to reclaim the island, and by 1511 the Portuguese had withdrawn, but not before constructing a church at the fortress they had conquered. The Mahris destroyed both the church and the fort.

The Portuguese maintained contact with the island off and on over the next century. Vitaly Naumkin notes in his book on Socotra that some of the Socotran mountain tribes had songs about how their ancestors were expelled to Socotra because of their sins. He suggests that the Portuguese may have used Socotra as an island of exile – the idea that the native Socotrans descended from the Portuguese has been widely circulated.

By the late 16th century the Christian elements of Socotra had rapidly deteriorated. There were no longer any priests on the island, and the islanders who did practice religion combined old rituals that they could no longer understand with aspects of astral worship. As the Mahri sultans regained control of Socotra, the islanders converted to Islam. Hardly any evidence of Christianity's presence on the island remains today.

In 1835, the British occupied Socotra after the ruling Mahri Sultan refused to sell the land to the Empire. The British intended to use the island as a coaling station but scrapped the idea after they founded the colony at Aden in 1838. Socotra reverted to Mahri control. In 1886, the Mahra Sultanate of Qishn and Socotra became the first sultanate in the area to sign a formal treaty with Britain and become a British protectorate. By the mid 20th century the Mahri sultans were living on Socotra, and they declined to join the Federation of South Arabia in the 1960s. In 1967, Socotra became a part of South Yemen.

LANGUAGE

In addition to Arabic, villagers on the island speak the unwritten Modern South Arabian language of Socotri. For more information and phrases, see *Appendix 1*, page 236.

GETTING THERE AND AWAY

There are weekly flights from Sana'a and Mukalla to Socotra and back on Mondays and Fridays. Monday flights to and from Sana'a require a stopover in Mukalla. The return airfare on Air Yemenia will cost about US$200, but it is possible to get great deals through **Yemenia Holidays** (✆ *01 211699;* e *holidays@yemenia.com; www.yemenia.com/new2/holydays/yemen.htm*), the travel agency branch of the airline. Return airfare, a three-night hotel stay and half board will cost under US$200 – an amazing bargain! Stop in at the Sana'a office on Zubayri Street or visit the website for more information.

There are currently no reliable means of transportation by boat to the island; tourist sailing trips to the island are currently at the developmental stage.

GETTING AROUND

The most common way to cover the long distances between points of interest on the island is by hiring a 4x4 and driver (US$40/day). For those with more time on their hands and interested in more eco-friendly means of travelling the country, camel tours are possible.

Another option is to bike the island; you will have to bring your own bike and equipment, though. Jan Leenknegt and Candida do Amaral made the trip around the island, and while disagreeing with noted cyclist Heinz Stücke that the trip was 'pure bliss', they noted that it was a very rewarding experience. A couple of particularly good treks to make are: the road between Hadibu and Qalansiya, the area around the Diksam region, and across the Nujed plain. Be sure you are completely self-sufficient, with plenty of bottled water, as water can be difficult to come by in some areas of the island.

If you are interested in seeing more endemic wildlife than Socotra has to offer, you can charter a boat (US$4,000/week) to take you to the even more secluded islands of the archipelago. A trip to the large island of Abd al-Kuri takes about six hours. Again, be sure you are completely self–sufficient, with food, water, and sleeping equipment.

HADIBU

The village of Hadibu is the only town on the island with hotels, and it is located close to the airport. It will most likely serve as your base for seeing the entire island. The age of the town is not known, although some scholars have identified it with the dazzling capital known as Panara, described by Diodorus of Sicily in the 1st century BC.

WHERE TO STAY

Summerland Hotel (13 rooms) ✆ 660350; 𝆑 660370; e summerland@yemen.net.ye. The most popular guesthouse on Socotra. Rooms are fine, although sparse, & the shared bathrooms have hot water. The Ritz Restaurant at the back of the hotel offers a wide selection of meals (& is the only place on the island to find freshly brewed coffee). The hotel's main attraction is its ability to arrange a variety of outings & services (fishing trips: US$50; camel tours: 6,000YR/day; diving guides: US$50/day; snorkel & fins: US$5; complete diving equipment: US$65/1 day, US$75/2 days). The management allows its guests to use the reception computer for internet access (10YR/min). $$$. HB.
Funduq Hafuf Tourism Hotel (15 rooms) ✆/𝆑 660469. Decent hotel located on the main road

of Hadibu. Six of the rooms come with private bathrooms.$$
Taj Socotra Hotel (21 rooms) ✆ 660627; 𝆑 660629. Pleasant rooms, some with couch & balcony. There are private Western bathrooms with no hot water. The attached Taj Socotra Restaurant serves typical chicken, fish, & vegetable dishes. The management can help you arrange tours of the island. $$
Al-Gazeera Hotel (6 rooms) ✆ 660447. The manager of this small hotel says that he is interested in 'friendship, not money', so expect a lot of unprompted visits while you are resting here. Most rooms come with shared Western bathrooms; 1 trpl room (#115) comes with a private bathroom. No hot water. $

✖ **WHERE TO EAT** There are three main restaurants in Hadibu – the **Ritz** at the Summerland Hotel, the **Taj Socotra Restaurant** (an outdoor restaurant at the hotel of the same name), and a small local restaurant that serves up decent fare on the nearest northern road parallel to the main street.

SHOPPING Located on the main street of Hadibu is the **Women's Centre**, a small not-for-profit store that sells handicrafts made by local women and then passes the earnings on to them.

ALBUQUERQUE'S FORT AND CHURCH Located just outside Hadibu are the remains of the Old Portuguese Fort and Church. In the early 16th century the Portuguese, under the command of Captain Alfonso de Albuquerque, captured the island of Socotra after conquering a Mahri fort located outside the Old City of **Souk**. During the four-year Portuguese occupation, the Europeans built a church at the fort to help foster the Christianity that was still being practised on the island. After they were expelled by Mahri forces, the Mahris destroyed both the fort and the church – either because the fortifications had previously failed them or because the previous foreign-occupied battlements were viewed as bad luck. The smallest remnants of church ruins remain here in the village of Souk near the fort. The ruins of Albuquerque's Fort sits at the top of the cliff (a 1½hr hike) – little remains but a few stones. There are some good coral reefs off the village.

EAST OF HADIBU

Dihamri Marine Protected Area (*entrance fee: 500YR; camping fee: 1,000YR*) Located about 30km to the east of Hadibu is one of the protected areas of the island. The Dihamri Marine Camp is located at a particularly gorgeous section of coral reef that makes for some of the best diving on the island. Even with just a pair of goggles and a snorkel, an amazing underwater world reveals itself.

There is a designated access point for entering the water to minimize damage to the corals. There have been plans for some time to open a diving centre in Dihamri, but they have not materialised yet.

The camp restaurant (**$$$**) serves fish and rice at lunchtime.

Qariya Lagoon The Qariya Lagoon is part of the **Khor Qaryah Nature Preserve**, a small area of the island that plays host to a variety of wildlife and which is located near Dihamri. The area around the lagoon is a good spot for birdwatching, and there are several small supply stores at the nearby town.

Homhill (*entrance fee: 500YR/person; camping fee: 1,000YR*) Homhill is the main region in Socotra for viewing the dragon's blood trees. A fancy sign welcomes you to the protected park, and while there are several clearly designated camping areas, you are allowed to camp in only one of them. If you are interested in staying the night here, the workers at the main tent will instruct you where you can stay. Meals at the camp are offered at breakfast, lunch and dinner. Although there is an extensive menu posted, most of the items are not available (**$$$**). There will probably be some young local boys selling frankincense and dragon's blood resin at the tent.

A trek along the mountain and through the frankincense trees is well worth it. There are some splendid views to the north at the edge of the cliff. A small brook of water gathers into a pool here, that later empties into the sea. Unlike other pools on the island, this one is not used for drinking water, and you can jump in for a quick swim if you so desire. Any trekking in the mountains or through the forests requires hiring a mandatory mountain guide (1,000YR). For 2,000YR, the guide can help you walk the long trek (4hrs) to the coast. A percentage of the tour guide and entrance fees go toward helping the locals here.

Hoq Caves Located in between the areas of Homhill and Ras Ersel, the Hoq Caves present another interesting aspect of Socotra Island. Recent archaeological discoveries have indicated that the cave served as an important place for merchants as early as the 2nd century AD. The reason for the importance remains unknown, but

The resin of the dragon's blood tree has long been known to Europe – it was written as a product of Socotra in the *Periplus of the Erythraean Sea* in the 1st century AD. Today the resin is mainly used as a dye, and at the women's centre in Hadibu you can buy incense burners that have been painted with the bright-red dye.

Some locals on the island still value the resin for its medicinal properties. According to some of the villagers, the extract of the trees is used still to cure disease generally and is taken by women after childbirth to limit blood loss. When the resin was exported to Europe over several centuries, it was used as a stain for violins and, according to some reports, by European women to win back lost loves. A C Wooton notes in his 1910 work *Chronicles of Pharmacy* that: 'maidens whose swains are unfaithful or neglectful procure a piece [of dragon's blood], wrap it in paper, and throw it on the fire, saying, "may he no pleasure or profit see, till he come back again to me."'

exploration of the cave has revealed that travellers and merchants of various spots of the world visited the region and the cave in particular. In 2001, archaeologists discovered a wooden tablet of a Syrian merchant dating to the 3rd century AD. There are multiple drawings in the cave in a variety of archaic languages.

To reach the cave, you will need to hire an additional local guide (3,000YR). The hiring of the guide is mandatory – part of the procedures that have been put in place to help protect the cave system. Hoq was mapped by a group of Belgian cavers early in the 2000s, and they have since left behind a series of roped paths through which visitors can walk with minimal disturbance to the cave.

Along the path there is a freshwater pool used by locals as a drinking source. You should not bathe or swim in the water, although you are free to drink from it. Additionally, refrain from touching the stalagmites or stalactites, as the oil from your skin will damage the formation process. Needless to say, the cave is immersed in complete darkness, so you need to bring your own lighting equipment.

The hike up the mountain to the cave entrance takes about two hours.

Ras Ersel The small fishing village of Ras Ersel is located on the eastern tip of the island. The village does quite a bit of shark fishing, as can be inferred from the countless carcasses that litter the area around the docks. The area is said to be good for diving, and that there is a number of small shipwrecks off the coast worth exploring.

There is a quite astonishing section of the island right before the village coming from Hadibu. A small spring exiting from a mountain makes a journey of about 200m or so before emptying into the sea, and lush green grass and vegetation springs forth on either side. Directly abutting this are large, white sand dunes. The grass and sand border each other only a few metres from the stream right along the coast. The contrast is lovely.

SOUTH OF HADIBU
Haghir Mountains The Haghir Mountains are located in the centre of Socotra, and they are praised by nearly every local Socotran as being his personal favourite place on the island. In terms of nature and scenery, the area is unbelievable, particularly the dragon's blood tree forests located on **Fermhin Mountain** and the **Skand Preserve**.

To have an excellent day of hiking, start early from the **Diksam Plateau** (an excellent area for viewing Socotran endemic birds) and walk down the slope to the base of **Wadi Dirhur**. The river that runs through the wadi forms natural swimming pools with small waterfalls, and it is permissible to swim in them. Continue up the opposite mountain toward Fermhin and the Skand Preserve.

Umag Beach Located on the southern coast of Socotra, Umag Beach is one of the most beautiful and relaxing beaches on the island. The sand is perfect and there is a little pavilion that has been built to provide shade.

If you are travelling from the southern **Nujed** region toward **Momi** and Homhill, you should stop by one of the local villages along the way and purchase some fresh fruit. Papaya (200YR) and watermelon (150YR) will be pulled straight from the source. The fruit makes a great snack and you get to help the villagers by buying directly from them. In addition to fruit, there are also villagers in the region hawking incense and handmade carpets.

WEST OF HADIBU
Qalansiya & the Ditwa Protected Area (*camping fee: 500YR*) On the northwest tip of Socotra, at the end of the road from Hadibu lies the small village of Qalansiya and the nearby area of Ditwa, which contains a shallow lagoon surrounded by mountains. The beach at Ditwa is very peaceful, although the water past the lagoon is rather rough and makes swimming difficult. The local village has no hotels or restaurants, but has some stores where you can stock up on water, snacks, and juice.

Ras Shu'ab The area of Ras Shu'ab is well known as one of the best diving spots on Socotra. An old shipwreck off the coast provides perfect cover for a vast variety of fish. You can hire a small fishing boat at Qalansiya to make the two-hour trip to Shu'ab for 8,000YR. Unfortunately, the fierce currents at the ends of the island make it hard for the fishermen to reach the area in anything but the calmest conditions. (It's not without good reason that there's a large shipwreck at Ras Shu'ab!)

Kadama Beach Lying along the road between Qalansiya and Hadibu, Kadama Beach is a known nesting site of sea turtles.

Monitor lizard

YEMENI DREAMS

Y E M E N 'S

ADVENTURE

C O M P A N Y

Sana'a - Khartoum St.
P.O.Box: 25303 SANA'A-YEMEN
Tel.: (+967) 1 514 028
        (+967) 1 514 029
Fax: (+967) 1 514 027
Mobile: (+967) 733 210 600
        (+967) 777 964 663
info@yemeni-dreams.com
www.yemeni-dreams.com
صنعاء – شارع الخرطوم (مجاهد سابقا)

Appendix I

LANGUAGE

ARABIC Arabic is a very elegant language, but it is often intimidating to the novice. The Arabic script, full of strange-sounding letters that change shape depending on their location in a word, is read from right to left. In truth, it is a very difficult language to master, but with a little work and determination, you should not find much difficulty in getting a handle on speaking or reading Arabic.

Arabic has a lot of regional variations. Each country in the region has its own take on the language, and there are often further differences within each country. It would not be surprising if a Moroccan, a Syrian and a Yemeni couldn't understand each other while all speaking their respective native tongues – a much more exaggerated version of the confusion that would ensue during a conversation between three individuals from York in the UK, Newfoundland in Canada and Pittsburgh in the US. To overcome this problem, Arabic speakers can resort to Modern Standard Arabic ('MSA'), the standard literary dialect understood by all Arabic speakers. As a rough approximation, think of our three friends from York, Newfoundland, and Pittsburgh who can't understand one another but who can all listen and understand the same CNN broadcast while sitting in the lobby of their Yemeni hotel.

Yemenis claim that their dialect is closest to the original Arabic language. Of course, you can undoubtedly find an Arabic speaker of any dialect who will claim the same for his own regional variant. Yemenis repeat the claim more frequently than others though, and there does seem to be some truth to the country's assertion of linguistic proximity.

In any event, the Yemeni locals will appreciate any attempt you make at speaking Arabic, and by throwing in a few Yemeni words or phrases, you'll quickly make a lot of new friends. This chapter presents an introduction to basic communication with Yemenis by presenting a mix of MSA and Yemeni Arabic. It includes a description of the Arabic script and pronunciation as well as a list of basic words and phrases. Naturally, if you are serious about learning the language you will have to look beyond these introductory materials.

Script and pronunciation The Arabic script contains 28 basic letters, including nine that represent sounds not found in the English language. The text is read from right to left, and the shape of a letter varies according to whether it appears by itself or in the beginning, middle or end of a word. Thus, the word *habbak* ('your love') is written as حبك, while reversing the letters yields KabH ('curb'), written as كبح. The notion of having to learn four different varieties of each letter seems daunting, but with a little practice you'll get the hang of it. Plus, the good news is that some of the letters only have two shapes!

Alone	Final	Middle	Initial	Name	Transliteration	Pronunciation
ا	ـا			alif	ā	as in 'always'
ب	ـب	ـبـ	بـ	ba	b	as in 'bat'
ت	ـت	ـتـ	تـ	ta	t	as in 'ton'
ث	ـث	ـثـ	ثـ	tha	th	as in '**th**ink'

AI

				Name	Translit.	Pronunciation
ج	ج	ـج	جـ	jeem	j	as in 'jam'
ح	ح	ـح	حـ	Ha	H	emphatic 'h' sound
خ	خ	ـخ	خـ	kha	kh	as in the Scottish 'loch'
د	ـد			daal	d	as in 'dad'
ذ	ـذ			dhaal	dh	as in 'the'
ر	ـر			raa	r	as in 'red'
ز	ـز			zay	z	as in 'zoo'
س	ـس	ـسـ	سـ	seen	s	as in 'sam'
ش	ـش	ـشـ	شـ	sheen	sh	as in 'shoe'
ص	ـص	ـصـ	صـ	Saad	S	emphatic 's'
ض	ـض	ـضـ	ضـ	Daad	D	emphatic 'd'
ط	ـط	ـطـ	طـ	Taa	T	emphatic 't'
ظ	ـظ	ـظـ	ظـ	Dhaa	DH	emphatic 'dh' or 'z'
ع	ـع	ـعـ	عـ	'ayn		strangled 'a' (see Pronunciation notes, below)
غ	ـغ	ـغـ	غـ	ghayn	gh	dry, gargled 'g' (see Pronunciation notes, below)
ف	ـف	ـفـ	فـ	faa	f	as in 'fat'
ق	ـق	ـقـ	قـ	qaaf	q	as in 'goat'
ك	ـك	ـكـ	كـ	kaaf	k	as in 'king'
ل	ـل	ـلـ	لـ	lam	l	as in 'long'
م	ـم	ـمـ	مـ	meem	m	as in 'man'
ن	ـن	ـنـ	نـ	noon	n	as in 'not'
ه	ـه	ـهـ	هـ	ha	h	as in 'home'
و	ـو			waw	w/ō/ū	as in 'wet' or as a vowel in 'boat' or 'food'
ي	ـي	ـيـ	يـ	ya	y/ī/ay	as in 'yet' or as a vowel in 'bean' or 'aim'

Pronunciation notes Most Arabic speakers hold that the letter Daad (ض) is the hardest sound for non-native speakers to reproduce. The sound was believed to be so unique to Arabic that the language is referred to as 'the language of Daad', and Muhammad is attributed as to having said that he was 'the most eloquent of those that utter the letter Daad'. The letter may have had a slightly different sound previously though. An over-pronounced, emphatic 'd' sound should approximate the letter closely enough. The related letter of Taa (ط) is just as unique to Arabic as Daad, but it doesn't share top billing with the latter because it is the rarest letter in the language. Officially, the sound is made by producing an emphatic 'dh', and this is maintained in some parts of the country. Many areas of Yemen, however, take the easier Middle Eastern approach of pronouncing the letter as an emphatic 'z'.

The two letters of 'ayn (ع) and ghayn (غ) are related, but each has a distinct sound unfamiliar to the English language. The letter 'ayn is a difficult sound for Arabic neonates to speak or hear. Though technically a consonant, the sound resembles a short 'a' spoken by one being strangled. Another technique for approximating the sound is to make a noise using the back muscle in your throat used when gagging or vomiting. The letter ghayn is a bit easier to master, although it is often mischaracterised as a Parisian 'r'. You can make the sound perfectly by gargling without water.

The letter qaaf (ق) is one of the hallmarks of Arabic, in part due to its place in the word 'Koran' and in part due to the baffling reaction it presents in transliteration. (How can there be a 'q' without a 'u'?) One author noted that writing using the 'q' sans 'u' in transliterations made Arabic to reek of savagery; moreover, English speakers simply didn't know how to pronounce it. In classical Arabic, the qaaf was pronounced like a 'k' sound back in the throat, similar to the sound you would make when imitating a crow. Making the sound takes some effort, and like most Arabs, Yemenis substitute easier sounds for the troublesome letter. In most of the country, the letter is pronounced with a 'g' sound, as in '**g**oat'. In Ta'iz, the letter is pronounced with 'gh' sound, similar to the letter ghayn. A local story relates that during the Sana'ani–Ta'izi War, the Imam of Sana'a would point to a cow (*baqqarah*) and ask those entering the city to tell him what it was. The Sana'anis would say *baggarah* and were admitted entrance, while those unfortunate Ta'izis who gave themselves up by saying *bagharah* were sent to the gallows. Luckily, no shibboleth is required nowadays to enter through the Bab al-Yemen. But just in case, remember the Sana'ani pronunciation of the word 'cow' is with a 'g' sound.

Words

Numbers Although Arabic text is read from right to left, numbers are read from left to right. Thus, if the price of your *shisha* is listed as '255', you should pay 255YR, and not 552YR, although the waiter no doubt would appreciate your 300YR tip.

0	*Sifr*	.	30	*thalathīn*	٣٠	
1	*wāHid*	١	40	*arba'īn*	٤٠	
2	*ithnayn*	٢	50	*khamsīn*	٥٠	
3	*thalatha*	٣	60	*sitīn*	٦٠	
4	*arba'a*	٤	70	*sab'aīn*	٧٠	
5	*khamsa*	٥	80	*thamanyīn*	٨٠	
6	*sitta*	٦	90	*tis'īn*	٩٠	
7	*sab'a*	٧	100	*mīa*	١٠٠	
8	*thamānya*	٨	101	*wāHad wa mīa*	١٠١	
9	*tis'a*	٩	200	*mīatayn*	٢٠٠	
10	*'ashara*	١٠	300	*thalātha mīa*	٣٠٠	
11	*āHad'asher*	١١	400	*arba'a mīa*	٤٠٠	
12	*ithn'asher*	١٢	500	*khamsa mīa*	٥٠٠	
13	*thalath'asher*	١٣	1,000	*ālf*	١٠٠٠	
20	*'ashrīn*	٢٠	2,000	*ālfayn*	٢٠٠٠	
21	*wāHad 'ashrīn*	٢١	10,000	*'ashara ālf*	١٠٠٠٠	

Days

Sunday	*yōm al-āHad* (the first day)	يوم الأحد
Monday	*yōm al-ithnayn* (the second day)	يوم الاثنين
Tuesday	*yōm ath-thalātha* (the third day)	يوم الثلاثة
Wednesday	*yōm al-arba'a* (the fourth day)	يوم الأربعاء
Thursday	*yōm al-khamīs* (the fifth day)	يوم الخميس
Friday	*yōm al-jum'a* (day of the mosque)	يوم الجمعة
Saturday	*yōm as-sebt* (day of the Sabbath)	يوم السبت
Today	*al-yōm*	اليوم
Tomorrow	*būkra*	بوكرة
Yesterday	*ams*	أمس

Months

January	*shaher wāHid*		July	*shaher sab'a*
February	*shaher ithnayn*		August	*shaher thamānya*
March	*shaher thalātha*		September	*shaher tis'a*
April	*shaher arba'a*		October	*shaher 'ashara*
May	*shaher khamsa*		November	*shaher āHad'ashar*
June	*shaher sitta*		December	*shaher ithn'asher*

Basics
Greetings

Hello	*salām 'alaykum* (literally 'peace be upon you')
Hello (response)	*wa 'alaykum as-salām* (lit 'and upon you, peace')
Hello (long response)	*salām 'alaykum wa rahmat allah*
	(lit 'peace and God's blessings upon you')
Goodbye	*ma'a salāma*
Good morning	*sabāH al-khayr*
	(response) *sabāH an-nūr*
Good afternoon/evening	*masā al-khayr*
	(response) *masā an-nūr*
Good night	*tisbaH 'ala khayr*
	(response) *tisbaH 'ala nūr*
Greetings!	*Haiyak allāh* (lit 'may God maintain your life')
	(response) *allāh yaHayyak* (same meaning)
Greetings!	*Hai allāh min ja*
	(lit 'may God maintain the life of the one who comes')
	(response) *allāh yaHayyak* (same meaning)

Responses

Yes	*aiwa*		Excuse me	*'afwān*
No	*lā*		Thank you	*shukrān*
Possibly	*mumkin*		You're welcome	*'afwān*
As you like	*mithil ma tāshti*		God willing	*in sha` allāh*
Please	*lō samāHt*		Never mind	*ma'alesh*
I'm sorry	*ānā muta'assif*		After you	*tafaDHal*

Meeting people

Do you speak English?	*tatakallam bil-inglīzi?*
I don't speak Arabic very well	*la atakallam bil-'arabi gōwī*
I don't understand	*ana mafHimsh*
How are you?	(m) *kayf Hālak?*
	(f) *kayf Hālish?*
I am fine	*ana tammam*
Thanks be to God	*al-Hamdu lillāh*
What is your name?	(m) *aysh ismak?*
	(f) *aysh ismish?*
My name is…	*ismī…*
Where are you from?	(m) *min wayn ent?*
	(f) *min wayn entī?*
I am from…	*ana min…*
What is your nationality?	(m/f) *aysh jinsīyatak/jinsīyatish?*
I am…	*ana…*
British (m/f)	*britāni/britānīya*
Irish (m/f)	*irlāndi/irlāndīya*
Scottish (m/f)	*scotlāndi/scotlāndīya*
American (m/f)	*amrīki/amrīkīya*
Australian (m/f)	*astrāli/astrālīya*
I am…	*ana…*
Muslim (m/f)	*muslim/muslima*
Christian (m/f)	*masīHi/masīHīya*
Jewish	(m/f) *yaHōdi/yaHōdīya*

Buddhist	(m/f) *buddhī/buddhīya*
Hindu	(m/f) *hindī/hindīya*
Can I do anything else for you?	*ayya khidimāt?*

Getting around

How do I get to the…?	*Wayn at-tarīq ila…?*
airport	*al-matār*
museum	*al-matHaf*
post office	*maktab al-barīd*
bank	*al-bank*
hospital	*al-mustashfa*
restaurant	*al-mata'am*
hotel	*al-funduq*
shared taxi stand	*al-furzāt*

right	*yamīn*	let's go	*yalla*
left	*yisār*	quickly	*fīsa'*
straight ahead	*'ala tūl*	slowly	*dalā dalā*
stop here	*'ala jamb*		

Food and drink

breakfast	*faTūr*	strawberry	*farawla*
lunch	*ghadā`*	pineapple	*ananās*
dinner	*'ashā`*	orange	*bortugāl*
restaurant	*maTa'am*	vegetables	*khudrā`*
bread	*khubs*	beans	*fasūlia*
cheese	*jubben*	potato	*biTāTa*
eggs	*bayD*	chicken	*dijāj*
honey	*'aSl*	meat (red)	*laHm*
yoghurt	*zabādi*	fish	*samak*
fruit	*fawākha*	rice	*rūz*
dates	*tammer*	water	*mā`*
banana	*mōz*	juice	*'aSīr*
apple	*tufa'*	coffee	*bunn*
mango	*manja*	tea	*shay*

| Thank you very much for the food | *karimtū salimtū* |

Accommodation

| I would like a room with | *lō samāht fia 'andak ghurfa* |
| a Western bathroom please | *fīha hamām aferānjī* |

Miscellaneous

Yemen is a beautiful country	*al-yaman bilād jamīl*
Yemen is great!	*al-yaman min Hāna!*
	(with your index finger, touch the side of your nose and flick across to the other side when saying '*Hāna*' – this literally means: 'Yemen is from here (the nose)', which is a great compliment.
That's none of your business!	*mush shughal abbuk!*
	(lit 'it's not your father's work')

Sneezing

(the sneezer initiates)

1	Thanks be to God!	*al-Hamdu li-llāh*
	(God bless you)	*yarHamak allāh*
2	God bless us and everyone	*yarHamina wa yarHamikum allāh*

SOCOTRI AND MAHRI The languages of **Mahri** and **Socotri** are known as **Modern South Arabian languages**. Mahri is spoken in the al-Mahra, the easternmost governorate of Yemen, as well as parts of western Oman and in communities of Mahra immigrants in Kuwait. Socotri is spoken on the island of Socotra. Other languages of Modern South Arabian include Jibbali, Harsusi, Bathari and Hobyot. These four languages are spoken in western Oman, and Bathari is also spoken in parts of eastern Yemen. All the languages of Modern South Arabian are unwritten.

Of the Modern South Arabian languages, Mahri and Socotri are the most widely spoken. That isn't saying much, seeing as the number of living speakers of all six languages is equivalent roughly to the population of Aberdeen or Baton Rouge. There are over 70,000 speakers of Mahri in Yemen, and about 50,000 speakers of Socotri on the island. While the languages are faring better than their Bathari neighbour (with roughly only 200 speakers), they are still in danger of extinction. This is especially true given the increasing communication advances and the corresponding rising need for Mahri and Socotri speakers to be fluent in Arabic as well.

There has been some research on the languages, and anyone who is seriously interested in learning either should turn to this. The Yemeni government has allowed researchers to study the languages, but it has not done much toward preserving them or doing any research of its own.

Pronunciation Naturally, because Mahri and Socotri are unwritten languages, there is no script to learn, however there have been attempts to transcribe the languages into an altered Latin or Arabic script. Here I will use a simplified Latin script that does not take into account all the complexities and nuances of the language but that should suffice in speaking some simple phrases to locals. (They will love it!)

A couple of notes should be made about some of the distinctive sounds of the language. The hardest sounds to make are the *ś* and the *ź*. The *ś* is pronounced like the Welsh 'll', done by attempting to pronounce the letters 'l' and 'h' simultaneously out of the side of your mouth. (For linguistic buffs, the letter is the voiceless lateral fricative: ɬ.) The *ź* sound is made by pronouncing 'dh' (as in 'the') and 'l' simultaneously out of the side of your mouth. (Again, for the linguistically inclined, the letter is the voiced lateral fricative: ɮ.) Acting as though you have a slight lisp can only aid your attempts.

The other sounds of note are the glottalised consonants d', k', s', and t' – a combination of the consonant and a glottal stop. A glottal stop is the sound produced when the vocal cords restrict the flow of air and then release, as in the cockney pronunciation of 'a bit of butter' ('a bi' of bu'er'). Thus the combination of the 'd' sound followed in quick succession by a glottal stop would produce the d` sound.

Transliteration

ś	voiceless lateral fricative, as in Welsh '**Ll**anelli' (see above)
ź	voiced lateral fricative (see above)
d`	d with a glottal stop (see above)
k`	k with a glottal stop (see above)
s`	s` with a glottal stop (see above)
t`	t` with a glottal stop (see above)
H	as in the Arabic ح
q	as in the Arabic ق
gh	dry gargling sound, as in the Arabic غ
'	as in the Arabic ع
a	as in '**bu**t'

ā	as in 'father'	
i	as in 'bit'	
ī	as in 'weed'	
e	as in 'let'	
o	as in 'not'	
ō	as in 'boat'	
u	as in 'but'	
ū	as is 'lute'	
ai	as in 'lied'	
ay	as in 'late'	
aw	as in 'bout'	

Words
Numbers

English	Socotri	Mahri
1	tōt	tawt
2	tera	thrū
3	silay	śażayt
4	orb'e	rebōt
5	haimī	khomū
6	yaht	yethīt
7	yehōb'e	yebayt
8	tamūnī	themenyīt
9	sa'h	sayt
10	ażur	aśerīt
20	ayśīre	aśerī

Days

English	Socotri	Mahri
Monday	al-itnayn	tenayn
Tuesday	at-tulūt	telūt
Wednesday	ar-rubō'	rubū
Thursday	al-khamīs	khomīs
Friday	al-jum'a	jemayt
Saturday	as-sabt	sabt
Sunday	al-aHad	Had
Today	Hīr	līmo
Tomorrow	qarī	gi'ima
Yesterday	amshān	leba`atten

Basics

English	Socotri	Mahri
Greetings!	laqedom 'akdīye!	Hay abbūk!
Good morning	mandiba 'āri	s`beHkum
(response)	libā'er 'akdīye	s`beHkum
Good night	neshi bā'er ladīye	Hellaykum
(response)	ula 'atshīqen dīye tinerho	Hellaykum
Goodbye	te'ātshak 'afīya	sehōlt
Nice to meet you	ya Hay fik	Hai usā`alla aś-śinkig
Thank you	yulayk allāh	mishkūr
You are welcome	smeHktek	'afwān
Excuse me/I'm sorry	saymeH to	samHi
Please	kad shafa'a hāk	qīb
Quickly	maHla	fīsa
Slowly	brīfe	khārkhō

English	Socotri	Mahri
Yes	*ahhū*	*yahō*
No	*la*	*la*
Maybe	*'aśe*	*wako`ina*

Meeting people

Do you speak English?	*chimōtel inglīzi?*	*tehōrij inglīzyet?*
I don't speak Socotri/Mahri	*al ayshmatāl sokātrī*	*la uhōrij mahrīyet*
I don't understand	*al aysh'īrob*	*la ūdak*
How are you?	*al ger'urk?*	*Hayt bi-khayr?*
I am fine	*al ger*	*bi-khayr*
Thanks be to God	*tayfu Hay 'āfīya*	*eHtemōd*
What is your name?	(m) *ful maksham?*	*Hemak mun?*
	(f) *ful miksham?*	*Hemik mun?*
My name is…	*man isham…*	*Hemmi…*
Where are you from?	*minu ayHen?*	*minhu k`habk?*
I am from…	*hōhun min…*	*k`habk min…*

Getting around

taxi	*taxi*	*taxi*
close	*shke*	*qarīb*
far	*shirHaq*	*rīHeq*
left	*śimhell*	*shōla*
right	*imhell*	*git*
straight ahead	*difa'ana*	*serōh mebūra*
Where is…?	*ah wa…?*	*…ghūa?*

Food and drink

food	*aqnīyo*	*qawt*
breakfast	*qas-him*	*fitār*
lunch	*feśo*	*feśīt*
dinner	*tadāma*	*iśīt*
chicken	*digāg*	*degōget*
sheep	*tīten*	*kabś*
goat	*ōz*	*arōt*
fish	*sōde*	*sayd*
yoghurt	*Halōāb*	*Hamś*
cheese	*gobna*	*ewfōk*
beans	*zer'e*	*āter*
vegetables	*khadra*	*khedra*
eggs	*qaHilhin*	*bīśayt*
bread	*es-hīroh*	*khabz*
camel	*ba'īrah*	*Hābū*
drink	*dōārah*	*tek*
water	*rīho*	*Hamū*
tea	*shāhi*	*shāhi*
coffee	*qahwah*	*kehwayt*
juice	*'asīr*	*'asīr*

Miscellaneous

May I take a picture?	*'aśe s`ōra?*	*wakō`ina s`ōt?*
Where is the market?	*ah wo suq?*	*suq ghūa?*
How much is this?	*kam temen dedha?*	*Kam qaimet dōma?*

Appendix 2

GLOSSARY

Abbasids   The ruling Islamic dynasty in Baghdad that appointed governors to and maintained control of Yemen from AD750–820.

Ayyubids   The Kurdish dynasty founded by Saladin that ruled much of Yemen from 1173–1228.

Bakil   The largest and second most powerful tribal confederation in Yemen.

Debub   A 'tank' or mini-van used as a shared taxi system for intra-city transport.

Diwan   Large sitting room used for formal occasions.

Fatimids   Members of an Isma'ili dynasty based in Egypt from the 10th–12th centuries, and which had influence over several ruling powers of Yemen.

Hadhramawt   A region of eastern Yemen; also the name of one of the ancient caravan kingdoms that existed from 1000BC–AD350, ruling from its capital of Shabwa.

Hamdanids   A family of local sultans who ruled from Sana'a in the 12th century.

Hashid   The most powerful tribal confederation in Yemen today.

Himyar   The final ancient kingdom of Yemen which existed from 110BC–AD525 and who ruled from the capital of Dhafar.

Ibadhis   Members of a moderate sect of the Kharajite branch of Islam (located primarily today in Oman) who revolted against the Umayyads in AD746.

Isma'ili   A minority Shi'a sect of Islam present in some of the mountainous regions of Yemen.

Koran   Holy book of Islam, believed to have been revealed to the Prophet Muhammad by the Angel Gabriel.

Madhij   The third-largest tribal confederation after Bakil and Hashid.

Mafraj   The top level of a house, used as a social room for chewing qat. Good views are a must.

Minaean   Seafaring kingdom of ancient Yemen that existed from 625BC–AD25.

Nabi   Prophet.

Ottoman   Turkish dynasty that occupied Yemen twice – once in the 16th century and again in the 19th.

Qamariya   A word used to refer either to the older translucent alabaster windows or the more modern stained-glass designs of tower houses.

Qat   A tree/shrub, the fresh leaves and shoots of which are chewed daily by Yemenis all across the country.

Qataban   Ancient kingdom that ruled parts of Yemen from 800BC–AD190.

Rasul   Prophet.

Rasulid   Successful dynasty that ruled Yemen from Ta'iz from 1229–1454.

Saba'   Ancient kingdom that ruled much of Yemen from its capital at Marib from early in the 1st millennium BC, when the famed Queen of Sheba is said to have made her visit to Solomon in the 3rd century AD.

Sayyid   Male descendant of the Prophet Muhammad.

Shafi'i	One of the four schools of Sunni jurisprudence prevalent in Yemen.
Souk	Market.
Zaydi	Technically a Shi'a sect, but called 'the fifth school of Sunni Islam' due to its dogmatic proximity to Sunni beliefs; prominent in the highlands of Yemen.

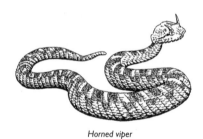

Horned viper

Appendix 3

FURTHER INFORMATION

BOOKS

Abdu, Rashid A *Journey of a Yemeni Boy* Dorrance Publishing Co, Inc, 2005.

Aithie, Charles and Patricia *Yemen: Jewel of Arabia* Stacey International, London, 2004.

Boxberger, Linda *On the Edge of Empire: Hadhramawt, Emigration, and the Indian Ocean, 1880s–1930s* State University of New York Press, Albany, 2002.

Breton, Jean-François (Albert LaFarge, trans) *Arabia Felix From the Time of the Queen of Sheba* University of Notre Dame Press, Notre Dame, 1999.

Burrows, Robert D *Historical Dictionary of Yemen* Scarecrow Press, Inc, London, 1995.

Caton, Steven C *Peaks of Yemen I Summon* University of California Press, London, 1990.

Caton, Steven C *Yemen Chronicle: An Anthropology of War and Mediation* Hill and Wang, New York, 2005.

Cheung, Catherine and DeVantier, Lyndon *Socotra: A Natural History of the Islands and their People* Odyssey, 2007.

Daum, Werner (ed) *Yemen: 3000 Years of Art and Civilisation in Arabia Felix* Pinguin-Verlag, Innsbruck, 1987.

Dresch, Paul *A History of Modern Yemen* Cambridge University Press, 2000.

Dresch, Paul *Tribes, Government and History in Yemen* Clarendon Press, Oxford, 1993.

Franck, Derek, Broad, Tom and Cheek, Linda *A Yemeni Passage* Azimuth Press, 1997.

Gunter, Ann C (ed) *Caravan Kingdoms: Yemen and the Ancient Incense Trade* Arthur M Sackler Gallery, Washington DC, 2005. The interactive website available at www.asia.si.edu/exhibitions/online/yemen.

Han, Carolyn *From the Land of Sheba: Yemeni Folk Tales* Interlink Publishing Group, Inc, Northampton, 2005.

Hansen, Eric *Motoring with Mohammed* Vintage Books, New York, 1991.

Ho, Engseng *The Graves of Tarim: Genealogy and Mobility across the Indian Ocean* University of California Press, 2006.

Ingrams, Leila *Yemen Engraved: Illustrations by Foreign Travellers 1690 to 1900* Interlink Publishing Group, Inc, Northampton, 2006.

al-Mad'ah, 'Abd al-Muhsin Mad'aj M *The Yemen in Early Islam 9-233/630-847, a political history* Ithaca Press, London, 1988.

de Maigret, Alessandro (Rebecca Thompson, trans) *Arabia Felix: an exploration of the archaeological history of Yemen* Stacey International, London, 2002.

Muchawsky-Schnapper, Ester *The Yemenites: Two Thousand Years of Jewish Culture* The Israel Museum, Jerusalem, 2000.

Naumkin, Vitaly V *Island of the Phoenix: An Ethnographic Study of the People of Socotra* Ithaca Press, Reading, 1993.

Rushby, Kevin *Eating the Flowers of Paradise: One Man's Journey Through Ethiopia and Yemen* St Martins Press, New York, 1999.

al-Salami, Khadija *The Tears of Sheba: Tales of Survival and Intrigue in Arabia* John Wiley & Sons, West Sussex, 2003.

Schippmann, Klaus (Allison Brown, trans) *Ancient South Arabia* Markus Wiener Publishers, Princeton, 2001.

Mackintosh-Smith, Tim *Yemen: The Unknown Arabia* Overlook Press, Woodstock, 2000.

Wali, Mohammad Abdul *They Die Strangers* CMES Modern Middle East Literature in Translation, University of Texas at Austin, 2002.

Weir, Shelagh *A Tribal Order: Politics and Law in the Mountains of Yemen* University of Texas Press, Austin, 2007.

WEBSITES

www.al-bab.com/bys British Yemeni Society.

www.aiys.org American Institute for Yemeni Studies.

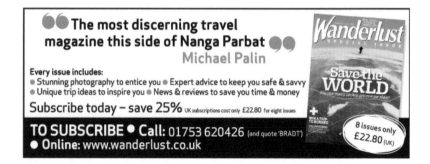

WIN £100 CASH!
READER QUESTIONNAIRE

Send in your completed questionnaire for the chance to win £100 cash in our regular draw

All respondents may order a Bradt guide at half the UK retail price – please complete the order form overleaf.

(Entries may be posted or faxed to us, or scanned and emailed.)

We are interested in getting feedback from our readers to help us plan future Bradt guides. Please answer ALL the questions below and return the form to us in order to qualify for an entry in our regular draw.

Have you used any other Bradt guides? If so, which titles? . . . .
. . . .

What other publishers' travel guides do you use regularly? . . . .
. . . .

Where did you buy this guidebook? . . . .

What was the main purpose of your trip to Yemen (or for what other reason did you read our guide)? eg: holiday/business/charity etc.. . . . .
. . . .

What other destinations would you like to see covered by a Bradt guide?
. . . .

Would you like to receive our catalogue/newsletters?

YES / NO (If yes, please complete details on reverse)

If yes – by post or email? . . . .

Age (circle relevant category) 16–25   26–45   46–60   60+

Male/Female (delete as appropriate)

Home country . . . .

Please send us any comments about our guide to Yemen or other Bradt Travel Guides. . . . .
. . . .
. . . .
. . . .

Bradt Travel Guides
23 High Street, Chalfont St Peter, Bucks SL9 9QE, UK
☏ +44 (0)1753 893444 f +44 (0)1753 892333
e info@bradtguides.com
www.bradtguides.com

CLAIM YOUR HALF-PRICE BRADT GUIDE!

Order Form

To order your half-price copy of a Bradt guide, and to enter our prize draw to win £100 (see overleaf), please fill in the order form below, complete the questionnaire overleaf, and send it to Bradt Travel Guides by post, fax or email.

Please send me one copy of the following guide at half the UK retail price

Title		*Retail price*	*Half price*
. . .	. . . .	. . . .	. . . .

Please send the following additional guides at full UK retail price

No	*Title*		*Retail price*	*Total*
. . .	. . . .	. . . .	. . . .
. . .	. . . .	. . . .	. . . .
. . .	. . . .	. . . .	. . . .

Sub total . . . .
Post & packing . . . .
(£1 per book UK; £2 per book Europe; £3 per book rest of world)
Total . . . .

Name . . . .

Address . . . .

Tel . . . .   Email . . . .

☐ I enclose a cheque for £. . . . . made payable to Bradt Travel Guides Ltd

☐ I would like to pay by credit card. Number: . . . .

Expiry date: . . . / . . .   3-digit security code (on reverse of card) . . . . .

Issue no (debit cards only) . . . . .

☐ Please add my name to your catalogue mailing list.

☐ I would be happy for you to use my name and comments in Bradt marketing material.

Send your order on this form, with the completed questionnaire, to:

Bradt Travel Guides YEM1
23 High Street, Chalfont St Peter, Bucks SL9 9QE
☏ +44 (0)1753 893444   **f** +44 (0)1753 892333
e info@bradtguides.com   www.bradtguides.com

Index

Page numbers in **bold** indicate main entries; those in *italics* indicate maps.